HOW DOES

A POEM MEAN?

HOW

A

by John Ciardi

DOES

POEM MEAN?

HOUGHTON MIFFLIN COMPANY BOSTON

The Riverside Press Cambridge

ACKNOWLEDGMENTS

The selections reprinted in this book are used by permission of and special arrangement with the proprietors of their respective copyrights. Grateful acknowledgment is made to the many authors and publishers who generously extended permission to include the selections in this Trade edition of *How Does a Poem Mean?*

Since this volume was first published, Langston Hughes' "Early Evening Quarrel," pages 984–985, has been reprinted in *Selected Poems of Langston Hughes,* published by Alfred A. Knopf, Inc. Copyright 1942 by Alfred A. Knopf, Inc.; copyright 1959 by Langston Hughes.

SEVENTH PRINTING   R

The Riverside Press
CAMBRIDGE · MASSACHUSETTS
PRINTED IN THE U.S.A.

PUBLISHER'S
NOTE

How Does a Poem Mean? was originally published by Houghton Mifflin Company as one section of a collaborative volume entitled *Introduction to Literature.* Considerable interest in Mr. Ciardi's discussion of poetry has been aroused outside of academic circles and Houghton Mifflin Company is now publishing a Trade edition of *How Does a Poem Mean?* The reader will observe that the pagination of the original printing has been retained.

PUBLISHER'S
NOTE

CONTENTS

CHAPTER FOUR · THE WORDS OF POETRY   762

Contents

Contents

Contents

Contents

HOW DOES

A POEM MEAN?

H O W

D O E S   A   P O E M

M E A N ?

Introductory

A poem is a formal structure in which many elements operate at the same time. In analysis, each element must be discussed separately. By nature, analysis is plodding at best. Were an aeronautical engineer to analyze the flight of a gull, for example, he would find himself involved in a great deal of crabbed detail. No one, however, would be tempted to believe that the analysis tried to take the place of the gull, or that it damaged the gull in any way. Many readers of poetry, however, seem to be hair-trigger ready to charge that analysis destroys a poem, and that any critic undertaking an analysis confuses his analysis with the thing analysed and thereby loses touch with poetry. When one excerpt from the present book was published, in a modified form, in the *Saturday Review,* a number of readers brought exactly such charges against the analysis in angry Letters to the Editor.

Analysis is never in any sense a substitute for the poem. The best any analysis can do is to prepare the reader to enter the poem more perceptively. By isolating for special consideration some of the many simultaneous elements of the poem, analysis makes them more visible in one sense, and less interesting in another. It is up to the reader, once the analysis is completed, to re-read the poem in a way that will restore the simultaneity and therefore the liveliness and interest of the poetic structure. The only reason for taking a poem apart is that it may then be put back together again more richly.

The present volume sets out simply to isolate some of the characteristics of poetry and to develop criteria by which parts of the poetic structure may be experienced in a more comprehensive way. The final chapter suggests a method whereby all the criteria developed in the preceding chapters may be applied to the comprehension of the total poem. What one must always comprehend of poetry is that it is an experience the reader must re-live. There is no other comprehension of the arts.

The final chapter is, therefore, the important one, but it will not be wholly meaningful until the earlier chapters have been read. Should the development of specific points in the earlier chapters give rise to any confusion, I hope the final chapter may serve to resolve at least some of them.

The title I have chosen is not intended in any way as a verbal trick. The usual question one hears of poetry is "What does a poem mean?" I am interested rather in "How" the poem means, how it goes about being a performance of itself. An alternative title might have been "How to talk about a poem without actually paraphrasing."

In 1951 when I was teaching at Harvard, a number of friends—all of them valued poets—organized a small group that met irregularly to talk about the poems each brought with him. That group continued to meet for two years or so through a number of memorable evenings. The regular core of that group consisted of Richard Eberhart, John Holmes, Archibald MacLeish, Richard Wilbur, and myself. I am indebted to those meetings for some of the happiest and best poet's talk I have ever heard. I have no doubt that I have worked into this book many ideas that were touched on in those meetings, but in expressing my gratitude to these good men, I must make it clear that they are in no way responsible for what I have said here. I simply confess that I have stolen from them, and that I wish I might have stolen more. Could I be sure of exactly what I have stolen, I would acknowledge my thefts in detail. My most gratitude to them is that they are rich enough to be worth stealing from.

I owe a similar debt to the staff and members of the Bread Loaf Writers' Conference—especially to Robert Frost, Theodore Morrison, Fletcher Pratt, Bernard DeVoto, and William Sloane—who year after year have stored me with ideas and insights I could not have come to by myself.

JOHN CIARDI
RUTGERS UNIVERSITY

Chapter One

HOW DOES A POEM MEAN?

"Bitzer," said Thomas Gradgrind, "your definition of a horse."
"Quadruped. Gramnivorous. Forty teeth, namely twenty-four grinders, four eye-teeth, and twelve incisive. Sheds coat in the spring; in marshy countries sheds hoofs too. Hoofs hard, but requiring to be shod with iron. Age known by marks in mouth." Thus (and much more) Bitzer.
"Now girl number twenty," said Mr. Gradgrind, "you know what a horse is."

Charles Dickens, *Hard Times*

The School of Hard Facts over which Mr. Gradgrind presided was a school of fixed answers. Mr. Gradgrind would have agreed with a recent anthologist who wrote that the inspection of a poem should be as certain as a chemical analysis. Mr. Gradgrind would have assured himself that he was a first-class critic, of poetry as of horses. "Now girl number twenty," he would have said looking up from his analysis, "you know what a poem is."

Today, a century later than Mr. Gradgrind's School of Hard Facts, the idea is still current that the methods of measurement evolved by the physical sciences can be applied to all human processes. And there still lingers the belief that a dictionary definition is a satisfactory description of an idea or of an experience.

There are many grounds on which dictionary definitions can be disputed, but only one need concern us here. Bitzer's definition of a horse was a dictionary definition. Note that it is put almost exclusively in terms of classification. In those terms, it may do as a table of physical characteristics of *Equus caballus*. But what can it possibly say of the experience one has had of the living animal? No horseman ever rode a "gramnivorous quadruped." No gambler ever bet on one. No sculptor ever dreamed one out of a block of stone. For horseman, gambler, and sculptor are involved in a living relation to a living animal, *and the kind of relation is expressed in the language each has evolved for his experience.* ("A good winded bay," says the horseman, "but he has a mouth like iron and won't answer to the bit. He's had bad schooling." Or the gambler: "A good four-year-old. Better than his performance to date. And a good mudder. He's due to win, especially on a wet track. And at nice odds." Or the sculptor: "The set of the stone suggested a rearing posture: the line of force curving down the haunches repeated in the straining line of the neck with the mouth held hard-down by the bit.") Whatever the "gramnivorous quad-

665

ruped" may be to the biologist, these three ways of speaking are three experiences of the living horse. As Tip O'Neill once wrote in a fine sarcastic line: "There's not a wedding in the world that's worth a running horse." Now try the line revised: "There is not a marriage ceremony in existence worthy of comparison with a gramnivorous quadruped of the genus *Equus caballus* in rapid motion."

The point is that *the language of experience is not the language of classification.* A boy burning with ambition to become a jockey does not study a text on zoology. He watches horses, he listens to what is said by those who have spent their lives around horses, he rides them, trains them, feeds them, curries them, pets them. He lives with intense feelings toward them. He may never learn how many incisors a horse has, nor how many yards of intestines. What does it matter? He is concerned with a *feel*, a response-to, a sense of the character and reaction of the living animal. And zoology cannot give him that. Not all the anatomizing of all the world's horses could teach a man horse-sense.

So for poetry. The concern is not to arrive at a definition and to close the book, but to arrive at an experience. There will never be a complete system for "understanding" or for "judging" poetry. Understanding and critical judgment are admirable goals, but neither can take place until the poem has been experienced, and even then there is always some part of every good work of art that can never be fully explained or categorized. It still remains true that the reader who has experienced most fully will finally be the best judge.

Poetry has only a remote place in the gross of our culture. As has, for example, the opera. Therefore, Americans generally need to be taught in school how to experience both poetry and the opera. In Milan, on the other hand, no one need go to school in order to learn how to experience an opera: the Milanese do not study opera, they *inhale* it. They would have to go to school to learn, for example, how to watch a baseball game in an experienceable way. Certainly no one in The Bronx need go to that school: in The Bronx it is baseball that is inhaled as a living thing, and opera and poetry that have to be learned.

If the reader cared enough for poetry, he would have no need to study it. He would *live into it.* As the Milanese citizen becomes an encyclopedia of opera information, and as even retarded boys in The Bronx are capable of reciting endlessly detailed baseball statistics, so the passionate reader of poetry becomes alive to it by natural process.

Any teaching of the poem by any other method owes the poem an apology. What greater violence can be done to the poet's experience than to drag it into an early morning classroom and to go after it as an item on its way to a Final Examination? The apology must at least be made. It is the experience, not the Final Examination, that counts. Though one must note with care—as in the case of the baseball fan—that passionate learning is full of very technical stuff. Why else would baseball statistics give rise to such heated argument as one can hear throughout the season?

And in poetry there is the step beyond: <u>once one has learned to ex-</u>perience the poem as a poem, there inevitably arrives a sense that one is <u>also experiencing himself as a human</u> being. It must certainly have been this second experience (to put it in another way, the point at which Art for Art's sake becomes Art for Life's sake) that Matthew Arnold had in mind when he wrote: "The grand power of poetry is its interpretative power . . . the power of so dealing with things as to awaken in us a wonderfully full, new, and intimate sense of them, and of our relations with them." But the grand power of a good sermon is also its interpretative power, and a sermon, it must be remembered, is not a poem.

Paradise Lost is, in one sense, a rhymed sermon written to justify God's ways to man. So is Michael Wigglesworth's *The Day of Doom.* Wigglesworth was a Puritan clergyman of the Massachusetts Bay Colony and for over two centuries Puritan children memorized large sections of his poem as part of their church training. Wigglesworth's theology is every bit as sound and as comprehensive as Milton's. Yet today *The Day of Doom* is all but unknown except as a scholar's curio. The difference is not in content but in the fact that Milton wrote a poem whereas Wigglesworth wrote only doggerel. Poetry, it follows, is more than simply "something to say." Nor is it simply an elaborate way of saying something or nothing.

W. H. Auden was once asked what advice he would give a young man who wished to become a poet. Auden replied that he would ask the young man why he wanted to write poetry. If the answer was "because I have something important to say," Auden would conclude that there was no hope for that young man as a poet. If on the other hand the answer was something like "because I like to hang around words and overhear them talking to one another," then that young man was at least interested in a fundamental part of the poetic process and there was hope for him.

When one "message-hunts" a poem (*i.e.*, goes through the poem with no interest except in its paraphraseable content) he is approaching the writing as did the young man with "something important to say." He is giving it the Wigglesworth treatment. The common question from which such an approach begins is "What Does the Poem Mean?" His mind closed on that point of view, the reader tends to "interpret" the poem rather than to experience it, seeking only what he can make over from it into a prose statement (or Examination answer) and forgetting in the process that it was originally a poem. Thus, students are too often headed by their teachers in the direction of reciting, almost like Bitzer: "Keats. 'When I have fears that I may cease to be.' Sonnet. Irregular. Consisting of three quatrains and a couplet, the third quatrain consisting of very close rhymes, thus: 'hour, more, power, shore.' Written on the theme of the vanity of earthly wishes, but given a strong romantic coloration of individualistic aspiration for the good pleasures of the world."

Poor Keats!

For what does the poem mean? is too often a self-destroying approach to poetry. A more useful way of asking the question is HOW DOES A POEM MEAN? Why does it build itself into a form out of images, ideas, rhythms? How do these elements become the meaning? How are they inseparable from the meaning? As Yeats wrote:

> O body swayed to music, o quickening glance,
> How shall I tell the dancer from the dance?

What the poem is, is inseparable from its own performance of itself. The dance is in the dancer and the dancer is in the dance. Or put in another way: where is the "dance"when no one is dancing it? and what man is a "dancer" except when he is dancing?

Above all else, poetry is a performance. Keats' overt subject in his sonnet was his own approaching death. But note this about poetry: Keats took the same *self-delighting pains* in writing about his death as he took in poems on overtly happy subjects, such as "On First Looking into Chapman's Homer" or the "Ode to a Nightingale." Here is the complete sonnet:

> When I have fears that I may cease to be
>   Before my pen has gleaned my teeming brain,
> Before high piled books, in charactery,
>   Hold like rich garners the full ripened grain;
> When I behold upon the night's starred face,
>   Huge cloudy symbols of a high romance,
> And think that I may never live to trace
>   Their shadows with the magic hand of chance;
> And when I feel, fair creature of an hour,
>   That I shall never look upon thee more,
> Never have relish in the faery power
>   Of unreflecting love;—then on the shore
> Of the wide world I stand alone, and think
> Till love and fame to nothingness do sink.

If this sonnet means "the vanity of human wishes given a strong romantic coloration, *etc.*," why did Keats take the trouble to bring his rhythms to a stop at the end of the fourth and eighth lines and in the middle of the twelfth? Sonnets normally divide into "octet" (the first eight lines) and "sestet" (the final six lines). Note that Keats' divisions occur in a very nearly symmetrical pattern. Why did Keats spend so much care on symmetry? What has symmetry to do with "the vanity of earthly wishes"? Why, too, did Keats bother to compare his mind to a field of grain, and the books he felt himself able to write, to storage bins? An elaborate figure. Why did Keats bother to construct it? Why did he search out such striking phrases as "the magic hand of chance"? If Keats were really convinced that all human wishes are vain, why did he wish to phrase his idea with such earthly care? If *nothingness* is all, why bother to make the something a poem is?

Robert Frost provided a valuable clue when he spoke of "the pleasure of taking pains." The paradox here is simply verbal. Frost meant precisely what the German critic Baumgarten meant when he spoke of the central impulse toward poetry (and toward all art) as the *Spieltrieb*, the play impulse.

An excellent native example of the play impulse in poetry is the child clapping its hands in response to a Mother Goose rhyme. What does a child care for "meaning"? What on earth is the "meaning" of the following poem?

> High Diddle diddle
> The cat and the fiddle
> The cow jumped over the moon;
> The little dog laughed
> To see such craft
> And the dish ran away with the spoon.

"Preposterous," says Mr. Gradgrind. But the child is wiser: he is busy having a good time with the poem. The poem pleases and involves him. He responds to it in an immediate muscular way. He recognizes its performance at once and wants *to act with it.*

This is the first level of play. As rhythm is the first element of music. The child claps hands, has fun, and the play involves practically no thoughtful activity. Beyond this level of response, there begins the kind of play whose pleasure lies for the poet in overcoming meaningful and thoughtful (and "feelingful") difficulties, and for the reader in identifying with the poet in that activity.

Nor is the word "difficulty" one to be afraid of. Chess is a play-activity, yet it is play only because the players deliberately make the game difficult in order to overcome the difficulties. The equation is simple: no difficulty, no fun. No chess player finds any real pleasure in playing an obviously inferior opponent. *Every game ever invented by mankind is a way of making things hard for the fun of it. The great fun, of course, is in making the hard look easy.* Too much difficulty is painful. The Freshman football coach does not send his squad to play last year's Rose Bowl winner. Neither does he send it to play grammar school teams. He tries to find opponents who will give his players a real chance to extend themselves, win or lose, and he hopes bit by bit to develop them for harder play.

Learning to experience poetry is not a radically different process from that of learning any other kind of play. The way to develop a poetic sense is by using it. And one of the real joys of the play-impulse is in the sudden discovery that one is getting better at it than he had thought he would be.

It is this self-delighting play impulse that the literalist and message-hunter overlooks, just as Mr. Gradgrind overlooked the living fun it is to ride a horse, even an undefined horse.

To summarize these same points in more formal terms: *no matter how*

serious the overt message of a poem, the unparaphraseable and undimin-
ishable life of the poem lies in the way it performs itself through the
difficulties it imposes upon itself. The way *in which* it means is *what*
it means.

What for example does a dance "mean"? Or what does music "mean"?
Or what does a juggler "mean" when we watch him with such admiration
of his skill? All of these forms—and poetry with them—have meaning
only as they succeed in being good performances.

One sees a wizard of a poet tossing his words in the air and catching
them and tossing them again—what a grand stunt! Then suddenly one
may be astonished to find that the poet is not simply juggling cups,
saucers, roses, rhymes and other random objects, but the very stuff of life.
And discovering that, one discovers that seeing the poet's ideas flash so
in the air, seeing them performed under such control, is not only a re-
ward in itself, but a living experience that deepens every man's sense of
life. One finds himself more alert to life, surer of his own emotions, wiser
than he would have been without that experience.—And he thought he
was just watching a show!

But only a poem can illustrate how a poem works. One of the purposes
of this volume is to provide beginning students with a reasonable bulk of
poems from the great tradition of English and American poetry. But great
as are the virtues of wide reading, they amount to nothing unless the
reading goes deep as well as wide. It is good to read much. It is even
more important to read a little in greater depth, for every poem one reads
closely will teach him something about how to read another poem.

What should such a close reading take into consideration?

Here is a poem, one of the master lyrics of American poetry, perhaps
the best known poem by an American poet:

Stopping by Woods on a Snowy Evening

Robert Frost

Whose woods these are I think I know.
His house is in the village though;
He will not see me stopping here
To watch his woods fill up with snow.

My little horse must think it queer
To stop without a farmhouse near
Between the woods and frozen lake
The darkest evening of the year.

He gives his harness bells a shake
To ask if there is some mistake.
The only other sound's the sweep
Of easy wind and downy flake.

The woods are lovely, dark and deep.
But I have promises to keep,
And miles to go before I sleep,
And miles to go before I sleep.

Note that the poem begins as a simple description of events, but that it ends in a way that suggests meanings far beyond the specific description. This movement *from the specific to the general* is one of the basic formulas of poetry. Such a poem, as Yvor Winter's "Before Disaster" (p. 1005), and Holmes' "The Chambered Nautilus" (p. 742) follow exactly this progression from the specific to the general, but the generalization in these poems is, in a sense, divided from the specific description or narration, and even seems additional to the specific action rather than intrinsically part of it. It is this sense of division that is signified when one speaks of "a tacked-on moral." Frost, however, is painstakingly careful to avoid the tacked-on moral. Everything in the poem pretends, on one level, to be part of the incident narrated. Yet one cannot miss the feeling that by the end of the poem, Frost has referred to something much more far-reaching than stopping by woods or than driving home to go to bed. There can be little doubt, in fact, that part of Frost's own pleasure in this poem was in making the larger intent *grow out* of the poem rather than in tacking it on. It is in the poem's own performance of itself that the larger meaning is made to emerge from the specific incident. A careful look at that performance will teach a great deal about the nature of poetry.

The poem begins with a situation. A man—knowing Robert Frost, we know it is a Vermont or New Hampshire man—is on his way somewhere at night-fall. It is snowing and as he passes a patch of woods he stops to watch the easy down-drift of the snow into the dark woods. We are told two other things: first that the man is familiar with these parts (he knows who owns these woods and where he lives) and second that no one sees him stop. More could be read into this opening (for example: why doesn't he say what errand he is on? why does he say he knows whose woods these are? what is the significance of watching another man's woods in this way?) Such questions can be multiplied almost endlessly without losing real point, but for present purposes let us assume that we have identified scene one of the poem's performance without raising these questions.

Note that the scene is set in the simplest possible terms. We have no trouble sensing that the man stopped because the scene moved him, but he neither tells us that it is beautiful nor that it moved him. A student writer, always ready to overdo, might have said that he was moved to stop and "to fill his soul with the slow steady stately sinking of that crystaline loveliness into the glimmerless profundities of the hushed primeval wood." Frost prefers to avoid such a spate of words, and to speak the incident in the simplest terms.

His choice illustrates two basic principles of writing of which every sensitive reader should be aware. Frost stated the first principle himself in "The Mowing" (p. 812) when he wrote "Anything *more* than the truth would have seemed too *weak*." (italics mine) Understatement is one of the principal sources of power in English poetry.

The second principle here illustrated is to let the action speak for itself. A good novelist who wishes us to know a character does not tell us that character is good or bad and leave it at that. Rather, he introduces the character, shows him in action, and lets his actions speak for him. This process is spoken of as *characterization in action*. One of the skills of a good poet is to enact his experiences rather than to talk about having had them. "*Show* it, don't *tell* it," he says, "make it happen, don't talk about its happening."

One part of this poem's performance, in fact, is *to act out* (and thereby to make us act out—*i.e.*, *feel out*—*i.e.*, *identify with*) just why the speaker did stop. The man is the principal actor of this little "drama of why" and in scene one he is the only character. In scene two (starting with the beginning of stanza two), however, a "foil" is introduced. In drama, a "foil" is a character who "plays against" a more important character; by presenting a different point of view or an opposed set of motives, the foil moves the more important character to react in ways that might not have found expression without such opposition. The more important character is thus more fully revealed, to the reader and to himself. The foil here is the horse.

The horse forces the first question in the drama of why. Why did the man stop? Until he comes to realize that his "little horse must think it queer" to stop this way, he has not asked himself why he stopped; he simply did. But he senses that the horse is confused by the stop. He imagines how the horse must feel about it—what *is* there to stop for out here in the cold, away from bin and stall and all that any self-respecting horse would value on such a night?

In imagining the horse's question, the man is of course led to examine his own reasons. In stanza two this question arises only as a feeling within the man. In stanza three, however, the horse acts definitely. He gives his harness bells a shake. "What's wrong," he seems to say, "what are we doing here?"

By now, obviously, the horse, without losing its identity as a horse has also become a symbol. A symbol is something that stands for something else. That something else may, perhaps, be taken as the order of life that does not understand why a man stops in the wintry middle of nowhere to watch snow come down. (Could the dark and the snowfall symbolize a death wish? that hunger for the last rest that man may feel, but not a beast?) So there is the man, there is that other order of life, and there is the third presence—the movement of the inanimate wind and snow (the all-engulfing?) across both their lives—with the difference that the man knows the second darkness of the dark while the horse does not.

The man has no ready answer to this combination of forces. They exist and he feels them—all three of them, himself included. We sense that he would like to remain here longer to ponder these forces, perhaps to yield to their total. But a fourth force prompts him. That fourth force can be given many names. It is almost certainly better, in fact, to give it many names than attempt to limit it to one. Social obligation, responsibility, personal commitment, duty, or just the realization that a man cannot indulge a mood forever—all of these things and more. He has a long way to go and it is time to be getting there (so there's something to be said for the horse, too). We find the man's inner conflict dramatized to this point by the end of scene two (which coincides with the end of stanza three).

Then and only then—his feelings dramatized in the cross tug of motives he has given form to—does the poet, a little sadly, venture on the comment of his final scene. "The woods are lovely, dark and deep." The very sound of the syllables lingers over the thought. But there is something to do yet before he can yield to the lovely dark-and-deep. "Not yet," he seems to say, "not yet." He has a long way to go—miles to go before he can sleep. Yes, miles to go. He repeats the line and the performance ends.

But why the repetition? The first time Frost writes "And miles to go before I sleep" there can be little doubt that he means, "I have a long way to go yet before I can get to bed tonight." The second time he says it, however, "miles to go" and "sleep" are suddenly transformed into symbols. What is the "something else" these symbols stand for? Hundreds of people have asked Mr. Frost that question in one form or another, and Mr. Frost has always turned the question away with a joke. He has turned it away primarily *because he cannot answer it.* He could answer some part of it. But some part is not enough.

For a symbol is like a rock dropped into a pool: it sends out ripples in all directions, and the ripples are in motion. Who can say where the last ripple disappears? One may have a sense that he at least knows approximately the center point of all those ripples, the point at which the stone struck the water. Yet even then he has trouble marking it precisely. How does one make a mark on water? Oh, very well—the center point of "miles to go" is probably approximately in the neighborhood of being close to meaning, perhaps, "the road of life," and "before I sleep" is maybe that close to meaning "before I take my final rest." (That rest-in-darkness that seemed so temptingly "lovely dark-and-deep" for the moment of the mood.) But the ripples continue to move and the light to change on the water and the longer one watches the more changes he sees. And such shifting-and-being-at-the-same-instant is of the very sparkle and life of poetry. Of poetry and of life itself. For the poem is a dynamic and living thing. One experiences it as one experiences life—as everybody but Mr. Gradgrind experiences life. One is never done with it: every time he looks he sees something new, and it changes even as he watches. And that very sense of continuity in fluidity is one of the kinds of knowledge, one of the ways of knowing, that only the arts can teach, poetry foremost among them.

Frost himself certainly did not ask what the lines "meant." They came to him and he received them; he "felt right" about them. And what he "felt right about" may perhaps be called their "meaning," but it is far more to the point to describe it as "their long possibility of meaning." For the poem is not a statement but a performance of forces, not an essay on life but a reenactment, and just as men must search their lives over and over again for the meaning of their deepest experiences, so the performance of a true poem is endless in being not a meaning but an act of existence.

Now look at the poem in another way. Did Frost know what he was going to do when he began? Considering the poem simply as a piece of juggling one cannot fail to respond to the magnificent turn at the end where, with one flip, seven of the simplest words in the language suddenly dazzle full of never-ending waves of thought and feeling; or—more precisely—of felt-thought. Certainly an equivalent stunt by a juggler— could there be such an equivalent—would bring the house down. Was it to cap his performance with that grand stunt that Frost wrote the poem?

Far from it: the fact that must not be overlooked is that *Frost did not know he was going to write those lines until he wrote them.* Then a second fact must be registered: *he wrote them because, for the fun of it, he had got himself into trouble.*

Let us start by saying that Frost began by playing a game with himself. The most usual way of writing a four line stanza with four feet to the line, is to rhyme the third line with the first, and the fourth line with the second. Even that much rhyme is so difficult that many poets and almost all the anonymous ballad makers do not bother to rhyme the first and third lines at all, settling for two rhymes in four lines. For the fact is that English is a rhyme-poor language. In Italian and in French, for example, so many words end with the same sounds that rhyming is relatively easy. English, being a more agglomerate language, has far more final sounds, hence fewer of them rhyme. When an Italian poet writes a line ending with "vita" (life) he has literally hundreds of possible rhyme words available. When an English poet writes "life" at the end of a line, he can summon "strife, wife, knife, fife, rife" and then he is in trouble. Now "life-strife," and "life-rife" and "life-wife" seem to offer a combination of ideas that are possibly related by more than rhyme. Inevitably, therefore, the poets have had to work, re-work, and over-work these combinations until the sparkle has gone out of them. Readers are normally tired of these combinations. When one encounters "life-strife" he is certainly entitled to suspect that the poet did not really want to say "strife"—that if there had been in English such as word as, say, "hife" meaning "infinite peace and harmony," he would gladly have used that word instead of "strife." So one feels that the writing is haphazard: that the rhyme is making the poet say things he doesn't really feel, and which, therefore, the reader does not feel. One likes to see the rhymes fall into place, but he must end up with the belief that it is the poet who is deciding what is said and not the rhyme scheme.

So rhyme is a kind of game, and an especially difficult one in English. As in every game, the fun of rhyme is to set one's difficulties high and then to meet them skillfully. As Frost himself once defined freedom, it consists of "moving easy in harness."

In "Stopping by Woods on a Snowy Evening" Frost took a long chance. He decided to rhyme not two lines, but three in each stanza. Not even Frost could have sustained that much rhyme in a long poem (as Dante, for example, with the advantage of writing in Italian sustained triple rhyme for thousands of lines in *The Divine Comedy*). He would have known instantly, therefore, when he took that first chance, that he was going to write a short poem. He would have had that much foretaste of it. So the first stanza emerged rhymed a a b a. And with the certain sense that this was to be a short poem, Frost decided to take a chance and redouble: in English three rhymes in four lines is enough—there is no need to rhyme the fourth line. For the fun of it, however, Frost set himself to pick up that loose rhyme and weave it into the pattern—thereby accepting the all but impossible burden of quadruple rhyme.

The miracle is that it worked. Despite that enormous freight of rhyme, the poem not only came out as a neat pattern, but managed to do so with no sense of strain. It is this unstrained fulfillment of one's difficulties Frost means by "moving easy in harness." Despite all his self-imposed restrictions the poem *seems* to go effortlessly. Every word falls into place as naturally as if there were no rhyme restricting the choice.

That ease is part of the success of the performance. One watches the skill-man juggle two balls, then three, then four—and every addition makes the trick more wonderful, but unless he makes the hard trick *seem* as easy as the easy one, then all is lost.

The real point, however, is not only that Frost took on a hard rhyme-trick and made it look easy. It is rather as if a juggler, carried away, had tossed up one more ball than he could really handle—and then amazed himself by actually handling it. So with the real triumph of this poem. Frost could not have known what a stunning effect his repetition of the last line was going to produce. He could not even have known he was going to repeat the line. He simply found himself up against a difficulty he probably had not foreseen: in picking up the rhyme from the third line of stanza one and carrying it over into stanza two, he had created an endless chain-link form. Each stanza left a hook sticking out for the next stanza to catch. So by stanza four, feeling the poem rounding to its end, Frost had to do something about his third-line rhyme.

He might have tucked it back in a third line rhyming with "know/ though/snow" of stanza one. That would have worked out to the mathematical symmetry of using each rhyme four times. But though such a device might be defensible in theory, a rhyme repeated after eleven lines is so far from its original rhyme sound that its feeling as rhyme must certainly be lost, and what good is theory if the reader is not moved by the writing?

It must have been in some such quandary that the final repetition suggested itself—a suggestion born of the very difficulty of what the poet had set out to do. So the point beyond mere ease in handling a hard thing: that the very difficulty of the restrictions the poet imposed upon himself offered the opportunity to do better than he had imagined. What—aside from having that happen to oneself—could be more self-delighting than to participate in its happening by one's reader-identification with the poem?

You will observe one further point: that the human-insight of the poem, and the technicalities of the poetic devices are inseparable. Each feeds the other. This interplay is the poem's meaning, a matter not of WHAT IT MEANS (nobody can say entirely what a good poem means) but HOW IT MEANS—a process one can come much closer to discussing.

Is it too frivolous to have compared this process to the act of juggling? Consider the following parable based on a short story by Anatole France, "The Juggler of Notre Dame."

The juggler wandered France from fair to fair and whenever he saw a chance to earn a few pennies he unrolled his rug, lay on his back, and juggled his paraphernalia with his hands and feet. It was all he knew how to do, he did it well, and he was happy in the doing.

As he grew older, however, misfortunes crowded him. One winter's day, ill and tired, he took refuge in a monastery and by the time he had recovered he decided to remain there. It was a pleasant monastery dedicated to the Virgin and each of the monks and brothers set himself a special task in her honor. One illuminated manuscripts to offer her, another decorated her altar, another raised flowers. Only the juggler had no productive art, only he produced nothing that could be set in place before her and stay tangibly in place. (This rendering takes a few liberties with the original for the sake of making a point.)

Finally, in despair, the juggler took to stealing into the chapel when no one else was about. There he would unroll his rug and juggle before the Virgin's statue. It was all he had to offer, the one thing he could do well.

One day a passing brother discovered the juggler at work before the statue and summoned the other monks in horror to witness the profanation of the chapel. Soon all the window-sills were lined with the heads of outraged monks come to verify the horrible report. They were just about to rush in and put an end to the sacrilege, when before their eyes the Virgin descended smiling from her pedestral and wiped the sweat from the juggler's brow. The offering was acceptable.

A note to residual Gradgrinds: This parable is not a religious excursion. It is an allegory. An allegory is a story in which each character and element is more important as a symbol (as something else) than as its presumably-literal self. Then all these symbols-put-together acquire further meanings by their interaction upon one another. —what does the Virgin stand for in poetic terms? What do the monks stand for? The juggler? How does juggling relate to Frost's definition of freedom (in poetry)? Why should juggling produce the miracle? How does the parable mean what it means?

Chapter Two

A BURBLE THROUGH THE
TULGEY WOOD

Everyone who has an emotion and a language knows something about poetry. What he knows may not be much on an absolute scale, and it may not be organized within him in a useful way, but once he discovers the pleasures of poetry, he is likely to be surprised to discover how much he always knew without knowing he knew it. He may discover, somewhat as the character in the French play discovered to his amazement that he had been talking prose all his life, that he has been living poetry. Poetry, after all, is about life. Anyone who is alive and conscious must have some information about it.

And like life, poetry is not uniformly serious. True, poetry is the natural language of man's most exalted thoughts. The rhythmic resemblance between prayer and poetry, for example, can hardly be missed. Yet the more exalted the thought, the more careful the poet must be, for poetic high-seriousness can fall into a burlesque of itself at a touch. William Wordsworth, for all his great powers as a poet, was yet capable of slipping from the intensely serious into the intensely inane. His "Idiot Boy," an intensely serious ballad about the natural unspoiled goodness of a young idiot, can hardly be said to survive such a line as "Burr, burr—now Johnny's lips they burr," a line in which the poet seeks to render soulfully the blubbering of a happy idiot, and falls into bathos. Percy Bysshe Shelley was similarly capable of a kind of labored excess that could turn sublime intention into ridiculous utterance. His "Epipsychidion" sets out to describe ideal love, but few readers today can suppress a smile at the last line: "I pant, I sink, I tremble, I expire!" So, too, when John Keats addresses an apostrophe to his love and lets slip the exclamation: "Those lips, O slippery blisses!"

Such lapses do not prove that Wordsworth, Shelley, and Keats were bad poets, but that they could strain so hard for high-seriousness that their voices cracked. If, however, some poets let themselves fall into unconsciously ridiculous positions, there are always others ready to pick up the slip and to have fun with it. One of the most pompous and flat-footedly moral of the English poets was Robert Southey. The performance of his poems tends always to center around a spike of moral Gradgrindism which the performer proceeds to drive in with such graceless energy that the hammer splits and leaves him holding a shattered stump of the handle. We in the audience see his laborious earnestness, but the act is so clumsy that we cannot resist laughing it off the stage.

Lewis Carroll, the ever-graceful author of *Alice in Wonderland*, had a great gift for such laughter. His "Father William," a direct take-off of Southey's "The Old Man's Comforts and How He Gained Them," is as devastating a spoof as one may find in English poetry:

The Old Man's Comforts
And how he gained them
Robert Southey

"You are old, Father William," the young man cried;
  "The few locks which are left you are gray;
You are hale, Father William,—a hearty old man:
  Now tell me the reason, I pray."

"In the days of my youth," Father William replied,
  "I remembered that youth would fly fast,
And abused not my health and my vigor at first,
  That I never might need them at last."

"You are old, Father William," the young man cried,
  "And pleasures with youth pass away;
And yet you lament not the days that are gone:
  Now tell me the reason, I pray."

"In the days of my youth," Father William replied,
  "I remembered that youth could not last;
I thought of the future, whatever I did,
  That I never might grieve for the past."

"You are old, Father William," the young man cried,
  "And life must be hastening away;
You are cheerful, and love to converse upon death:
  Now tell me the reason, I pray."

"I am cheerful, young man," Father William replied;
  "Let the cause thy attention engage;
In the days of my youth, I remembered my God,
  And He hath not forgotten my age."

Father William

Lewis Carroll

"You are old, Father William," the young man said,
　"And your hair has become very white,
And yet you incessantly stand on your head—
　Do you think, at your age, it is right?"

"In my youth," Father William replied to his son,
　"I feared it might injure the brain;
But now that I'm perfectly sure I have none,
　Why, I do it again and again."

"You are old," said the youth, "as I mentioned before,
　And have grown most uncommonly fat;
Yet you turned a back-somersault in at the door—
　Pray, what is the reason of that?"

"In my youth," said the sage, as he shook his gray locks,
　"I kept all my limbs very supple
By the use of this ointment—one shilling the box—
　Allow me to sell you a couple?"

"You are old," said the youth," and your jaws are too weak
　For anything tougher than suet;
Yet you finished the goose, with the bones and the beak—
　Pray, how did you manage to do it?"

"In my youth," said his father, "I took to the law,
　And argued each case with my wife;
And the muscular strength which it gave to my jaw
　Has lasted the rest of my life."

"You are old," said the youth, "one would hardly suppose
　That your eye was as steady as ever;
Yet you balanced an eel on the end of your nose—
　What made you so awfully clever?"

"I have answered three questions, and that is enough,"
　Said his father; "don't give yourself airs!
Do you think I can listen all day to such stuff?
　Be off, or I'll kick you downstairs!"

　　The fun that Carroll had with his spoof is obvious, but it should not obscure an awareness of his skill in building his poem—his "act," as a juggler might say. The first question put to Father William, for example, accuses Southey of being turned upside down, and Father William's first reply openly accuses Southey of being brainless. There is really not much more one can say against a poet, yet Carroll, having already assassinated Southey, manages to keep his poem lively for three more question-an-answer turns. If each question-and-answer turn is thought of as a scene, what is the principle on which the scenes follow one another? Are they increasingly serious? Increasingly ludicrous? Increasingly trivial? Increasingly revealing of Father William's character? What is the order of progression in Southey's poem? What are the three virtues Southey's old man extolls to the youth, and why did Southey develop them in the order given? Carroll found himself having such fun with his parody that he went on for one more question-and-answer than the original. What are the four points Carroll makes about Father William's character, and how does each parody comment on the points Southey makes?

Very often, when one is uncertain about a given poem, he may find useful clues to better understanding in other poems by the same poet. Carroll wrote a number of happy parodies, all of them aimed at deflating overserious morality. Another of Carroll's most memorable parodies is "The Crocodile," a spoof of Isaac Watts' "How Doth the Little Busy Bee":

How Doth the Little Busy Bee

Isaac Watts

How doth the little busy bee
    Improve each shining hour,
And gather honey all the day
    From every opening flower!

How skillfully she builds her cell!
    How neat she spreads the wax!
And labors hard to store it well
    With the sweet food she makes.

In works of labor or of skill
    I would be busy too;
For Satan finds some mischief still
    For idle hands to do.

In books, or work, or healthful play,
    Let my first years be passed,
That I may give for every day
    Some good account at last.

The Crocodile

Lewis Carroll

How doth the little crocodile
  Improve his shining tail,
And pour the waters of the Nile
  On every shining scale!

How cheerfully he seems to grin,
  How neatly spreads his claws,
And welcomes little fishes in
  With gently smiling jaws!

Southey's Father William and Carroll's speak in what seem to be the same terms, yet to very different ends. Watts' little busy bee and Carroll's crocodile are also presented in similar terms. Both are described with a kind of pious unctuousness, yet the two are engaged in activities of quite a different moral color. Is it too much to argue that the crocodile is a happy hypocrite piously gobbling up the trusting fishes (including the poor fishes among the readers who are willing to take Watt's prettily-shallow morality as a true rule of life)? Is it too much again to claim that the crocodile and Father William have a good deal in common—that both of them, in fact, accuse their originals of hypocrisy?

If Carroll's aim in these two poems is to show the ludicrousness and hypocrisy of the poems he lampoons, how do the lampoons achieve that aim? (How does a poem mean?) Clearly the two old men, the little busy bee, and the crocodile are symbols. Of what? One must never be in a hurry to "define" symbols for, as already noted, symbols are not pat equivalents but areas of meaning. What must not be missed, however, is that the real performance of Carroll's parodies arises from the way the symbol "crocodile" plays against the symbol "little busy bee." How many such interplays of meaning suggest themselves?

Whether or not one can identify Carroll's great skills as a poetic performer, no reader can fail to respond to Carroll's sense of fun. He has such a good time within his own mind that inevitably the reader is made happy in his mind. One of the most unusual and certainly one of the most delightful of Carroll's performances is "Jabberwocky":

Jabberwocky

Lewis Carroll

'Twas brillig, and the slithy toves
   Did gyre and gimble in the wabe;
All mimsy were the borogoves,
   And the mome raths outgrabe.

"Beware the Jabberwock, my son!
   The jaws that bite, the claws that catch!
Beware the Jubjub bird, and shun
   The frumious Bandersnatch!"

He took his vorpal sword in hand;
   Long time the manxome foe he sought—
So rested he by the Tumtum tree,
   And stood awhile in thought.

And, as in uffish thought he stood,
   The Jabberwock, with eyes of flame,
Came whiffling through the tulgey wood,
   And burbled as it came!

One, two! One, two! And through and through
   The vorpal blade went snicker-snack!
He left it dead, and with its head
   He went galumphing back.

"And hast thou slain the Jabberwock?
   Come to my arms, my beamish boy!
O frabjous day! Callooh! Callay!
   He chortled in his joy.

'Twas brillig, and the slithy toves
   Did gyre and gimble in the wabe;
All mimsy were the borogoves,
   And the mome raths outgrabe.

Everyone knows that "Jabberwocky" is a "nonsense" poem: it may be found so listed in any number of anthologies. The word "jabber" in the title, followed by "wocky" (whatever that may mean) is itself descriptive: if there were such a thing as a "wocky" this is the way it might "jabber."

In case there were any doubt about the fun, Carroll "explains" this poem in *Through the Looking Glass*. There, Alice and Humpty Dumpty discuss it, and Humpty Dumpty, after an unenlightening explanation of "brillig," goes on to explain "slithy":

> Well, "slithy" means "lithe and slimy."
> "Lithe" is the same as active. You see
> it's like a portmanteau—there are two
> meanings packed up in one word.

Later he identifies "mimsy" as another portmanteau word made up of "flimsy and miserable."

And with Humpty Dumpty's encouragement a number of people have hunted through "Jabberwocky" for other portmanteau words and for what has been packed into them. Such word-hunting is pleasant enough as a game, and it is clearly founded in the author's own directive. Where, moreover, there is such good reason for believing the poem to be "nonsense," little will be served by denying its character as such. But what is "nonsense"? Is it the same as "non-sense"? Suppose that Carroll had written not a poem but an orchestral *scherzo*, a simple but brilliant piece of fun-music: would one be so readily tempted to call such music "nonsense"? Let the Wocky jabber as it will—and beautiful jabber it is—there is still a second sort of performance to which the appearance of "non-sense" gives an especially apt flavor. And that second performance involves a great deal of "sense" if by "sense" one means "meaningful comment upon an identifiable subject."

One must go a long way round to identify the subject and the comment upon it. Even then his identifications cannot be more than good guesses. The long way round, however, has the advantage of rambling through some of the most attractive and most native of English poetry, and it will further serve to raise some basic questions about the nature of the poetic performance.

Assume for the sake of exploration that the performance of "Jabberwocky" does involve "sensible" comment on a subject. What sort of performance is it, and what clues are there to the nature of its subject? The beamish (whatever that is) boy is warned about a monster called The Jabberwock. The boy is warned to shun it, and also the Jubjub bird and the frumious (furious, ruminous, gloomious?) Bandersnatch (who "snatches at banter"?) Instead of shunning it, however, the boy hunts its, slays it, and is welcomed back as a conquering hero. Clearly, the tone of all this is mock-heroic.

"Father William" and "The Crocodile" provide any reader with reason enough to look for mockery in Carroll's poems. But what could he be mocking here? A first clue lies in the devices Carroll uses in his poetic performance. The poem is deeply indebted to the techniques of English ballads. Stanzas one and two of "Jabberwocky," for example, utter some sort of dark prophecy. In disregard of that prophecy, the hero goes forth to mortal combat. He succeeds in overcoming his dark fate and returns victorious to a hero's welcome. Variants of this basic action may be found in countless ballads. Sometimes the hero returns victorious to be greeted with joy, sometimes he returns dying to be saluted with a lament, sometimes the action takes a different turn. The pattern itself, however, is unmistakable, and in order to sense meaningfully what Carroll is doing with this pattern, the reader will have to take an excursion through English balladry, both "folk" and "literary."

Folk Ballads

The introductions to the various ballads that follow will point out specific characteristics of the form, but a brief guide at the outset will be useful.

The folk ballad is an anonymous product of the native culture, put together by many unknown folk-singers. Folk ballads were not set down on paper at their point of origin, but were sung. Others heard the ballads and repeated them. Such singers had no original text to which they felt they must be faithful. They were simply attracted to a moving song-story. When they came on something in the ballad that did not suit them, they changed it. When they came on something that seemed unimportant, they simply forgot it. Thus the ballad has gone through a process of evolution by natural selection. No "literary" judges passed upon it. It either made itself unforgettable or it was forgotten. This process of oral transmission through many centuries has amounted to an ethnic experiment in the nature of poetry and of story telling. It follows that what survives such transmission must be inseparable from the "poetic pulse" of the language. The ballads, therefore, demonstrate principles of poetry and of story telling in a way that must be basic to both arts. Ballads have been remembered by the culture only because they are memorable.

It is easier to remember the high spots of an action than to remember all the connecting detail: so the folk ballad leaps from peak to peak of the story's action, skipping the incidentals. It is easier to remember an action than it is to keep straight the moral comment upon it: so the folk ballad tends to consist of action for its own sake, and to avoid moralization. It is easier, obviously, to remember an effective image, phrases, or detail than it is to remember an ordinary or ineffective one: so the folk ballad, its weak points weeded out, has become a treasury of a sort of poetry that English-speaking people have found unforgettable. Finally, the folk-mind is most likely to be attracted to larger rather than smaller kinds of action: so the folk ballad is full of tales of life and death—of tragic loves, of bloody betrayals, of heroic deeds; and so the action tends to be direct and uncomplicated by subtleties and minor motives.

The literary ballad, as will be discussed below, is a conscious imitation of the folk form by a single poet.

The following ballads are meant to be read for pleasure. Most of them, moreover—to combine business with pleasure—have some story elements in common with those Carroll uses in "Jabberwocky." In the course of the reading, all such elements should be noted and marked for later discussion.

Childe Maurice

Childe Maurice hunted the Silver Wood,
    He whistled as he sang:
I think I see the woman yonder
    That I have lovèd lang."

He called to his bonnie boy:
    "You do not see what I see.
Yonder's the very first woman
    That ever lovèd me."

"Woe's me for you, my master,
    Your name it waxes wide;
It is not for your rich, rich robes,
    Nor yet for your great pride,
But all is for yon lord's ladie
    That lives on Ithan side."

"Go take her this green mantel,
    Lined all with fur it is;
And bid her come to the Silver Wood
    To speak with Childe Maurice.

And take to her this silken shirt,
    Her own hand sewed the sleeve;
And bid her come to the Silver Wood
    And ask not Burnard's leave."

The boy got to the castle.
    He ran right through the gate.
Until he came to the high, high hall
    Where the company sat at meat.

"God make you safe you ladies all,
    God make you safe and sure;
But Burnard's lady among you all,
    My errand is to her.

Take you here this green mantel,
    Lined all with fur it is;
You're bidden come to the Silver Wood
    And speak to Childe Maurice.

Take you here this silken shirt,
    Your own hand sewed the sleeve:
You're bidden come to the Silver Wood,
    And ask not Burnard's leave."

Then out and spake him bold Burnard,
    Behind the door stood he:
"I'll go unto the Silver Wood
    And see what he may be.

Come, bring to me the gowns of silk,
    Your petticoats so small,
And I will go to the Silver Wood
    And try him with a fall."

Childe Maurice stood in the Silver Wood,
    He whistled and he sang:
"I think I see the woman come
    That I have lovèd lang."

"What now, what now, Childe Maurice.
    What now, and how do ye?
How long have you my lady lovèd?
    This day come tell to me."

He's taken out a long long sword
    And flashed it through the air,
And he's taken off Childe Maurice's head,
    And put it on a spear:
The soberest boy in all the court
    Childe Maurice's head did bear.

He's put the head in a basin wide
    And brought it to the hall,
And laid it in his lady's lap,
    Saying, "Lady, here's a ball!

Now play with it, my lady," he said,
    "Now play from hall to bower;
Play all ye please with Childe Maurice's head
    Who was your paramour."

                                        (modified excerpt)

Johnie Armstrong

Johnie Armstrong was a robber baron of the Scottish border. The Scottish king, both jealous and afraid of his power, summoned him to court with all his men under promise of good treatment and then ordered that Johnie and all his men be executed. In almost all of the (much longer) existing folk-versions, Johnie not only protests his loyalty to the king and offers him great gifts and armed support, but makes clear his claim that he has raided only the English and never turned his force against a Scottish subject. The King refuses his gifts (once Johnie is dead, all his possessions will be forfeit to the crown) and Johnie and his men go down fighting rather than submit. The last three stanzas, and especially the final one, are great examples of the power of the ballad.

There dwelt a man in fair Westmorland,
    Johnie Armstrong men did him call.
He had neither lands nor rents coming in,
    Yet he kept eight score men in his hall.

He had horses and harness for them all.
    There goodly steeds were all milk-white.
O the golden bands all about their necks!
    Their weapons, they were all alike.

The news was brought unto the king
    That there was such a one as he
That lived like a bold out-law,
    And robbed all the north-countree.

The king he writ a letter then,
    A letter which was large and long,
And signed it with his own hand,
    And he promised to do him no wrong.

When this letter came to Johnie,
    His heart was as blythe as birds on the tree:
"Never was I sent for before any king,
    My father, my grandfather, nor none but me.

And if we go the king before,
    I would we went most orderly;
Let everyman wear his scarlet cloak
    Laced up with silver laces three.

Let everyman wear his velvet coat
    Laced with silver lace so white.
O the golden bands all about your necks!
    Black hats, white feathers, all alike."

By the morrow morning at ten of the clock,
    Towards Edenburough gone was he,
And with him all his eight score men.
    Good lord, it was a goodly sight to see!

When Johnie came before the king,
　He fell down on his knee.
"O pardon my sovereign liege," he said,
　"O pardon my eight score men and me!"

"Thou shalt have no pardon, thou traitor strong,
　For thy eight score men nor thee;
For tomorrow morning by ten of the clock
　Both thou and them shall hang on the gallow-tree."

But Johnie looked over his left shoulder,
　Good Lord, what a grievous look looked he!
Saying, "Asking grace of a graceless face—
　Why there is none for you nor me."

But Johnie had a bright sword by his side,
　And it was made of the mettle so free,
That had not the king stept his foot aside,
　He had smitten his head from his fair bodie.

Saying: "Fight on, my merry men all,
　And see that none of you be taine;
For rather than men shall say we were hanged,
　Let them say how we were slain."

Then, God wot, fair Edenburough rose,
　And so beset poor Johnie round,
That four score and ten of his best men
　Lay gasping all upon the ground.

Then like a mad man Johnie laid about,
　And like a mad men then fought he,
Until a false Scot come Johnie behind
　And ran him through the fair bodie.

Saying: "Fight on, my merry men all,
　And see that none of you be taine;
For I will lie down and bleed awhile,
　And then I will rise and fight again."

　　　　　　　　　　　　　　(condensed version)

Sir Patrick Spens

Sir Patrick Spens (or Spence) is certainly the best known of the
Scottish ballads and may well be taken as a model for the ballad form.
I have modernized the language but a few points of difficulty remain.
In stanza three "a broad letter" probably means "an official letter, a royal

command." In stanza eight the "shoon" means "shoes" and "aboon," means "above." "Their hats they swam aboon," means "Their hats floated above them" (*i.e.* the crew sank leaving their hats floating on the surface).

The King sits in Dumferling town,
    Drinking the blood-red wine:
"O where will I get good sailors
    To sail this ship of mine?"

Up and spoke an old knight,
    Sat at the King's right knee:
"Sir Patrick Spens is the best sailor
    That sails upon the sea."

The King has written a broad letter,
    And signed it with his hand,
And sent it to Sir Patrick Spens,
    Was walking on the sand.

The first line that Sir Patrick read
    A loud laugh laughed he:
The next line that Sir Patrick read,
    A tear blinded his ee.

"O who is this has done this deed,
    This ill deed done to me,
To send me out this time of the year
    To sail upon the sea?

Make haste, make haste, my merry men all,
    Our good ship sails at morn."
"O say not so, my master dear,
    For I fear a deadly storm.

Late, late last night I saw the new moon
    with the old moon in her arm,
And I fear, I fear, my master dear,
    That we will come to harm."

O our Scots nobles were right loth
    To wet their cork-heeled shoon;
But long ere all the play was played,
    Their hats they swam aboon.

O long, long will their ladies sit
    With their fans into their hand,
Before they see Sir Patrick Spens
    Come sailing to the land.

O long, long will the ladies stand
   With their gold combs in their hair,
Waiting for their own dear lords,
   For they'll see them no mair.

Half-o'er, half-o'er to Abadour
   'Tis fifty fathoms deep,
And there lies good Sir Patrick Spens
   With the Scots lords at his feet.

A Lyke-Wake Dirge

Since the present chapter is, among other things, a ramble through some specimen English ballads, there is no reason to avoid inviting by-paths. The "Lyke-Wake Dirge" is very far indeed from "Jabberwocky," but certainly it must not be omitted from any discussion of the ballad tradition, though it is not strictly speaking a ballad but a folk-dirge for a departed soul, as moving a knell for the departed as any in the English language.

The idea of the "lyke-wake" survives in the modern Irish wake, the custom of sitting up with the dead. "Lyke" meant body or corpse. In this dirge, the soul is described as going first to "Whinny-muir," a moor grown with "whins" or thorny furze bushes. If in life the departed had "given shoes" (been generous) his soul would have them now; if not, the thorns would prick him to the bone. "Brig o' Dread" is bridge of dread, between this world and the next. The idea of a bridge to immortality, or a bridge between the real world and the world of fairyland, was not uncommon in medieval literature.

This ae nighte, this ae nighte,
   —*Every nighte and alle,*
Fire and sleet and candle-lighte,
   And Christe receive thy saule.

When thou from hence away art past,
   —*Every nighte and alle,*
To Whinny-muir thou com'st at last;
   And Christe receive thy saule.

If ever thou gavest hosen and shoon,
   —*Every nighte and alle,*
Sit thee down and put them on;
   And Christe receive thy saule.

If hosen and shoon thou ne'er gav'st nane
   —*Every nighte and alle,*
The whinnes sall prick thee to the bare bane;
   And Christe receive thy saule.

From Whinny-muir when thou may'st pass,
—*Every nighte and alle,*
To Brig o' Dread thou com'st at last;
And Christe receive thy saule.

From Brig o' Dread when thou may'st pass,
—*Every nighte and alle,*
To Purgatory fire thou com'st at last;
And Christe receive thy saule.

If ever thou gavest meat or drink,
—*Every nighte and alle,*
The fire sall never make thee shrink;
And Christe receive thy saule.

If meat or drink thou ne'er gav'st nane,
—*Every nighte and alle,*
The fire will burn thee to the bare bane;
And Christe receive thy saule.

This ae nighte, this ae nighte,
—*Every nighte and alle,*
Fire and sleet and candle-lighte,
And Christe receive thy saule.

this ae nighte: this very night. **hosen and shoon:** stockings and shoes. **whinnes:** furze. **bane:** bone. **sall:** shall.

Edward

To illustrate the great vitality of the ballad and its diffusion through many cultures, the ballad of Edward is here reproduced in a Scottish form and also in a version recorded in North Carolina. The two texts are taken from Albert B. Friedman's *The Viking Book of Folk Ballads of the English Speaking World* (The Viking Press, New York, 1956). "Lord Randal" is added as an example of a similar but independent ballad. It also exists in many Scotch, English, and American forms, and Mr. Friedman thinks it may originally have been transplanted from Italy. The form of text A of "Edward" follows Mr. Friedman's text without modernization. The following note is excerpted from his introduction to the ballad:

Entirely developed through dialogue, the ballad manages to generate enormous dramatic tension. As a result, there is no more powerful climax in any ballad than the surprise revelation of the mother's guilt in the last lines of "Edward." Some scholars suspect the folk tradition had literary assistance here. . . . The "Edward" story has proved too "strong" for the American folk: a brother or a brother-in-law, not the sufferer's father, is the victim in American versions, and the mother has no share in the crime . . . . the American ballads may be nearer the original form of the story since a brother was also the victim in the lost English or Scottish version from which the Scandinavian ballads on this theme descended. In A, Edward intends to go into exile. Another Scottish version has him setting his foot in a "bottomless boat," thus suggesting that in an ancient form of the story Edward submitted himself to exposure in an open boat, a medieval punishment for fratricide. Text B from North Carolina repre‚ sents the American tradition.

— A —

"Why dois your brand sae drap wi' bluid,
        Edward, Edward?
Why dois your brand sae drip wi' bluid?
    And why sae sad gang yee, O?"
"O, I hae killed my hauke sae guid,
        Mither, mither,
O, I hae killed my hauke sae guid,
    And I had nae mair bot hee, O."

"Your haukis bluid was nevir sae reid,
        Edward, Edward,
Your haukis bluid was nevir sae reid,
    My deir son I tell thee, O."
"O, I hae killed my reid-roan steid,
        Mither, mither,
O, I hae killed my reid-roan steid,
    That erst was sae fair and frie, O."

"Your steid was auld, and yee hae gat mair,
        Edward, Edward,
Your steid was auld, and yee hae gat mair,
    Sum other dule ye drie, O."
"O, I hae killed my fadir deir,
        Mither, mither,
O, I hae killed my fadir deir,
    Alas, and wae is mee, O!"

"And whatten penance wul yee drie for that,
        Edward, Edward?
And whatten penance wul yee drie for that?
    My deir son, now tell me, O."
"Ile set my feit in yonder boat,
        Mither, mither,
Ile set my feit in yonder boat,
    And Ile fare ovir the sea, O."

"And what wul yee doe wi' your towirs and your ha',
　　　　Edward, Edward?
And what wul yee doe wi' your towirs and your ha',
　　That were sae fair to see, O?
"Ile let thame stand tul they doun fa',
　　　　Mither, mither,
Ile let thame stand tul they doun fa',
　　For here nevir mair maun I bee, O."

"And what wul yee leive to your bairns and your wife,
　　　　Edward, Edward?
And what wul yee leive to your bairns and your wife,
　　When yee gang ovir the sea, O?"
"The warldis room, late them beg thrae life,
　　　　Mither, mither,
The warldis room, late them beg thrae life,
　　For thame nevir mair wul I see, O."

"And what wul yee leive to your ain mither deir,
　　　　Edward, Edward?
And what wul yee leive to your ain mither deir?
　　My deir son, now tell me, O."
"The curse of hell frae me sall yee beir,
　　　　Mither, mither,
The curse of hell frae me sall yee beir,
　　Sic counseils yee gave to me, O."

— B —

"How comes that blood all over your shirt?
My son, come tell it to me."
"It's the blood of my little guinea pig—
O mother, please let me be.
Its the blood of my little guinea pig—
O mother, please let me be.

"Your guinea pig's blood is not so red.
My son come tell it to me."
"It's the blood of my little hunting dog
That played in the field for me . . ."

"Your dog lies yonder, O my son,
And this it could not be."
"It is the blood of my old roan horse
That pulled the plow for me . . ."

"How comes that blood all over your shirt?
My son, you must tell to me."
"It's the blood of my little brother Bill
Who I killed in the field today."

"And what will you do when your father comes home?
My son, come tell it to me."
"I'll put my feet in the bottom of a boat
I'll put my feet in the bottom of a boat
And sail across the sea.
And sail across the sea."

brand: sword. **sae:** so. **haukis:** hawk's. **dule:** dole, grief. **drie:** endure. **bairns:** children. **the warldis room:** the world's room, *i.e.,* the length and breadth of the world. **thrae:** through. **gang:** go. **sic counseils:** such counsels.

Lord Randal

"O where hae ye been, Lord Randal, my son?
  O where hae ye been, my handsome young man?"
"I hae been to the wild wood; mother, make my bed soon,
  For I'm weary wi' hunting, and fain wald lie down."

"Where gat ye your dinner, Lord Randal, my son?
  Where gat ye your dinner, my handsome young man?"
"I din'd wi' my true-love; mother, make my bed soon,
  For I'm weary wi' hunting, and fain wald lie down."

"What gat ye to your dinner, Lord Randal, my son?
  What gat ye to your dinner, my handsome young man?"
"I gat eels boil'd in broth; mother, make my bed soon,
  For I'm weary wi' hunting, and fain wald lie down."

"What became of your bloodhounds, Lord Randal, my son?
  What became of your bloodhounds, my handsome young man?"
"O they swell'd and they died; mother, make my bed soon,
  For I'm weary wi' hunting, and fain wald lie down."

"O I fear ye are poisoned, Lord Randal, my son!
  O I fear ye are poisoned, my handsome young man!"
"O yes! I am poison'd; mother, make my bed soon,
  For I'm sick at the heart, and fain wald lie down."

Literary Ballads

From Chaucer's time to the eighteenth century, the ballad had a relatively small place in "serious" English poetry, but following the eighteenth century's revival of interest in England's literary antiquities and the wider awareness of the ballad as a form, it was inevitable that poets should find the ballad way of telling a story irresistible. Thousands of ballads, good, bad, and miserably bad were written in the nineteenth century. "Written" here is used literally: these ballads were composed by a single man deliberately re-working the ballad form for his own purposes. "The Old Man's Comforts" is a ballad heavily invested with morality. (The folk ballad seldom bothers to draw a moral; its native interest is in telling a story.) Many literary balladeers hoaxed-up the ballad form with so much flummery and so many perfumed asides that it tended to die of over-decoration. Others strove for the heroic strain and succeeded only in achieving a mock-heroic pastiche.

Of the ballads that follow, the excerpt from "Marco Bozzaris" may be taken as a fair example of the mock-heroic smother. "A Ballad of Hell" may be taken as a relatively successful, though unmistakably literary imitation, of the pure ballad. "The Yarn of the Nancy Bell" may be taken as a happy example of a poet having fun with the ballad form.

QUESTIONS

1. Compare the following poems with "Johnie Armstrong." Which elements of the performance of each poem seem to make the difference in tone? The Scottish border lords proudly recorded Johnie Armstrong's death as an example of tyranny resisted, and Halleck certainly sings Bozzaris' praises for the same reason. Is Halleck more interested in the story or in the moral he derives from it?

2. Assuming that "Marco Bozzaris" were memorable enough to undergo folk-transmission, which parts of it might survive and which parts would most probably be dropped in oral transmission?

3. What differences between ballad and poem can you identify in the language, in the tone, and in the kind of incident? In "Sir Patrick Spens" the description of the crew drowning ("Their hats they swam aboon") is a classic trope known as *synechdoche*, a figure of speech in which a part is used to represent the whole. Note that there are no shrieks of the dying, no final prayers, no moral pronouncements, but simply the statement that long before the Scot's lords crossed the water their hats floated above them on the tide. The tremendous last stanza of "Johnie Armstrong" on the other hand is a *hyperbole* (an exaggeration), but a hyperbole made with such understatement (paradoxical as that may seem) that it leaves no sense of over-reaching for effect.

4. Compare Bozzaris' exhortation to his band in stanza three. Had Marine sergeants on Guadalcanal been required to make all their orders quotations from English poetry, and had one of them had to cheer his men on during a battle, would he have been more tempted to quote Bozzaris or Johnie Armstrong? That is to say, which is better "fight-talk"?

Marco Bozzaris

(April 20, 1823)

Fitz-Greene Halleck

At midnight, in his guarded tent,
   The Turk was dreaming of the hour
When Greece, her knee in suppliance bent,
   Should tremble at his power:
In dreams, through camp and court, he bore
The trophies of a conqueror;
   In dreams his song of triumph heard;
Then wore his monarch's signet ring:
Then pressed that monarch's throne—a king;
As wild his thoughts, and gay of wing,
   As Eden's garden bird.

At midnight, in the forest shades,
   Bozzaris ranged his Suliote band,
True as the steel of their tried blades,
   Heroes in heart and hand.
There had the Persian's thousands stood,
There had the glad earth drunk their blood
   On old Platæa's day;
And now there breathed that haunted air
The sons of sires who conquered there,
With arm to strike, and soul to dare,
   As quick, as far as they.

An hour passed on—the Turk awoke;
   That bright dream was his last;
He woke—to hear his sentries shriek,
"To arms! they come! the Greek! the Greek!"
He woke—to die midst flame, and smoke,
And shout, and groan, and sabre-stroke,
   And death-shots falling thick and fast
As lightnings from the mountain-cloud;
And heard, with voice as trumpet loud,
   Bozzaris cheer his band:
"Strike—till the last armed foe expires;
Strike—for your altars and your fires;
Strike—for the green graves of your sires;
   God—and your native land!"

They fought—like brave men, long and well;
   They piled that ground with Moslem slain,

They conquered—but Bozzaris fell,
　Bleeding at every vein.
His few surviving comrades saw
His smile when rang their proud hurrah,
　And the red field was won;
Then saw in death his eyelids close
Calmly, as to a night's repose,
　Like flowers at set of sun.

Come to the bridal-chamber, Death!
　Come to the mother's, when she feels,
For the first time, her first-born's breath;
　Come when the blessed seals
That close the pestilence are broke,
And crowded cities wail its stroke;
Come in consumption's ghastly form,
The earthquake shock, the ocean storm;
Come when the heart beats high and warm
　With banquet-song, and dance, and wine;
And thou art terrible—the tear,
The groan, the knell, the pall, the bier,
And all we know, or dream, or fear
　Of agony, are thine.

But to the hero, when his sword
　Has won the battle for the free,
Thy voice sounds like a prophet's word;
And in its hollow tones are heard
　The thanks of millions yet to be.
Come, when his task of fame is wrought—
Come, with her laurel-leaf, blood-bought—
　Come in her crowning hour—and then
Thy sunken eye's unearthly light
To him is welcome as the sight
　Of sky and stars to prisoned men:
Thy grasp is welcome as the hand
Of brother in a foreign land;
Thy summons welcome as the cry
That told the Indian isles were nigh
　To the world-seeking Genoese,
When the land wind, from woods of palm,
And orange groves, and fields of balm,
　Blew o'er the Haytian seas.

Bozzaris! with the storied brave
　Greece nurtured in her glory's time,
Rest thee—there is no prouder grave,
　Even in her own proud clime.

She wore no funeral-weeds for thee,
  Nor bade the dark hearse wave its plume
Like torn branch from death's leafless tree
In sorrow's pomp and pageantry,
  The heartless luxury of the tomb;
But she remembers thee as one
Long loved, and for a season gone;
For thee her poet's lyre is wreathed,
Her marble wrought, her music breathed;
For thee she rings the birthday bells;
Of thee her babes' first lisping tells;
For thine her evening prayer is said
At palace-couch and cottage-bed;
Her soldier, closing with the foe,
Gives for thy sake a deadlier blow;
His plighted maiden, when she fears
For him, the joy of her young years,
Thinks of thy fate, and checks her tears:
  And she, the mother of thy boys,
Though in her eye and faded cheek
Is read the grief she will not speak,
  The memory of her buried joys,
And even she who gave thee birth,
Will, by their pilgrim-circled hearth,
  Talk of thy doom without a sigh:
For thou art Freedom's now, and Fame's:
One of the few, the immortal names,
  That were not born to die.

                                        (excerpt)

All criticism of poetry begins fundamentally with "I like it" or "I don't like it." It seems impossible to imagine a reader of "A Ballad of Hell" who does not find himself liking the heroine. She certainly performs superbly the role of the ballad heroine, and finding her unforgettable, the reader can scarcely forget the poem. Yet certainly, had the ballad undergone folk-transmission a number of its details would have disappeared. Both the heroine and Sir Patrick receive alarming letters and take action as a result of them. The time between the receipt of the letter and the beginning of the consequent action may reasonably be called—by analogy to a play—"the letter scene." Compare the two Letter Scenes. Which is the more effective performance? Could anything be added to Sir Patrick's reaction to make it more effective? Could anything be subtracted from the heroine's?

In general, could anything well be added to Sir Patrick or subtracted from "A Ballad of Hell"? How long does the heroine take to kill herself? How long might she have taken had she been a true ballad product?

ranged: drew up into battle formation, arranged.

How long does it take her to get to Hell, once she has died? How "devilish" is the Devil? Compare the heroine's defiance of the Devil and of Hell with Johnie Armstrong's defiance of the Scottish King.

A Ballad of Hell

John Davidson

"A letter from my love today!
　Oh, unexpected, dear appeal!"
She struck a happy tear away
　And broke the crimson seal.

"My love, there is no help on earth,
　No help in heaven; the dead-man's bell
Must toll our wedding; our first hearth
　Must be the well-paved floor of hell."

The color died from out her face,
　Her eyes like ghostly candles shone;
She cast dread looks about the place,
　Then clenched her teeth and read right on.

"I may not pass the prison door;
　Here must I rot from day to day,
Unless I wed whom I abhor,
　My cousin, Blanche of Valencay.

"At midnight with my dagger keen,
　I'll take my life; it must be so.
Meet me in hell tonight, my queen,
　For weal and woe."

She laughed, although her face was wan,
　She girded on her golden belt,
She took her jewelled ivory fan,
　And at her glowing missal knelt.

Then rose, "And am I mad?" she said.
　She broke her fan, her belt untied;
With leather girt herself instead,
　And stuck a dagger at her side.

She waited, shuddering in her room,
　Till sleep had fallen on all the house.
She never flinched; she faced her doom:
　They two must sin to keep their vows.

Then out into the night she went,
 And, stooping, crept by hedge and tree;
Her rose-bush flung a snare of scent,
 And caught a happy memory.

She fell, and lay a minute's space;
 She tore the sward in her distress;
The dewy grass refreshed her face;
 She rose and ran with lifted dress.

She started like a morn-caught ghost
 Once when the moon came out and stood
To watch; the naked road she crossed,
 And dived into the murmuring wood.

The branches snatched her streaming cloak;
 A live thing shrieked; she made no stay!
She hurried to the trysting-oak—
 Right well she knew the way.

Without a pause she bared her breast,
 And drove her dagger home and fell,
And lay like one that takes her rest,
 And died and wakened up in hell.

She bathed her spirit in the flame,
 And near the center took her post;
From all sides to her ears there came
 The dreary anguish of the lost.

The devil started at her side,
 Comely, and tall, and black as jet.
"I am young Malespina's bride;
 Has he come hither yet?"

"My poppet, welcome to your bed."
 "Is Malespina here?"
"Not he! Tomorrow he must wed
 His cousin Blanche, my dear!"

"You lie, he died with me tonight."
 "Not he! it was a plot" . . . "You lie."
"My dear, I never lie outright."
 "We died at midnight, he and I."

The devil went. Without a groan
 She, gathered up in one fierce prayer,
Took root in hell's midst all alone,
 And waited for him there.

She dared to make herself at home
    Amidst the wail, the uneasy stir.
The blood-stained flame that filled the dome,
    Scentless and silent, shrouded her.

How long she stayed I cannot tell;
    But when she felt his perfidy,
She marched across the floor of hell;
    And all the damned stood up to see.

The devil stopped her at the brink.
    She shook him off; she cried, "Away!"
"My dear, you have gone mad, I think."
    "I was betrayed: I will not stay."

Across the weltering deep she ran;
    A stranger thing was never seen:
The damned stood silent to a man;
    They saw the great gulf set between.

To her it seemed a meadow fair;
    And flowers sprang up about her feet;
She entered heaven; she climbed the stair;
    And knelt down at the mercy-seat.

Seraphs and saints with one great voice
    Welcomed that soul that knew not fear.
Amazed to find it could rejoice,
    Hell raised a hoarse, half-human cheer.

The Yarn of the Nancy Bell

William Schwenck Gilbert

"The Yarn of the Nancy Bell" was written in 1866 and offered to *Punch* but was rejected on the grounds that cannibalism was too offensive a theme. By "a theme" one generally understands "what the writer set out to say." To what extent did the writer set out to write about cannibalism?

Is it possible that his real intent was to write a parody of Coleridge's "Ancient Mariner"? (p. 721)

How "real" is the cannibalism? Note that in the first line of stanza eleven the survivors had neither "wittles (victuals) nor drink." Yet in stanza eighteen it is clear that the cook not only has water, but a very large kettle, salt and pepper, shalot (along with something to chop it with) and sage and parsley—practically an epicure's kitchen. Could one explain this contradiction to Mr. Gradgrind's satisfaction?

'Twas on the shores that round our coast
   From Deal to Ramsgate span,
That I found alone on a piece of stone
   An elderly naval man.

His hair was weedy, his beard was long,
   And weedy and long was he,
And I heard this wight on the shore recite
   In a singular minor key:

"Oh, I am a cook and a captain bold,
   And the mate of the *Nancy* brig,
And a bo'sun tight, and a midshipmite,
   And the crew of the captain's gig."

And he shook his fists, and he tore his hair,
   Till I really felt afraid,
For I couldn't help thinking the man had been drinking,
   And so I simply said:

"Oh elderly man, it's little I know
   Of the duties of men of the sea,
And I'll eat my hand if I understand
   However you can be

At once a cook, and a captain bold,
   And the mate of the *Nancy* brig,
And a bo'sun tight, and a midshipmite,
   And the crew of the captain's gig."

Then he gave a hitch to his trousers, which
   Is a trick all seamen larn,
And having got rid of a thumping quid,
   He spun this painful yarn:

" 'Twas in the good ship *Nancy Bell*
   That we sailed to the Indian Sea,
And there on a reef we came to grief,
   Which has often occurred to me.

And pretty nigh all the crew was drowned
   (There was seventy-seven o' soul),
And only ten of the *Nancy's* men
   Said 'Here!' to the muster-roll.

There was me and the cook and the captain bold,
   And the mate of the *Nancy* brig,

Deal and Ramsgate: Seaside resorts on the coast of Kent. **thumping quid:** of chewing tobacco. **seventy-seven o' soul:** seventy-seven souls.

And the bo'sun tight, and a midshipmite,
  And the crew of the captain's gig.

For a month we'd neither wittles nor drink,
  Till a-hungry we did feel,
So we drawed a lot, and, accordin' shot
  The captain for our meal.

The next lot fell to the *Nancy's* mate,
  And a delicate dish he made;
Then our appetite with the midshipmite
  We seven survivors stayed.

And then we murdered the bo'sun tight,
  And he much resembled pig;
Then we wittled free, did the cook and me,
  On the crew of the captain's gig.

Then only the cook and me was left,
  And the delicate question, 'Which
Of us two goes to the kettle?' arose,
  And we argued it out as sich.

For I loved that cook as a brother, I did,
  And the cook he worshiped me;
But we'd both be blowed if we'd either be stowed
  In the other chap's hold, you see.

'I'll be eat if you dines off me,' says Tom;
  'Yes, that,' says I, 'you'll be—'
'I'm boiled if I die, my friend,' quoth I;
  And 'Exactly so,' quoth he.

Says he, 'Dear James, to murder me
  Were a foolish thing to do,
For don't you see that you can't cook *me*,
  While I can—and will—cook *you!*'

So he boils the water, and takes the salt
  And the pepper in portions true
(Which he never forgot) and some chopped shalot,
  And some sage and parsley too.

'Come here,' says he, with a proper pride
  Which his smiling features tell,
' 'Twill soothing be if I let you see
  How extremely nice you'll smell.'

And he stirred it round and round and round,
  And he sniffed at the foaming froth;

When I ups with his heels, and smothers his squeals
  In the scum of the boiling broth.

And I eat that cook in a week or less,
  And—as I eating be
The last of his chops, why, I almost drops,
  For a wessel in sight I see!

❁   ❁   ❁   ❁

And I never larf, and I never smile,
  And I never lark nor play,
But sit and croak, and a single joke
  I have—which is to say:

'Oh, I am a cook and a captain bold,
  And the mate of the *Nancy* brig,
And a bos'sun tight, and a midshipmite,
  And the crew of the captain's gig!' "

Jabberwocky Revisited

With some knowledge of the ballad in his background, one is prepared to see in "Jabberwocky" a number of devices that might not have been visible at first reading. The first stanza of "Jabberwocky," for example, is unmistakably based on a ballad motif that may be called "the opening contest of dark forces" (see the beginning of "Marco Bozzaris"). The second stanza reinforces the dark mood of the opening forces with a ballad motif that may be called "the dark warning" (see stanza 7 of "Sir Patrick Spens"). Stanzas three through five describe some vastly heroic action of arms (see the death of Childe Maurice and Johnie Armstrong's final battle). Stanza six presents the hero returning in triumph (see Hallecks' final windy salute to Bozzaris. The beamish boy was luckier than Bozzaris, but both receive an accolade).

Carroll, however, uses these heroic patterns only to blow them up by exaggeration into the mock-heroic. The Jabberwock and the frumious Bandersnatch may be dark forces, but they are more ridiculous than frightful. The conquering hero, a bit of an "uffish" oaf at best, does not ride back in state but goes "galumphing back." He is greeted not as "Bozzaris! with the storied brave!" but as my "beamish boy." Nor can one fail to note that the final voice, like the hero himself, is slightly cracked and queer.

But what is Carroll inflating so carefully into a kind of ultimate ridiculousness? Carroll's is a playful mind, and playful poets always tend to be evasive. As Robert Frost wrote of his neighbor in "Mending Wall":

I could say "Elves" to him,
But it's not elves exactly, and I'd rather
He said it for himself.

Carroll, like Frost, would rather the reader said it for himself. And while a discerning reader will take care not to define rigidly what was meant to be felt rather than defined, Carroll has left clues enough to guide such a reader's guesses. We have already observed that Carroll found a special delight in deflating such pompous moral hypocrisies as many Victorian readers warmed to in Southey and Watts. And no one who has read Carroll's *Alice* can have failed to note the number of pompous bugaboos that present themselves to Alice only to be deflated by her natural logic. The Duchess is one such bugaboo. She confuses Alice at first and gives her a great deal of trouble, but Alice has only to say at the end "Why, you're nothing but a pack of cards," and the whole elaborate pretense of Wonderland blows up. The Jabberwocky, the Jubjub bird, and the Bandersnatch are also bugaboos. Is it too far-fetched to speculate that all of Carroll's bugaboos are related, and that all of them have their origin in Carroll's sense of the grotesque pompousness of a great deal of Victorian morality and social pretense?

So, over and over again, Carroll finds delight in deflating the pompous. Nothing deflates pomposity as does ridicule. And nonsense is one of the natural languages for ridiculing non-sense. Had Carroll set out with the announced aim of writing a ballad that would express a deep personal sense of one part of the Victorian character, it is impossible to imagine how he could have done better than he does in "Jabberwocky." Nonsense is the surface of the poem and its language of attack. But the very use of nonsense makes excellent sense. The nonsense surface-performance is one part of a very meaningful comment upon an identifiable subject. "Jabberwocky" is a happy and a graceful performance, but it is unmistakably— like almost everything else Carroll wrote—also a direct satire upon the mental habits of his own age. As noted, Carroll refuses to say directly that the subject is *X* or is not *X*. He might say *X*, but it's not *X* exactly. And he'd rather you said it for yourself. Nevertheless that second performance is certainly there: an effort (very much like that a choreographer might make for a Victorian Ballet Suite) to find poses, groupings, and actions that would present an accurately ridiculous sense of what was ridiculous in Carroll's age. "Jabberwocky" may be read with perfect coherence as a series of postures that interpret Victorian pomposity.

This function of poetry as a series of interpretive pictures is too seldom recognized and then usually too late in one's awareness of the poetic process, but the idea of this function is certainly not hard to grasp. Had there survived from Early and Middle English times only a series of ballad fragments, snatches describing sea captains drowned on impossible voyages, robber barons cheering the battle as they lay dying, betrayed lovers, sons cursing their mothers, and such like, there can be no doubt that the reader of such fragments would emerge with some rather definite impressions of what the age valued, *i.e.*, of how it felt about its mortal problems, and of *what sort of picture it had of itself*.

Most readers tend to lose sight of this force in poetry—of this sub-surface release of pictures from the psyche—because they tend to think of poems as made of words only. As they tend to think that all thinking is done with words. Words are inseparable from poetry and forever ready to release unforeseeable magic into the poetic performance. But no poem is made of words alone. Just as no thought exists in words alone. Feelings, suggestions, images arise out of the words and run free of them.

Nor, finally, are words our only language. Music is a language capable of communication. So is a painting. Watch a good mechanic listening to an engine that has come up for repair; can there be any doubt that the engine's noises are "talking" to the man, telling him what he needs to know? What the mechanic has in his mind is probably an intimate diagram of the engine's parts. He listens, relates the sounds to the picture in his mind, and comes to a conclusion: a pure case of a nonverbal thought process.

Or suppose that there existed somewhere a religious order that imposed a vow not only of eternal silence but against all verbalization even of one's thoughts. Initiates, suppose further, must pray a certain number of hours each day but *they must dance their prayers.* (The temple dancers of certain religious sects, for that matter, come very close to doing exactly that.) Can there be any doubt that the kinds of postures and the sequences of actions such dancers fall into could constitute not only a language but a language susceptible of great refinement?

In very much this way, the performance of a good poem is very likely to contain under its verbalization a dance of images, postures, and attitudes, and such motions, both separately and in their sequences, are an indispensable part of the poetic performance—a deep part, and a complicated one to discuss outside itself, but a part to which one cannot help responding whether or not he realizes what he is responding to. Pattern is a profound and active part of everyman's life. The dance of such patterns through his mind may even be the fundamental basis of all his thinking. But though that idea may be a difficult one to grasp in such terms as these, there is fortunately no difficulty in grasping examples of this sort of life-performance. The temple dancers are one such illustration. The revealing gestures a badly trained public-speaker makes on a platform—gestures that are from his basic nervous pattern and that have only the most tenuous connection with the words he may be speaking (or no connection at all if he is fidgeting through the recital of a memorized "piece")—are another such illustration. There are the words in his mouth and there are the patterns of fidget-and-twitch from his basic nervous life.

A poem has a similar sort of existence in that it has both a surface of words and an inner nervous life, but in a good poem there is the essential difference that the words and the nervous dance are two closely related parts of one thing.

Jabberwocky is an example of just such a poem. The surface of nonsense words goes happily on in its own self-entertaining way. But under the words there is a release of grotesque postures and pictures that amount to a series of dance-caricatures of the moral flaws in the poet's age, as he sees them. What must finally be seen is that the dance occurs not only under but with the words, one reinforcing the other. And though thousands upon thousands of readers have found delight in "Jabberwocky" without being aware of this interplay, it is exactly this interplay that has been the source of their delight.

Chapter Three

BY RIPPLING POOLS

"Symbolism" may be a frightening, or at least a mysterious, word. It may even be that a few, not necessarily representative, critics of poetry have used "symbolism" and similar terms in somewhat the way medieval alchemists used elaborate symbols—as a way of keeping the discussion private while releasing the suggestion that they were possessed of profound and secret knowledge. Actually, once the alchemist's myserious symbols are explained they generally turn out to be nothing more mysterious than signs for "salt," "iron," or for some simple chemical process.

Argument by analogy is not argument in good intellectual order unless the analogy can be shown to be apt at all points. It would be absurd to imply that literary criticism and alchemy are the same thing. They obviously are not. But though nothing can be concluded from such an analogy, it may still serve to illustrate the general principle that not everything surrounded by a mysterious aura need be taken as mysterious. The fact is we have already discussed symbolism. At this point we have merely added a technical name to the discussion. Basically, a symbol is *something that stands for something else*. A traffic light is a fixed symbol: it uses three different colors to stand for three commands. A dollar bill is also a symbol, but though it seems a fixed and clear symbol, it stands for a theory of wealth and of money-exchange that economists do not yet pretend wholly to understand. One can see, therefore, that even very simple symbols, upon careful reflection, tend to represent "areas of meaning in motion" rather than static equivalents. It follows that symbolism should offer a natural sort of language to the poet, interested as he must be to keep his "meaning" in motion.

The poems that follow in the present ramble include some of the best known narrative poems in the English language. Each one tells a story or part of a story. Read them for the pleasure to be found in a story well told. But as an exercise in more perceptive reading, concentrate on identifying and examining the force of every symbolic element in the narrative. Such a reading will demonstrate clearly that symbolism, far from being a mysterious and unknown device, is an essential part of good fictional technique. Coleridge's albatross, for example, in "The Rhyme of the Ancient Mariner," is a symbol. Its symbolic nature begins in the fact that it seems from the start to signify something more than its literal self. That symbolic nature is further made clear in the fact that it goes on adding significances (the widening of the ripples) as the story progresses. Far from being mysterious, this device is so common that few if any story tellers have ever managed to hold an audience long without such symbolic assistance.

The beginning reader will also see, on very little reflection, that he himself is constantly using symbolism and that human communication would be impossible without it. The Flag of the United States, for example, is a symbol made up of a complex of symbols. Taken in the most literal way, the fifty stars, the thirteen stripes, and the three colors, all have precisely fixed meanings. Each of the stars, for example, is assigned to represent one particular state, and no other, in the order of the state's admission into the union.

Any flag manual will run on with pages of such exact specifications. Thus, these literal and fixed meanings may be taken as a code. It is worth noting, too, that in the legislation that established this flag as the symbol of The United States, and in the discussion preceding the legislation, all of these code-symbols had to be discussed in more or less literal terms. Such discussion and legislation would not necessarily be unemotional, but it would certainly have to be considerably less emotional than, let us say, the present-day orator's attitudes toward the flag.

It seems clear that not only in poetry but in history itself—which is to say in the very motion of men's lives—symbols acquire emotional expansion and intensity in the process of being sustained over a period of time. As the flag became associated with more and more of the nation's struggles and triumphs, it tended to become less and less evidently the pre-determined legislative code it was at birth, and increasingly the symbol of a much broader emotional force. That emotional force, moreover, became so powerful that in many ways the flag tended to lose its character as a symbol and to become a living force in itself. Everyone today is familiar with the—unfortunately very bad—sculpture of the Marines raising the Flag on Iwo Jima. It is difficult to believe that those Marines afire with the life-and-death of battle were consciously concerned with symbolism. Hoisting the Flag is, of course, a symbolic action. But those Marines were mortally involved in what certainly must have seemed to them a self-sufficient action. The enmarveling power of all symbolism is exactly in the way symbols tend to become forces in themselves. They never do, in fact, lose their secondary character as representatives of whole other areas of meaning, but in the illusion of one's received sense-impressions, as in the illusion of art, the emotional force of a powerfully developed symbol seems to become a force in itself. One of the qualifications of a good reader is his ability to receive that emotional force *as if* it were self-evidently itself, without losing sight of the secondary symbolic force. For convenience it will be useful to think of these two forces as the *literal force* of the symbol on the one hand, and its *symbolic force* on the other.

There is another quality of symbolism that any man can recognize from his own life once his awareness has been directed. In few, if any, of his life activities does a man feel one way and only one way about anything. His total attitude tends to be made up of a whole complex of conflicting attitudes. A simple example of a man possessed of conflicting attitudes is the situation of a voter who after long analysis of a national election announced: "I'm going to hold my nose and vote the straight Democratic ticket." Endless examples of attitudes made up of conflicting feelings lie about and in everyman's life. No one likes to pay taxes, yet he knows it is his duty to pay them, as he also knows that those taxes buy for him the necessary services of government, as he also knows that it still hurts to pay them—he ends up by grumbling about the hopeless complexity of the forms he must fill out, lets out several hot pronouncements about more efficiency in government, and he pays. John loves Elizabeth, but he knows that Jane is also attractive and has money besides: he finally marries Elizabeth but he still regrets, if only a very little bit, that Elizabeth is poor. Frank is William's assistant in the advertising agency and thinks of himself as William's good friend. William falls ill, and Frank—who happens to be badly in debt—realizes that he will receive a substantial promotion should William fail to recover. Frank is a decent fellow and would never dream of wishing William ill. And still he realizes that his promotion can come about only through the elimination of William. And still he likes William. You may be sure that when Frank visits the hospital with a large basket of fruit, he is feeling more than one way at once.

So with symbols: they often manage to feel more than one way at once. Even more often, a poem develops counter-sets of symbols. The snarling trumpets and the Beadsman of Keats' "Eve of St. Agnes" are, among other things, counter-symbols within the main narrative (in which the hero and heroine themselves are symbols of a kind of human aspiration toward youth and love).

This way of multi-feeling is termed "ambivalence" by psychologists and critics. It is possible to argue that ambivalence is not necessarily a universal characteristic of poetry, but without involving needless critical subtleties at this point, ambivalence may certainly be asserted to be so pervasive in poetry that it is safe enough to assume its presence in some measure in every poem we shall here examine. The symbol, because it tends, like those ripples on the pond, to expand in all directions (and "all" must include opposite directions), is certainly the most natural way of expressing ambivalence.

All the immediately following poems tell a story of some sort and all to some extent use symbolism. For present purposes the symbolic elements may be defined as (1) areas of refusal to be specific in order to emphasize some larger possibility of meaning, or (2) devices introduced into the poem in whole or in part to stand for something else.

Lanier's "Revenge of Hamish" and Morris's "Haystack in the Floods" may reasonably be taken as making the least use of symbolism, yet Hamish himself may be argued to be an illustration, though a terrible one, of the human rebellion from tyranny, and Morris's Jehane and Robert may be argued to stand for a principle of tragic love—which is to say they may have more validity as types of a human action than as specific dramatic entities. At the other extreme, de la Mare's Traveler (note that

Traveler is capitalized) in "The Listeners" has almost no specific charac-
teristics, nor have the Listeners. The astonishing suggestiveness of the poem
arises from the fact that de la Mare has given his principal actors so little
specific identity that they not only have to suggest *something* else but
somehow seem to suggest almost *everything* else.

"The Listeners," one may well argue, is not even remotely about a man
riding up to an empty house at night and knocking on the door. All that
about his horse and the house and the forest's ferny floor has only an
illusory connection with what the poem is *about*. The incident is simply
what the poem is doing. More precisely, the incident is what the poem
pretends to be doing while it is actually doing something else—a kind of
poetic performance that should become instantly clear if one turns to
Brooke's "Heaven" (p. 877) and asks: "Is this poem about fish?" The
poem has a great deal to say about fish, but any reader who can believe
that Brooke's performance in this poem is literally about fish, is a reader
forever lost to poetry.

With such touchstones to identify nearly pure cases of one sort of
poetic performance and another, it should be possible for a willing reader
to sense the way the other poems here presented perform in a mixed way.
Robinson's "Mr. Flood's Party," for example, presents an incident and a
character in great detail. Old Eben Flood securely, drunkenly singing
with "only two moons listening" becomes a specific and unforgettable
person. Yet his very name is a pun—Eben Flood, ebb 'n flood, the going
and the coming tide. Of what? Of life, and feeling, of the old order and
the new, of the world that changes out from under a man leaving him
silly and tragic and lovable and lost—all that and more, to the last ripple
at the last edge of the pool at whose center this sort of thought waits.

QUESTIONS

In an approximate way the following questions might be asked of all
these poems. For the sake of clarity, let the questions be phrased in terms
of the albatross in "The Rhyme of the Ancient Mariner." The albatross is
simply one example of a thing not wholly specified and suggestive of some-
thing else. By changing the referent from "albatross" to whatever element
seems pertinent in the specific poem, the same questions will serve for all.

1. What is the albatross if taken literally? (How might Gradgrind
identify it?)

2. How is the albatross transformed into a symbolic force? (How does
it come to acquire meanings that would elude Gradgrind?)

3. Does the albatross have its symbolic force at the beginning, or does
it enter strictly as its literal self?

4. Does that symbolic force seem to expand (do the ripples spread) as
the poem progresses, and if so, how? by what devices? what are some of
the areas of implication released by the albatross at the end of the nar-
rative, and which of those areas was not present—at least not immediately
visible—in the beginning?

5. Are such symbolic elements as the albatross simply embellishments or do they have an essential part in the narrative performance?

Additional point for the willing reader to consider: In the most common sort of discussion of poetry, the structure and performance of a poem are treated as if they were more or less like the structure and performance of an expository essay. The poem, that is, is parsed out as if it consisted of a series of topic assertions which are developed and left behind in the process of moving on to the next assertion, and as if the true key to the poem were to be found in a logical analysis of its statements, almost as if they were so many syllogisms.

It is far better to think of the poem as a kind of thematic structure, like music, moving forward, but harking back upon itself, one theme playing against the other. This essentially thematic quality of poetic structure must be discussed in a detailed way later, but any reader willing to keep his imagination open to this possibility beforehand, must certainly be invited to do so.

Poems for Study

The Revenge of Hamish

Sidney Lanier

It was three slim does and a ten-tined buck in the bracken lay;
    And all of a sudden the sinister smell of a man,
    Awaft on a wind-shift, wavered and ran
Down the hill-side and sifted along through the bracken and passed that
    way.

Then Nan got a-tremble at nostril; she was the daintiest doe;
    In the print of her velvet flank on the velvet fern
    She reared, and rounded her ears in turn.
Then the buck leapt up, and his head as a king's to a crown did go

Full high in the breeze, and he stood as if Death had the form of a deer;
    And the two slim does long lazily stretching arose,
    For their day-dream slowlier came to a close,
Till they woke and were still, breath-bound with waiting and wonder and
    fear.

Then Alan the huntsman sprang over the hillock, the hounds shot by,
    The does and the ten-tined buck made a marvellous bound,
    The hounds swept after with never a sound,
But Alan loud winded his horn in sign that the quarry was nigh.

For at dawn of that day proud Maclean of Lochbuy to the hunt had
    waxed wild,
  And he cursed at old Alan till Alan fared off with the hounds
  For to drive him the deer to the lower glen-grounds:
"I will kill a red deer," quoth Maclean, "in the sight of the wife and the
    child."

So gayly he paced with the wife and the child to his chosen stand;
  But he hurried tall Hamish the henchman ahead: "Go turn"—
  Cried Maclean—"if the deer seek to cross to the burn,
Do thou turn them to me: nor fail, lest thy back be as red as thy hand."

Now hard-fortuned Hamish, half blown of his breath with the height of
    the hill,
  Was white in the face when the ten-tined buck and the does
  Drew leaping to burn-ward; huskily rose
His shouts, and his nether lip twitched, and his legs were o'er-weak for
    his will.

So the deer darted lightly by Hamish and bounded away to the burn.
  But Maclean never baiting his watch tarried waiting below;
  Still Hamish hung heavy with fear for to go
All the space of an hour; then he went, and his face was greenish and
    stern,

And his eye sat back in the socket, and shrunken the eye-balls shone,
  As withdrawn from a vision of deeds it were shame to see.
  "Now, now, grim henchman, what is't with thee?"
Brake Maclean, and his wrath rose red as a beacon the wind hath upblown.

"Three does and a ten-tined buck made out," spoke Hamish, full mild,
  "And I ran for to turn, but my breath it was blown, and they passed;
  I was weak, for ye called ere I broke me my fast."
Cried Maclean: "Now a ten-tined buck in the sight of the wife and the
    child

I had killed if the gluttonous kern had not wrought me a snail's own
    wrong!"
  Then he sounded, and down came kinsmen and clansmen all:
  "Ten blows, for ten tine, on his back let fall,
And reckon no stroke if the blood follow not at the bite of the thong!"

So Hamish made bare, and took him his strokes; at the last he smiled.
  "Now I'll to the burn," quoth Maclean, "for it still may be,
  If a slimmer-paunched henchman will hurry with me,
I shall kill me the ten-tined buck for a gift to the wife and the child!"

Then the clansmen departed, by this path and that; and over the hill
  Sped Maclean with an outward wrath for an inward shame;

And that place of the lashing full quiet became;
And the wife and the child stood sad; and bloody-backed Hamish sat still.

But look! red Hamish has risen; quick about and about turns he.
    "There is none betwixt me and the crag-top!" he screams under breath.
    Then, livid as Lazarus lately from death,
He snatches the child from the mother, and clambers the crag toward the
    sea.

Now the mother drops breath; she is dumb, and her heart goes dead for
    a space,
    Till the motherhood, mistress of death, shrieks, shrieks through the glen,
    And that place of the lashing is live with men,
And Maclean, and the gillie that told him, dash up in a desperate race.

Not a breath's time for asking; an eye-glance reveals all the tale untold.
    They follow mad Hamish afar up the crag toward the sea,
    And the lady cries: "Clansmen, run for a fee!—
Yon castle and lands to the first two hands that shall hook him and hold

Fast Hamish back from the brink!"—and ever she flies up the steep,
    And the clansmen pant, and they sweat, and they jostle and strain.
    But mother, 'tis vain; but, father, 'tis vain;
Stern Hamish stands bold on the brink, and dangles the child o'er the
    deep.

Now a faintness falls on the men that run, and they all stand still.
    And the wife prays Hamish as if he were God, on her knees,
    Crying: "Hamish! O Hamish! but please, but please
For to spare him!" and Hamish still dangles the child, with a wavering
    will.

On a sudden he turns; with a sea-hawk scream, and a gibe, and a song,
    Cries: "So; I will spare ye the child if, in sight of ye all,
    Ten blows on Maclean's bare back shall fall,
And ye reckon no stroke if the blood follow not at the bite of the thong!"

Then Maclean he set hardly his tooth to his lip that his tooth was red,
    Breathed short for a space, said: "Nay, but it never shall be!
    Let me hurl off the damnable hound in the sea!"
But the wife: "Can Hamish go fish us the child from the sea, if dead?

"Say yea!—Let them lash *me*, Hamish?"—"Nay!"—"Husband, the lashing
    will heal;
    But, oh, who will heal me the bonny sweet bairn in his grave?
    Could ye cure me my heart with the death of a knave?
Quick Love! I will bare thee—so—kneel!" Then Maclean 'gan slowly to
    kneel

With never a word, till presently downward he jerked to the earth.
   Then the henchman—he that smote Hamish—would tremble and lag;
   "Strike, hard!" quoth Hamish, full stern, from the crag;
Then he struck him, and "One!" sang Hamish, and danced with the child
   in his mirth.

And no man spake beside Hamish; he counted each stroke with a song.
   When the last stroke fell, then he moved him a pace down the height,
   And he held forth the child in the heartaching sight
Of the mother, and looked all pitiful grave, as repenting a wrong.

And there as the motherly arms stretched out with the thanksgiving
   prayer—
   And there as the mother crept up with a fearful swift pace,
   Till her finger nigh felt of the bairnie's face—
In a flash fierce Hamish turned round and lifted the child in the air,

And sprang with the child in his arms from the horrible height in the sea,
   Still screeching, "Revenge!" in the wind-rush; and pallid Maclean,
   Age-feeble with anger and impotent pain,
Crawled up on the crag, and lay flat, and locked hold of dead roots of a
   tree—

And gazed hungrily o'er, and the blood from his back drip-dripped in
   the brine,
   And a sea-hawk flung down a skeleton fish as he flew,
   And the mother stared white on the waste of blue,
And the wind drove a cloud to seaward, and the sun began to shine.

The Haystack in the Floods

William Morris

Had she come all the way for this,
To part at last without a kiss?
Yea, had she borne the dirt and rain
That her own eyes might see him slain
Beside the haystack in the floods?

Along the dripping, leafless woods,
The stirrup touching either shoe,
She rode astride as troopers do;
With kirtle kilted to her knee,
To which the mud splashed wretchedly;
And the wet dripp'd from every tree
Upon her head and heavy hair,
And on her eyelids broad and fair;
The tears and rain ran down her face.

By fits and starts they rode apace,
And very often was his place
Far off from her; he had to ride
Ahead to see what might betide
When the roads cross'd; and sometimes, when
There rose a murmuring from his men,
Had to turn back with promises.
Ah me! she had but little ease;
And often for pure doubt and dread
She sobb'd, made giddy in the head
By the swift riding; while, for cold,
Her slender fingers scarce could hold
The wet reins; yea, and scarcely, too,
She felt the foot within her shoe
Against the stirrup: all for this,
To part at last without a kiss
Beside the haystack in the floods.

For when they near'd that old soak'd hay,
They saw across the only way
That Judas, Godmar, and the three
Red running lions dismally
Grinn'd from his pennon, under which,
In one straight line along the ditch,
They counted thirty heads.

                    So then,
While Robert turn'd round to his men,
She saw at once the wretched end,
And, stooping down, tried hard to rend
Her coif the wrong way from her head,
And hid her eyes; while Robert said:
"Nay, love, 'tis scarcely two to one,
At Poictiers where we made them run
So fast—why, sweet my love, good cheer.
The Gascon frontier is so near,
Nought after this."

                    But, "O," she said,
"My God! my God! I have to tread
The long way back without you; then
The court at Paris; those six men;
The gratings of the Chatelet;
The swift Seine on some rainy day
Like this, and people standing by,
And laughing, while my weak hands try
To recollect how strong men swim.
All this, or else a life with him,

For which I should be damned at last.
Would God that this next hour were past!"

He answer'd not, but cried his cry,
"St. George for Marny!" cheerily;
And laid his hand upon her rein.
Alas! no man of all his train
Gave back that cheery cry again;
And, while for rage his thumb beat fast
Upon his sword-hilts, some one cast
About his neck a kerchief long,
And bound him.

        Then they went along
To Godmar; who said: "Now, Jehane,
Your lover's life is on the wane
So fast, that, if this very hour
You yield not as my paramour,
He will not see the rain leave off—
Nay, keep your tongue from gibe and scoff,
Sir Robert, or I slay you now."

She laid her hand upon her brow,
Then gazed upon the palm, as though
She thought her forehead bled, and—"No!"
She said, and turn'd her head away,
As there were nothing else to say,
And everything were settled: red
Grew Godmar's face from chin to head:
"Jehane, on yonder hill there stands
My castle, guarding well my lands:
What hinders me from taking you
And doing that I list to do
To your fair wilful body, while
Your knight lies dead?"

        A wicked smile
Wrinkled her face, her lips grew thin,
A long way out she thrust her chin:
"You know that I should strangle you
While you were sleeping; or bite through
Your throat, by God's help—ah!" she said,
"Lord Jesus, pity your poor maid!
For in such wise they hem me in,
I cannot choose but sin and sin,
Whatever happens: yet I think
They could not make me eat or drink
And so should I just reach my rest."

By Rippling Pools

"Nay, if you do not my behest,
O Jehane! though I love you well,"
Said Godmar, "would I fail to tell
All that I know?" "Foul lies," she said.
"Eh? lies, my Jehane? by God's head,
At Paris folks would deem them true!
Do you know, Jehane, they cry for you,
'Jehane the brown! Jehane the brown!
Give us Jehane to burn or drown!'—
Eh!—gag me Robert!—sweet my friend,
This were indeed a piteous end
For those long fingers, and long feet,
And long neck, and smooth shoulders sweet;
An end that few men would forget
That saw it—So, an hour yet:
Consider, Jehane, which to take
Of life or death!"

        So, scarce awake,
Dismounting, did she leave that place,
And totter some yards: with her face
Turn'd upward to the sky she lay,
Her head on a wet heap of hay,
And fell asleep: and while she slept,
And did not dream, the minutes crept
Round to the twelve again; but she,
Being waked at last, sigh'd quietly,
And strangely childlike came, and said:
"I will not." Straightway Godmar's head,
As though it hung on strong wires, turn'd
Most sharply round, and his face burn'd.

For Robert—both his eyes were dry,
He could not weep, but gloomily
He seem'd to watch the rain; yea, too,
His lips were firm; he tried once more
To touch her lips; she reach'd out, sore
And vain desire so tortured them,
The poor grey lips, and now the hem
Of his sleeve brush'd them.

        With a start
Up Godmar rose, thrust them apart;
From Robert's throat he loosed the bands
Of silk and mail; with empty hands
Held out, she stood and gazed and saw
The long bright blade without a flaw
Glide out from Godmar's sheath, his hand

In Robert's hair; she saw him bend
Back Robert's head; she saw him send
The thin steel down; the blow told well—
Right backward the knight Robert fell,
And moan'd as dogs do, being half dead,
Unwitting, as I deem: so then
Godmar turn'd grinning to his men,
Who ran, some five or six, and beat
His head to pieces at their feet.

Then Godmar turn'd again and said:
"So, Jehane, the first fitte is read!
Take note, my lady, that your way
Lies backward to the Chatelet!"
She shook her head and gazed awhile
At her cold hands with a rueful smile,
As though this thing had made her mad.

This was the parting that they had
Beside the haystack in the floods.

The Listeners

Walter De la Mare

"Is there anybody there?" said the Traveler,
    Knocking on the moonlit door;
And his horse in the silence champed the grasses
    Of the forest's ferny floor.
And a bird flew up out of the turret,
    Above the Traveler's head:
And he smote upon the door again a second time;
    "Is there anybody there?" he said.
But no one descended to the Traveler;
    No head from the leaf-fringed sill
Leaned over and looked into his gray eyes,
    Where he stood perplexed and still.
But only a host of phantom listeners
    That dwelt in the lone house then
Stood listening in the quiet of the moonlight
    To that voice from the world of men:
Stood thronging the faint moonbeams on the dark stair
    That goes down to the empty hall,
Hearkening in an air stirred and shaken
    By the lonely Traveler's call.

And he felt in his heart their strangeness,
   Their stillness answering his cry,
While his horse moved, cropping the dark turf,
   'Neath the starred and leafy sky;
For he suddenly smote on the door, even
   Louder, and lifted his head:—
"Tell them I came, and no one answered,
   That I kept my word," he said.
Never the least stir made the listeners,
   Though every word he spake
Fell echoing through the shadowiness of the still house
   From the one man left awake:
Aye, they heard his foot upon the stirrup,
   And the sound of iron on stone,
And how the silence surged softly backward,
   When the plunging hoofs were gone.

The Rime of the Ancient Mariner

Samuel Taylor Coleridge

At the end of Part IV the Mariner breathes forth unawares a blessing upon the creatures of the deep and immediately the guilty weight of the Albatross falls from him and sinks "Like lead into the sea."

Students are often tempted to interpret this action as symbolizing the Mariner's forgiveness and release from pain. But to accept this interpretation is to ignore the words of the spirit at the end of Part V: "The man hath penance done, And penance more will do." The Mariner suffers when the Albatross is about his neck, and he continues to suffer when he is released from its weight. Obviously, however, the nature of his suffering has changed. Until love touches his soul he suffers in one way. As soon as love has touched him the mood changes: a sleep refreshes him and he wakens from it to a visitation and a whole new motion of events.

The key to an understanding of this change lies in basic Christian theology, in which love is the beginning of redemption. Until love touches the Mariner he has suffered as a damned soul suffers, without hope. As soon as love touches him his sufferings become a penance rather than a doom. Penance is a state of grace for, however painful it may be, it leads to salvation. The Mariner has not been released from pain at the moment the Albatross falls from him, nor is he admitted into Heaven, his sin forgiven: he has rather passed from the state of Hell (pain without purification) to the state of Purgatory (purifying penance).

How many other religious symbolisms can be related to this center of the poem? How many Christ-symbols are suggested in connection with the Albatross? Can the shooting of the Albatross reasonably be related to Original Sin? Does the fact that the crew comes to condone the Mariner's act in shooting the Albatross implicate them in the act? If so why? Why does Coleridge allow a brief spell of improved weather to follow the death of the Albatross? What does the crew then do to the Mariner when things begin to deteriorate? Why? If the Mariner has committed something like Original Sin, that fact would suggest that he is a sort of Adam— what then must the crew symbolize?

PART I

An ancient Mariner meeteth three Gallants bidden to a wedding-feast, and detaineth one.

It is an ancient Mariner,
And he stoppeth one of three.
"By thy long gray beard and glittering eye,
Now wherefore stopp'st thou me?

The Bridegroom's doors are opened wide,
And I am next of kin;
The guests are met, the feast is set:
May'st hear the merry din."

He holds him with his skinny hand,
"There was a ship," quoth he.
"Hold off! unhand me, gray-beard loon!"
Eftsoons his hand dropt he.

The Wedding-Guest is spellbound by the eye of the old seafaring man, and constrained to hear his tale.

He holds him with his glittering eye—
The Wedding-Guest stood still,
And listens like a three years' child:
The Mariner hath his will.

The Wedding-Guest sat on a stone:
He cannot choose but hear;
And thus spake on that ancient man,
The bright-eyed Mariner.

"The ship was cheered, the harbor cleared,
Merrily did we drop
Below the kirk, below the hill,
Below the lighthouse top.

The Mariner tells how the ship sailed southward with a good wind and fair weather, till it reached the Line.

The sun came up upon the left,
Out of the sea came he!
And he shone bright, and on the right
Went down into the sea.

Higher and higher every day,
Till over the mast at noon—"
The Wedding-Guest here beat his breast,
For he heard the loud bassoon.

The Wedding-Guest heareth the bridal music; but the Mariner continueth his tale.

The bride hath paced into the hall,
Red as a rose is she;
Nodding their heads before her goes
The merry minstrelsy.

The Wedding-Guest he beat his breast,
Yet he cannot choose but hear;
And thus spake on that ancient man,
The bright-eyed Mariner.

The ship driven by a storm toward the south pole.

"And now the storm-blast came, and he
Was tyrannous and strong:
He struck with his o'ertaking wings,
And chased us south along.

With sloping masts and dipping prow,
As who pursued with yell and blow
Still treads the shadow of his foe,
And forward bends his head,
The ship drove fast, loud roared the blast,
And southward aye we fled.

And now there came both mist and snow,
And it grew wondrous cold:
And ice, mast-high, came floating by,
As green as emerald.

The land of ice, and of fearful sounds where no living thing was to be seen.

And through the drifts the snowy clifts
Did send a dismal sheen:
Nor shapes of men nor beasts we ken—
The ice was all between.

The ice was here, the ice was there,
The ice was all around:
It cracked and growled, and roared and howled,
Like noises in a swound!

Till a great sea-bird, called the Albatross, came through the snow-fog, and was received with great joy and hospitality.

At length did cross an Albatross,
Thorough the fog it came;
As if it had been a Christian soul,
We hailed it in God's name.

It ate the food it ne'er had eat,
And round and round it flew.
The ice did split with a thunder-fit;
The helmsman steered us through!

And lo! the Albatross proveth a bird of good

And a good south wind sprung up behind;
The Albatross did follow,

omen, and
followeth the
ship as it re-
turned north-
ward through
fog and
floating ice.

And every day, for food or play,
Came to the mariners' hollo!

In mist or cloud, on mast or shroud,
It perched for vespers nine;
Whiles all the night, through fog-smoke white,
Glimmered the white moon-shine."

The ancient
Mariner in-
hospitably
killeth the
pious bird of
good omen.

"God save thee, ancient Mariner!
From the fiends, that plague thee thus!—
Why look'st thou so?"—"With my cross-bow
I shot the Albatross.

PART II

"The Sun now rose upon the right:
Out of the sea came he,
Still hid in mist, and on the left
Went down into the sea.

And the good south wind still blew behind,
But no sweet bird did follow,
Nor any day for food or play

His ship-
mates cry out
against the
ancient
Mariner, for
killing the
bird of good
luck.

Came to the mariners' hollo!

And I had done a hellish thing,
And it would work 'em woe:
For all averred, I had killed the bird
That made the breeze to blow.
'Ah wretch!' said they, 'the bird to slay,
That made the breeze to blow!'

But when the
fog cleared
off, they
justify the
same, and
thus make
themselves
accomplices
in the crime.

Nor dim nor red, like God's own head,
The glorious Sun uprist:
Then all averred, I had killed the bird
That brought the fog and mist.
' 'Twas right,' said they, 'such birds to slay,
That bring the fog and mist.'

The fair
breeze con-
tinues; the
ship enters
the Pacific
Ocean, and
sails north-
ward, even
till it reaches
the Line

The fair breeze blew, the white foam flew,
The furrow followed free;
We were the first that ever burst
Into that silent sea.

The ship hath
been suddenly
becalmed.

Down dropt the breeze, the sails dropt down,
'Twas sad as sad could be;
And we did speak only to break
The silence of the sea!

All in a hot and copper sky,
The bloody Sun, at noon,
Right up above the mast did stand,
No bigger than the Moon.

Day after day, day after day,
We stuck, nor breath nor motion;
As idle as a painted ship
Upon a painted ocean.

And the Albatross begins to be avenged.

Water, water, everywhere,
And all the boards did shrink;
Water, water, everywhere
Nor any drop to drink.

A Spirit had followed them; one of the invisible inhabitants of this planet, neither departed souls nor angels; concerning whom the learned Jew, Josephus, and the Platonic Constantinopolitan, Michael Psellus, may be consulted. They are very numerous, and there is no climate or element without one or more.

The very deep did rot: O Christ!
That ever this should be!
Yea, slimy things did crawl with legs
Upon the slimy sea.

About, about, in reel and rout
The death-fires danced at night;
The water, like a witch's oils,
Burnt green, and blue, and white.

And some in dreams assured were
Of the Spirit that plagued us so:
Nine fathom deep he had followed us
From the land of mist and snow.

The shipmates, in their sore distress, would fain throw the whole guilt on the ancient Mariner: in sign whereof they hang the dead sea-bird round his neck.

And every tongue, through utter drought,
Was withered at the root;
We could not speak, no more than if
We had been choked with soot.

Ah! well a-day! what evil looks
Had I from old and young!
Instead of the cross, the Albatross
About my neck was hung.

PART III

The ancient Mariner beholdeth a sign in the element afar off.

"There passed a weary time. Each throat
Was parched, and glazed each eye.
A weary time! a weary time!
How glazed each weary eye,
When looking westward, I beheld
A something in the sky.

At first it seemed a little speck,
And then it seemed a mist;
It moved and moved, and took at last
A certain shape, I wist.

A speck, a mist, a shape, I wist!
And still it neared and neared:
As if it dodged a water-sprite,
It plunged and tacked and veered.

At its nearer approach, it seemeth him to be a ship; and at a dear ransom he freeth his speech from the bonds of thirst.

With throats unslaked, with black lips baked,
We could nor laugh nor wail;
Through utter drought all dumb we stood!
I bit my arm, I sucked the blood,
And cried, 'A sail! a sail!'

With throats unslaked, with black lips baked,
Agape they heard me call;
Gramercy! they for joy did grin,
And all at once their breath drew in,
As they were drinking all.

A flash of joy;

And horror follows. For can it be a ship that comes onward without wind or tide?

'See! see! (I cried) she tacks no more!
Hither to work us weal;
Without a breeze, without a tide,
She steadies with upright keel!'

The western wave was all a-flame;
The day was well nigh done!
Almost upon the western wave
Rested the broad bright Sun;
When that strange shape drove suddenly
Betwixt us and the Sun.

It seemeth him but the skeleton of a ship.

And straight the Sun was flecked with bars
(Heaven's Mother send us grace!)
As if through a dungeon-grate he peered
With broad and burning face.

Alas! (thought I, and my heart beat loud)
How fast she nears and nears!
Are those her sails that glance in the Sun,
Like restless gossameres?

And its ribs are seen as bars on the face of the setting Sun. The Spectre-Woman and

Are those her ribs through which the Sun
Did peer, as through a grate?
And is that Woman all her crew?
Is that a Death? and are there two?
Is Death that woman's mate?

her Death-
mate, and no
other on
board the
skeleton-
ship.
Like vessel,
like crew!

Her lips were red, her looks were free,
Her locks were yellow as gold:
Her skin was as white as leprosy,
The nightmare Life-in-Death was she,
Who thicks man's blood with cold.

Death and
Life-in-
Death have
diced for the
ship's crew,
and she (the
latter)
winneth the
ancient
Mariner.

The naked hulk alongside came,
And the twain were casting dice;
'The game is done! I've won! I've won!'
Quoth she, and whistles thrice.

No twilight
within the
courts of the
Sun.

The Sun's rim dips; the stars rush out:
At one stride comes the dark;
With far-heard whisper, o'er the sea,
Off shot the spectre-bark.

At the rising
of the Moon,

We listened and looked sideways up!
Fear at my heart, as at a cup,
My life-blood seemed to sip!
The stars were dim, and thick the night,
The steersman's face by his lamp gleamed white;
From the sails the dew did drip—
Till clomb above the eastern bar
The horned Moon, with one bright star
Within the nether tip.

One after
another,

One after one, by the star-dogged Moon,
Too quick for groan or sigh,
Each turned his face with a ghastly pang,
And cursed me with his eye.

His ship-
mates drop
down dead.

Four times fifty living men
(And I heard nor sigh nor groan)
With heavy thump, a lifeless lump,
They dropped down one by one.

But Life-in-
Death
begins her
work on the
ancient
Mariner.

The souls did from their bodies fly—
They fled to bliss or woe!
And every soul, it passed me by,
Like the whizz of my cross-bow!"

PART IV

The Wed-
ding-Guest
feareth that
a Spirit is
talking to
him;

"I fear thee, ancient Mariner!
I fear thy skinny hand!
And thou art long, and lank, and brown,
As is the ribbed sea-sand.

I fear thee and thy glittering eye,
And thy skinny hand, so brown."—
"Fear not, fear not, thou Wedding-Guest!
This body dropt not down.

Alone, alone, all, all alone,
Alone on a wide, wide sea!
And never a saint took pity on
My soul in agony.

The many men, so beautiful!
And they all dead did lie:
And a thousand thousand slimy things
Lived on; and so did I.

I looked upon the rotting sea,
And drew my eyes away;
I looked upon the rotting deck,
And there the dead men lay.

I looked to heaven, and tried to pray;
But or ever a prayer had gusht,
A wicked whisper came, and made
My heart as dry as dust.

I closed my lids, and kept them close,
And the balls like pulses beat;
For the sky and the sea, and the sea and the sky
Lay like a load on my weary eye,
And the dead were at my feet.

The cold sweat melted from their limbs,
Nor rot nor reek did they:
The look with which they looked on me
Had never passed away.

An orphan's curse would drag to hell
A spirit from on high;
But oh! more horrible than that
Is the curse in a dead man's eye!
Seven days, seven nights, I saw that curse,
And yet I could not die.

The moving Moon went up the sky,
And nowhere did abide:
Softly she was going up,
And a star or two beside—

Her beams bemocked the sultry main,
Like April hoar-frost spread;
But where the ship's huge shadow lay,
The charmed water burnt alway
A still and awful red.

Beyond the shadow of the ship,
I watched the water-snakes:
They moved in tracks of shining white,
And when they reared, the elfish light
Fell off in hoary flakes.

Within the shadow of the ship
I watched their rich attire:
Blue, glossy green, and velvet black,
They coiled and swam; and every track
Was a flash of golden fire.

O happy living things! no tongue
Their beauty might declare:
A spring of love gushed from my heart,
And I blessed them unaware:
Sure my kind saint took pity on me,
And I blessed them unaware.

The selfsame moment I could pray;
And from my neck so free
The Albatross fell off, and sank
Like lead into the sea.

PART V

"Oh sleep! it is a gentle thing,
Beloved from pole to pole!
To Mary Queen the praise be given!
She sent the gentle sleep from Heaven,
That slid into my soul.

The silly buckets on the deck,
That had so long remained,
I dreamt that they were filled with dew;
And when I awoke, it rained.

My lips were wet, my throat was cold,
My garments all were dank;
Sure I had drunken in my dreams,
And still my body drank.

everywhere the blue sky belongs to them, and is their appointed rest, and their native country and their own natural homes, which they enter unannounced, as lords that are certainly expected and yet there is a silent joy at their arrival.

By the light of the Moon he beholdeth God's creatures of the great calm.

Their beauty and their happiness.

He blesseth them in his heart.

The spell begins to break.

By grace of the holy Mother, the ancient Mariner is refreshed with rain.

I moved, and could not feel my limbs;
I was so light—almost
I thought that I had died in sleep,
And was a blessed ghost.

*He heareth
sounds and
seeth strange
sights and
commotions
in the sky
and the
element.*

And soon I heard a roaring wind:
It did not come anear;
But with its sound it shook the sails,
That were so thin and sere.

The upper air burst into life!
And a hundred fire-flags sheen,
To and fro they were hurried about!
And to and fro, and in and out,
The wan stars danced between.

And the coming wind did roar more loud,
And the sails did sigh like sedge;
And the rain poured down from one black cloud;
The Moon was at its edge.

The thick black cloud was cleft, and still
The Moon was at its side:
Like waters shot from some high crag,
The lightning fell with never a jag,
A river steep and wide.

The loud wind never reached the ship,
Yet now the ship moved on!
Beneath the lightning and the Moon
The dead men gave a groan.

*The bodies
of the ship's
crew are in-
spired, and
the ship
moves on.*

They groaned, they stirred, they all uprose,
Nor spake, nor moved their eyes;
It had been strange, even in a dream,
To have seen those dead men rise.

The helmsman steered, the ship moved on;
Yet never a breeze up blew;
The mariners all 'gan work the ropes,
Where they were wont to do;
They raised their limbs like lifeless tools—
We were a ghastly crew.

The body of my brother's son
Stood by me, knee to knee:
*But not by
the souls of*
The body and I pulled at one rope
But he said nought to me."

the men, nor by daemons of earth or middle air, but by a blessed troop of angelic spirits, sent down by the invocation of the guardian saint.

"I fear thee, ancient Mariner!"
"Be calm, thou Wedding-Guest!
'Twas not those souls that fled in pain,
Which to their corses came again,
But a troop of spirits blest:

For when it dawned—they dropped their arms,
And clustered round the mast;
Sweet sounds rose slowly through their mouths,
And from their bodies passed.

Around, around, flew each sweet sound,
Then darted to the Sun;
Slowly the sounds came back again,
Now mixed, now one by one.

Sometimes a-dropping from the sky
I heard the sky-lark sing;
Sometimes all little birds that are,
How they seemed to fill the sea and air
With their sweet jargoning!

And now 'twas like all instruments,
Now like a lonely flute;
And now it is an angel's song,
That makes the heavens be mute.

It ceased; yet still the sails made on
A pleasant noise till noon,
A noise like of a hidden brook
In the leafy month of June,
That to the sleeping woods all night
Singeth a quiet tune.

Till noon we quietly sailed on,
Yet never a breeze did breathe:
Slowly and smoothly went the ship,
Moved onward from beneath.

The lonesome Spirit from the south pole carries on the ship as far as the Line, in obedience to the angelic troop, but still requireth vengeance.

Under the keel nine fathom deep,
From the land of mist and snow,
The Spirit slid: and it was he
That made the ship to go.
The sails at noon left off their tune,
And the ship stood still also.

The Sun, right up above the mast,
Had fixed her to the ocean:

But in a minute she 'gan stir,
With a short uneasy motion—
Backwards and forwards half her length
With a short uneasy motion.

Then like a pawing horse let go,
She made a sudden bound:
It flung the blood into my head,
And I fell down in a swound.

The Polar Spirit's fellow-daemons, the invisible inhabitants of the element, take part in his wrong; and two of them relate, one to the other, that penance long and heavy for the ancient Mariner hath been accorded to the Polar Spirit, who returneth southward.

How long in that same fit I lay,
I have not to declare;
But ere my living life returned,
I heard and in my soul discerned
Two voices in the air.

'Is it he?' quoth one, 'Is this the man?
By Him who died on cross,
With his cruel bow he laid full low
The harmless Albatross.

The Spirit who bideth by himself
In the land of mist and snow,
He loved the bird that loved the man
Who shot him with his bow.'

The other was a softer voice,
As soft as honey-dew:
Quoth he, 'The man hath penance done,
And penance more will do.'

PART VI

First Voice

" 'But tell me, tell me! speak again,
Thy soft response renewing—
What makes that ship drive on so fast?
What is the ocean doing?

Second Voice

'Still as a slave before his lord,
The ocean hath no blast;
His great bright eye most silently
Up to the Moon is cast—

If he may know which way to go;
For she guides him smooth or grim.
See, brother, see! how graciously
She looketh down on him.'

First Voice

The Mariner
hath been
cast into a
trance; for
the angelic
power caus-
eth the vessel
to drive
northward
faster than
human life
could en-
dure.

'But why drives on that ship so fast,
Without or wave or wind?'

Second Voice

'The air is cut away before,
And closes from behind.

Fly, brother, fly! more high, more high!
Or we shall be belated:
For slow and slow that ship will go,
When the Mariner's trance is abated.'

The super-
natural
motion is
retarded;
the Mariner
awakes, and
his penance
begins anew.

I woke, and we were sailing on
As in a gentle weather:
'Twas night, calm night, the Moon was high,
The dead men stood together.

All stood together on the deck,
For a charnel-dungeon fitter:
All fixed on me their stony eyes,
That in the Moon did glitter.

The pang, the curse, with which they died,
Had never passed away:
I could not draw my eyes from theirs,
Nor turn them up to pray.

The curse is
finally ex-
piated.

And now this spell was snapt: once more
I viewed the ocean green,
And looked far forth, yet little saw
Of what had else been seen—

Like one, that on a lonesome road
Doth walk in fear and dread,
And having once turned round walks on,
And turns no more his head;
Because he knows a frightful fiend
Doth close behind him tread.

But soon there breathed a wind on me,
Nor sound nor motion made:
Its path was not upon the sea,
In ripple or in shade.

It raised my hair, it fanned my cheek
Like a meadow-gale of spring—
It mingled strangely with my fears,
Yet it felt like a welcoming.

Swiftly, swiftly flew the ship,
Yet she sailed softly too:
Sweetly, sweetly blew the breeze—
On me alone it blew.

And the
ancient Ma-
riner be-
holdeth his
native
country.

Oh! dream of joy! is this indeed
The light-house top I see?
Is this the hill? is this the kirk?
Is this mine own countree?

We drifted o'er the harbor-bar,
And I with sobs did pray—
O let me be awake, my God!
Or let me sleep alway.

The harbor-bay was clear as glass,
So smoothly it was strewn!
And on the bay the moonlight lay,
And the shadow of the Moon.

The rock shone bright, the kirk no less,
That stands above the rock:
The moonlight steeped in silentness
The steady weathercock.

And the bay was white with silent light
Till rising from the same,
Full many shapes, that shadows were,
In crimson colors came.

The angelic
spirits leave
the dead
bodies,

A little distance from the prow
Those crimson shadows were:
I turned my eyes upon the deck—
Oh, Christ, what saw I there!

And appear
in their own
forms of light.

Each corse lay flat, lifeless and flat,
And, by the holy rood!
A man all light, a seraph-man,
On every corse there stood.

This seraph-band, each waved his hand;
It was a heavenly sight!
They stood as signals to the land,
Each one a lovely light;

This seraph-band, each waved his hand,
No voice did they impart—
No voice; but oh! the silence sank
Like music on my heart.

But soon I heard the dash of oars,
I heard the Pilot's cheer;
My head was turned perforce away,
And I saw a boat appear.

The Pilot and the Pilot's boy,
I heard them coming fast:
Dear Lord in Heaven! it was a joy
The dead men could not blast.

I saw a third—I heard his voice:
It is the Hermit good!
He singeth loud his godly hymns
That he makes in the wood.
He'll shrieve my soul; he'll wash away
The Albatross's blood.

PART VII

The Hermit
of the Wood.

"This Hermit good lives in that wood
Which slopes down to the sea.
How loudly his sweet voice he rears!
He loves to talk with marineres
That come from a far countree.

He kneels at morn, and noon, and eve—
He hath a cushion plump:
It is the moss that wholly hides
The rotted old oak-stump.

The skiff-boat neared: I heard them talk,
'Why, this is strange, I trow!
Where are those lights so many and fair,
That signal made but now?'

Approacheth
the ship with
wonder.

'Strange, by my faith!' the Hermit said—
'And they answered not our cheer!
The planks look warped! and see those sails,
How thin they are and sere!
I never saw aught like to them
Unless perchance it were

Brown skeletons of leaves that lag
My forest-brook along;
When the ivy-tod is heavy with snow,
And the owlet whoops to the wolf below,
That eats the she-wolf's young.'

'Dear Lord! it hath a fiendish look—
(The Pilot made reply)
I am a-feared'—'Push on, push on!'
Said the Hermit cheerily.

The boat came closer to the ship,
But I nor spake nor stirred;
The boat came close beneath the ship,
And straight a sound was heard.

Under the water it rumbled on,
Still louder and more dread:
It reached the ship, it split the bay;
The ship went down like lead.

The ship suddenly sinketh.

Stunned by that loud and dreadful sound,
Which sky and ocean smote,
Like one that hath been seven days drowned
My body lay afloat;
But swift as dreams, myself I found
Within the Pilot's boat.

The ancient Mariner is saved in the Pilot's boat.

Upon the whirl, where sank the ship,
The boat spun round and round;
And all was still, save that the hill
Was telling of the sound.

I moved my lips—the Pilot shrieked
And fell down in a fit;
The holy Hermit raised his eyes,
And prayed where he did sit.

I took the oars: the Pilot's boy,
Who now doth crazy go,
Laughed loud and long, and all the while
His eyes went to and fro.
'Ha! ha!' quoth he, 'full plain I see,
The Devil knows how to row.'

And now, all in my own countree,
I stood on the firm land!
The Hermit stepped forth from the boat,
And scarcely he could stand.

The ancient Mariner earnestly entreateth the Hermit to shrieve him;

'O shrieve me, shrieve me, holy man!'
The Hermit crossed his brow.
'Say quick,' quoth he, 'I bid thee say—
What manner of man art thou?'

and the
penance of
life falls on
him.

Forthwith this frame of mine was wrenched
With a woful agony,
Which forced me to begin my tale;
And then it left me free.

And ever
and anon
throughout
his future life
an agony
constraineth
him to travel
from land to
land,

Since then, at an uncertain hour,
That agony returns:
And till my ghastly tale is told,
This heart within me burns.

I pass, like night, from land to land;
I have strange power of speech;
That moment that his face I see,
I know the man that must hear me:
To him my tale I teach.

What loud uproar bursts from that door!
The wedding-guests are there:
But in the garden-bower the bride
And bride-maids singing are:
And hark the little vesper bell
Which biddeth me to prayer!

O Wedding-Guest! this soul hath been
Alone on a wide, wide sea;
So lonely 'twas, that God himself
Scarce seemed there to be.

O sweeter than the marriage-feast,
'Tis sweeter far to me,
To walk together to the kirk
With a goodly company!—

To walk together to the kirk,
And all together pray,
While each to his great Father bends,
Old men, and babes, and loving friends,
And youths and maidens gay!

And to teach,
by his own
example,
love and rev-
erence to all
things that
God made
and loveth.

Farewell, farewell! but this I tell
To thee, thou Wedding-Guest!
He prayeth well, who loveth well
Both man and bird and beast.

He prayeth best, who loveth best
All things both great and small;
For the dear God who loveth us,
He made and loveth all."

The Mariner, whose eye is bright,
Whose beard with age is hoar,
Is gone: and now the Wedding-Guest
Turned from the Bridegroom's door.

He went like one that hath been stunned,
And is of sense forlorn:
A sadder and a wiser man,
He rose the morrow morn.

Mr. Flood's Party

Edwin Arlington Robinson

Old Eben Flood, climbing alone one night
Over the hill between the town below
And the forsaken upland hermitage
That held as much as he should ever know
On earth again of home, paused warily.
The road was his with not a native near;
And Eben, having leisure, said aloud,
For no man else in Tilbury Town to hear:

"Well, Mr. Flood, we have the harvest moon
Again, and we may not have many more;
The bird is on the wing, the poet says,
And you and I have said it here before.
Drink to the bird." He raised up to the light
The jug that he had gone so far to fill,
And answered huskily: "Well, Mr. Flood,
Since you propose it, I believe I will."

Alone, as if enduring to the end
A valiant armor of scarred hopes outworn,
He stood there in the middle of the road
Like Roland's ghost winding a silent horn.
Below him, in the town among the trees,
Where friends of other days had honored him,
A phantom salutation of the dead
Rang thinly till old Eben's eyes were dim.

Then, as a mother lays her sleeping child
Down tenderly, fearing it may awake,
He set the jug down slowly at his feet
With trembling care, knowing that most things break;

From *Collected Poems*, by Edward Arlington Robinson. Reprinted by permission of The Macmillan Company.

And only when assured that on firm earth
It stood, as the uncertain lives of men
Assuredly did not, he paced away,
And with his hand extended paused again:

"Well, Mr. Flood, we have not met like this
In a long time; and many a change has come
To both of us, I fear, since last it was
We had a drop together. Welcome home!"
Convivially returning with himself,
Again he raised the jug up to the light;
And with an acquiescent quaver said:
"Well, Mr. Flood, if you insist, I might.

"Only a very little, Mr. Flood—
For auld lang syne. No more, sir; that will do."
So, for the time, apparently it did,
And Eben evidently thought so too;
For soon amid the silver loneliness
Of night he lifted up his voice and sang,
Secure, with only two moons listening,
Until the whole harmonious landscape rang—

"For auld lang syne." The weary throat gave out,
The last word wavered; and the song being done,
He raised again the jug regretfully
And shook his head, and was again alone.
There was not much that was ahead of him,
And there was nothing in the town below—
Where strangers would have shut the many doors
That many friends had opened long ago.

Eve

Ralph Hodgson

Eve, with her basket, was
Deep in the bells and grass,
Wading in bells and grass
Up to her knees.
Picking a dish of sweet
Berries and plums to eat,
Down in the bells and grass
Under the trees.

FROM *Poems,* by Ralph Hodgson. Reprinted by permission of The Macmillan Company.

Mute as a mouse in a
Corner the cobra lay,
Curled round a bough of the
Cinnamon tall. . . .
Now to get even and
Humble proud heaven and
How was the moment or
Never at all.

"Eva!" Each syllable
Light as a flower fell,
"Eva!" he whispered the
Wondering maid,
Soft as a bubble sung
Out of a linnet's lung,
Soft and most silverly
"Eva!" he said.

Picture that orchard sprite;
Eve, with her body white,
Supple and smooth to her
Slim finger tips;
Wondering, listening,
Listening, wondering,
Eve with a berry
Half-way to her lips.

Oh, had our simple Eve
Seen through the make-believe.
Had she but known the
Pretender he was!
Out of the boughs he came,
Whispering still her name,
Tumbling in twenty rings
Into the grass.

Here was the strangest pair
In the world anywhere,
Eve in the bells and grass
Kneeling, and he
Telling his story low. . . .
Singing birds saw them go
Down the dark path to
The Blasphemous Tree.

Oh, what a clatter when
Titmouse and Jenny Wren
Saw him successful and
Taking his leave!

How the birds rated him,
How they all hated him!
How they all pitied
Poor motherless Eve!

Picture her crying
Out side in the lane,
Eve, with no dish of sweet
Berries and plums to eat,
Haunting the gate of the
Orchard in vain. . . .
Picture the lewd delight
Under the hill tonight—
"Eva!" the toast goes round,
"Eva!" again.

The Glove and the Lions

Leigh Hunt

King Francis was a hearty king, and loved a royal sport,
And one day, as his lions fought, sat looking on the court.
The nobles filled the benches, and the ladies in their pride,
And 'mongst them sat the Count de Lorge, with one for whom he sighed:
And truly 'twas a gallant thing to see the crowning show,
Valor and love, and a king above, and the royal beasts below.

Ramped and roared the lions, with horrid laughing jaws;
They bit, they glared, gave blows like beams, a wind went with their paws;
With wallowing might and stifled roar they rolled on one another,
Till all the pit with sand and mane was in a thunderous smother;
The bloody foam above the bars came whisking through the air;
Said Francis then, "Faith, gentlemen, we're better here than there."

De Lorge's love o'erheard the King, a beauteous lively dame,
With smiling lips and sharp bright eyes, which always seemed the same;
She thought, "The Count, my lover, is brave as brave can be;
He surely would do wondrous things to show his love of me;
King, ladies, lovers, all look on; the occasion is divine;
I'll drop my glove to prove his love; great glory will be mine."

She dropped her glove, to prove his love, then looked at him and smiled;
He bowed, and in a moment leaped among the lions wild;
The leap was quick, return was quick, he has regained his place,
Then threw the glove, but not with love, right in the lady's face.
"By Heaven," said Francis, "rightly done!" and he rose from where he sat;
"No love," quoth he, "but vanity, sets love a task like that."

The Chambered Nautilus

Oliver Wendell Holmes

This is the ship of pearl, which, poets feign,
   Sails the unshadowed main,—
   The venturous bark that flings
On the sweet summer wind its purpled wings
In gulfs enchanted, where the Siren sings,
   And coral reefs lie bare,
Where the cold sea-maids rise to sun their streaming hair.

Its webs of living gauze no more unfurl!
   Wrecked is the ship of pearl!
   And every chambered cell,
Where its dim dreaming life was wont to dwell,
As the frail tenant shaped his growing shell,
   Before thee lies revealed,—
Its irised ceiling rent, its sunless crypt unsealed!

Year after year beheld the silent toil
   That spread his lustrous coil;
   Still, as the spiral grew,
He left the past year's dwelling for the new,
Stole with soft step its shining archway through,
   Built up its idle door,
Stretched in his last-found home, and knew the old no more.

Thanks for the heavenly message brought by thee,
   Child of the wandering sea,
   Cast from her lap forlorn!
From thy dead lips a clearer note is born
Than ever Triton blew from wreathèd horn!
   While on mine ear it rings,
Through the deep caves of thought I hear a voice that sings:—

Build thee more stately mansions, O my soul,
   As the swift seasons roll!
   Leave thy low-vaulted past!
Let each new temple, nobler than the last,
Shut thee from heaven with a dome more vast,
   Till thou at length art free,
Leaving thine outgrown shell by life's unresting sea!

Ulysses

Alfred, Lord Tennyson

It little profits that an idle king,
By this still hearth, among these barren crags,
Matched with an aged wife, I mete and dole
Unequal laws unto a savage race,
That hoard, and sleep, and feed, and know not me.
I cannot rest from travel: I will drink
Life to the lees: all times I have enjoyed
Greatly, have suffered greatly, both with those
That loved me, and alone; on shore, and when
Through scudding drifts the rainy Hyades
Vext the dim sea. I am become a name;
For always roaming with a hungry heart
Much have I seen and known: cities of men
And manners, climates, councils, governments,
Myself not least, but honored of them all,—
And drunk delight of battle with my peers,
Far on the ringing plains of windy Troy.
I am a part of all that I have met;
Yet all experience is an arch wherethrough
Gleams that untraveled world, whose margin fades
For ever and for ever when I move.
How dull it is to pause, to make an end,
To rust unburnished, not to shine in use!
As though to breathe were life! Life piled on life
Were all too little, and of one to me
Little remains: but every hour is saved
From that eternal silence, something more,
A bringer of new things; and vile it were
For some three suns to store and hoard myself,
And this gray spirit yearning in desire
To follow knowledge, like a sinking star,
Beyond the utmost bound of human thought.
     This is my son, mine own Telemachus,
To whom I leave the scepter and the isle—
Well-loved of me, discerning to fulfill
This labor, by slow prudence to make mild
A rugged people, and through soft degrees
Subdue them to the useful and the good.
Most blameless is he, centered in the sphere
Of common duties, decent not to fail
In offices of tenderness, and pay
Meet adoration to my household gods,
When I am gone. He works his work, I mine.

There lies the port: the vessel puffs her sail:
There gloom the dark broad seas. My mariners,
Souls that have toiled, and wrought, and thought with me—
That ever with a frolic welcome took
The thunder and the sunshine, and opposed
Free hearts, free foreheads—you and I are old;
Old age hath yet his honor and his toil;
Death closes all: but something ere the end,
Some work of noble note, may yet be done,
Not unbecoming men that strove with Gods.
The lights begin to twinkle from the rocks:
The long day wanes: the slow moon climbs: the deep
Moans round with many voices. Come, my friends,
'Tis not too late to seek a newer world.
Push off, and sitting well in order smite
The sounding furrows; for my purpose holds
To sail beyond the sunset, and the baths
Of all the western stars, until I die.
It may be that the gulfs will wash us down:
It may be we shall touch the Happy Isles,
And see the great Achilles, whom we knew.
Though much is taken, much abides; and though
We are not now that strength which in old days
Moved earth and heaven, that which we are, we are,—
One equal temper of heroic hearts,
Made weak by time and fate, but strong in will
To strive, to seek, to find, and not to yield.

The Eve of St. Agnes

John Keats

St. Agnes' Eve—Ah, bitter chill it was!
The owl, for all his feathers, was a-cold;
The hare limped trembling through the frozen grass,
And silent was the flock in woolly fold:
Numb were the Beadsman's fingers while he told
His rosary, and while his frosted breath,
Like pious incense from a censer old,
Seemed taking flight for heaven, without a death,
Past the sweet Virgin's picture, while his prayer he saith.

His prayer he saith, this patient, holy man;
Then takes his lamp, and riseth from his knees,
And back returneth, meager, barefoot, wan,
Along the chapel aisle by slow degrees:
The sculptured dead, on each side, seem to freeze,

Imprisoned in black, purgatorial rails:
Knights, ladies, praying in dumb orat'ries,
He passeth by, and his weak spirit fails
To think how they may ache in icy hoods and mails.

Northward he turneth through a little door,
And scarce three steps, ere Music's golden tongue
Flattered to tears this aged man and poor;
But no—already had his death-bell rung:
The joys of all his life were said and sung:
His was harsh penance on St. Agnes' Eve:
Another way he went, and soon among
Rough ashes sat he for his soul's reprieve,
And all night kept awake, for sinners' sake to grieve.

That ancient Beadsman heard the prelude soft;
And so it chanced, for many a door was wide,
From hurry to and fro. Soon, up aloft,
The silver, snarling trumpets 'gan to chide:
The level chambers, ready with their pride,
Were glowing to receive a thousand guests.
The carved angels, ever eager-eyed,
Stared, where upon their heads the cornice rests,
With hair blown back, and wings puts crosswise on their breasts.

At length burst in the argent revelry,
With plume, tiara, and all rich array,
Numerous as shadows haunting faerily
The brain new-stuffed, in youth, with triumphs gay
Of old romance. These let us wish away,
And turn, sole-thoughted, to one Lady there,
Whose heart had brooded, all that wintry day,
On love, and winged St. Agnes' saintly care,
As she had heard old dames full many times declare.

They told her how, upon St. Agnes' Eve,
Young virgins might have visions of delight,
And soft adorings from their loves receive
Upon the honeyed middle of the night,
If ceremonies due they did aright;
As, supperless to bed they must retire,
And couch supine their beauties, lily white;
Nor look behind, nor sideways, but require
Of Heaven with upward eyes for all that they desire.

Full of this whim was thoughtful Madeline:
The music, yearning like a God in pain,
She scarcely .eard: her maiden eyes divine,

Fixed on the floor, saw many a sweeping train
Pass by—she heeded not at all: in vain
Came many a tiptoe, amorous cavalier,
And back retired; not cooled by high disdain,
But she saw not: her heart was otherwhere;
She sighed for Agnes' dreams, the sweetest of the year.

She danced along with vague, regardless eyes,
Anxious her lips, her breathing quick and short:
The hallowed hour was near at hand: she sighs
Amid the timbrels, and the thronged resort
Of whisperers in anger or in sport;
'Mid looks of love, defiance, hate, and scorn,
Hoodwinked with faery fancy; all amort,
Save to St. Agnes and her lambs unshorn,
And all the bliss to be before tomorrow morn.

So, purposing each moment to retire,
She lingered still. Meantime, across the moors,
Had come young Porphyro, with heart on fire
For Madeline. Beside the portal doors,
Buttressed from moonlight, stands he, and implores
All saints to give him sight of Madeline,
But for one moment in the tedious hours,
That he might gaze and worship all unseen;
Perchance speak, kneel, touch, kiss—in sooth such things have been.

He ventures in: let no buzzed whisper tell,
All eyes be muffled, or a hundred swords
Will storm his heart, Love's feverous citadel:
For him, those chambers held barbarian hordes,
Hyena foemen, and hot-blooded lords,
Whose very dogs would execrations howl
Against his lineage; not one breast affords
Him any mercy in that mansion foul,
Save one old beldame, weak in body and in soul.

Ah, happy chance! the aged creature came,
Shuffling along with ivory-headed wand,
To where he stood, hid from the torch's flame,
Behind a broad hall pillar, far beyond
The sound of merriment and chorus bland.
He startled her: but soon she knew his face,
And grasped his fingers in her palsied hand,
Saying, "Mercy, Porphyro! hie thee from this place;
They are all here tonight, the whole bloody-thirsty race!

"Get hence! get hence! there's dwarfish Hildebrand:
He had a fever late, and in the fit

He cursed thee and thine, both house and land:
Then there's that old Lord Maurice, not a whit
More tame for his gray hairs—Alas me! flit!
Flit like a ghost away."—"Ah, Gossip dear,
We're safe enough; here in this arm-chair sit,
And tell me how—" "Good saints! not here, not here!
Follow me, child, or else these stones will be thy bier."

He followed through a lowly arched way,
Brushing the cobwebs with his lofty plume;
And as she muttered "Well-a—well-a-day!"
He found him in a little moonlight room,
Pale, latticed, chill, and silent as a tomb.
"Now tell me where is Madeline," said he,
"O tell me, Angela, by the holy loom
Which none but secret sisterhood may see,
When they St. Agnes' wool are weaving piously."

"St. Agnes! Ah! it is St. Agnes' Eve—
Yet men will murder upon holy days.
Thou must hold water in a witch's sieve,
And be liege-lord of all the Elves and Fays
To venture so: it fills me with amaze
To see thee, Porphyro!—St. Agnes' Eve!
God's help! my lady fair the conjurer plays
This very night: good angels her deceive!
But let me laugh awhile,—I've mickle time to grieve."

Feebly she laugheth in the languid moon,
While Porphyro upon her face doth look,
Like puzzled urchin on an aged crone
Who keepeth closed a wondrous riddle-book,
As spectacled she sits in chimney nook.
But soon his eyes grew brilliant, when she told
His lady's purpose; and he scarce could brook
Tears, at the thought of those enchantments cold,
And Madeline asleep in lap of legends old.

Sudden a thought came like a full-blown rose,
Flushing his brow, and in his pained heart
Made purple riot: then doth he propose
A stratagem, that makes the beldame start:
"A cruel man and impious thou art!
Sweet lady, let her pray, and sleep and dream
Alone with her good angels, far apart
From wicked men like thee. Go, go! I deem
Thou canst not surely be the same that thou didst seem."

"I will not harm her, by all saints I swear!"
Quoth Porphyro: "O may I ne'er find grace
When my weak voice shall whisper its last prayer,
If one of her soft ringlets I displace,
Or look with ruffian passion in her face.
Good Angela, believe me, by these tears;
Or I will, even in a moment's space,
Awake, with horrid shout, my foemen's ears,
And beard them, though they be more fanged than wolves and bears."

"Ah! why wilt thou affright a feeble soul?
A poor, weak, palsy-stricken, churchyard thing,
Whose passing-bell may ere the midnight toll;
Whose prayers for thee, each morn and evening,
Were never missed." Thus plaining, doth she bring
A gentler speech from burning Porphyro;
So woeful, and of such deep sorrowing,
That Angela gives promise she will do
Whatever he shall wish, betide her weal or woe.

Which was, to lead him, in close secrecy,
Even to Madeline's chamber, and there hide
Him in a closet, of such privacy
That he might see her beauty unespied,
And win perhaps that night a peerless bride,
While legioned fairies paced the coverlet,
And pale enchantment held her sleepy-eyed.
Never on such a night have lovers met,
Since Merlin paid his Demon all the monstrous debt.

"It shall be as thou wishest," said the Dame:
"All cates and dainties shall be stored there
Quickly on this feast-night: by the tambour frame
Her own lute thou wilt see: no time to spare,
For I am slow and feeble, and scarce dare
On such a catering trust my dizzy head.
Wait here, my child, with patience: kneel in prayer
The while. Ah! thou must needs the lady wed,
Or may I never leave my grave among the dead."

So saying she hobbled off with busy fear.
The lover's endless minutes slowly passed;
The dame returned, and whispered in his ear
To follow her; with aged eyes aghast
From fright of dim espial. Safe at last
Through many a dusky gallery, they gain
The maiden's chamber, silken, hushed and chaste;
Where Porphyro took covert, pleased amain.
His poor guide hurried back with agues in her brain.

Her faltering hand upon the balustrade,
Old Angela was feeling for the stair,
When Madeline, St. Agnes' charmed maid,
Rose, like a missioned spirit, unaware:
With silver taper's light, and pious care,
She turned, and down the aged gossip led
To a safe level matting. Now prepare,
Young Porphyro, for gazing on that bed;
She comes, she comes again, like ring-dove frayed and fled.

Out went the taper as she hurried in;
Its little smoke, in pallid moonshine, died:
She closed the door, she panted, all akin
To spirits of the air, and visions wide:
No uttered syllable, or, woe betide!
But to her heart, her heart was voluble,
Paining with eloquence her balmy side;
As though a tongueless nightingale should swell
Her throat in vain, and die, heart-stifled, in her dell.

A casement high and triple-arched there was,
All garlanded with carven imageries,
Of fruits, and flowers, and bunches of knot-grass,
And diamonded with panes of quaint device,
Innumerable of stains and splendid dyes,
As are the tiger-moth's deep-damasked wings;
And in the midst, 'mong thousand heraldries,
And twilight saints, and dim emblazonings,
A shielded scutcheon blushed with blood of queens and kings.

Full on this casement shone the wintry moon,
And threw warm gules on Madeline's fair breast,
As down she knelt for Heaven's grace and boon;
Rose-bloom fell on her hands, together prest,
And on her silver cross soft amethyst,
And on her hair a glory, like a saint:
She seemed a splendid angel, newly drest,
Save wings, for heaven:—Porphyro grew faint:
She knelt, so pure a thing, so free from mortal taint.

Anon his heart revives: her vespers done,
Of all its wreathed pearls her hair she frees;
Unclasps her warmed jewels one by one;
Loosens her fragrant bodice; by degrees
Her rich attire creeps rustling to her knees:
Half-hidden, like a mermaid in sea-weed,
Pensive awhile she dreams awake, and sees,
In fancy, fair St. Agnes in her bed,
But dares not look behind, or all the charm is fled.

Soon, trembling in her soft and chilly nest,
In sort of wakeful swoon, perplexed she lay,
Until the poppied warmth of sleep oppressed
Her soothed limbs, and soul fatigued away;
Flown, like a thought, until the morrow-day;
Blissfully havened both from joy and pain;
Clasped like a missal where swart Paynims pray;
Blinded alike from sunshine and from rain,
As though a rose should shut, and be a bud again.

Stolen to this paradise, and so entranced,
Porphyro gazed upon her empty dress,
And listened to her breathing, if it chanced
To wake into a slumberous tenderness;
Which when he heard, that minute did he bless,
And breathed himself: then from the closet crept,
Noiseless as fear in a wide wilderness,
And over the hushed carpet, silent, stept,
And 'tween the curtains peeped, where, lo!—how fast she slept.

Then by the bed-side, where the faded moon
Made a dim, silver twilight, soft he set
A table, and, half anguished, threw thereon
A cloth of woven crimson, gold, and jet:—
O for some drowsy Morphean amulet!
The boisterous, midnight, festive clarion,
The kettle-drum, and far-heard clarinet,
Affray his ears, though but in dying tone:—
The hall-door shuts again, and all the noise is gone.

And still she slept an azure-lidded sleep,
In blanched linen, smooth, and lavendered,
While he from forth the closet brought a heap
Of candied apple, quince, and plum, and gourd;
With jellies soother than the creamy curd,
And lucent syrops, tinct with cinnamon;
Manna and dates, in argosy transferred
From Fez; and spiced dainties, every one,
From silken Samarcand to cedared Lebanon.

These delicates he heaped with glowing hand
On golden dishes and in baskets bright
Of wreathed silver: sumptuous they stand
In the retired quiet of the night,
Filling the chilly room with perfume light.—
"And now, my love, my seraph fair, awake!
Thou art my heaven, and I thine eremite:
Open thine eyes, for meek St. Agnes' sake,
Or I shall drowse beside thee, so my soul doth ache."

Thus whispering, his warm, unnerved arm
Sank in her pillow. Shaded was her dream
By the dusk curtains:—'twas a midnight charm
Impossible to melt as iced stream:
The lustrous salvers in the moonlight gleam;
Broad golden fringe upon the carpet lies:
It seemed he never, never could redeem
From such a stedfast spell his lady's eyes;
So mused awhile, entoiled in woofed phantasies.

Awakening up, he took her hollow lute,—
Tumultuous,—and, in chords that tenderest be,
He played an ancient ditty, long since mute,
In Provence called, "La belle dame sans mercy":
Close to her ear touching the melody;—
Wherewith disturbed, she uttered a soft moan:
He ceased—she panted quick—and suddenly
Her blue affrayed eyes wide open shone:
Upon his knees he sank, pale as smooth-sculptured stone.

Her eyes were open, but she still beheld,
Now wide awake, the vision of her sleep:
There was a painful change, that nigh expelled
The blisses of her dream so pure and deep
At which fair Madeline began to weep,
And moan forth witless words with many a sigh,
While still her gaze on Prophyro would keep;
Who knelt, with joined hands and piteous eye,
Fearing to move or speak, she looked so dreamingly.

"Ah, Porphyro!" said she, "but even now
Thy voice was at sweet tremble in mine ear,
Made tuneable with every sweetest vow;
And those sad eyes were spiritual and clear:
How changed thou art! how pallid, chill, and drear!
Give me that voice again, my Porphyro,
Those looks immortal, those complainings dear!
Oh, leave me not in this eternal woe,
For if thou diest, my Love, I know not where to go."

Beyond a mortal man impassioned far
At these voluptuous accents, he arose,
Ethereal, flushed, and like a throbbing star
Seen 'mid the sapphire heaven's deep repose;
Into her dream he melted, as the rose
Blendeth its odor with the violet,—
Solution sweet: meantime the frost-wind blows
Like Love's alarum, pattering the sharp sleet
Against the window-panes; St. Agnes' moon hath set.

'Tis dark: quick pattereth the flaw-blown sleet.
"This is no dream, my bride, my Madeline!"
'Tis dark: the iced gusts still rave and beat:
"No dream, alas! alas! and woe is mine!
Porphyro will leave me here to fade and pine.
Cruel! what traitor could thee hither bring?
I curse not, for my heart is lost in thine,
Though thou forsakest a deceived thing;—
A dove forlorn and lost with sick unpruned wing."

"My Madeline! sweet dreamer! lovely bride!
Say, may I be for aye thy vassal blest?
Thy beauty's shield, heart-shaped and vermeil-dyed?
Ah, silver shrine, here will I take my rest
After so many hours of toil and quest,
A famished pilgrim,—saved by miracle.
Though I have found, I will not rob thy nest,
Saving of thy sweet self; if thou think'st well
To trust, fair Madeline, to no rude infidel.

"Hark! 'tis an elfin-storm from faery land,
Of haggard seeming, but a boon indeed:
Arise—arise! the morning is at hand;—
The bloated wassailers will never heed;—
Let us away, my love, with happy speed;
There are no ears to hear, or eyes to see,—
Drowned all in Rhenish and the sleepy mead:
Awake! arise! my love, and fearless be,
For o'er the southern moors I have a home for thee."

She hurried at his words, beset with fears,
For there were sleeping dragons all around,
At glaring watch, perhaps, with ready spears—
Down the wide stairs a darkling way they found;
In all the house was heard no human sound.
A chain-drooped lamp was flickering by each door;
The arras, rich with horseman, hawk, and hound,
Fluttered in the besieging wind's uproar;
And the long carpets rose along the gusty floor.

They glide, like phantoms, into the wide hall;
Like phantoms, to the iron porch they glide,
Where lay the Porter, in uneasy sprawl,
With a huge empty flagon by his side:
The wakeful bloodhound rose, and shook his hide,
But his sagacious eye an inmate owns:
By one, and one, the bolts full easy slide:—
The chains lie silent on the footworn stones;
The key turns, and the door upon its hinges groans.

And they are gone: aye, ages long ago
These lovers fled away into the storm.
That night the Baron dreamt of many a woe,
And all his warrior-guests with shade and form
Of witch, and demon, and large coffin-worm,
Were long be-nightmared. Angela the old
Died palsy-twitched, with meager face deform;
The Beadsman, after thousand aves told,
For aye unsought-for slept among his ashes cold.

The Death of the Hired Man

Robert Frost

Mary sat musing on the lamp-flame at the table
Waiting for Warren. When she heard his step,
She ran on tip-toe down the darkened passage
To meet him in the doorway with the news
And put him on his guard. "Silas is back."
She pushed him outward with her through the door
And shut it after her. "Be kind," she said.
She took the market things from Warren's arms
And set them on the porch, then drew him down
To sit beside her on the wooden steps.

"When was I ever anything but kind to him?
But I'll not have the fellow back," he said.
"I told him so last haying, didn't I?
'If he left then,' I said, 'that ended it.'
What good is he? Who else will harbor him
At his age for the little he can do?
What help he is there's no depending on.
Off he goes always when I need him most.
'He thinks he ought to earn a little pay,
Enough at least to buy tobacco with,
So he won't have to beg and be beholden.'
'All right,' I say, 'I can't afford to pay
Any fixed wages, though I wish I could.'
'Someone else can.' 'Then someone else will have to.'
I shouldn't mind his bettering himself
If that was what it was. You can be certain,
When he begins like that, there's someone at him
Trying to coax him off with pocket-money,—
In haying time, when any help is scarce.
In winter he comes back to us. I'm done."

"Sh! not so loud: he'll hear you," Mary said.

"I want him to: he'll have to soon or late."

"He's worn out. He's asleep beside the stove.
When I came up from Rowe's I found him here,
Huddled against the barn-door fast asleep,
A miserable sight, and frightening, too—
You needn't smile—I didn't recognize him—
I wasn't looking for him—and he's changed.
Wait till you see."

             "Where did you say he'd been?"

"He didn't say. I dragged him to the house,
And gave him tea and tried to make him smoke.
I tried to make him talk about his travels,
Nothing would do: he just kept nodding off."

"What did he say? Did he say anything?"

"But little."

       "Anything? Mary, confess
He said he'd come to ditch the meadow for me."

"Warren!"

        "But did he? I just want to know."

"Of course he did. What would you have him say?
Surely you wouldn't grudge the poor old man
Some humble way to save his self-respect.
He added, if you really care to know,
He meant to clear the upper pasture, too.
That sounds like something you have heard before?
Warren, I wish you could have heard the way
He jumbled everything. I stopped to look
Two or three times—he made me feel so queer—
To see if he was talking in his sleep.
He ran on Harold Wilson—you remember—
The boy you had in haying four years since.
He's finished school, and teaching in his college.
Silas declares you'll have to get him back.
He says they two will make a team for work:
Between them they will lay this farm as smooth!
The way he mixed that in with other things.
He thinks young Wilson a likely lad, though daft

On education—you know how they fought
All through July under the blazing sun,
Silas up on the cart to build the load,
Harold along beside to pitch it on."

"Yes, I took care to keep well out of earshot."

"Well, those days trouble Silas like a dream.
You wouldn't think they would. How some things linger!
Harold's young college boy's assurance piqued him.
After so many years he still keeps finding
Good arguments he sees he might have used.
I sympathize. I know just how it feels
To think of the right thing to say too late.
Harold's associated in his mind with Latin.
He asked me what I thought of Harold's saying
He studied Latin like the violin
Because he liked it—that an argument!
He said he couldn't make the boy believe
He could find water with a hazel prong—
Which showed how much good school had ever done him,
He wanted to go over that. But most of all
He thinks if he could have another chance
To teach him how to build a load of hay—"

"I know, that's Silas' one accomplishment.
He bundles every forkful in its place,
And tags and numbers it for future reference,
So he can find and easily dislodge it
In the unloading. Silas does that well.
He takes it out in bunches like birds' nests.
You never see him standing on the hay
He's trying to lift, straining to lift himself."

"He thinks if he could teach him that, he'd be
Some good perhaps to someone in the world.
He hates to see a boy the fool of books.
Poor Silas, so concerned for other folk,
And nothing to look backward to with pride,
And nothing to look forward to with hope,
So now and never any different."

Part of a moon was falling down the west,
Dragging the whole sky with it to the hills.
Its light poured softly in her lap. She saw
And spread her apron to it. She put out her hand
Among the harp-like morning-glory strings,
Taut with the dew from garden bed to eaves,

As if she played unheard the tenderness
That wrought on him beside her in the night.
"Warren," she said, "he has come home to die:
You needn't be afraid he'll leave you this time."

"Home," he mocked gently.

                    "Yes, what else but home?
It all depends on what you mean by home.
Of course he's nothing to us, any more
Than was the hound that came a stranger to us
Out of the woods, worn out upon the trail."

"Home is the place where, when you have to go there,
They have to take you in."

              "I should have called it
Something you somehow haven't to deserve."

Warren leaned out and took a step or two,
Picked up a little stick, and brought it back
And broke it in his hand and tossed it by.
"Silas has better claim on us, you think,
Than on his brother? Thirteen little miles
As the road winds would bring him to his door.
Silas has walked that far no doubt today.
Why didn't he go there? His brother's rich,
A somebody—director in the bank."

"He never told us that."

                  "We know it though."

"I think his brother ought to help, of course.
I'll see to that if there is need. He ought of right
To take him in, and might be willing to—
He may be better than appearances.
But have some pity on Silas. Do you think
If he'd had any pride in claiming kin
Or anything he looked for from his brother,
He'd keep so still about him all this time?"

"I wonder what's between them."

                  "I can tell you.
Silas is what he is—we wouldn't mind him—
But just the kind that kinsfolk can't abide.
He never did a thing so very bad.

He don't know why he isn't quite as good
As anyone. He won't be made ashamed
To please his brother, worthless though he is."

"I can't think Si ever hurt anyone."

"No, but he hurt my heart the way he lay
And rolled his old head on that sharp-edged chair-back.
He wouldn't let me put him on the lounge.
You must go in and see what you can do.
I made the bed up for him there tonight.
You'll be surprised at him—how much he's broken.
His working days are done; I'm sure of it."

"I'd not be in a hurry to say that."

"I haven't been. Go, look, see for yourself.
But, Warren, please remember how it is:
He's come to help you ditch the meadow.
He has a plan. You mustn't laugh at him.
He may not speak of it, and then he may.
I'll sit and see if that small sailing cloud
Will hit or miss the moon."

It hit the moon.
Then there were three there, making a dim row,
The moon, the little silver cloud, and she.

Warren returned—too soon, it seemed to her,
Slipped to her side, caught up her hand and waited.

"Warren?" she questioned.

"Dead," was all he answered.

The Love Song of J. Alfred Prufrock

T. S. Eliot

*S'io credesse che mia risposta fosse
A persona che mai tornasse al mondo,
Questa fiamma staria senza piu scosse.
Ma perciocche giammai di questo fondo
Non torna vivo alcun, s'i'odo il vero,
Senza tema d'infamia ti rispondo.*

FROM *Collected Poems 1909-1936* by T. S. Eliot, copyright, 1936, by Harcourt, Brace and Company, Inc.

Let us go then, you and I,
When the evening is spread out against the sky
Like a patient etherized upon a table;
Let us go, through certain half-deserted streets,
The muttering retreats
Of restless nights in one-night cheap hotels
And sawdust restaurants with oyster-shells:
Streets that follow like a tedious argument
Of insidious intent
To lead you to an overwhelming question. . . .
Oh, do not ask, "What is it?"
Let us go and make our visit.

In the room the women come and go
Talking of Michelangelo.

The yellow fog that rubs its back upon the window-panes,
The yellow smoke that rubs its muzzle on the window-panes,
Licked its tongue into the corners of the evening,
Lingered upon the pools that stand in drains,
Let fall upon its back the soot that falls from chimneys,
Slipped by the terrace, made a sudden leap,
And seeing that it was a soft October night,
Curled once about the house, and fell asleep.

And indeed there will be time
For the yellow smoke that slides along the street,
Rubbing its back upon the window-panes;
There will be time, there will be time
To prepare a face to meet the faces that you meet;
There will be time to murder and create,
And time for all the works and days of hands
That lift and drop a question on your plate;
Time for you and time for me,
And time yet for a hundred indecisions,
And for a hundred visions and revisions,
Before the taking of a toast and tea.

In the room the women come and go
Talking of Michelangelo.

And indeed there will be time
To wonder, "Do I dare?" and, "Do I dare?"
Time to turn back and descend the stair,
With a bald spot in the middle of my hair—
(They will say: "How his hair is growing thin!")
My morning coat, my collar mounting firmly to the chin,
My necktie rich and modest, but asserted by a simple pin—

(They will say: "But how his arms and legs are thin!")
Do I dare
Disturb the universe?
In a minute there is time
For decisions and revisions which a minute will reverse.

For I have known them all already, known them all:
Have known the evenings, mornings, afternoons,
I have measured out my life with coffee spoons;
I know the voices dying with a dying fall
Beneath the music from a farther room.
   So how should I presume?

And I have known the eyes already, known them all—
The eyes that fix you in a formulated phrase,
And when I am formulated, sprawling on a pin,
When I am pinned and wriggling on the wall,
Then how should I begin
To spit out all the butt-ends of my days and ways?
   And how should I presume?

And I have known the arms already, known them all—
Arms that are braceleted and white and bare
(But in the lamplight, downed with light brown hair!)
Is it perfume from a dress
That makes me so digress?
Arms that lie along a table, or wrap about a shawl,
   And should I then presume?
   And how should I begin?

     .   .   .   .

Shall I say, I have gone at dusk through narrow streets
And watched the smoke that rises from the pipes
Of lonely men in shirt-sleeves, leaning out of windows? . . .

I should have been a pair of ragged claws
Scuttling across the floors of silent seas.

     .   .   .   .   .   .

And the afternoon, the evening, sleeps so peacefully!
Smoothed by long fingers,
Asleep . . . tired . . . or it malingers,
Stretched on the floor, here beside you and me.
Should I, after tea and cakes and ices,
Have the strength to force the moment to its crisis?
But though I have wept and fasted, wept and prayed,
Though I have seen my head (grown slightly bald) brought in upon a
   platter,

I am no prophet—and here's no great matter;
I have seen the moment of my greatness flicker,
And I have seen the eternal Footman hold my coat, and snicker,
And in short, I was afraid.

And would it have been worth it, after all,
After the cups, the marmalade, the tea,
Among the porcelain, among some talk of you and me,
Would it have been worth while,
To have bitten off the matter with a smile,
To have squeezed the universe into a ball
To roll it toward some overwhelming question,
To say: "I am Lazarus, come from the dead,
Come back to tell you all, I shall tell you all"—
If one, settling a pillow by her head,
   Should say: "That is not what I meant at all;
   That is not it, at all."

And would it have been worth it, after all,
Would it have been worth while,
After the sunsets and the dooryards and the sprinkled streets,
After the novels, after the teacups, after the skirts that trail along the
    floor—
And this, and so much more?—
It is impossible to say just what I mean!
But as if a magic lantern threw the nerves in patterns on a screen:
Would it have been worth while
If one, settling a pillow or throwing off a shawl,
And turning toward the window, should say:
   "That is not it at all,
   That is not what I meant, at all."

     .   .   .   .

No! I am not Prince Hamlet, nor was meant to be;
Am an attendant lord, one that will do
To swell a progress, start a scene or two,
Advise the prince; no doubt, an easy tool,
Deferential, glad to be of use,
Politic, cautious, and meticulous;
Full of high sentence, but a bit obtuse;
At times, indeed, almost ridiculous—
Almost, at times, the Fool.

I grow old. . . . I grow old. . . .
I shall wear the bottoms of my trousers rolled.

Shall I part my hair behind? Do I dare to eat a peach?
I shall wear white flannel trousers, and walk upon the beach.
I have heard the mermaids singing, each to each.

I do not think that they will sing to me.

I have seen them riding seaward on the waves
Combing the white hair of the waves blown back
When the wind blows the water white and black.
We have lingered in the chambers of the sea
By sea-girls wreathed with seaweed red and brown
Till human voices wake us, and we drown.

Chapter Four

THE WORDS OF POETRY

Something about Words

Poetry is made of not-words
Karl Shapiro

Few people in any age use their own language to the limit of its resources. One manages to get himself understood in one way or another, and for most people that seems to do. When, occasionally, one is moved to wonder about a particular word, he may go so far as to turn to the dictionary. He then "looks up what the word means" and he thereby "builds his vocabulary." He has found out about the word.

A good dictionary is, of course, indispensable to the man who hopes to use the language well. But the dictionary itself cannot be wholly useful until one realizes four basic qualities of all words. They are qualities not simply of words in poetry but of words used in any context. The good poet makes deliberate and impassioned use of these qualities, but had human history not produced a single poem, these qualities would still be observable as living forces of the language. Once one is aware of these qualities his very use of a dictionary will be changed, for he will then be appraising in a very different way what the dictionary tells him.

1. A word is a feeling.

Words do, to be sure, have areas of agreed-upon "meaning," or "dictionary definitions." "Rat," for example, is the label agreed upon in English to identify a rodent that resembles a mouse but is larger and marked by a different sort of tooth structure. This "identifying" function of the word is its *denotation*.

But what has happened to the word when a gangster refers to an accomplice as "a rat," or when he makes the word into a verb and says "he ratted on me," *i.e.*, "he gave information against me to the police"? The gangster does not mean that his accomplice is a rodent resembling a mouse but larger and having a different tooth-structure. For man, the language-animal, not only invents words as labels (denotations), but tends to associate the word with the thing it labels. Most people think of rats as despicable, vicious, and filthy. So the word takes on that "feel." The gangster is not at all concerned with the zoological classification of *genus Rattus*. He has dropped the denotation in order to use the feeling of the word (connotation).

762

The following are more or less random examples of different labels used to identify the same objects. What is the difference in feeling implied in using one label instead of another?

Label A	Label B	Label C
Fish	Finny folk	Denizens of the deep
Earth	La machine ronde (The round machine)	The little O, the earth
Alderman John J. McGinnis	That man four-square	That thieving skunk
Can of cat food	Ground fish-heads	Pussy-Purr Preparation
Digitaria sanguinalis	Crab grass	Pestiferous weeds
Elizabeth Jukes	Sweetie-pie	Big Bess

These examples will demonstrate that we commonly select language for its feeling (connotation) rather than for purposes of identification (denotation). That is to say we are often less concerned with identifying a thing than we are with expressing a feeling toward it. If I point to a candidate and say "Yes" and you point to a candidate and say "No," we have both pointed to the same person but we have expressed different feelings about him. So with Alderman John J. McGinnis in the table above. Neither Label A nor Label B is really intended to identify him. Each label is a different vote. Each seeks to persuade to a different course of action toward Mr. McGinnis.

But man is a suggestible animal and it often happens not only that his attitudes influence his labels, but that his labels influence his attitudes. Were one to pose as a strolling reporter and stop every mother out pushing a baby carriage to ask her "Are you willing to have your child killed in the defense of our National Policy?" he would probably get a negative answer. Were he to ask instead, "Do you believe we should defend our National Policy at all cost?" he would probably get a largely affirmative set of answers. We are all likely to feel well-disposed toward defending "Our National Policy," and mothers seem to have strong feelings against having their children killed. Yet the phrase "at all cost" in question two must certainly include the cost of killing some sons of some mothers, and to that extent the two questions are the same. It is the emphasis and the aura of the question that changes the response.

One last instance. In England a man "stands" for Parliament. In America he "runs" for Congress. "Standing" certainly seems to suggest a process rather different from "running." Is there any merit in the argument that a major difference between American and English politics can be summed up in the difference of feeling (connotation) released by these two words? The speculation is more important than the answer. What must be understood is the fact that if "meaning" equals "denotation" (*i.e.*, identification), then everyone uses many words without "meaning," selecting them primarily for the way they feel rather than for the accuracy with which they point-to.

The difference between this process in normal speech and in poetry is simply that the poet makes his selections with more acute attention to the various forces within the word. For the person who is a language-sensitive, every word has its own personality. Billingsgate, riparian, pismire, omnium-gatherum, rasp, bang, bodacious, lazy-susan, crepuscular—every word releases its own aura of feeling.

2. A word involves the muscles.

An inseparable but special part of the feeling of words lies in the fact that they have to be produced by a human body—with an exception noted for parrots and such-like. The act of producing a word involves breath and muscle, and various kinds of muscular activity tend to produce various kinds of feeling. Thus, aside from all other considerations, the bodily involvement in sounding the word is a distinct part of the word's personality. "Elate" feels one way and "thud" feels another. So for sheets, burble, spit, clack, snip, bang, buzz, alleluia, prestidigitation, indubitably, liquescent, ululate, majestic, and anything else one cares to cite from the total language—some words involve more specific and more localized muscular play than others, and some have their denotations more involved in the resulting sound than others, but every word has a muscular feel of its own. When the muscular play tends more or less definitely to enact the denotation of the word as in "prestidigitation" or "oily" (one has only to protract the "oi" sound to produce an oily suggestion), then the word may be called *mimetic*. When the sound of a word imitates the sound of what the word denotes (as in buzz, plink, splash, crunch), then the word may be called *onomatopoetic*. Any conversation attentively listened to will offer examples of both kinds of words. The more excited the conversation becomes, the easier it will be to see in the emphases and gestures of the speakers how the muscles and the whole body are involved in the process of speech and its meaning.

3. A word is a history.

Languages die but words tend to be immortal. Catch-words, slang, and technical terms often disappear after a brief run, but many become established parts of the language, and once so established they persist. Hosts of Greek and Latin words are in use in dozens of the world's present-day languages. It is mainly the order in which words are used, the ways in which they are joined together (syntax), and their inflections that change. Like the stones of an ancient ruin, the words fall out of their original organization but survive to be used again, though they are usually re-shaped in the process. There is hardly a tenement hovel in the old section of modern Rome that was not built in part with stones from ancient ruins. There is hardly a phrase in a modern American's vocabulary that has not been built up from pieces fallen out of other languages.

To the attentive collector of ancient fragments, however, each unit tends to keep its history. It is so and more so with words, for the history tends to remain in them as an immediate and intrinsic force. Thus a person sensitive to language could conceivably object to the sentence "On the eighth day we arrived at our mid-ocean rendezvous and refueled." "Arrive" is simply a slightly changed way of spelling and pronouncing the Latin *ad ripa,* meaning "to the shore." It offends the history of a perfectly good word to speak of "arriving" at mid-ocean.

And just as a firm awareness of the history of words leads one to more precise usage, so can it yield rewarding pleasures. Hearing a New England farmer calling in his cows with a "Ho! Boss! Ho! Boss!" one may be both surprised and delighted to realize that what he is hearing is almost pure Greek. Centuries before Christ, the same cry rang over the hills of Greece, the call meaning literally "The Cow! The Cow!" One may take such awareness as simply ornamental information, or he may find in it a moving example of the continuity of human experience. For the poet, as for any man passionately concerned with words as living forces, the realization is bound to have a touch of excitement in it.

Often, an awareness of a word's history will not only make clear but will dramatize its meaning. "Supercilious" is an Anglicized form of Latin supercilium (*super,* above, and *cilium,* eye-lid); hence, an eyebrow. Hence a supercilious expression is "an eyebrow expression," one with raised eyebrows. Nor need one know Latin to come by such an awareness. Good dictionaries not only define words but give their histories in brief. Any one truly concerned to make his speech precise will stop to learn such roots when he consults the dictionary. Having done so, he is less likely to be tempted into such unhistorical imprecisions as the construction, "A supercilious wave of the hand."

Chaucer, at one point, refers to "Christ sterved (starved) on the cross." In Chaucer's day "sterven"—from Anglo Saxon *steorfan,* which in turn derived from Old Norse—meant any slow death, as by exposure, torture, hunger, or thirst. "To starve" acquired its present limited meaning long after Chaucer's day. Towns under attack were often besieged and "starved out." That is, they were exposed to slow death by being shut off from the means of life. As it happened, however, it was almost invariably the food that gave out first in those days of no refrigeration and poor storage. Thus "to die of lack of food" came to usurp the whole meaning of the original word. In sensitive usage, however, the old meaning is still there, still available for some situation in which it can enrich the total communication. "The starved thief of the wind and the hanging tree," is an invented example. Were it an authentic line of poetry, its effect would depend on many allusions. Nor does the writing demand full awareness of such allusions: the general sense of the line is suggestive even when its "meaning" has not been located. But certainly there is an added richness hidden away in "starved" and waiting for the reader who can unlock it. Many poets like to hide away such happy additions: they do not insist that every reader respond to them; it is enough that such touches delight the writer and are ready to delight the reader who is able to respond to them.

Denham's lines on Cowley (p. 791) and John Crowe Ransom's *Blue Girls* (p. 802) will provide examples of how richly a deep sense of the history hidden in words can sharpen and excite the language, teaching the reader precisions and distinctions of which he had not been aware.

For with a few exceptions every word traced back far enough is either a metaphor or an onomatopoeia. Nor can an awareness of that fact fail to suggest a deep truth about the nature of man's mind and of his sense of the universe. Let us leave onomatopoeia out of present consideration, and consider only specimens of the metaphors, *i.e.*, the pictures, locked up in words. "Hippopotamus" is from the Greek *hippo* (horse) and *potamos* (river), hence "the river horse." "Billingsgate" (foul and vituperative language) is derived from the name of a London fishmarket (compare: "swore like a fishwife") and conceals within it a picture of the whole wrangling, competitive, and coarse squabbling of a penny-grabbing street market. A semi-related word, "aspersion," on the other hand (a calumny, a calumnious remark) is from latin *ad* (to, toward) and *spargere* (to sprinkle). The distinctions revealed by the histories of these words permit precision of usage that is not possible to those who lack a sense of word-history. "My opponent has interpreted my remarks as an aspersion upon his character and has given substance to the interpretation by his own spew of billingsgate." Note how nicely the word "spew" trumps the hidden "sprinkle" in "aspersion."

The following words all have some area of denotation in common. In a good dictionary (preferably the many-volumed Oxford English Dictionary available in the library, though a Webster's will do) look up the *history* of each word. Note how the word's history makes possible distinctions that are not apparent in the simple dictionary definition:

> vituperation, condemnation, denunciation, censure,
> criticism, vilification, calumniation, objurgation,
> execration, abuse, invective, obloquy, scurrility.

Note especially that an awareness of the word's history eventually identifies the word's meaning in terms of a root-picture or root-metaphor. This picture-making power, already touched upon, is the fourth indispensable function in determining the feel of the word.

4. A word is a picture.

The word "daisy" points to a common flower and lightly conceals the root-picture "day's eye." "Goodbye" is the noise socially agreed upon for basic leave-taking, and just behind it sounds the benediction from which it is derived: "God be wi' ye." As soon as one takes into account this picture-behind-the-word, there simply are no synonyms any more. The whole idea of synonyms is an invention of the habit of dictionary definition. Conceivably there might be sets of identical twins among the words of the world, but they are rare by the very nature of language. For all practical purposes words are most richly conceived as individuals, each with its own history, each with its own locked-in picture.

The problem of the translator will illustrate. The English verb "to burke" is derived from the practices of a famous felon of Edinburgh, one William Burke, well-hanged in 1829. Burke began as a corpse-snatcher for a medical school, and when newly buried corpses were unprocurable, or when it became too dangerous to steal them from the guarded grave-yards, he simplified matters by making his corpses to order. As a result of its derivation the word "to burke" means, in its fully extended sense, "to smother a victim by pinching his nose between the fingers while pressing the butt of the palm against his mouth in such a way as to produce a corpse with no visible signs of violence and therefore readily saleable to a medical school." It must be obvious without further investigation that there is small chance of finding any word in any other language that has exactly the same dramatization as "to burke."

What is less obvious is that no two words—unless they are derived from the same roots, or except by extraordinary chance, can have the four basic qualities here discussed in anything like the same combination. Each word is peculiarly itself. (A happy word, "peculiar," in that it derives from Latin *peculium*, "private property." "Private," moreover, is from *privatus*, "apart from the state," *i.e.*, "not held in common." A certain amount of redundance in the roots may help to underline the idea: *every word is peculiarly its exclusive self apart from all common holding*. Within the "state" of common usage, words may seem to have some parts of their dictionary definitions in common, but never within their peculiar private properties.

Even as simple a word as "daisy" is untranslatable. In French, for example, the flower is called a *marguerite*, a pleasant enough suggestion of girls named Marguerite. It is, moreover, derived from Greek *margaron*, "pearl." Two happy pictures in themselves—but what has happened to the lovely English picture, "day's eye"?

Anyone who listens carefully to common speech is bound to realize that though most people respond as if instinctively to the feeling and to the muscular quality of words, few pay attention to the histories and the root-pictures words can release. Those neglected qualities are there, however, and the poets have always found them a self-delighting source of excitement. The reader without some awareness of these qualities must inevitably remain insensitive to a substantial part of the life of a good poem.

EXERCISE: Look up the following words in one of the dictionaries mentioned above. Pay special attention to their derivations (histories) and to their root-pictures. Note how many of them you have used over and over without real awareness of all their meaning.

explicit	publish	algebra
buckaroo	establish	amen
two-bits	rhododendron	gentle
progress	aspiration	subscribe
agony	ambition	clown
sympathy	jargon	pants
nice	distinguish	comfort

The Word in the Poem

> So spake the enemy of mankind, enclosed
> In serpent, inmate bad, and toward Eve
> Addressed his way, not with indented wave,
> Prone on the ground, as since, but on his rear
> Circular base of rising folds, that towered
> Fold above fold a surging maze; his head
> Crested aloft, and carbuncle his eyes;
> With burnished neck of verdant gold, erect
> Against his circling spires that on the grass
> Floated redundant.
>
> John Milton, *Paradise Lost*

John Milton had a peculiar problem in the foregoing passage in which he describes the serpent's approach to Eve. Milton's theology demanded the belief that the serpent was condemned to crawl on its belly for its crime in tempting Eve. It follows, then, that serpents originally moved in some other way, and that theological point forces Milton to invent a rather fanciful rear-wheel drive, the details of which he well-advisedly keeps a bit vague.

Readers with long memories may recall that something very much like the same point was raised in the course of the famous Evolution Trial in Tennessee as part of the defending attorney's cross-examination of witnesses. An assiduous digger through European archives, moreover, might well expect to turn up a number of ponderous essay-treatises on snake-locomotion before and after. By the world's evidence, then, as well as his own conviction, Milton is dealing with facts. There was a time not too long since when the study of such facts was very nearly all there was to the study of poetry in our universities, and there is still a marked tendency among many readers to think they have made a sufficient contact with the poem when they have identified and placed such central facts.

Because the natural form for the exposition of facts seems to be the essay, such a fact-centered reading of poetry may be thought of as "the essay approach." The true nature of a poem's performance of itself, however, is so lightly concerned with its essay-content, that it may reasonably serve the purposes of good reading to pretend that there are no facts in the poem. A poet must believe *something* passionately enough to have strong feelings about it, but what that *something* is in actual fact is the item of least consequence as far as participating in the poetic performance is concerned.

The essay has satisfied its essential requirements when it has followed the facts—facts, opinions, argument, all in general that it "has to say." Music, on the other hand, follows itself, the first sound calling the second into being, and it the third, and so on until those inner calls become feelingly involved and feelingly solve themselves. Music has no facts. It is its own fact.

Poetry does, as noted, involve itself with facts, but the poetic essence is so much nearer that of music than it is that of the essay, that to stress facts in poetry is often the quickest way to lose sight of the poem. *The essence of a poem is that one thing in it requires another.* As far as the words of poetry are concerned that inner-requirement is so little a matter of external meaning (denotation) and so much an inner-dialogue of connotations (feelings, sounds, and historical and pictorial roots) that it will at least serve to redress the balance to pretend that denotation has no function, and to practice the experience of a poem in something like pure musical terms.

The French critic Boileau called the essence of poetry a *je-ne-sais-quoi*, an "I-don't-know-what." Line by line and passage by passage the poem comes to the poet from sources he feels strongly but does not pretend to understand. At least at the beginning of the poem. Very soon, however, whatever comes to him from the *je-ne-sais-quoi* had better start coming in response to what he has already written down or he is not going to have a poem. Maybe the first line comes from nowhere. And maybe the second comes from a second-theme nowhere. But whatever part of what follows continues to come to him from his nowhere, it has to come from those first lines as well. The poem, that is, is forever generating its own context. Like a piece of music, it exists as a self-entering, self-generating, self-complicating, self-resolving form.

To answer to that musicality within the structure of the poem is to answer to the poem itself. Milton's rear-wheel-snake-passage, ridiculous as its essay-content is bound to seem, is an example of poetry elevated to sublimity by the rich and powerful development of its diction into music-like themes.

The first characteristic of Milton's diction here is precision. Note especially the rightness of "indented." Milton wished to ascribe to the post-Paradisal snake a wave-like motion. Now a wave may be conceived in many ways—as a single peak, as a trough-and-crest, as a long roller. But the clear historical meaning of "indented" is "cut into tooth-like points." For Milton—so passionate a Latinist that he could speak of "elephants endorsed with towers"—that root image of "indented" establishes all. For clearly a single wave cannot be indented. At least two are required to make an indentation. In poetry, the force of a given sense is readily extended: as soon as the pluralness of the wave is established, the suggested picture at once becomes not a picture of two waves but of many.

Parenthetically, it must be noted that the process of selection going on in the poet's mind (or the recognition of that process in the mind of a good reader) is not spread out across a paragraph of description. It is most likely to happen as an instantaneous, surprising, and happy discovery. The rightness of the choice is felt in many ways at once. It is the explanation that labors, not the poem. The one point of the explanation is to guide the reader back to the poem with a sharper awareness of what he must learn to experience instantaneously.

Now note the last phrase, "floated redundant." As the snake rears its jeweled head, the remaining coils lie on the grass as if they floated. "Floated," of course, once more suggests the wave-image, and in combination with "redundant" it urges a picture of many slow coils lying at ease on the waters, resting but still keeping a slow, endless, easy motion.

But why "redundant"? Why not "superfluous"? "remaining"? "excessive"? Milton's choice was partly determined by the sound of the word, to be sure, but much more urgently because of the picture hidden in the Latin roots of the word (redundare, to overflow; from unda, a wave). "Superfluous" also means "to overflow" but with a single, continuous outward motion, as of a river rather than with the better-related suggestion of a wave's surging and receding motion.

Quite clearly Milton has chosen his words not only, nor even primarily, for the rightness of their denotation (essay-wise) but for the interconnection of their connotations (musically); not for their exactness to the "facts" but for the way they follow from other words in the passage. "Floated redundant," for example, might factually have been expressed "sprawled out in excess loops and coils"; but then the interplay of one wave suggestion with another would have been lost. The point cannot be made often enough that it is exactly such interplays that determine the poem as a poem, and that such interplays, far from being merely ornamental, are inseparable from the poem's "meaning." They *are* the meaning, and if they are not there is no defense for poetry, nor any meaningful way of preferring it to embroidery, cross-word puzzles, or the day's prose-from-Washington.

Having located "indented wave" and "floated redundant" as specific kinds of watery motion, one may now look back and see that "surging," too, is at root a watery motion. Its base picture is of a spring bubbling up, its waters agitated in all directions around it. Thus in nine-and-a-fraction lines, that suggestion of watery motion has been three times urged upon the reader. What could be more like the way in which the fragments of a musical theme are picked up, dropped, and picked up again? If the jargon is not objectionable, this sort of poetic development may reasonably be called an "overtone theme." Just as certain characters in opera are identifiable by a musical theme that accompanies them through the action, so the serpent is carried through this description to the theme of a constant wavering watery motion.

And having noted one theme, the reader can hardly fail to note another: the snake also moves like an oriental monarch. His elevation is regal: ("towered," "crested aloft," "spires"). His ornaments are all magnificence: ("crested"—*i.e.*, crowned, "carbuncled"—*i.e.*, diamonded, and "gold"). Thus the theme of watery motion is accompanied by a theme of regal splendor. Again the poem performs itself much as does a piece of music.

And much as in a piece of music, the two themes join. Waves "tower" and kings may be said to "tower" above men. "Crested aloft" suggests a wave at peak, and it also means "crowned on high."

Now if one re-reads the passage he can note three groupings of over-tone themes: watery-motion, regal-splendor, and the two together. Arranged in three columns the words and phrases that might be related to each of these themes would appear so:

Watery motion	*Regal splendor and Watery motion*	*Regal splendor*
indented wave	towered	carbuncle
circular base	crested aloft	burnished
rising folds		gold
fold upon fold		circling spires
surging maze		
floated redundant		

Whatever the value of such a tabulation, it cannot fail to make clear, first, that a unified principle of selection is at work in this diction, and second, that the words are being selected from inside their connotations and in answer to one another's connotations, rather than from inside their denotation.

For poetry, it must be understood, is a made thing. It does not *record* reality nor even imagination; it *selects* from them. The ideal newspaper account of an incident, for example, aims at recording what happened; a good short story selects and shapes. Whatever the short story's take-off from fact, it must end by shaping itself to itself. The fact that a given event happened in "real life" does not make it happen in an art form; art is its own way of happening. A good painting is neither a photograph nor a blueprint but an interpretation and an intensification achieved by emphasizing some things, subordinating others, and by following the inner-requiredness of the composition. For that matter, even a photographer selects. Nature does not care where and in what sequence as seen from what vantage point the mountains of Maine fall into the sea or thrust up again as islands: they are simply there. But let the most amateur photographer decide to take a photo of that coastline, and the instant he has framed it in his view-finder he begins to move the camera about in the attempt to find a relation within the frame. Put a dab of paint on an endless surface and it does not matter where it falls. But put a frame around it, and immediately the one dab requires another, and the two a third, until some sort of composition has been achieved.

These scattering examples are all to the point that every art form presents its material within a convention and a limitation, and that the material does not exist meaningfully in that art form until it has become involved in the inner-requiredness of its formal limitations. Until the perception of a poem becomes a perception of that inner-requiredness, the poem has not come into view. To paraphrase a statement by I. A. Richards, "One talks about the subject of a poem when he does not know what to do with the poemness of the poem." That "poemness" exists nowhere but in the poem's performance of itself from itself into itself.

A simpler and perhaps more pointed example of this inner-relationship of words within the poem occurs in Keats' "The Eve of St. Agnes" (p. 744). In stanza xxvi, Keats is faced with a delicate problem, for in a poem concerned with idealized love, Keats finds himself describing the hero in the potentially satyr-like situation of hiding in a closet and watching the heroine undress for bed. The tone is delicate, yet the material in this particular scene has been the immemorial property of coarse humor from fabliaux to burlesque show. Keats' original worksheets, now in the collection of Harvard's Houghton Library, trace out in interesting detail the poet's difficulties in making his choices.

With Porphyro looking on from the closet, Madeline enters, says her prayers, and prepares for bed. The tone of that opening description is all airiness and delicacy:

> her vespers done
> Of all its wreathed pearls she frees her hair,
> Unclasps her warmed jewels one by one

Keats' choice of adjectives has been much and justly praised. "Wreathed" is light, graceful, ideal, with a suggestion of a halo about it. And "warmed" (warmed by her flesh) is precisely the kind of rich sensuous yet not sensual detail Keats loved to lavish upon his poems. All goes well so far.

But Keats has already survived one difficulty. The first draft of the manuscript reads not as above in the third line, but "Unclasps her bosom jewels." This reading Keats immediately struck out. One must note in the final version that though Madeline undresses in this stanza, there is not one word that mentions flesh. Certainly there is no reason except the narrowest kind of prurience against mentioning "bosom" as a fact of the world. But the word does not fit the mood Keats is seeking to establish. The flesh remains in the revised line, but it is sublimated and suggested in the richness of "warmed" rather than baldly stated.

In the next line Keats encounters exactly the same difficulty, but here his trouble is more persistent. He begins:

> Loosens the bodice from her . . .

But what can she loosen her bodice from, other than the naked fact Keats is seeking to avoid? He crosses out that reading and tries again even more disastrously:

> Loosens her bursting bodice . . .

But he realizes at once that "bursting" will not do. In succeeding attempts he tries:

> Loosens her bodice lace-strings . . .

then

> Loosens her bodice, and her bosom bare . . .

then

> Loosens her fragrant bodice and doth bare
> Her . . .

And in this last form, he has conquered the most of his problem, but "bare" as demanded by the rhyme with "hair" is still wrong. At this point Keats backed up, inserted a new rhyme word into line two, and seems to have gone straight to the perfection of his final version:

> Anon his heart revives: her vespers done,
> Of all its wreathed pearls her hair she frees;
> Unclasps her warmed jewels one by one;
> Loosens her fragrant bodice; by degrees
> Her rich attire creeps rustling to her knees:
> Half-hidden, like a mermaid in sea-weed,
> Pensive awhile she dreams awake and sees,
> In fancy, fair St. Agnes in her bed,
> But dares not look behind, or all the charm is fled.

Two things seem to emerge clearly from a careful look at Keats' choices and revisions here. First, Keats seems originally to have conceived of Madeline as definitely buxom, *but no hint of that original conception survives the revisions.* Keats seems to have changed, or at least to have suppressed his original conception of the facts, and to have done so with no hint of unfaithfulness to facts, but rather in a joyous pursuit of something else. *Poets seem easily inclined to change the denotations of what they write about in order to control the connotations.*

The second fact to emerge from such a work-sheet examination is the care with which those connotations have been related to one another. "Wreathed . . . warmed . . . fragrant" release an intimately inter-related series of connotations. "Wreathed" establishes the lightness and grace of the theme. "Warmed" richly suggests the vitality of Madeline's bodily presence. And "fragrant" repeats exactly that suggestion. "Warmed" and "fragrant," in a sense, are brother-and-sister words, and they are cousins of "wreathed."

It is upon such "family" relations within words that the poet lavishes his love and attention. Milton, a Latinist, "felt" his words most richly in terms of their root sense. Keats, a lover of the sensuous fact of the world, "felt" his words in terms of the sensations they released. Both were concerned with the way their words worked in context with one another. Both used words as poets dream of doing, with a kind of life words rarely possess except in poetry.

The Phrase as a Form

Words are, in one sense, distinct units. In another, however, they are forever shaping themselves into rhythmic phrases in which the words themselves become parts of a large unit. This tendency of words to form together is a basic process in all language. Poetry makes rich use of this force but the force itself is pre-poetic and is best illustrated by such forms as the battle-cry and the proverb, forms of intense and direct natural language in which the phrasing is *muscular, irreducible,* and *memorable.*

The *muscularity* of good phrasing is obvious at a glance. "Saint George and the Dragon for Merrie England" is not simply a statement; it is a rhythmic unit to which a man on a horse can swing his sword arm. The phrase involves the whole body in its muscular spasm. And that muscular spasm is far more important than the precise meaning of the statement. The cry is intimately linked with an action. Its function is to make the muscles twitch. A captain leading his men into battle sounds the cry waving his sword over his head and his men give it back in a single animal roar as they rush forward. Does the statement have meaning? A philosophical captain might have gathered his men quietly about him and said in thoughtful tones: "Men of England, here at this brink of battle, let us summon to mind the triumphant image of Saint George the Dragon slayer, and with him ever in our minds as a symbol of our high heritage, let us move resolutely against the foe. Thank you." Is that statement the same thing? Unfortunately the paraphrase has taken the muscular twitch from it. There is about the same difference between the paraphrase and the original statement as there is between the Official Rule Book for Intercollegiate Football and the kick-off of the Rose Bowl Game.

The fact is that battle-cries have no real need to mean, only to be. (See Archibald MacLeish's *Ars Poetica,* p. 909.) Here are a few of the many battle-cries men have fought and died to. Self evidently the power of such phrasing is not in its paraphrasable meaning:

Courage mes amis, le diable est mort.

Banzai. (The literal meaning is something like "May you live a thousand years.)

Ding how! (The literal meaning is something like "perfect.")

Bonnie Dundee!

Hundred and third!

Examples could be multiplied indefinitely, but it should be amply clear that whatever meaning might be locked into the cry (as in "Remember the Alamo!") the real function of such a cry is to release pent up emotion. Any noise will serve so long as those who cry it are emotionally identified with it. The bark-and-snarl of dogs is essentially a battle cry.

What is reduced to a single outburst in such cries is used in much more subtle ways in poetic phrasing, but the basic principle of all such phrasing remains firm: *good language involves the body, the more powerful and the more simple its emotion, the greater the bodily involvement is likely to be.*

The language of such cries is also *irreducible.* One cannot find an excess word in them. Proverbs are generally subtler examples of basic phrasing than are battle cries, but the same irreducibility of the phrase is the basis of their effect. "A bird in the hand is worth two in the bush." "Be sure to sell your horse before he dies." "Pretty is as pretty does." "A stitch in time saves nine." The proverb or the proverb-shaped poetic line can be extended into long passages of paraphrase. The second example above is a line from a Robert Frost poem. How many words would one need to write in order to explain everything the line means? The essence of its success is exactly that it says so much in so little. Every word counts: remove any one and the meaning is lost. A whole area of meaning has been reduced to what must certainly be the fewest possible words.

And partly because such phrasing is indeed irreducible, it is also *memorable.* The memorableness of proverbs is assisted by their rhythms, by their turns of phrase, and by their ability to convert a thought into a picture. "A stitch in time saves nine," for example, is rhythmically definite and inevitably suggests some picture of a "nine-stitch rip" as opposed to the same fabric kept whole by the timely taking of a single stitch. A proverb is essentially a rhythmic word-portrait of a thought. Still, were the rhythm to become too complex, or the portrait to run to too many words, the force would be lost. For all of these reasons, its irreducibility first among them, the proverb seems to hook onto the memory almost by itself.

These qualities of *muscularity, irreducibility,* and *memorableness* function in many complex ways in the language of poetry, but they are forever inseparable from powerful emotional effect.

The Language of Poetry

Neither the deadness of bad poetry nor the liveliness of good poetry can be located exclusively in the way the poet uses words. Yet certainly whatever is most characteristic of a good poet must begin with a special sensitivity to language. As in Auden's measure of the potential poet, the man must want to hang around words in order to overhear them talking to one another. That "hanging around," however, is not a passive occupation. The poet's necessary sensitivity involves a life-time of bringing his joyous attention to the ways in which words whisper to one another. And the words of good poetry must be those of the poet's native tongue, the words that echo most deeply into his memory and response.

Thus one may hear poets speaking of words in ways that are not immediately clear; of "hard" words and "soft" ones, of "thin" or "echoing" or "square" words. There is a feeling at the root of such talk, but the labels themselves lack precision. The fact that deeply felt things are often the hardest to define must not, however, obscure the point that such strange talk arises from a real feeling, and that those who have such feelings most urgently, are likely to use the language in the most living way.

Robert Burns is perhaps the outstanding example of a poet who had a genius for the quality of one sort of language and almost none whatever for the quality of another. His poems in Scottish dialect ring true to the very roots of the language. His poems in English are never more than merely correct. Burns could overhear the broad Scots words talking to one another, hear their echoes to the depths of his consciousness, but he had no such feeling for the sound and echo of English. Here, for example, are the first three stanzas of a poem in his native language:

To James Smith

Dear Smith, the sleest, paukie thief,
That e'er attempted stealth or rief,
Ye surely hae some warlock-breef
    Owre human hearts;
For ne'er a bosom yet was prief
    Against your arts.

For me, I swear by sun and moon,
And every star that blinks aboon,
Ye've cost me twenty pair o' shoon
    Just gaun to see you;
And ev'ry ither pair that's done,
    Mair taen I'm wi' you.

That auld, capricious carlin, Nature,
To make amends for scrimpit stature,
She's turned you aff, a human creature
    On her first plan,
And in her freaks, on ev'ry feature,
    She's wrote, "The Man."

sleest: slyest. **paukie:** cunning, sly. **warlock-breef:** wizard's contract (with the devil). **prief:** proof. (Sense: no human heart could fail to answer to the quality of your friendship.) **aboon:** above. **shoon:** shoes. (Sense: Burns has worn out twenty pairs of shoes walking to Smith's house and finds himself more and more drawn to Smith with each new pair of shoes he wears out on that road.) **carlin:** old woman. **scrimpit stature:** scanty and slight of build, not tall. (Sense: To make amends for having made you so small, Nature, in one of her freaks of mood, has stamped your every feature with qualities that say "This is Man.")

The language of such a dialect poem is, of course, a difficulty, but the notes should take care of that. Even beyond the strangeness of the language, however, the poem requires careful attention. One is not used to reading of friendship in these (anti-poetic) terms. Were the turning of the poem closer to the standard copybook sentiments on friendship, one might run his eyes over it once lightly and perceive all there is in it. Fortunately for the reader's pleasure, the poem is close to life rather than to the copybook. It does require some effort (perhaps as much effort of the attention as it takes to play a tight hand of bridge). Yet despite the effort, there can be no mistaking the liveliness of the poem. One has the sense that only a man who has actually walked many miles (and many times) to the house of his friend could have written of his friendship in this way. One has the sense, too, that the description in stanza three—at once tender and humorous—could only have been drawn from a man the poet knew well and loved dearly. And with this depth of feeling, the words come alive. Burns did not have to go to school to learn to use words in this way, and no school could have taught him. For the character and depth of the words echo up from the subconscious of the language. They are leaping, laughing, tender, easy, dear words to Burns. No matter that he could not have defined their quality as he felt it. What counts is that he did feel it. Here on the other hand are the first three stanzas of a Burns poem in English, this one also written to a specific and known person:

Verses

Intended to be written below a Noble Earl's Picture

> Whose is that noble dauntless brow?
>   And whose that eye of fire?
> And whose that generous princely mien
>   Even rooted foes admire?
>
> Stranger, to justly shew that brow
>   And mark that eye of fire,
> Would take His hand, whose vernal tints
>   His other works admire.
>
> Bright as a cloudless summer sun,
>   With stately port he moves;
> His guardian seraph eyes with awe
>   The noble ward he loves.

Verses is a poetic or fashionable poem, a standard sort of inscriptive piece out of the copybook of eighteenth century manners, though rather badly overdone. "Only God's hand," the second stanza asserts, "painting on something like the same scale on which He paints the world's greenery *etc.* could portray the noble Earl *etc.*"—surely a gross, insincere, and even irreverent bit of flattery. Heaven knows what Burns hoped to gain by it but his need was at times great and servility was one of the ways of moving an influential patron to provide the means of life.

But the point to be made is one of diction. It is almost impossible, if not absolutely impossible, for a poet to cheat emotionally in this way without betraying himself in the flatness and triteness of his language. There is not a phrase in the poem that is not cliché-ridden. "Noble brow" and "dauntless brow" are both clichés: Burns gives the reader both for good measure. Pausing for a single cliché in "eye of fire," he once more doubles the charge with "generous princely mien." Then, to round off the first stanza, he reaches blithely into the file of poetic stereotypes for the image of the last line. And so on through "vernal tints," "bright sun," "cloudless summer," "stately port" (for "stately bearing"), and "noble ward." There is no sort of pleasure in counting the insincerities a good poet may fall into, but sooner a small offense than to allow clichés to go unrecognized for lack of sufficient examples. There is not one of these phrases that could not be compiled a hundred times over from the works of a hundred bad poets before and since Burns.

One may argue, to be sure, that such a piece of rhymed flattery composed in the hope of bread must necessarily be stilted. The fact is, however, that Burns always tended to fall into lifeless and unconvincing language when he wrote in English. Here, for example, is a lament of exactly the sort he wrote so well in Scottish dialect. Like all of Burns' Scottish lyrics, it was specifically meant to be sung:

A Mother's Lament for the Death of Her Son

Tune—"Finlayston House"

Fate gave the word, the arrow sped,
    And pierced my darling's heart;
And with him all the joys are fled
    Life can to me impart!
By cruel hands the sapling drops,
    In dust dishonour'd laid:
So fell the pride of all my hopes,
    My age's future shade.

The mother-linnet in the brake
    Bewails her ravish'd young;
So I, for my lost darling's sake,
    Lament the live-day long.
Death, oft I've feared thy fatal blow,
    Now fond, I bare my breast,
O, do thou kindly lay me low
    With him I love at rest.

Despite Burns' successes with such songs in the Scottish dialect, there is no life in this one. Death as the arrow that pierces the heart, the young man as the sapling chopped down before it could become a tree, the mother bird lamenting her lost fledgling, the baring of the mourner's own breast to the stroke of death—all are worn poetic counters. And, inseparably, the diction goes slack as the impulse goes dead, over-familiar phrase following over-familiar phrase.

"Poetry," wrote John Wheelwright, "is a way of knowing." Language, one might paraphrase, is a way of feeling. It has been said somewhere that one can write poetry only in the language in which he first learned to say "Mamma," and the fact is that though some prose-writers (Joseph Conrad, to mention one outstanding example) have distinguished themselves in an acquired language, no poet has ever done so. This fact, and the example of Burns' failures in his English poems, will suggest how deeply the language of good poetry must be felt, and how many shadings of response must go into the selection of the right and moving word. The language must not only be overheard, it must be overheard echoing all the way back to one's birth, before the poet can achieve a way of speaking that reveals to the reader not only how well an experience may be perceived, but how well the language can be spoken by one who is live-involved in it.

1. A sense of the whole language stirring.

If it is understood that language used at its full depth involves complications as profound and as undefinable as those of life itself, it will then be possible to discuss some questions of language in poetry that will at least help to phrase the final question. That final question, it must be remembered, remains a fundamental one. What is the nature of poetic language? What is the nature of life? How does the planet come to be inhabited? These are all fundamental questions and they are fundamental precisely because they are finally unanswerable. What matters is to raise the question in the most meaningful way possible.

The fact that a good poem will never wholly submit to explanation is not its deficiency but its very life. One lives every day what he cannot define. It is feeling that is first. What one cannot help but sense in good poetry is a sense of the whole language stirring toward richer possibilities than one could have foreseen. To consider some of the impressions that can be isolated from that total feeling, and to speculate on their possible causes, is at least to enter the question of how language functions in a poem. One must remember, however, that such impressions do not exist in isolation in the poem. To separate them for analysis is pointless unless one then attempts to put them back in context. One does not take a poem apart for the love of dissection but only in order to put it back together more meaningfully.

2. Language and diction.

The Irish critic Donald Davie makes a useful distinction between language and diction. Certain poets, he points out, give off a sense that any word in the language could find a place in their works. Others, on the other hand, deliberately exclude certain words. Their work, as Davie puts it, gives off a sense "of words thrusting to be let into the poem but being fended off from it."

In the process of such fending off these poets are, in essence, either following or developing a "poetic." In our own time, American poets have made free use of all sorts of technical terms, whereas French poets have refused to allow such terms into their work. The point of the example is not that all American poets write in a language, but that to the extent that French poets fend off all technical terms *they* are writing a diction. Such terms have been branded "unpoetic" and have been deliberately excluded. Davie cites Goldsmith on Homer to illustrate a similar difference in point of view:

> Homer has been blamed for the bad choice of his similes on some particular occasions. He compares Ajax to an ass, in the *Iliad*, and Ulysses to a steak broiling on the coals, in the *Odyssey*. His admirers have endeavored to excuse him, by reminding us of the simplicity of the age in which he wrote; but they have not been able to prove that any ideas of dignity or importance were, even in those days, affixed to the character of an ass, or the quality of a beef collop; therefore they were very improper illustrations for any situation in which a hero ought to be represented.

If one agrees with Goldsmith on what is dignified and important, one must agree with his censure of Homer. One must not miss the point, however, that diction is more than a matter of stylish word-choices. A man's diction involves the whole of his attitude toward himself and toward everything else. Cleanth Brooks, in his *Modern Poetry and the Tradition,* makes nearly the same distinction when he speaks of the *poets of wit* as opposed to the *poets of high seriousness.* The poets of wit (John Donne will do as an example) strive toward a language and welcome into their poems the rush of every sort of experience. The poets of high seriousness (William Wordsworth will do as an example) strive toward a diction and exclude all that is not "dignified and important."

Quite clearly most poets, especially the American and English poets of the eighteenth and nineteenth centuries, wrote a diction. And a diction is certainly a lesser thing than a language. On the other hand a poet who practices a diction, Alexander Pope for example, may achieve what he achieves not in spite of his diction, but because of it. Poetry remains large enough to be all things to all who care to read. Even as considerable a poet as Milton wrote essentially a diction. One would certainly have no trouble imagining good English words that Milton would not have accepted. Like Goldsmith, he will allow no beefsteaks in Eden. And he will not allow them precisely because he has excluded from the Eden of his poetic imagination those concepts which such excluded words express.

Finally, it seems to be true that poets who write in a diction tend to be more ornamental, and poets who write in a language to be more direct.

Once again, no judgment for or against is implied in pointing out this difference. The aim is to identify. Poetry is the one, the other, and both together. Hamlet's "So I have heard and do, in part, believe" is an example of the direct unornamented line. Tennyson's "The mellow ousel fluted in the elm," is an example of the richly ornamented line.

There are real pleasures in either manner, but the highest effects of passionately moving speech seem to occur in the simplicity of poetic language as distinct from diction. The more passionate the statement the more simple the form it tends to take.

Perhaps the best example of this difference in a single passage is the speech Dante puts into the mouth of Pier delle Vigne on the journey through Hell. Since it occurs in a complicated context, a little advance explanation will assist the reading.

The spirit of Pier delle Vigne is condemned among the suicides. Since these are sinners who destroyed their own bodies, they are denied a bodily form and grow as trees in a dark wood of Hell. Thus the reference to the "trunk" and the oath "by the new roots of this tree" (delle Vigne has been dead only a short time). In life, delle Vigne was the powerful minister of Frederick II until he was accused of treachery, imprisoned and blinded. It was to escape further torture that he killed himself. (The "Caesar" of line 10 is a generic term for "Emperor.")

Pier delle Vigne was also famous for his eloquence and for his mastery of the ornate and intricate poetry of the Provençal-inspired Sicilian School. He was an embroiderer of words. It may help to think of him as a slightly more elegant but equally pompous Polonius.

Thus as he begins to speak, he carefully announces that he will wind up slowly (line 3). He then proceeds through a series of little rhetorical exercises, such as the balanced construction of line 5, and the double and triple repetitions of key words in the passage that follows. In the middle of line 18, however, the elaborate courtly prologue ends abruptly, and in a sudden rush of language (as distinct from diction), he speaks his grief from the heart, simply and passionately.

Pier delle Vigne

Dante Alighieri

Translated by John Ciardi

And the trunk: "So sweet those words to me that I
    cannot be still, and may it not annoy you
    if I seem somewhat lengthy in reply.

I am he who held both keys to Frederick's heart,
    locking, unlocking with so deft a touch
    that scarce another soul had any part

in his most secret thoughts. Through every strife
  I was so faithful to my glorious office
  that for it I gave up both sleep and life.

That harlot, Envy, who on Caesar's face
  keeps fixed forever her adulterous stare,
  the common plague and vice of court and palace,

inflamed all minds against me. These inflamed
  so inflamed him that all my happy honors
  were changed to mourning. Then, unjustly blamed,

my soul in scorn, and thinking to be free
  of scorn in death, made me at last, though just,
  unjust to myself. By the new roots of this tree

I swear to you that never in word or spirit
  did I break faith to my lord and emperor
  who was so worthy of honor in his merit.

If ever you regain the world, speak for me,
  to vindicate in the memory of men
  one who lies prostrate from the blows of Envy."

In case the distinction is not wholly clear, imagine how different the effect of this passage would have been had delle Vigne continued his elaborate rhetoric to the end, as for example:

By the firm root of this tree

I firmly swear my faith was ever firm
  to him who was my lord, as to the Lord
  who was our Lord alike. If at the term

of your dark way you make your way to light
  I pray you lighten the dark memory
  Envy's brief day cast to eternal night.

3. A poem is a machine for making choices.

A poet who writes in a diction is constantly making one sort of choice; a poet who writes in a language is constantly making another. A poem may well be conceived as a machine for making choices. At any given point in the poem, the poet must select the next thing to do. He must choose a word, an idea, an image—all these together. He must decide to add ornamentation or to thrust for the statement and center of his feeling. If nothing else he must choose from the total language one word and not another.

Keats' "Epistle to Charles Cowden Clarke" is an early poem. Clarke had been instrumental in turning Keats to the pleasures of poetry. Among other things, Clarke has introduced Keats to Spenser's poetry. Keats responded with a sense of uncontainable and joyous excitement at such discoveries. Keats writes to thank Clarke for having taught him:

> all the sweets of song:
> The grand, the sweet, the terse, the free, the fine;
> What swelled with pathos, and what right divine:
> Spenserian vowels that . . .

That what? What will his choice be? Having equated Spenser's verse to vowels, what shall he say about it? He has a new rhyme at his disposal (the "Epistle" is written in couplets) and is therefore free of rhyme demand. Shall he say

> Spenserian vowels, that divinely lilt?

or: Spenserian vowels, delicate and light?

He wrote instead:

> Spenserian vowels that elope with ease.

And what a magnificent choice "elope" is in this context! "Divinely lilt" could not be objected to. Nor could "delicate and light." But nothing distinguishes them; one could easily improvise choices that good. These, in fact, were improvised on the typewriter. But "elope" contains that shiver of real poetry that Emily Dickinson had in mind when she spoke of "the desirable gooseflesh which is poetry." And at least three reasons can be pointed out for the rush of pleasure that arises from this source. First, the word is *both surprising and surprisingly right*. One could not have foreseen it, but he is immediately convinced by it; he has made a happy discovery. Second, the sound of "elope" exactly illustrates the Spenserian vowel: *the thing itself echoes through the word*. Third, the overtone of "elope" is delicate, light and divinely lilting. *All that the adjectives of the lesser choices labor to say, the exactly right choice releases, seemingly without labor, and directly into our sensations.* Moreover, one knows, from having read Keats' later poems, that the overtone is exactly right to Keats' own deepest point of view—a romantic, light, incomplete, and loving action. What the lovers on the Grecian Urn are yearning to (p. 808) and what Porphyro and Madeline dramatise in an actual elopement at the end of "The Eve of St. Agnes" (p. 744) is already germinally in this loving usage of "elope."

As Keats himself later described this quality of poetry, it "should surprise with a fine excess, and not by singularity; it should strike the reader as a wording of his own thoughts, and appear almost a remembrance."

Whether a poet writes in a language or a diction (and hereafter unless one or the other is specified it should be assumed that the discussion applies to both) this "fine excess" is inseparable from the richness and muscular-stir of good poetry. A good poem is always better than one could have expected. Even on re-reading, and even on many re-readings, the truly achieved poem stays richer than one's best memory of it.

Here, for example, is Hamlet's familiar soliloquy from Act IV, scene iv. Hamlet has just seen Fortinbras lead his army away to battle for a plot of ground worthless in itself but involving a small point of honor. This grand tossing of life and death for such minute reasons is the occasion that informs against Hamlet, damning him in his own eyes for having hesitated so long in the much greater cause of avenging his father:

> How all occasions do inform against me,
> And spur my dull revenge! What is a man
> If his chief good and market of his time
> Be but to sleep and feed? a beast, no more.
> Sure, he that made us with such large discourse
> Looking before and after, gave us not
> The capability of god-like reason
> To fust in us unused. Now, whether it be
> Bestial oblivion, or some craven scruple
> Of thinking too precisely on the event—
> A thought which, quartered, hath but one part wisdom,
> And ever three parts coward—I do not know
> Why yet I live to say "This thing's to do,"
> Sith I have cause, and will, and strength, and means
> To do't. Examples gross as earth exhort me:
> Witness this army of such mass and charge,
> Led by a delicate and tender prince,
> Whose spirit, with divine ambition puffed,
> Makes mouths at the invisible event,
> Exposing what is mortal and unsure
> To all that fortune, death, and danger dare,
> Even for an eggshell. Rightly to be great
> Is not to stir without great argument,
> But greatly to find quarrel in a straw
> When honor's at the stake. How stand I then
> That have a father killed, a mother stained,
> Excitements of my reason and my blood,
> And let all sleep? while to my shame I see
> The imminent death of twenty thousand men,
> That for a fantasy and trick of fame
> Go to their graves like beds, fight for a plot
> Whereon the numbers cannot try the cause,
> Which is not tomb enough and continent
> To hide the slain? O, from this time forth
> My thoughts be bloody, or be nothing worth.

The total effect of such a passage cannot, certainly, be said to spring simply from its word choices. The rhythms and the dramatic pauses and contrasts determine its pace. Hamlet's narrative situation helps create an identity with him (empathy). And the whirl of many images glimpsed and gone (the sharpness of "spur," the sleeping beast, the heraldic suggestion of "quartered," as if Hamlet were thinking of an escutcheon for his state of mind) populates the mind's eye. Still, considered simply as a series of word choices delivering each thought (denotation) wrapped in the aura of its precisely felt and precisely suggestive overtone, the passage certainly gives off a sense that English cannot be better selected than this. Let it stand as a high example of *that kind of poetry which is written* in a *language as distinct from a diction and with the impulse toward passionate simplicity rather than toward ornamentation.* What are some of its characteristics? How does one measure the firmness of its selection?

Marie Gilchrist offers one measure that should never be lost sight of:

> Verbs and words derived from verbs are of great importance. When you say that your object does something, rather than that it is something or like something else, you give it life and movement. Nouns stand for ideas, names, and things. Each noun is a complete picture. Nouns and verbs are almost pure metal. Adjectives are cheaper ore; they have less strength of meaning, since they stand for just one aspect of a thing, one characteristic, and do not represent it in its entirety.[1]

Adjectives, then, may be said to be relatively inactive. And with this in mind one may formulate a valuable principle:

4. The language of good poetry is active.

No all-encompassing rules work in poetry, yet here is one which, used with discretion, can offer a simple, tangible, and still basically sound measure of the quality of a poem's language: *count the adjectives and the verbs; good writing (active writing) will almost invariably have more verbs.*

There seems always to be some difference of opinion on the adjective count. Should "quartered" (line 11), for example, be argued as an adjective ("a quartered thought") or as a verb ("quarter the thought and you will see")? As it falls in the text, it certainly is presented as a verb. And still its force could be argued to be adjectival. The point at issue, however, does not require any real concern with such hair-splitting. When in doubt let it count as an adjective. The Hamlet passage will still turn up a count of approximately two verbs per adjective: forty-six verbs to twenty-four adjectives.

The nearly two-to-one ratio is not exorbitant (as a count through the poems in this volume will demonstrate) and it seems to be a general rule

[1]Marie Gilchrist, *Writing Poetry*. Boston: Houghton Mifflin Company.

that passages of poetry (one must, of course, assume a passage of suffi-
cient length to be representative) that have generally been agreed upon
as good English poetry by critics of various ages of taste, always seem to
hit toward this ratio.

Note, too, that the rule (as a simplification) has been restricted to
verbs and adjectives. Were adverbs to be added to the adjective count
and nouns to the verb count, the ratio would mount sharply in favor of
nouns-and-verbs. (Suggestion: Count the adverbs and the nouns in the
Hamlet passage and add that count to the adjective-verb ratio of twenty-
four to forty-six. What is the new ratio?)

The idea of such a count is not to show that adjectives cannot be well
used in poetry, but rather to underline the fact that they *must* be well
used, or not at all. Chaucer, in summarizing his description of the Knight
in the General Prologue to the *Canterbury Tales* makes memorable use
of piled-on adjectives:

> He was a verray, parfit, gentil Knyght.

It must be remembered, however, that Chaucer piled on his adjectives
only after twenty-eight lines of detailed description at the end of which
the three adjectives precisely sum up the merit of the knight and are con-
ferred upon him almost as a title. And it is worth noting, too, that though
the passage from which this line is taken is one of introductory physical
description rather than one of narrated action or of re-invoked experience,
there are still in the preceding twenty-eight lines twenty-four verbs to
seventeen adjectives. In the description of a person's appearance a writer
will find it all but impossible to avoid some more than normal inflow of
adjectives. Aside from passages of such introductory description, and
aside from those least interesting passages of Chaucer where he piles
elaboration upon elaboration with a medieval gusto for brocading, the
verb-adjective ratio of Chaucer's language will mount sharply in favor of
the verbs. In any case a diction in which every noun is propped up by an
adjective may almost flatly be said to be a bad one.

A second and indispensable characteristic of an active poetic language
derives from the basic characteristics of a good English sentence. Reduced
to its essence, a good English sentence is a *statement (in idiomatic word
order) that an agent (the subject of the sentence) performed an action
(the verb) upon something (the object).* However complex the demands
and resources of language that norm must not long be lost: *active voice,
idiomatic word order, and agent-action-object order.*

"The odor of cooking cabbage was wafted to my nostrils" is a bad way
of saying "I smelled cabbage cooking." In the inert passive voice it seems
to be the "odor of cooking cabbage" which is the agent of the action. No
such thing. The agent is "I." Good prose, as Coleridge pointed out, is
words in their best order and good poetry is the best words in the best
order. The idiom of English, whether in poetry or in prose, establishes a
sense of sequence and that sense is basically keyed to statement in the

active voice, with the passive voice serving not as a ready and elegant substitute for all occasions, but rather standing by to be used for special purposes. Imagine, if you will, how Hamlet's speech might have run had it been keyed to the passive voice and had the agent of the action consistently been obscured:

> How I am informed against by all,
> Till my revenge do spur me. What is a man
> If sleep and food together constitute
> His time's chief good and mart? a beast, no more.
> Sure, made as we have been, such large discourse
> Looking before and after, given us . . .

But enough of that. The point of such vandalism is not to make Shakespeare sound like Browning in one of his worst moments, but to re-emphasize what must not be lost sight of even at the cost of redundancy: *The norm of good language is the active voice. The norm of a good sentence is a subject which appears first in the sentence.*

It may be argued perhaps that all of the Hamlet passage can be reduced to the last line and a half:

> O, from this time forth
> My thoughts be bloody or be nothing worth!

A good muscular exclamation, and one that states the essence of Hamlet's determination. But how could one *feel* Hamlet's situation in the last line and a half, without the preceding lines as a preparation? The communication of a poem is an involvement. The reader must be made to enter Hamlet's state of mind in telling detail. In this sense then, the irreducibility of a passage of poetry may be seen as the long way round, but always as the most direct line to our involvement. What must be cut away from the poem is not words, but those parts of the poem, if any, that do not serve to involve us. The best conductor is not the man who can lead the orchestra through a Mozart symphony in the shortest elapsed time, but the one who can bring the orchestra to the fullest involvement in the music and to its fullest suggestion. It is the density of the suggestion that counts. Suppose for example, that Shakespeare had inserted after the first half of line twenty-one, some such lines as:

> I have heard
> Saints and philosophers aver alike
> That greatness is the measure of the will
> Not of the object sought, its formal cause
> Being but the vessel that the spirit fills,
> Costly or worthless. Rightly to be great
> Is not to stir . . . etc. . . . .

Quite obviously the intrusive lines are worthless, but even assuming by some large effort of the imagination that they are worthy of Shakespeare, they certainly could serve only to delay the passage. The irreducibility of the poem must be seen *not as the shortest verbal line between two points, but as the shortest completely involving line.*

5. *The language of good poetry is exact.*

When Milton speaks of locusts "warping" on the Eastern wind, nothing spectacular has happened, to be sure, but the word is obviously being used in a precise way. There is a quality of motion involved in the verb "to warp" which is not available in any other single word of English, and that quality is exactly the one Milton sought. "Weaving," for example, is close to "warping" in some ways, but it is still not exactly right for the motion Milton intended.

The only other way in which Milton could have achieved exactly that shade of meaning, would have been to use a less specific verb ("moving" or "progressing" or "advancing," for example) followed by a string of modifiers. Thus, he might have spoken of "locusts advancing on the Eastern wind with a motion that. . . ." And he would then have been committed to adding something like the dictionary definition of "to warp" —a necessarily laborious and necessarily forceless way of writing.

A minimum qualification of good poetic language is the ability to find the word that is exactly right to the physical fact. "Waddle," "sidle," "lurch," "march," "stumble," are all verbs of motion and each locates a specific kind of motion. The least that one can expect of language well used is the precision of such choices. The examples above have all been verbs, but true precision must obviously extend to all parts of speech. One can scarcely admire, for example, a writer who finds it necessary to write "He was a man who amassed wealth simply for the joy of possession rather than for the good things of life that it could bring him" when the same idea might as well be rendered simply "He was a miser."

Often, however, the poets have found that the words they seek do not exist ready made, and they have forced words to perform duties not normally expected of them. Thus Shakespeare refers to a flag across the water "lackeying the tide." "Lackeying" is of course from "lackey" and implies a servile bowing and fluttering. Its intent obviously is not only to catch the exact motion but to couple it with a precise overtone. Suppose for example that Shakespeare had spoken of the flag as "sweeping the tide." There would still be a sense of the back and forth fluttering motion, but the overtone of servility would have disappeared.

There is, of course, the fact that such wrenchings of one part of speech into another can seem forced and thereby call attention to themselves rather than to their communication. Shakespeare's using of "lackeying" is not an especially offensive example, and yet it might reasonably be argued that it does seem strained. When, on the other hand, Emily Dickinson says of a snake "it wrinkled and was gone," "wrinkled" comes not only as a delightful surprise but seems to enter the line with no resistance whatever from the language. The doubt one may have about "lackeying" is from the opposite source; there is a sense that English resists making "lackey" into a verb, perhaps only because "lackeying" is difficult to say.

One asks of the language of good poetry, then, *exactness without strain.* If that exactness may be said to begin with exactness of denotation, it must also be seen to carry over to a point at which denotation is all but irrelevant. Hamlet's use of "puffed" in line 18 is worth careful attention:

> Led by a delicate and tender prince
> Whose spirit with divine ambition puffed,
> Makes mouths at the invisible event

Hamlet might have said, for example, "swelled" instead of "puffed." But "swelled" has an overtone of heaviness, of being "swollen" as in a bruise; whereas "puffed" is lighter and airier. Fortinbras, Hamlet has seen, is staking everything "even for an eggshell." He and his men go to their deaths for a "fantasy and trick of fame." Obviously the lightness of "puffed" is better keyed to "eggshell" to "fantasy" and to "trick" than would have been the weightier "swelled."

Note, however, that it is relatively difficult to fix an exact denotation for "puffed." Some sort of inflation of the spirit, yes. But certainly nothing that can be fixed with the physical exactness of "warping."

By the very nature of language in general, and of the language of poetry in particular, words and phrases may be used with what seems to be no denotation at all. "Wet sea," for example, presents a problem of redundancy but none of denotation. What happens, however, when someone speaks of a "dry sea"? Milton comes very close to doing so when he speaks of Satan pacing up and down on a "windy sea of land":

> As when a vulture on Imaus bred,
> Whose snowy ridge the roving Tartar bounds,
> Dislodging from a region of scarce prey
> To gorge the flesh of lambs or yearling kids
> On hills where flocks are fed, flies toward the springs
> Of Ganges or Hydaspes, Indian streams;
> But on his way lights on the barren plains
> Of Sericana where Chineses drive
> With sails and wind their cany wagons light:
> So on this windy sea of land, the Fiend
> Walked up and down alone, bent on his prey,
> Alone for other creatures in this place,
> Living or lifeless, to be found was none.

Here, of course, Milton is using the language of *as if*: the endless stretch of the high plateau is land, to be sure, but it presents itself to the eye *as if* it were a sea, an *is if* already suggested by the fantastic image of lightly built wagons moved by sail, as if they were boats. In Milton's description of Satan's fall, however, there is no such *as if*:

> Him the Almighty Power
> Hurled headlong flaming from the ethereal sky
> With hideous ruin and combustion down
> To bottomless perdition.

And while no word can be wholly free of some element of denotation, it certainly seems to be true in such a line as "With hideous ruin and combustion down" that the words are being selected for their large suggestiveness and sound rather than for their denotation. They are, that is, being *exact to the feeling rather than to the physical detail* of the scene.

Milton, in fact, made such considerable use of this sort of word choice that this quality of his style has been labeled "the Miltonic vague." In the line cited, for example, "ruin" is a conceptual word. As such, it has relatively little denotation. And "combustion" is certainly the most abstract of possible words to denote "kinds of burning." Any number of more specific kinds of combustion suggest themselves: "flaming," "fire-spewing," "blazing," "incandescence." "Combustion" is the one word that includes them all, and it can do so only by being the least specific. The line, then, is built on a concept and an abstraction. And it is modified by another concept, "hideous."

Poetry generally strives for more specific effect than this, but Milton's principle of selection remains firm. The "big" sound of the line is obviously part of what Milton intended. One cannot, moreover, be specific in dealing with the Primal: ultimate Good and Evil defy exact definition. Milton chose exactly for the effect of the necessary feeling.

Thus, poetry may achieve high effect by the power of suggestion (overtone) rather than by its specific identification (denotation). John William Burgon, an English poet of the nineteenth century, wrote many poems but survives only as the author of one line describing the Trans-Jordan city of Petra:

> A rose-red city half as old as time.

The "rose-red" is clearly intended to convey the color of the sandstone from which the city is built. In another context it might suggest the sunset stain on white walls. In either case the effect is denotative. But the truly memorable quality of the line certainly rests in "half as old as time," a phrase about as far from denotation as language seems able to go this side of nonsense syllables.

6. *The language of good poetry is exact to its own roots and distinctions.*

Everyone, at one time or another, has had pointed out to him the precision of the distinction Edgar Allan Poe locates in

> The glory that was Greece
> And the grandeur that was Rome.

In common speech one tends to ignore such distinctions. When the newspapers haul out their standard banner heads on "The grand and glorious Fourth," "grand" and "glorious" seem to blur together into one thing. Poe saves the distinction by putting it into such a context that one is reminded of the quality and force of each word. At once and without strain, one understands what he had always known but had tended to forget, that "glory" is a spiritual achievement and "grandeur" a material one. By the exactness of good poetic usage, that is to say, the language is made new. It is one of the functions of the poet, wrote the French critic Paul Valéry, to "purify the language of the tribe."

Thus, in the seventeenth century Beaumont wrote in praise of Ben Jonson's language that it quickened the speech of the whole succeeding age:

> His wit and language still remain the same
> In all men's mouths; grave preachers did it use
> As golden pills, by which they might infuse
> Their heavenly physic; ministers of state
> Their grave dispatches in his language wrate;
> Ladies made curt'sies in it, courtiers legs,
> Physicians bills;—perhaps, some pedant begs
> He may not use it, for he hears 'tis such
> As in few words a man may utter much.
> Could I have spoken in his language too,
> I had not said as much, as now I do,
> To whose clear memory I this tribute send,
> Who dead's my Wonder, living was my Friend.

Beaumont here makes the essential connection between economy and precision. The exact placement of one shade of meaning against another certainly makes for an irreducible kind of saying. One has only to attempt to state Poe's distinction without the precise counterbalancing of "glory" against "grandeur," to realize with Beaumont that:

> Could I have spoken in his language too,
> I had not said as much as now I do.

A superb example of this power of exact selection occurs in Denham's lines on Cowley:

> To him no author was unknown,
> Yet what he wrote was all his own;
> Horace's wit and Virgil's state,
> He did not steal, but emulate!
> And when he would like them appear,
> Their garb, but not their cloaths, did wear.

To make a leg: to make a formal bow (in this context, to bow while delivering a complimentary phrase).
I had not said: I would not have said. As much: as many words as.

As one comes on the turn of "he did not steal, but emulate" there can certainly be no doubt that language is being well and irreducibly used here. The kind of "taking" which is involved in "steal" and the kind which is involved in "emulate" seem precisely played, one against the other. But it is in the distinction between "garb" and "clothes" that the language truly arrives to us refreshed. As in the case of the "grand and glorious Fourth" the level of ordinary attention tends to run these words one into the other. Before reading Denham, one would probably have used "garb" and "clothes" as synonyms. With Denham's awakening of the exact possibilities of these two words, however, their root suggestion is precisely purified. "Clothes," of course, derives from "cloth" and, strictly speaking, our clothes are the actual physical tissues we have on. "Garb," however, derives from the Italian *garbo* meaning "grace" and has come to mean by extension "bearing, manner, fashion, style." "Garb" is not the cloth but the cut. So Cowley is no rag picker, but an emulator of grace. It seems impossible to find a better example of the poet finding his delight in "hanging around words" to overhear them talking to one another:

Thus Hamlet in:

> How all occasions do inform against me
> And spur my dull revenge

is obviously displaying Shakespeare's relish in placing "spur" against "dull." Thus, too, in a line much quoted since the British critic F. R. Leavis drew special attention to it, Samuel Johnson wrote (italics mine):

> The festal blazes, the triumphant show,
> The ravished standard and the captive foe,
> The senate's thanks, the gazette's pompous tale,
> With force resistless o'er the brave prevail.
> Such bribes the rapid Greek o'er Asia whirled,
> *For such the steady Romans shook the world.*

One does not normally think of being shaken by that which is steady: the line arrives first in an instant of surprise. "Shook the world," moreover, is certainly a cliché. But the presence of that "steady" lifts it away from vague stereotype. Consider in how many ways the Roman Legions could be called "steady." Certainly, in this context, the steady tread of their marching feet is the first effect to suggest itself. Consider, too, the precise relation of the line to the physical phenomenon known as "resonance." A rhythmic repetition of blows can often cause a wave effect that may result in a constant increase of vibration. Thus columns of foot soldiers marching across a weak bridge break step, since the rhythmic falling of thousands of feet may build up a wave of resonance that could topple the bridge. It is such a combination of surprising rightnesses that offers the

the rapid Greek: Alexander the Great.

reader his reward. One's very expectation of what language can accomplish is enlarged in the process of seeing it so well used.

7. *Some notes on adjectives.*

Adjectives and, to a lesser extent, adverbs are the points at which the weakness of a weak diction are likely to be most apparent. It is still true, however, that adjectives may be the source of major effect. Poetry will suffer no absolute rules. Short of the absolute, however, and assuming some discretion on the part of the reader, one may still defend a few useful rules of thumb. It is at least possible to distinguish kinds of adjectives and to observe that some kinds are more likely to occur in bad writing than in good.

A useful first distinction can be made by dividing all adjectives (and by extension, all modifiers) into those which present *evidence* and those which present *judgments.*

When one speaks of "the blonde girl," the adjective "blonde" offers evidence which helps to identify the girl. When one speaks of "the bad girl," however, "bad" does not help identify the girl unless one knows the speaker well enough to have some notion of his ideas of good and bad. "Blonde" is evidence; "bad" is a judgment. One can see the blondeness for himself; he cannot meaningfully see the "badness" until it is located in some observable characteristic.

The speaker himself, before he could reasonably judge the girl to be bad must have observed some evidence on which to base his judgment. He may even be of the school that believes lipstick to be the mark of a lost woman. For him, then, "bad girl" may mean no more than "girl wearing lipstick." Had he presented such evidence for his judgment one would have a clear basis for rejecting it. If, on the other hand, he had mentioned that there was an automatic in her purse and that her picture was on the postoffice wall, one might reasonably conclude that the girl was something less than wholly virtuous. The point is that the reader could then reach his own judgment. In general it is much better to let the reader reach his own judgments than to make them for him. "The armed and wanted girl" or "the girl wearing lipstick" are more self-evident phrases than "the bad girl."

Good writing tends to present evidence rather than judgments. When the evidence is well presented, the reader's judgments will agree with those implicit in the writing. But nothing is more disastrous to the communication between writer and reader than a series of implicit judgments with which the reader cannot agree, or which he finds to be simply silly (see "My Garden," p. 813; and "Threnody," p. 813), or for which he is given no evidence he can respect.

It follows that poems in which *judgment* adjectives appear with any sort of regularity are reasonably suspect as bad poems unless some special principle of selection is operating to achieve a special effect. And barring such special intent, a good starting orientation is the assumption that adjectives presenting *evidence* are better than adjectives asserting unsupported judgments.

Nevertheless it remains difficult at times to distinguish adjectives of evidence from those of judgments. "Serene twilight" is a cliché, to be sure, and the fact is that the root meaning of "serene" already includes the idea of twilight, whereby a certain amount of objectionable redundancy (consult the dictionary for the root meanings of "serene") calls the whole phrasing into question. Nevertheless we may fairly ask: is "serene" a judgment or a statement of physical characteristics? The answer will have to be left to the individual's own search of the dictionary and to his own assessment of the root implications of the word.

Or in the case of Milton's "With hideous ruin and combustion down," is "hideous" an adjective of judgment or of evidence? Once more the question is more important than the answer. One might ask, what makes it "hideous" and argue that no denotation can be found as evidence of the hideousness of the ruin and combustion. Or one might argue that the whole ringing overtone of the word amply suggests the idea of the hideous, whereby the asserted judgment and the active suggestion of the word fuse into one. But the pro and con has point only as it opens both sides to view. Each case must determine itself.

One category of judgment adjectives, however, seems particularly defensible. Thus Ben Jonson speaks of the "spacious theatre" and Richard Wilbur speaks of "beasts in their major freedom." "Spacious" and "major" deserve a separate category as "philosophical" or "thinking" adjectives. It is not the physical dimensions of the theatre that "spacious" calls forth, but its intellectual dimension. The theatre is spacious because its illusion can reach into all dimensions of space and time. The stage is a space in which anything can be imagined. Thus "spacious" manages to summarize the whole idea of the theatre and the reader welcomes it as an expansion of his own concept of the theatre. It *thinks,* and thought is always welcome in poetry. As Kant observed: "Art without mind is horrid." And as Frost stated the corollary:

> No one knows how glad I am to find
> On any sheet the least display of mind.

Richard Wilbur's use of "major" responds to the same criteria. To speak of "beasts in their major freedom" does not seem to identify the freedom so much as to judge it. But if the freedom of beasts is major, there must also be a minor freedom, and that must be man's freedom. Any number of ways in which this implicit distinction is valid immediately suggest themselves.

We may go a step further then and speculate that what is really required of a modifier is *a principle of selection that displays both integrity and imagination.* We may summarize some rules of thumb:

Adjectives that present evidence may generally be judged by their freshness, by their responsiveness to the actuality of the thing modified, and by their ability to sharpen our perceptions. Some examples of single phrases that present this power of the well selected adjective are: "the tiger moth's *deep-damasked* wing," "vertical New York," "the stucco faces" (of people glaring in the sun), "the running fuse of surf" (*i.e.*, the running-fuse surf).

Adjectives that present judgments rather than physical or sensory evidence may generally be judged on the basis of how much emotional or philosophical depth speaks from their selection.

One last class of adjectives may be called "redundant" and may almost categorically be taken as an evidence of language poorly selected. A redundant adjective is one that asserts a quality already implicit in the noun it modifies. Thus, "green grass," "strong steel," "the hushed calm of evening," "distant sunset," and "blue sky."

Grass may of course be brown, or it may conceivably be stained by chemicals from a nearby factory. In one way or another a case can be made for almost any possibility. The fact remains that unmodified "grass" is automatically green, and that unless one is distinguishing a field of burned grass from a field of (perhaps irrigated) green grass, "green" has no function. Similarly, it may be argued that certain kinds of steel, depending upon their alloys and preparations, are "stronger" than other kinds. A technical manual on the strength of materials must certainly consider such differences carefully. It would be simply silly, however, to argue that "steel" in poetry is anything but strong. The case is even simpler for "hushed calm" and "distant sunset": one need only try to imagine an *unhushed* calm or a *nearby* sunset, to realize that such adjectives must tend above all else to indicate the incompetence of the writer. The least one should expect of poetry, is that it find for itself a language (or a diction) better than the reader could improvise.

Poems for Study—I. The Word Choice

Burning the Letters

Gwendolyn Grew

One flutter of memory, then all becomes
First blaze, then char. A Fall of after-thought,
And leaf by leaf, a slant wind numbs
Summer from the bone-tree. "Nothing is not

Something," she thinks. And it is nothing now
To send a season blazing. Day by day
What greened, a sun-machine upon its bough,
Unsuns, ungreens, discolors toward decay.

Up from the bed now she can see the pale
Last glow of paper X-rayed by the bright
Underglow of the flame. A becalmed sail
It stirs, uncertain. Then it bursts a-light.

Like leaf-veins, the black lines stand in relief
As fire travels them clean. Then a black bloat
Riffles the page. Footless as a night-thief
The fire draft stirs them then, sets them afloat

And sucks them up to darkness, each a bat.
Till the last line has swollen and gone out
With its black mouse-bird. "How long have I sat
Here in self pity?" she begins to doubt.

And still she kneels, and with a poker stirs
A last bird from the blaze, loving its flight.
Nursing the not-much hurt. But it is hers,
And nurse it she will through one more acted night.

QUESTIONS

1. The words of poetry do not needlessly repeat what has already been established. It is sometimes difficult, however, to decide what is "needless" repetition. Line 8 offers a fair test case. What is the function of "discolors"? Could it be argued that "Unsuns" and "ungreens" have already, in effect, "discolored" the leaf? Which of the three words most meaningfully suggests "discoloration"?

2. In the same line, can "decay" be justified? Can a leaf "discolor" toward anything but "decay"?

3. It is dangerous to rhyme on an adjective, for if it is less than brilliantly chosen it will seem that the poet selected that adjective not in faithfulness to the experience he is presenting, but only to pad out the rhyme. In line 9, could "pale" be considered rhyme-forced? Is the paper on which one writes love letters likely to be anything but "pale"? If it is "X-rayed by the bright underglow," can it still be "pale"?

4. In the same line, how apt a choice is "X-rayed"? Is it physically accurate? Physically wrong? Is it a natural-seeming word choice?

5. In stanzas 4 and 5 we are told that a "night-thief" does several things to the papers: he "stirs" them; he "sets them afloat"; he "sucks them up to darkness." Do these three specific actions seem natural to the work of a "night-thief"?

6. Other words and phrases that might well be closely considered are: line 3, "slant"; line 11, "travels them clean"; line 12, "riffles" and "footless"; line 18, "swollen"; line 19, "black mouse-bird"; line 24, "acted."

Burning Love Letters

Howard Moss

I

Fire that cancels all that is
Devours paper and pen,
And makes of the heart's histories
A cold hearth warm again.
It could as well consume a branch,
Blank paper or black coal
That now in ashy avalanche,
Scatters the heart whole.

II

What words led to the end of words?
Coldly, all separate sighs
Shiver in flame, flying upwards,
Merged into burnt lies.
In somersaults of light, words burn
To nothingness, then roll
In dead scrolls, delicate as fern,
Or hiss like a waterfall.

III

From partial feast to total fast
From object to mirage
An animal that cannot last
Appears in fire's cage:

REPRINTED from *The Toy Fair* by Howard Moss with permission of Charles Scribner's Sons. Copyright 1954 Howard Moss.

Love's crazy dog in a cold sweat
Far from its neighborhood,
Circles the puzzle of regret,
On fire in the wood.

IV

Love's ashes lie and will not rise
As fire dies to a black sun
And makes of the heart's histories
A warm hearth cold again.
Cremation's scattered dust confronts
Dead vision, and in these
Ashes I write your name once,
Bending on cold knees.

QUESTIONS

1. Part II is a physical description of paper in a fire. The last four stanzas of Gwendolyn Grew's "Burning the Letters" offer a description of the same physical experience. Which seems more convincingly fiery?

2. Can "pen" (line 2) be justified? Does the fire that consumes love letters consume the pen? Or is the poem opening with a general statement that fire consumes all? If so, is it an acceptable general statement?

3. What sort of adjective is "black" in line six? Would anything be lost from the poem (leaving rhythm out of consideration) if "black" were omitted? Is it fair to argue that "coal" already contains the idea "black"?

4. Lines 7 and 8 speak of an avalanche as "scattering." Suppose line 8 had ready "Bury the heart whole." What would the difference be? Is an avalanche a "scattering" phenomenon?

5. What is the effect of "partial" in line 1 of Stanza III? What may have dictated the author's choice of "partial"?

A Narrow Fellow in the Grass

Emily Dickinson

A narrow fellow in the grass
Occasionally rides;
You may have met him — did you not?
His notice sudden is.

The grass divides as with a comb,
A spotted shaft is seen;
And then it closes at your feet
And opens further on.

He likes a boggy acre,
A floor too cool for corn.
Yet when a boy, and barefoot,
I more than once, at morn,

Have passed, I thought, a whip lash
Unbraiding in the sun,—
When, stooping to secure it,
It wrinkled, and was gone.

Several of nature's people
I know, and they know me;
I feel for them a transport
Of cordiality;

But never met this fellow,
Attended or alone,
Without a tighter breathing,
And Zero at the Bone.

QUESTIONS

1. What is the effect of calling a snake "a narrow fellow"? Does the phrasing seem more nearly direct and felt or artful and coy?

2. Suppose similarly (disregarding consideration of rhyme) that the last line had read not "And Zero at the Bone" but "And a shudder deep inside." Which would be the more forceful? Why?

3. In earlier drafts Emily Dickinson wrote the Fourth line, "His notice instant is." Is "instant" better or worse than "sudden" in this context?

4. Line 11 appears in some worksheets with "But when a boy, and barefoot." Is there any reason for the poet to have hesitated between "Yet" and "But"? Having so hesitated, is there any reason for the poet to decide on "Yet"?

Snake

D. H. Lawrence

A snake came to my water-trough
On a hot, hot day, and I in pyjamas for the heat,
To drink there.

In the deep, strange-scented shade of the great dark carob-tree
I came down the steps with my pitcher
And must wait, must stand and wait, for there he was at the trough
    before me.

He reached down from a fissure in the earth-wall in the gloom
And trailed his yellow-brown slackness soft-bellied down, over the edge
    of the stone trough
And rested his throat upon the stone bottom,
And where the water had dripped from the tap, in a small clearness,
He sipped with his straight mouth,
Softly drank through his straight gums, into his slack long body,
Silently.

Someone was before me at my water-trough,
And I, like a second comer, waiting.

He lifted his head from his drinking, as cattle do,
And looked at me vaguely, as drinking cattle do,
And flickered his two-forked tongue from his lips, and mused a moment,
And stooped and drank a little more,
Being earth brown, earth golden from the burning burning bowels of the
    earth
On the day of Sicilian July, with Etna smoking.

The voice of my education said to me
He must be killed
For in Sicily the black, black snakes are innocent, the gold are venomous.

And voices in me said, If you were a man
You would take a stick and break him now, and finish him off.

But I must confess how I liked him,
How glad I was he had come like a guest in quiet, to drink at my water-
    trough
And departed peaceful, pacified, and thankless,
Into the burning bowels of the earth.

Was it cowardice, that I dared not kill him?
Was it perversity, that I longed to talk to him?
Was it humility, to feel so honoured?
I felt so honoured.

And yet those voices:
If you were not afraid, you would kill him!

And truly I was afraid, I was most afraid,
But even so, honoured still more
That he should seek my hospitality
From out the dark door of the secret earth.

He drank enough
And lifted his head, dreamily, as one who has drunken,

And flickered his tongue like a forked night on the air, so black,
Seeming to lick his lips,
And looked around like a god, unseeing, into the air,
And slowly turned his head,
And slowly, very slowly, as if thrice adream,
Proceeded to draw his slow length curving round
And climb again the broken bank of my wall-face.

And as he put his head into that dreadful hole,
And as he slowly drew up, snake-easing his shoulders, and entered farther,
A sort of horror, a sort of protest against his withdrawing into that horrid
    black hole,
Deliberately going into the blackness, and slowly drawing himself after,
Overcame me now his back was turned.

I looked round, I put down my pitcher,
I picked up a clumsy log
And threw it at the water trough with a clatter.

I think it did not hit him,
But suddenly that part of him that was left behind convulsed in un-
    dignified haste,
Writhed like lightning, and was gone
Into the black hole, the earth lipped fissure in the wall-front,
At which, in the intense still noon, I stared with fascination.

And immediately I regretted it.
I thought how paltry, how vulgar, what a mean act!
I despised myself and the voices of my accursed human education.

And I thought of the albatross,
And I wished he would come back, my snake.

For he seemed to me again like a king,
Like a king in exile, uncrowned in the underworld,
Now due to be crowned again.

And so I missed my chance with one of the lords
Of life.
And I had something to expiate;
A pettiness.

QUESTIONS

1. Compare this treatment of the snake with Emily Dickinson's.
Lawrence keeps his statement to a kind of primitive simplicity, Emily
Dickinson carefully jewels her phrasing. What difference of feeling re-
sults? Which poem reacts more profoundly to the earth-trace of the
snake? Which, to put it another way, has its zero deeper in the bone?

2. Lawrence seems so wholly taken with the presence of the snake that even clichés are admitted into the poem ("undignified haste," "writhed like lightning," "stared with fascination"). Can such phrasing be admitted as part of the merit of the poem, or should the poem be said to succeed in spite of such phrasing?

3. Underline each adjective Lawrence uses and consider it as presenting evidence or a judgment, as essential or inessential. Can the language of this poem be said to be even throughout? Compare the description of the snake's arrival (lines 7–10) with the description of the snake's departure (lines 50–55). What differences, if any, are observable?

4. Which of these two poems seems written in a diction, which in a language?

5. Lines 9–10: "straight mouth . . . straight gums . . . slack long body." Is "straight" a good adjective choice? Note its play against "slack long body."

6. Compare the snake's sudden motion in lines 59–60 with Emily Dickinson's "It wrinkled and was gone."

Blue Girls

John Crowe Ransom

Twirling your blue skirts, traveling the sward
Under the towers of your seminary,
Go listen to your teachers old and contrary
Without believing a word.

Tie the white fillets then about your lustrous hair
And think no more of what will come to pass
Than bluebirds that go walking on the grass
And chattering on the air.

Practice your beauty, blue girls, before it fail;
And I will cry with my loud lips and publish
Beauty which all our power shall never establish,
It is so frail.

For I could tell you a story which is true:
I know a lady with a terrible tongue,
Blear eyes fallen from blue,
All her perfections tarnished — and yet it is not long
Since she was lovelier than any of you.

QUESTIONS

1. The choice of "publish" and "establish" in stanza three is immediately striking and the effect of these words must certainly depend

REPRINTED from *Selected Poems* by John Crowe Ransom, by permission of Alfred A. Knopf, Inc. Copyright 1927, 1945 by Alfred A. Knopf, Inc.

on an awareness of their root meanings. In the habit of common usage one tends to lose sight of the fact that "publish" means not "to issue a book or magazine" but (Latin: publicare) "to make public." Similarly, one tends to think of the current meaning of "establish" and to forget the root meaning "to make stable, to bring into balance" which still survives as a term in logic, "to establish a proposition." The first shock of surprise and the immediate apprehension of rightness in such word choices acts as a true re-invigoration of the language. It comes as no surprise to learn that John Crowe Ransom is a classical scholar, but even without this information, one must be aware that he is choosing his words from the root.

2. With this clue plainly "established", a second reading more readily calls other key words to more than usual scrutiny. "Practice" and "perfection," both deriving from the root meaning "to do, to make" (check your dictionary), seem especially suggestive. An awareness of this root relationship between the girls ("doing") and the old woman ("done") certainly adds a dimension of meaning to the poem. Note, however, that the poem is complete without this addition. The relationship is an *addition* of pleasure.

3. Note, too, that in line 1 the girls "travel" the sward and in line 7 the bluebirds "walk" on it. Aware as one must be that John Crowe Ransom selects his words with care, what reasons could be offered for his choice of the one word for the girls and the other for the bluebirds?

The Christian Militant

Robert Herrick

A man prepared against all ills to come
That dares to dead the fire of martyrdom:
That sleeps at home, and sailing there at ease,
Fears not the fierce sedition of the Seas;
That's counter-proof against the Farm's mishaps,
Undreadful too of courtly thunderclaps:
That wears one face (like heaven) and never showes
A change, when Fortune either comes, or goes:
That keeps his own strong guard in the despight
Of what can hurt by day, or harm by night:
That takes and re-delivers every stroke
Of Chance, (as made up all of rock and oak:)
That sighs at others' death; smiles at his own
Most dire and horrid crucifixion.
Who for true glory suffers thus; we grant
Him to be here our *Christian militant.*

QUESTIONS

1. "Dares to dead" in line 2 equals "dare to the point of death."

2. "Sail" in line 3 derives from cognates in many languages, all of which derive in turn from Latin *secare*, "to saw." Does Herrick (an ac-

complished Latinist) intend this learned pun? *i.e.*, "That sleeps at home, and sawing there at ease"? (snoring?)

3. Line 10 seems to offer a distinction between "hurt" and "harm." Compare with similar juxtapositions already cited: ("The glory that was Greece/And the grandeur that was Rome." "Their garb, but not their cloaths, did wear.") The examples in parenthesis certainly leave no possibility of reversing the key words. Would it make any difference if Herrick's key words were reversed? Is a distinction possible between "hurt" and "harm"? Does one bear more correspondence to "day" and the other to "night"?

Compare the following possible variants with the original.

      1. Of what can clash by day or steal by night.
      2. Of what can leap by day or creep by night.
      3. Of what can hurt his soul by day or night.

Can any one of these be preferred to the original?

Upon M. Ben. Jonson. Epigram

Robert Herrick

After the rare Arch-Poet JONSON died
The Sock grew loathsome, and the Buskin's pride,
Together with the Stage's glory stood
Each like a poor and pitied widowhood.
The Cirque profaned was; and all postures rackt:
For men did strut, and stride, and stare, not act.
Then temper flew from wordes; and men did squeak,
Look red, and blow, and bluster, but not speake:
No Holy-Rage, or frantic-fires did stir,
Or flash about the spacious Theater.
No clap of hands, or shout, or praises-proof

Sock: originally a kind of slipper worn by comic actors in Greece and Rome, hence a symbol of Comic Drama. **Buskin:** the leather half-boot worn by tragic actors, hence Tragedy. **Sock and Buskin,** therefore, symbolize all drama. **Cirque:** cf. circus. The amphitheatre of ancient drama. Here, the playhouse. **and all postures** (were) **rackt:** "To rack" means "to torment by stretching on a rack," hence, to stiffen unnaturally, to pull out of joint. It also means "to pervert the meaning of." **arrant ignorance:** "Arrant" by Herrick's time had come to mean "outright," as "an arrant knave." Originally, however, it meant "wandering," as "an arrant (or errant) thief" or a "Knight errant." Note how in both **rackt** and **arrant** the second meanings assist the force of the word. **Then temper flew from wordes:** *i.e.*, Words lost their temper. A concealed pun? They lost their temper in two senses: (*a*) as a piece of metal loses temper, which is strictly "the proper mixture of elements," and (*b*) the popular extension of that sense, as in "temper-tantrum." Herrick extends the implication to the very throats of the actors, as if their voice-boxes themselves had gone slack and palsied.

Note that what "rackt" does for the posture and gesture of the actors, "temper flew from wordes" does for their speaking. A nice equivalence.

Did crack the Play-house sides, or cleave her roof.
Artless the Scene was; and that monstrous sin
Of deep and arrant ignorance came in;
Such ignorance as theirs was, who once hist
At thy unequaled play, the Alchymist:
Oh fie upon 'em! Lastly too, all wit
In utter darkness did, and still will sit
Sleeping the luckless Age out, till that she
Her Resurrection has again with Thee.

The End of Love

from *Modern Love*

George Meredith

As the poem opens, the husband and wife ("he" and "she") have come
to realize that they no longer love one another. Lying in bed by his wife's
side, the husband hears her crying in the dark. He does not know whether
she is awake or crying in her sleep, but when his hand moves near her
head in what little light there is, her sobbing changes and he knows she
has seen him and is awake. It is no dream but reality that calls forth her
tears.

By this he knew she wept with waking eyes:
That, at his hand's light quiver by her head,
The strange low sobs that shook their common bed
Were called into her with a sharp surprise,
And strangled mute, like little gaping snakes,
Dreadfully venomous to him. She lay
Stone-still, and the long darkness flowed away
With muffled pulses. Then, as midnight makes
Her giant heart of Memory and Tears
Drink the pale drug of silence, and so beat
Sleep's heavy measure, they from head to foot
Were moveless, looking through their dead black years,
By vain regret scrawled over the blank wall.
Like sculptured effigies they might be seen
Upon their marriage tomb, the sword between;
Each wishing for the sword that severs all.

QUESTIONS

1. What is the effect of "strangled" and of "gaping" in line 5? Does
this poem seem more nearly written in a language or in a diction?

2. Lines 8-11 seem to say that midnight makes her heart drink. Can
the idea of a heart drinking be justified?

The Cancer Cells

Richard Eberhart

Today I saw a picture of the cancer cells,
Sinister shapes with menacing attitudes.
They had outgrown their test-tube and advanced,
Sinister shapes with menacing attitudes,
Into a world beyond, a virulent laughing gang.
They looked like art itself, like the artist's mind,
Powerful shaker, and taker of new forms.
Some are revulsed to see these spiky shapes;
It is the world of the future too come to.
Nothing could be more vivid than their language,
Lethal, sparkling and irregular stars,
The murderous design of the universe,
The hectic dance of the passionate cancer cells.
O just phenomena to the calculating eye,
Originals of imagination. I flew
With them in a piled exuberance of time,
My own malignance in their racy, beautiful gestures
Quick and lean: and in their riot too
I saw the stance of the artist's make,
The fixed form in the massive fluxion.

I think Leonardo would have in his disinterest
Enjoyed them precisely with a sharp pencil.

QUESTION

1. Of all the words available in English to designate a group, Eberhart chose "gang" in line 5. Why? What is the relation between "gang" and, in line 18, "riot"?

Lines

from *Nepenthe*

George Darley

Hurry me Nymphs! O, hurry me
Far above the grovelling sea,
Which, with blind weakness and base roar
Casting his white age on the shore
Wallows along that slimy floor;

From *Selected Poems* by Richard Eberhart. 1951. Reprinted by permission of Oxford University Press, Inc.

With his widespread webbed hands
Seeking to climb the level lands
But rejected still to rave
Alive in his uncovered grave.

QUESTIONS

1. Darley personifies the sea as a kind of aged raving madman and carries his pathetic fallacy throughout these lines. What is the overtone of "grovelling"? (Suppose, for example, Darley had said instead "restless.")

2. "Roar" and "rave," it might be argued, are words that suggest strength. "Blind weakness," "white age," and perhaps "wallows," on the other hand, suggest the opposite. What principle of selection seems to be at work? Does the diction seem firm to its purpose?

A Dream

Thomas Lovell Beddoes

Last night I looked into a dream; 'twas drawn
On the black velvet of a midnight sleep
And set in woeful thoughts; and there I saw
A thin pale Cupid, with bare, ragged wings
Like skeletons of leaves in autumn,
That sift the frosty air. One hand was shut,
And in its little hold of ivory
Fastened a May morn zephyr, frozen straight,
Made deadly with a hornet's rugged sting,
Gilt with the influence of an adverse star.
Such was his weapon, and he traced with it,
Upon the waters of my thoughts, these words:
"I am the death of flowers, and nightingales,
And small-lipped babies, that give their souls to summer
To make a perfumed day with: I shall come,
A death no larger than a sigh to thee,
Upon a sunset hour." And so he passed
Into a place where faded rainbows are,
Dying along the distance of my mind
As down the sea Europa's hair-pearls fell
When through the Cretan waves the curly bull
Dashed tugging at a stormy plough, whose share
Was of the northern hurricane—

QUESTIONS

1. Beddoes was a poet of considerable verbal and imaginative power who came to maturity at the time when the Romantic tradition in poetry had reached exhaustion and when no new force had formed. Lacking a vigorous intellectual direction, he turned to ornate fantasies and a kind of derangement of the imagination. (It was in a somewhat similar intellectual climate that Mary Shelley turned to the writing of *Frankenstein.*) His starveling Cupid must be seen as an image from a literary dead end. Granted its eccentricity, however, Beddoes' verbal power offers real delights.

2. Note "sift" in line 6. Its function is clearly to reinforce the skeletal quality of the leaves. Could a non-skeletal leaf be said to "sift" the air?

3. What is the second suggestion of "hold" in line 7?

4. "Adverse star" is a phrase from astrology, *i.e.*, "a star of bad influence." Look up the root meaning of "influence." What does it add to the suggestion?

5. Is there any denotation for "Into a place where faded rainbows are"? Can this be taken as an example of pure verbal suggestion?

Ode on a Grecian Urn

John Keats

I

Thou still unravished bride of quietness,
 Thou foster-child of silence and slow time,
Sylvan historian, who canst thus express
 A flowery tale more sweetly than our rhyme:
What leaf-fringed legend haunts about thy shape
  Of deities or mortals, or of both,
   In Tempe or the dales of Arcady?
 What men or gods are these? What maidens loth?
What mad pursuit? What struggle to escape?
  What pipes and timbrels? What wild ecstacy?

II

Heard melodies are sweet, but those unheard
 Are sweeter; therefore, ye soft pipes, play on;
Not to the sensual ear, but, more endeared,
 Pipe to the spirit ditties of no tone:
Fair youth, beneath the trees, thou canst not leave
 Thy song, nor ever can those trees be bare;
  Bold Lover, never, never, canst thou kiss,
Though winning near the goal—yet, do not grieve;
  She cannot fade, though thou hast not thy bliss.
  For ever wilt thou love, and she be fair!

III

Ah, happy, happy boughs! that cannot shed
 Your leaves, nor ever bid the Spring adieu;

And, happy melodist, unwearied,
   For ever piping songs forever new;
More happy love! more happy, happy love!
   For ever warm and still to be enjoyed,
     For ever panting, and for ever young;
All breathing human passion far above,
   That leaves a heart high-sorrowful and cloyed,
     A burning forehead, and a parching tongue.

IV

Who are these coming to the sacrifice?
   To what green altar, O mysterious priest,
Lead'st thou that heifer lowing at the skies,
   And all her silken flanks with garlands drest?
What little town by river or sea shore,
   Or mountain-built with peaceful citadel,
     Is emptied of this folk, this pious morn?
And, little town, thy streets for evermore
   Will silent be; and not a soul to tell
     Why thou art desolate, can e'er return.

V

O Attic shape! Fair attitude, with brede
   Of marble men and maidens overwrought,
With forest branches and the trodden weed;
   Thou, silent form, dost tease us out of thought
As doth eternity: Cold Pastoral!
   When old age shall this generation waste,
     Thou shalt remain, in midst of other woe
Than ours, a friend to man, to whom thou say'st,
   "Beauty is truth, truth beauty,"—that is all
     Ye know on earth and all ye need to know.

QUESTIONS

1. There are more adjectives than verbs in this poem. "Happy," for example, occurs six times in five lines of stanza three. What reasons suggest themselves for Keats' profusion of adjectives? The two stanzas in which the adjectives outnumber the verbs are I and III. Note that stanza one is built on an extended parallel construction in which the verbs are implicit rather than stated.

   What men or gods are these? What maidens loth (are these)?
   What mad pursuit (is this)? etc.

2. What would happen to the adjective-verb count if these implicit verbs were counted? Note that stanza III is an invocation. What special situation does that involve that might affect the number of verbs?

3. The exact word: In line 5 of Stanza I Keats uses "haunt." He might have used "wreathes" or "surrounds" (omitting considerations of rhythm). What special overtone makes "haunt" the exactly right choice?

In line 4 of IV Keats originally wrote "sides" and later changed it to "flanks." Why?

Line 9 of I originally read: "What love? what dance? what struggle to escape?" and was revised to "What mad pursuit? What struggle to escape?" Before the revision was there anything to "escape" from?

4. One of the basic themes of this poem is the idea of the still serenity of eternally arrested motion. How many words can you locate in it whose overtones contribute directly to this theme?

Medusa

Louise Bogan

I had come to the house, in a cave of trees,
Facing a sheer sky.
Everything moved,—a bell hung ready to strike,
Sun and reflection wheeled by.

When the bare eyes were before me
And the hissing hair,
Held up at a window, seen through a door.
The stiff bald eyes, the serpents on the forehead
Formed in the air.

This is a dead scene forever now.
Nothing will ever stir.
The end will never brighten it more than this,
Nor the rain blur.

The water will aways fall, and will not fall,
And the tipped bell make no sound.
The grass will always be growing for hay
Deep on the ground.

And I shall stand here like a shadow
Under the great balanced day,
My eyes on the yellow dust, that was lifting in the wind,
And does not drift away.

QUESTIONS

1. This poem, like the Ode on a Grecian Urn, is built about a kind of arrested motion. Keats however centered his impression in the serenity of

FROM *Collected Poems*: 1923-53, by Louise Bogan. Reprinted by permission of The Noonday Press.

a Grecian urn. Louise Bogan centers hers about the terrible image of the snake-headed Medusa whose look changed men to stones. Accordingly there is one moment of motion (in the first stanza)—the moment of the change; then all is frozen.

2. "Bare eyes" and "stiff bald eyes" are strikingly strange usages, as is "hissing hair." "Hissing," of course, is a direct reference to the fact that Medusa's hair is made of snakes. What is the force of "bare" and "stiff bald" when applied to Medusa?

3. Why are the snakes said to be "formed" in the air?

4. Why is the bell "tipped"? Is there any connection between "tipped" bell and "balanced" day?

Poems for Study—II. "Hard" and "Soft" Diction

Cards and Kisses

John Lyly

Cupid and my Campaspe played
At cards for kisses—Cupid paid:
He stakes his quiver, bow, and arrows,
His mother's doves, and team of sparrows;
Loses them too; then down he throws
The coral of his lips, the rose
Growing on's cheek (but none knows how);
With these, the crystal of his brow,
And then the dimple of his chin:
All these did my Campaspe win.
At last he set her both his eyes—
She won, and Cupid blind did rise.
    O Love! hath she done this to thee?
    What shall, alas! become of me?

Sonnet CXXX

William Shakespeare

My mistress' eyes are nothing like the sun;
Coral is far more red than her lips' red:
If snow be white, why then her breasts are dun;
If hairs be wires, black wires grow on her head.
I have seen roses damasked, red and white,
But no such roses see I in her cheeks;
And in some perfumes is there more delight
Than in the breath that from my mistress reeks.

I love to hear her speak—yet well I know
That music hath a far more pleasing sound;
I grant I never saw a goddess go—
My mistress, when she walks, treads on the ground.
And yet, by Heaven, I think my love as rare
As any she belied by false compare.

QUESTIONS

1. "Cards and Kisses" is an elaborate rhymed compliment to the poet's lady, a compliment so fulsome that is saved only by its own graceful playfulness. Lyly is clearly playing a game of compliments and having fun doing so. Such rhymed compliments were traditional among Elizabethan poets. It should not be hard to imagine that the game if taken too seriously by a poet less graceful than Lyly might well become cloying.

2. It was in reaction to the second sort of false praise that Shakespeare wrote Sonnet cxxx. The sonnet may be taken in fact as a short catalogue of the most familiarly trite and familiarly false ways of detailing the ladies' beauty. Eyes like suns, coral lips, snow-white breasts, hairs like golden wires, *etc.* ran without end through the flutter of bad poems. Shakespeare deliberately set himself to argue against the falseness of this tradition, puncturing its pretty and false compliments one by one. Underline in Sonnet cxxx the phrases that paraphrase the compliments Shakespeare is satirizing and then bracket the phrases in which Shakespeare describes his own mistress. What can be said of the difference between the words so underlined and the words so bracketed? Note particularly "dun" and "reeks." Why did Shakespeare settle on such "strong" words?

Mowing

Robert Frost

There was never a sound beside the wood but one,
And that was my long scythe whispering to the ground.
What was it it whispered? I knew not well myself;
Perhaps it was something about the heat of the sun,
Something, perhaps, about the lack of sound—
And that was why it whispered and did not speak.
It was no dream of the gift of idle hours,
Or easy gold at the hand of fay or elf:
Anything more than the truth would have seemed too weak
To the earnest love that laid the swale in rows,
Not without feeble-pointed spikes of flowers
(Pale orchises), and scared a bright green snake.
The fact is the sweetest dream the labor knows.
My long scythe whispered and left the hay to make.

QUESTIONS

1. Robert Frost would have agreed with Shakespeare's impulse in Sonnet cxxx. What Shakespeare says about his refusal to "belie by false compare" Frost says in a different way in the lines "Anything more than the truth would have seemed too weak" and "The fact is the sweetest dream the labor knows." Both poems are declarations of the poets' mortal intention to speak the fact of the world in the most faithful rather than the most elaborate terms.

2. In the two poems that follow immediately mark any phrase that you believe Frost might have taken to be "more than the truth" or that Shakespeare might have suspected of "belying by false compare." What can be said of the quality of the diction of those phrases?

My Garden

Janice Appleby Succorsa

There's a faerie at the bottom of my garden.
  I see her when the dew is on the rose,
And the bumble bee is bumbling, "Oops! Beg pardon"
  As he bumps along the shining iris-rows.

Oh, of course, it's only sunlight if you say so
  Making spangled stars when it begins to rise
And shine on all my dew-drenched pretty flower show;
  But I can tell the shine's my faerie's eyes.

And oh, the happy hours we've shared together!
  And oh, the happy garden paths we've trod!
Year in, year out, in every sort of weather,
  Finding our way to Beauty—and to God!

Threnody

I. O. Scherzo

Truth is a golden sunset far away
Above the misty hills. Its burning eye
Lights all the fading world. A bird flies by
Alive and singing on the dying day.
Oh mystic world, what shall the proud heart say
When beauty flies on beauty beautifully
While blue-gold hills look down to watch it die
Into the falling miracle of clay?

Say: "I have seen the wing of sunset lift
Into the golden vision of the hills

And truth come flooding proud through the cloud **rift,**
And known that souls survive their mortal ills."
Say: "Having seen such beauty in the air,
I have seen truth and will no more despair."

A Sort of a Song

William Carlos Williams

Let the snake wait under
his weed
and the writing
be of words, slow and quick, **sharp**
to strike, quiet to wait,
sleepless

—through metaphor to reconcile
the people and the stones.
Compose. (No ideas
but in things) Invent!
Saxifrage is my flower that **splits**
the rocks.

The Lyric Pulse

a paraphrase of *A Sort of a Song*

Let the serpent bide under
his frond
and the vision
be of words, languid and lithe, **tempered**
to thrust, silent to bide,
undreaming.

—through fantasy to harmonize
spiritual and material.
Create! (No dream
but in being) Give form!
Saxifrage is my bloom that **cleaves**
the crags.

QUESTION

"The Lyric Pulse" was written in an effort to "soften" Williams' "hard"
diction in "A Sort of a Song." Wherever possible the editor has substituted

for Williams' words others with larger, vaguer, or more specifically literary connotations. Where no such words offered readily, he tried for the most lifeless possible equivalent. Compare the diction of the two poems word for word, applying the criteria already discussed. Which words would Shakespeare and Robert Frost have preferred? Which would Miss Succorsa and Scherzo have preferred?

The Lover Showeth How He Is Forsaken of Such as He Sometime Enjoyed

Sir Thomas Wyatt

They flee from me, that sometime did me seek,
With naked foot stalking within my chamber.
Once have I seen them gentle, tame, and meek,
That now are wild, and do not once remember
That sometime they have put themselves in danger
To take bread at my hand; and now they range,
Busily seeking in continual change.

Thanked be fortune it hath been otherwise,
Twenty times better; but once especial,
In thin array, after a pleasant guise,
When her loose gown did from her shoulders fall,
And she me caught in her arms long and small,
And therewithal so sweetly did me kiss
And softly said, Dear heart, how like you this?

It was no dream, for I lay broad awaking.
But all is turned now, through my gentleness,
Into a bitter fashion of forsaking;
And I have leave to go of her goodness,
And she also to use newfangleness.
But since that I unkindly so am served,
How like you this? what hath she now deserved?

The Frailty and Hurtfulness of Beauty

Henry Howard, Earl of Surrey

Brittle beauty that nature made so frail,
Whereof the gift is small, and short the season,
Flowering today, tomorrow apt to fail,
Tickle treasure, abhorred of reason,
Dangerous to deal with, vain, of none avail,
Costly in keeping, past not worth two peason,
Slipper in sliding as an eelës tail,

Hard to attain, once gotten not geason,
Jewel of jeopardy that peril doth assail,
False and untrue, enticèd oft to treason,
En'my to youth (that most may I bewail!),
Ah, bitter sweet! infecting as the poison,
Thou farest as fruit that with the frost is taken:
Today ready ripe, tomorrow all to-shaken.

QUESTION

The two preceding poems were written during the earlier half of the XVIth Century. Most critics since that time have thought of Surrey's poem as a dull poetic exercise and of Wyatt's as a moving capture of a sincere emotion. Analyze the diction of the poems, and basing the discussion upon that analysis, agree or disagree with the general verdict of the critics.

To Helen

Edgar Allan Poe

Helen, thy beauty is to me
   Like those Nicaean barks of yore,
That gently o'er the perfumed sea,
   The weary, wayworn wanderer bore
   To his own native shore.

On desperate seas long wont to roam,
   Thy hyacinth hair, thy classic face,
Thy Naiad airs have brought me home
   To the glory that was Greece
   And the grandeur that was Rome.

Lo! in yon brilliant window-niche
   How statue-like I see thee stand,
The agate lamp within thy hand!
   Ah, Psyche, from the regions which
   Are Holy Land.

Tickle: delicate. **slipper:** slippery. **eelës:** eel's. **geason:** rare. **to-shaken:** shaken apart, cf. German use of prefix *ver* as in *spielen*, to play, *verspielen*, to play away, to lose in gambling. **Nicaean:** Nicaea was the ancient name of modern Nice. "Nicaean barks" probably meant the ships of the Greeks (perhaps of Ulysses) sailing past Nicaea. The classic seas of such a voyage (perfumed sea) are powerfully contrasted with the "desperate seas" (of Poe's life? of his times?) in which the author finds himself astray and from which he is brought to his classic peace by Helen's virtue and beauty. **hyacinth hair** is borrowed from Homer. **Naiad:** a Greek water nymph. **Psyche:** the classic personification of the Soul. She was loved by Cupid who came to her only in darkness so that she might not see him, until one night, while he slept, she stood above him with a lamp and discovered how beautiful he was. Hence "the agate lamp." Note that all these references are to the classic, the perfumed sea. Only the one reference to "desperate seas" gives us Poe's distance from his wish.

Love Poem

John Frederick Nims

My clumsiest dear, whose hands shipwreck vases,
At whose quick touch all glasses chip and ring,
Whose palms are bulls in china, burs in linen,
And have no cunning with any soft thing

Except all ill at ease fidgeting people:
The refugee uncertain at the door
You make at home; deftly you steady
The drunk clambering on his undulant floor.

Unpredictable dear, the taxi drivers' terror,
Shrinking from far headlights pale as a dime
Yet leaping before red apoplectic streetcars—
Misfit in any space. And never on time.

A wrench in clocks and the solar system. Only
With words and people and love you move at ease.
In traffic of wit expertly manoeuvre
And keep us, all devotion, at your knees.

Forgetting your coffee spreading on our flannel,
Your lipstick grinning on our coat,
So gayly in love's unbreakable heaven
Our souls on glory of split bourbon float.

Be with me darling early and late. Smash glasses—
I will study wry music for your sake.
For should your hands drop white and empty
All the toys of the world would break.

QUESTION

Poe and Nims both seem to have written love poems but Poe has idealized his love into a single emotion of passionate yearning, and Nims has taken an emotional position closer to that of everyday love. Poe worships from afar in total seriousness. Nims pokes gentle but loving fun. With no suggestion that one poem need be better than the other, which seems closer to your own sense of things? How does the diction reflect this difference? Which poem is more nearly written in a diction, and which more nearly in a language? Is Poe s poem really about love?

Because the two elegies that follow are long, it may be well to set a few directions before rather than after the reading. Both poems were

FROM *The Iron Pastoral*, by John Frederick Nims, copyright 1947 by John Frederick Nims, by permission of William Sloane Associates, Inc.

written by poets on the deaths of fellow poets. Shelley did not know Keats intimately; nor did Auden, Yeats. Both poems are more nearly motivated by an idea of what a life-value should be than by an intense personal grief.

Even upon a glancing reading, however, it should be clear that Auden's view is very different from Shelley's. Shelley writes as if he were personally grief stricken, as if nature itself has been impoverished by Keats' death, as if nature itself wept for Keats' passing. Auden very carefully refuses to indulge any such *as if's*. One cannot fail to note, in fact, that "In Memory of W. B. Yeats" is not only a thoughtful statement of what a poet's life and death finally mean, but that it is in part a poem written against "Adonais." Nor need that additional motive imply that Auden believes "Adonais" is a bad poem. "Adonais" was written in another age, in a different literary tradition, with a different view of human destiny. Inevitably its tone is set by that complex. As Auden's tone is set by the complex of his own human position in time.

QUESTIONS

1. How would you describe Shelley's tone? How does the diction release that tone? How, similarly, would you describe Auden's tone and what part does the diction play in establishing it? How would the diction of the two poems measure against Frost's statement that anything more than the truth would be too weak?

2. What other devices of the two poems contribute notably to the tone? (Imagery? rhythm? form? grammatical structure?)

Adonais

Percy Bysshe Shelley

I weep for Adonais—he is dead!
Oh, weep for Adonais! though our tears
Thaw not the frost which binds so dear a head!
And thou, sad Hour, selected from all years
To mourn our loss, rouse thy obscure compeers,
And teach them thine own sorrow! Say: "With me
Died Adonais; till the Future dares
Forget the Past, his fate and fame shall be
An echo and a light unto eternity."

Where wert thou, mighty Mother, when he lay,
When thy son lay, pierced by the shaft which flies
In darkness? Where was lorn Urania
When Adonais died? With veiled eyes,
'Mid listening Echoes, in her Paradise
She sate, while one, with soft enamored breath,
Rekindled all the fading melodies,

With which, like flowers that mock the corse beneath,
He had adorned and hid the coming bulk of death.

Oh, weep for Adonais—he is dead!
Wake, melancholy Mother, wake and weep!
Yet wherefore? Quench within their burning bed
Thy fiery tears, and let thy loud heart keep,
Like his, a mute and uncomplaining sleep;
For he is gone, where all things wise and fair
Descend—oh, dream not that the amorous Deep
Will yet restore him to the vital air;
Death feeds on his mute voice, and laughs at our despair.

Most musical of mourners, weep again!
Lament anew, Urania!—He died—
Who was the Sire of an immortal strain,
Blind, old, and lonely, when his country's pride,
The priest, the slave, and the liberticide,
Trampled and mocked with many a loathed rite
Of lust and blood; he went, unterrified,
Into the gulf of death; but his clear Sprite
Yet reigns o'er earth—the third among the sons of light.

Most musical of mourners, weep anew!
Not all to that bright station dared to climb;
And happier they their happiness who knew,
Whose tapers yet burn through that night of time
In which suns perished; others more sublime,
Struck by the envious wrath of man or god,
Have sunk, extinct in their refulgent prime;
And some yet live, treading the thorny road,
Which leads, through toil and hate, to Fame's serene abode.

But now, thy youngest, dearest one has perished,
The nursling of thy widowhood, who grew,
Like a pale flower by some sad maiden cherished,
And fed with true-love tears, instead of dew;
Most musical of mourners, weep anew!
Thy extreme hope, the loveliest and the last,
The bloom, whose petals, nipped before they blew,
Died on the promise of the fruit, is waste;
The broken lily lies—the storm is overpast.

To that high Capital, where kingly Death
Keeps his pale court in beauty and decay,
He came; and bought, with price of purest breath,
A grave among the eternal.—Come away!

He: Milton.

Haste, while the vault of blue Italian day
Is yet his fitting charnel-roof! while still
He lies, as if in dewy sleep he lay;
Awake him not! surely he takes his fill
Of deep and liquid rest, forgetful of all ill.

He will awake no more, oh, never more!—
Within the twilight chamber spreads apace
The shadow of white Death, and at the door
Invisible Corruption waits to trace
His extreme way to her dim dwelling-place;
The eternal Hunger sits, but pity and awe
Soothe her pale rage, nor dares she to deface
So fair a prey, till darkness and the law
Of change shall o'er his sleep the mortal curtain draw.

Oh, weep for Adonais!—The quick Dreams,
The passion-winged Ministers of thought,
Who were his flocks, whom near the living streams
Of his young spirit he fed, and whom he taught
The love which was its music, wander not—
Wander no more, from kindling brain to brain,
But droop there, whence they sprung; and mourn their lot
Round the cold heart, where, after their sweet pain,
They ne'er will gather strength, or find a home again.

And one with trembling hands clasps his cold head,
And fans him with her moonlight wings, and cries:
"Our love, our hope, our sorrow, is not dead;
See, on the silken fringe of his faint eyes,
Like dew upon a sleeping flower, there lies
A tear some Dream has loosened from his brain."
Lost Angel of a ruined Paradise!
She knew not 'twas her own; as with no stain
She faded, like a cloud which had outwept its rain.

One from a lucid urn of starry dew
Washed his light limbs as if embalming them;
Another clipped her profuse locks, and threw
The wreath upon him, like an anadem,
Which frozen tears instead of pearls begem;
Another in her willful grief would break
Her bow and winged reeds, as if to stem
A greater loss with one which was more weak;
And dull the barbed fire against his frozen cheek.

Another Splendor on his mouth alit,
That mouth, whence it was wont to draw the breath

Which gave it strength to pierce the guarded wit,
And pass into the panting heart beneath
With lightning and with music; the damp death
Quenched its caress upon his icy lips;
And, as a dying meteor stains a wreath
Of moonlight vapor, which the cold night clips,
It flushed through his pale limbs, and passed to its eclipse.

And others came—Desires and Adorations,
Winged Persuasions and veiled Destinies,
Splendors, and Glooms, and glimmering Incarnations
Of hopes and fears, and twilight Phantasies;
And Sorrow, with her family of Sighs,
And Pleasure, blind with tears, led by the gleam
Of her own dying smile instead of eyes,
Came in slow pomp—the moving pomp might seem
Like pageantry of mist on an autumnal stream.

All he had loved, and molded into thought
From shape, and hue, and odor, and sweet sound,
Lamented Adonais. Morning sought
Her eastern watchtower, and her hair unbound,
Wet with the tears which should adorn the ground,
Dimmed the aërial eyes that kindle day;
Afar the melancholy thunder moaned,
Pale Ocean in unquiet slumber lay,
And the wild winds flew round, sobbing in their dismay.

Lost Echo sits amid the voiceless mountains,
And feeds her grief with his remembered lay,
And will no more reply to winds or fountains,
Or amorous birds perched on the young green spray,
Or herdsman's horn, or bell at closing day;
Since she can mimic not his lips, more dear
Than those for whose disdain she pined away
Into a shadow of all sounds—a drear
Murmur, between their songs, is all the woodmen hear.

Grief made the young Spring wild, and she threw down
Her kindling buds, as if she Autumn were,
Or they dead leaves; since her delight is flown,
For whom should she have waked the sullen year?
To Phoebus was not Hyacinth so dear
Nor to himself Narcissus, as to both
Thou, Adonais. Wan they stand and sere
Amid the faint companions of their youth,
With dew all turned to tears; odor, to sighing ruth.

Thy spirit's sister, the lorn nightingale,
Mourns not her mate with such melodious pain;
Not so the eagle, who like thee could scale
Heaven, and could nourish in the sun's domain
Her mighty youth with morning, doth complain,
Soaring and screaming round her empty nest,
As Albion wails for thee. The curse of Cain
Light on his head who pierced thy innocent breast,
And scared the angel soul that was its earthly guest!

Ah, woe is me! Winter is come and gone,
But grief returns with the revolving year;
The airs and streams renew their joyous tone;
The ants, the bees, the swallows reappear;
Fresh leaves and flowers deck the dead Seasons' bier;
The amorous birds now pair in every brake,
And build their mossy homes in field and brere;
And the green lizard, and the golden snake,
Like unimprisoned flames, out of their trance awake.

Through wood and stream and field and hill and ocean
A quickening life from the earth's heart has burst,
As it has ever done, with change and motion,
From the great morning of the world when first
God dawned on Chaos; in its stream immersed,
The lamps of heaven flash with a softer light;
All baser things pant with life's sacred thirst,
Diffuse themselves, and spend in love's delight
The beauty and the joy of their renewèd might.

The leprous corpse, touched by this spirit tender,
Exhales itself in flowers of gentle breath;
Like incarnations of the stars, when splendor
Is changed to fragrance, they illumine death
And mock the merry worm that wakes beneath;
Naught we know, dies. Shall that alone which knows
Be as a sword consumed before the sheath
By sightless lightning?—the intense atom glows
A moment, then is quenched in a most cold repose.

Alas! that all we loved of him should be,
But for our grief, as if it had not been,
And grief itself be mortal! Woe is me!
Whence are we, and why are we? Of what scene
The actors or spectators? Great and mean
Meet massed in death, who lends what life must borrow.
As long as skies are blue, and fields are green,
Evening must usher night, night urge the morrow,
Month follow month with woe, and year wake year to sorrow.

He will awake no more, oh, never more!
"Wake thou," cried Misery, "childless Mother, rise
Out of thy sleep, and slake, in thy heart's core,
A wound more fierce than his with tears and sighs."
And all the Dreams that watched Urania's eyes,
And all the Echoes whom their sister's song
Had held in holy silence, cried: "Arise!"
Swift as a Thought by the snake Memory stung,
From her ambrosial rest the fading Splendor sprung.

She rose like an autumnal Night, that springs
Out of the East, and follows wild and drear
The golden Day, which, on eternal wings,
Even as a ghost abandoning a bier,
Had left the earth a corpse. Sorrow and fear
So struck, so roused, so rapt Urania;
So saddened round her like an atmosphere
Of stormy mist; so swept her on her way
Even to the mournful place where Adonais lay.

Out of her secret Paradise she sped,
Through camps and cities rough with stone, and steel,
And human hearts, which to her aëry tread
Yielding not, wounded the invisible
Palms of her tender feet where'er they fell;
And barbed tongues, and thoughts more sharp than they,
Rent the soft Form they never could repel,
Whose sacred blood, like the young tears of May,
Paved with eternal flowers that undeserving way.

In the death chamber for a moment Death,
Shamed by the presence of that living Might,
Blushed to annihilation, and the breath
Revisited those lips, and life's pale light
Flashed through those limbs, so late her dear delight.
"Leave me not wild and drear and comfortless,
As silent lightning leaves the starless night!
Leave me not!" cried Urania. Her distress
Roused Death; Death rose and smiled, and met her vain caress.

"Stay yet awhile! speak to me once again;
Kiss me, so long but as a kiss may live;
And in my heartless breast and burning brain
That word, that kiss, shall all thoughts else survive.
With food of saddest memory kept alive,
Now thou art dead, as if it were a part
Of thee, my Adonais! I would give
All that I am to be as thou now art!
But I am chained to Time, and cannot thence depart!

"O gentle child, beautiful as thou wert,
Why didst thou leave the trodden paths of men
Too soon, and with weak hands though mighty heart
Dare the unpastured dragon in his den?
Defenseless as thou wert, oh, where was then
Wisdom the mirrored shield, or scorn the spear?
Or hadst thou waited the full cycle, when
Thy spirit should have filled its crescent sphere,
The monsters of life's waste had fled from thee like deer.

"The herded wolves, bold only to pursue;
The obscene ravens, clamorous o'er the dead;
The vultures to the conqueror's banner true,
Who feed where Desolation first has fed,
And whose wings rain contagion—how they fled,
When like Apollo, from his golden bow,
The Pythian of the age, one arrow sped
And smiled!—The spoilers tempt no second blow;
They fawn on the proud feet that spurn them lying low.

"The Sun comes forth, and many reptiles spawn;
He sets, and each ephemeral insect then
Is gathered into death without a dawn,
And the immortal stars awake again;
So is it in the world of living men:
A godlike mind soars forth, in its delight
Making earth bare and veiling heaven, and when
It sinks, the swarms that dimmed or shared its light
Leave to its kindred lamps the spirit's awful night."

Thus ceased she; and the mountain shepherds came,
Their garlands sere, their magic mantles rent;
The Pilgrim of Eternity, whose fame
Over his living head like heaven is bent,
An early but enduring monument,
Came, veiling all the lightnings of his song
In sorrow; from her wilds Ierne sent
The sweetest lyrist of her saddest wrong,
And love taught grief to fall like music from his tongue.

Midst others of less note, came one frail Form,
A phantom among men, companionless
As the last cloud of an expiring storm

The Pythian of the age: Byron. As Apollo struck down the Python, so Byron struck down the critics. The Pilgrim of Eternity: Byron. Ierne: Ireland. The sweetest lyrist: Thomas Moore. One frail Form: Shelley himself.

Whose thunder is its knell; he, as I guess,
Had gazed on Nature's naked loveliness,
Actaeon-like, and now he fled astray
With feeble steps o'er the world's wilderness,
And his own thoughts, along that rugged way,
Pursued, like raging hounds, their father and their prey.

A pardlike Spirit beautiful and swift—
A Love in desolation masked—a Power
Girt round with weaknesses:—it can scarce uplift
The weight of the superincumbent hour;
It is a dying lamp, a falling shower,
A breaking billow—even whilst we speak
Is it not broken? On the withering flower
The killing sun smiles brightly; on a cheek
The life can burn in blood, even while the heart may break.

His head was bound with pansies overblown,
And faded violets, white, and pied, and blue;
And a light spear topped with a cypress cone,
Round whose rude shaft dark ivy-tresses grew
Yet dripping with the forest's noonday dew,
Vibrated, as the ever-beating heart
Shook the weak hand that grasped it; of that crew
He came the last, neglected and apart;
A herd-abandoned deer, struck by the hunter's dart.

All stood aloof, and at his partial moan
Smiled through their tears; well knew that gentle band
Who in another's fate now wept his own;
As, in the accents of an unknown land,
He sung new sorrow; sad Urania scanned
The Stranger's mien, and murmured, "Who art thou?"
He answered not, but with a sudden hand
Made bare his branded and ensanguined brow,
Which was like Cain's or Christ's—Oh! that it should be so!

What softer voice is hushed over the dead?
Athwart what brow is that dark mantle thrown?
What form leans sadly o'er the white deathbed,
In mockery of monumental stone,
The heavy heart heaving without a moan?
If it be He, who, gentlest of the wise,
Taught, soothed, loved, honored the departed one,
Let me not vex with inharmonious sighs
The silence of that heart's accepted sacrifice.

Our Adonais has drunk poison—oh!
What deaf and viperous murderer could crown
Life's early cup with such a draught of woe?
The nameless worm would now itself disown.
It felt, yet could escape, the magic tone
Whose prelude held all envy, hate, and wrong,
But what was howling in one breast alone,
Silent with expectation of the song,
Whose master's hand is cold, whose silver lyre unstrung.

Live thou, whose infamy is not thy fame!
Live! fear no heavier chastisement from me,
Thou noteless blot on a remembered name!
But be thyself, and know thyself to be!
And ever at thy season be thou free
To spill the venom when thy fangs o'erflow.
Remorse and self-contempt shall cling to thee;
Hot shame shall burn upon thy secret brow,
And like a beaten hound tremble thou shalt—as now.

Nor let us weep that our delight is fled
Far from these carrion kites that scream below;
He wakes or sleeps with the enduring dead;
Thou canst not soar where he is sitting now.—
Dust to the dust! but the pure spirit shall flow
Back to the burning fountain whence it came,
A portion of the Eternal, which must glow
Through time and change, unquenchably the same,
Whilst thy cold embers choke the sordid hearth of shame.

Peace, peace! he is not dead, he doth not sleep—
He hath awakened from the dream of life—
'Tis we who, lost in stormy visions, keep
With phantoms an unprofitable strife,
And in mad trance strike with our spirit's knife
Invulnerable nothings.—*We* decay
Like corpses in a charnel; fear and grief
Convulse us and consume us day by day,
And cold hopes swarm like worms within our living clay.

He has outsoared the shadow of our night;
Envy and calumny and hate and pain,
And that unrest which men miscall delight,
Can touch him not and torture not again;
From the contagion of the world's slow stain

The nameless worm: Shelley (falsely) attributed Keats's death to a vicious unsigned review of Keats's *Endymion*.

He is secure, and now can never mourn
A heart grown cold, a head grown gray in vain;
Nor, when the spirit's self has ceased to burn,
With sparkless ashes load an unlamented urn.

He lives, he wakes—'tis Death is dead, not he;
Mourn not for Adonais.—Thou young Dawn,
Turn all thy dew to splendor, for from thee
The spirit thou lamentest is not gone;
Ye caverns and ye forests, cease to moan!
Cease, ye faint flowers and fountains, and thou Air,
Which like a mourning veil thy scarf hadst thrown
O'er the abandoned Earth, now leave it bare
Even to the joyous stars which smile on its despair!

He is made one with Nature; there is heard
His voice in all her music, from the moan
Of thunder, to the song of night's sweet bird;
He is a presence to be felt and known
In darkness and in light, from herb and stone,
Spreading itself where'er that Power may move
Which has withdrawn his being to its own;
Which wields the world with never-wearied love,
Sustains it from beneath, and kindles it above.

He is a portion of the loveliness
Which once he made more lovely; he doth bear
His part, while the one Spirit's plastic stress
Sweeps through the dull, dense world, compelling there
All new successions to the forms they wear;
Torturing th' unwilling dross that checks its flight
To its own likeness, as each mass may bear;
And bursting in its beauty and its might
From trees and beasts and men into the Heaven's light.

The splendors of the firmament of time
May be eclipsed, but are extinguished not;
Like stars to their appointed height they climb
And death is a low mist which cannot blot
The brightness it may veil. When lofty thought
Lifts a young heart above its mortal lair,
And love and life contend in it for what
Shall be its earthly doom, the dead live there
And move like winds of light on dark and stormy air.

The inheritors of unfulfilled renown
Rose from their thrones, built beyond mortal thought,
Far in the Unapparent. Chatterton

Rose pale; his solemn agony had not
Yet faded from him. Sidney, as he fought
And as he fell and as he lived and loved,
Sublimely mild, a Spirit without spot,
Arose. And Lucan, by his death approved—
Oblivion, as they rose, shrank like a thing reproved.

And many more, whose names on earth are dark
But whose transmitted effluence cannot die
So long as fire outlives the parent spark,
Rose, robed in dazzling immortality.
"Thou art become as one of us," they cry,
"It was for thee yon kingless sphere has long
Swung blind in unascended majesty,
Silent alone amid an Heaven of Song.
Assume thy winged throne, thou Vesper of our throng!"

Who mourns for Adonais? oh, come forth,
Fond wretch! and know thyself and him aright.
Clasp with thy panting soul the pendulous Earth;
As from a center, dart thy spirit's light
Beyond all worlds, until its spacious might
Satiate the void circumference. Then shrink
Even to a point within our day and night;
And keep thy heart light, lest it make thee sink,
When hope has kindled hope, and lured thee to the brink.

Or go to Rome, which is the sepulchre,
Oh, not of him, but of our joy; 'tis naught
That ages, empires, and religions there
Lie buried in the ravage they have wrought;
For such as he can lend—they borrow not
Glory from those who made the world their prey;
And he is gathered to the kings of thought
Who waged contention with their time's decay,
And of the past are all that cannot pass away.

Go thou to Rome—at once the Paradise,
The grave, the city, and the wilderness;
And where its wrecks like shattered mountains rise,
And flowering weeds and fragrant copses dress
The bones of Desolation's nakedness,
Pass, till the Spirit of the spot shall lead
Thy footsteps to a slope of green access
Where, like an infant's smile, over the dead
A light of laughing flowers along the grass is spread.

And gray walls molder round, on which dull Time
Feeds, like slow fire upon a hoary brand;

And one keen pyramid with wedge sublime,
Pavilioning the dust of him who planned
This refuge for his memory, doth stand
Like flame transformed to marble; and beneath,
A field is spread, on which a newer band
Have pitched in Heaven's smile their camp of death,
Welcoming him we lose with scarce extinguished breath.

Here pause. These graves are all too young as yet
To have outgrown the sorrow which consigned
Its charge to each; and if the seal is set,
Here, on one fountain of a mourning mind,
Break it not thou! too surely shalt thou find
Thine own well full, if thou returnest home,
Of tears and gall. From the world's bitter wind
Seek shelter in the shadow of the tomb.
What Adonais is, why fear we to become?

The One remains, the many change and pass;
Heaven's light forever shines, earth's shadows fly;
Life, like a dome of many-colored glass,
Stains the white radiance of Eternity,
Until Death tramples it to fragments.—Die,
If thou wouldst be with that which thou dost seek!
Follow where all is fled!—Rome's azure sky,
Flowers, ruins, statues, music, words, are weak
The glory they transfuse with fitting truth to speak.

Why linger, why turn back, why shrink, my Heart?
Thy hopes are gone before; from all things here
They have departed; thou shouldst now depart!
A light is past from the revolving year,
And man, and woman; and what still is dear
Attracts to crush, repels to make thee wither.
The soft sky smiles—the low wind whispers near;
'Tis Adonais calls! oh, hasten thither,
No more let Life divide what Death can join together.

That Light whose smile kindles the universe,
That Beauty in which all things work and move,
That Benediction which the eclipsing Curse
Of birth can quench not, that sustaining Love
Which, through the web of being blindly wove
By man and beast and earth and air and sea,
Burns bright or dim, as each are mirrors of
The fire for which all thirst, now beams on me,
Consuming the last clouds of cold mortality.

The breath whose might I have invoked in song
Descends on me; my spirit's bark is driven
Far from the shore, far from the trembling throng
Whose sails were never to the tempest given;
The massy earth and sphered skies are riven!
I am borne darkly, fearfully, afar;
Whilst, buring through the inmost veil of Heaven,
The soul of Adonais, like a star,
Beacons from the abode where the Eternal are.

In Memory of W. B. Yeats

W. H. Auden

I

He disappeared in the dead of winter:
The brooks were frozen, the air-ports almost deserted,
And snow disfigured the public statues;
The mercury sank in the mouth of the dying day.
O all the instruments agree
The day of his death was a dark cold day.

Far from his illness
The wolves ran on through the evergreen forests,
The peasant river was untempted by the fashionable quays;
By mourning tongues
The death of the poet was kept from his poems.

But for him it was his last afternoon as himself,
An afternoon of nurses and rumours;
The provinces of his body revolted,
The squares of his mind were empty,
Silence invaded the suburbs,
The current of his feeling failed: he became his admirers.

Now he is scattered among a hundred cities
And wholly given over to unfamiliar affections;
To find his happiness in another kind of wood
And be punished under a foreign code of conscience.
The words of a dead man
Are modified in the guts of the living.

But in the importance and noise of to-morrow
When the brokers are roaring like beasts on the floor of the Bourse,
And the poor have the sufferings to which they are fairly accustomed,

And each in the cell of himself is almost convinced of his freedom;
A few thousand will think of this day
As one thinks of a day when one did something slightly unusual.

O all the instruments agree
The day of his death was a dark cold day.

II

You were silly like us: your gift survived it all;
The parish of rich women, physical decay,
Yourself; mad Ireland hurt you into poetry.
Now Ireland has her madness and her weather still,
For poetry makes nothing happen: it survives
In the valley of its saying where executives
Would never want to tamper; it flows south
From ranches of isolation and the busy griefs,
Raw towns that we believe and die in; it survives,
A way of happening, a mouth.

III

Earth receive an honored guest;
William Yeats is laid to rest:
Let the Irish vessel lie
Emptied of its poetry.

Time that is intolerant
Of the brave and innocent,
And indifferent in a week
To a beautiful physique,

Worships language and forgives
Everyone by whom it lives;
Pardons cowardice, conceit,
Lays its honours at their feet.

Time that with this strange excuse
Pardoned Kipling and his views,
And will pardon Paul Claudel,
Pardons him for writing well.

In the nightmare of the dark
All the dogs of Europe bark,
And the living nations wait,
Each sequestered in its hate;

Intellectual disgrace
Stares from every human face,
And the seas of pity lie
Locked and frozen in each eye.

Follow, poet, follow right
To the bottom of the night,
With your unconstraining voice
Still persuade us to rejoice;

With the farming of a verse
Make a vineyard of the curse,
Sing of human unsuccess
In a rapture of distress;

In the deserts of the heart
Let the healing fountain start,
In the prison of his days
Teach the free man how to praise.

Poems for Study—III. Inter-Relation of Overtones

Naming of Parts

Henry Reed

Today we have naming of parts. Yesterday,
We had daily cleaning. And tomorrow morning,
We shall have what to do after firing. But today,
Today we have naming of parts. Japonica
Glistens like coral in all of the neighbouring gardens,
    And today we have naming of parts.

This is the lower sling swivel. And this
Is the upper sling swivel, whose use you will see,
When you are given your slings. And this is the piling swivel,
Which in your case you have not got. The branches
Hold in the gardens their silent, eloquent gestures,
    Which in our case we have not got.

This is the safety-catch, which is always released
With an easy flick of the thumb. And please do not let me
See anyone using his finger. You can do it quite easy
If you have any strength in your thumb. The blossoms
Are fragile and motionless, never letting anyone see
    Any of them using their finger.

And this you can see is the bolt. The purpose of this
Is to open the breech, as you see. We can slide it

Rapidly backwards and forwards: we call this
Easing the spring. And rapidly backwards and forwards
The early bees are assaulting and fumbling the flowers:
  They call it easing the Spring.

They call it easing the Spring: it is perfectly easy
If you have any strength in your thumb: like the bolt,
And the breech, and the cocking-piece, and the point of balance,
Which in our case we have not got; and the almond-blossom
Silent in all of the gardens and the bees going backwards and
     forwards,
  For today we have naming of parts.

QUESTIONS

"Naming of Parts" describes a young soldier's reaction to his basic training in the manual of arms. He stands gun-in-hand in the full hour of Spring caught between two voices, one the Army's, the other Spring's. What is the quality of the diction in the voice of the Army? In the voice of the Spring? One of the special successes of this poem is in its ability to slide one voice into the other in a series of puns and near puns (as in "easing the spring"). How many other phrases in the poem have double meanings and what part do the two basically opposed overtone themes have in making these double meanings function?

A Long-Tail Simile

from *The Faerie Queene*

Edmund Spenser

Like as the tide that comes from th' Ocean main,
  Flows up the Shenan with *contrary force*,
  And *overruling* him in his own *rayne*,
  Drives back the current of his kindly course,
  And makes it seem to have some other source:
  But when the flood is spent, then back again
  His borrowed waters *forced to redisbourse*,
  He sends the sea his own with double gain,
  And *tribute* eke withal, as to his *Souveraine*.

Thus did the battle vary to and fro . . .

QUESTION

What do the italicized words have in common? Compare the metaphor implied in their connotations with that of stanza three of Auden's *In Memory of W. B. Yeats*. To what is Yeats' death compared by implication? How does the diction release that implication?

The Heart

Harvey Shapiro

In the midst of words your wordless image
Marches through the precincts of my night
And all the structures of my language lie undone:
The bright cathedrals clatter, and the moon-
Topped spires break their stalks.
Sprawled before that raid, I watch the towns
Go under. And in the waiting dark, I loose
Like marbles spinning from a child
The crazed and hooded creatures of the heart.

QUESTIONS

1. "The Heart" is another poem based on a single comparison. The image of the loved one moves through the lover's midnight like a military raid.

2. Underline every word and phrase that could be taken as a literal description of a military raid. Note that the raid is presented not as an air-raid but as one that comes marching (line two), a foray. What causes the bright cathedrals to "clatter"? (clatter down?) the spires to "break their stalks"?

3. Is it possible that the poet is confused and that he is describing air-raid damage in connection with a raid that comes marching? Or are his choices coherent and defensible?

Polo Grounds

Rolfe Humphries

Time is of the essence. This is a highly skilled
And beautiful mystery. Three or four seconds only
From the time that Riggs connects till he reaches first,
And in those seconds Jurges goes to his right,
Comes up with the ball, tosses to Witek at second
For the force on Reese, Witek to Mize at first,
In time for the out — a double play.

(Red Barber crescendo. Crowd noises, obbligato;
Scattered staccatos from the peanut boys,
Loud in the lull, as the teams are changing sides) . . .

Hubbell takes the sign, nods, pumps, delivers —
A foul into the stands. Dunn takes a new ball out,
Hands it to Danning, who throws it down to Werber;
Werber takes off his glove, rubs the ball briefly,
Tosses it over to Hub, who goes to the rosin bag,
Takes the sign from Danning, pumps, delivers —
Low, outside, ball three. Danning goes to the mound,
Says something to Hub, Dunn brushes off the plate,
Adams starts throwing in the Giant bullpen,
Hub takes the sign from Danning, pumps, delivers,
Camilli gets hold of it, a *long* fly to the outfield,
Ott goes back, back, back, against the wall, gets under it,
Pounds his glove, and takes it for the out.
That's all for the Dodgers. . . .

Time is of the essence. The rhythms break,
More varied and subtle than any kind of dance;
Movement speeds up or lags. The ball goes out
In sharp and angular drives, or long, slow arcs,
Comes in again controlled and under aim;
The players wheel or spurt, race, stoop, slide, halt,
Shift imperceptibly to new positions,
Watching the signs, according to the batter,
The score, the inning. Time is of the essence.

Time is of the essence. Remember Terry?
Remember Stonewall Jackson, Lindstrom, Frisch,
When they were good? Remember Long George Kelly?
Remember John McGraw and Benny Kauff?
Remember Bridwell, Tenney, Merkel, Youngs,
Chief Meyers, Big Jeff Tesreau, Shufflin' Phil?
Remember Matthewson, and Ames, and Donlin,
Buck Ewing, Rusie, Smiling Mickey Welch?
Remember a left-handed catcher named Jack Humphries,
Who sometimes played the outfield, in '83?

Time is of essence. The shadow moves
From the plate to the box, from the box to second base,
From second to the outfield, to the bleachers.

Time is of the essence. The crowd and players
Are the same age always, but the man in the crowd
Is older every season. Come on, play ball!

QUESTIONS

1. "Polo Grounds," like "Naming of Parts," is a poem basically con-
trived of two voices playing against one another. One voice sets itself to
capture the tone of the radio announcer who describes the action of the

baseball game taking place at the Polo Grounds. The second voice is that of the writer commenting upon the action. There is a further complication in the fact that the second voice divides again into two kinds of voices. In one of his personal voices the writer takes on the role of an enthusiastic fan relishing not only what he sees but what he remembers of the game. In stanza five, the author summons this voice to think back over the history of baseball, naming a long list of past players and ending with one Jack Humphries whose climactic place in the series would suggest that he is the author's father. In the second of his personal voices, the writer speaks not so much as a baseball fan but as an aesthete: in this voice he runs to such terms as "beautiful mystery," "crescendo," "obbligato."

2. What is the effect of combining these tones? What motivates the author in mixing "rhythms more varied and subtle than any kind of dance" (is that a reasonable claim to make for baseball? might a professional choreographer agree or disagree?) with such tough-lunged "regular talk" as "Come on, play ball!"?

3. Are there traces of still a third personal voice?

4. What is the effect of the frequent repetition of "Time is of the essence"? In what voice is that phrase spoken? The phrase itself is clearly a cliché: does it justify itself in the course of the poem, or must it be put down as a device that failed?

5. When all of the author's personal voices are put together into the composite-second-voice, what principle or principles of selection manifest themselves?

Dover Beach

Matthew Arnold

The sea is calm to-night.
The tide is full, the moon lies fair
Upon the straits;—on the French coast the light
Gleams and is gone; the cliffs of England stand,
Glimmering and vast, out in the tranquil bay.
Come to the window, sweet is the night-air!
Only, from the long line of spray
Where the sea meets the moon-blanched land,
Listen! you hear the grating roar
Of pebbles which the waves draw back, and fling,
At their return, up the high strand,
Begin, and cease, and then again begin,
With tremulous cadence slow, and bring
The eternal note of sadness in.

Sophocles long ago
Heard it on the Ægean, and it brought
Into his mind the turbid ebb and flow
Of human misery; we

Find also in the sound a thought,
Hearing it by this distant northern sea.
The Sea of Faith
Was once, too, at the full, and round earth's shore
Lay like the folds of a bright girdle furled.
But now I only hear
Its melancholy, long, withdrawing roar,
Retreating, to the breath
Of the night-wind, down the vast edges drear
And naked shingles of the world.

Ah, love, let us be true
To one another! for the world, which seems
To lie before us like a land of dreams,
So various, so beautiful, so new,
Hath really neither joy, nor love, nor light,
Nor certitude, nor peace, nor help for pain;
And we are here as on a darkling plain
Swept with confused alarms of struggle and flight,
Where ignorant armies clash by night.

QUESTIONS

1. Assume "the eternal note of sadness" to be a key statement of this poem. How many of the words and phrases of the poem are keyed to the same overtone of sad-and-everlasting-things?

2. Note that after a major division following stanza two, the poem pursues a very different tone. What is the difference in tone of the two parts of the poem?

3. Assume "confused alarms of struggle and flight" to be a key statement of part two. How many of the other words and phrases in this part have the same overtone of meaningless-and-ephemeral-things?

4. Love, on the other hand, tries to imagine a land-of-dreams-and-certitude. Which words and phrases in the second part are keyed to this overtone? How does this overtone relate to the other two? It is obviously in opposition to "meaningless-and-ephemeral." Is it the same thing as "sad-and-everlasting"? Or is it truly a third theme lost to both the others?

The Coming of Dusk Upon a Village in Haiti

Henry Rago

The island that had flowered to the sun
Folded the night into its dark hills. Slow
Gestures of wind signed over it with sleep.
A dust of silver weighed upon the leaves
And touched the village roofs half into air.

Soft, soft, the air insisted: all things now
Be muted to the night, be drugged, be dumb,
Like that brown girl and boy who gravely move,
Sleepwalking, toward each other; like these leaves,
Huge in a dream, luxurious with fatigue.

And darkness, subtle as an undersea,
Became the secret touch upon the ferns,
Smothered the burning poinciana, quenched
All but the deepest red. All that could live
Lived only in one swollen influence.

O from the sea of jasmine, where no word
Could find its breath, and tambours from the hills
Spoke to the night, the helpless mind turned still
Its pale look upward, so the heart, that last
Bloom of conspiracy, would not be lost!

QUESTIONS

1. "Gravely move" in line eight and "sleepwalking" in line nine both describe the motion of the young people. Is the poet justified in describing the same motion twice? Is "sleepwalking," *per se,* a "grave motion"? (If the answer is yes, one must conclude that "grave motion" is wasted in redundancy. If the answer is no, he must decide how one description assists the other or contributes to the total effect of the poem.)

2. What is the modern meaning of "influence" (line 15)? What is its root meaning? Assume (what seems clear enough) that Rago meant both meanings to function at once. What does such a double-sense contribute to the poem's performance?

3. Take "slow gestures" to be a key phrase. How many of the words and phrases have overtones that relate to "slow gestures"?

Deciduous Branch

Stanley Kunitz

Winter, that coils in the thickets now,
Will glide from the fields; the swinging rain
Be knotted with flowers; on every bough
A bird will meditate again.

Lord in the night if I should die,
Who entertained your thrilling worm,
Corruption wastes more than the eye
Can pick from this imperfect form.

FROM *Selected Poems of Stanley Kunitz,* by permission of Little, Brown & Company. Copyright 1930, 1944, by Stanley Kunitz.

I lie awake hearing the drip
Upon my sill; thinking, the sun
Has not been promised; we who strip
Passion to seed shall be undone.

Now, while the antler of the eaves
Liquifies, drop by drop, I brood
On a Christian thing: unless the leaves
Perish, the tree is not renewed.

If all our perishable stuff
Be nourished to its rot, we clean
Our trunk of death, and in our tough
And final growth are evergreen.

QUESTIONS

1. In what way does winter "coil" in thickets? (The present editor be lieves that Kunitz means to release a picture of a coil of snow remaining in the shade of a thicket after the thaw has cleaned the unshaded fields. Such interpretation, however, is hardly final legislation.)

2. Note the major word-choices in stanza one: coil—glide—swinging —knotted—meditate. How does each function? Have they anything in common?

3. Why is the worm "thrilling" in line six? How is "antler of the eaves" to be taken? "Nourished to its rot" is a paradox: how does it function? How does the theme "winter thawing into spring" relate to the theme "corruption and renewal"?

Impromptu

Suggested by a view in 1766 of the seat and ruins of a deceased Nobleman at Kingsgate, Kent

Thomas Gray

Old and abandoned by each venal friend,
    Here Holland formed the pious resolution
To smuggle a few years, and strive to mend
    A broken character and constitution.

On this congenial spot he fix'd his choice;
    Earl Goodwin trembled for his neighbouring sand;
Here sea-gulls scream, and cormorants rejoice,
    And mariners, though shipwrecked, dread to land.

Holland: Lord Holland.

Here reign the blustering North and blighting East,
  No tree is heard to whisper, bird to sing;
Yet Nature could not furnish out the feast,
  Art he invokes new horrors still to bring.

Here mouldering fanes and battlements arise,
  Turrets and arches nodding to their fall,
Unpeopled monast'ries delude our eyes,
  And mimic desolation covers all.

"Ah!" said the sighing peer, "had Bute been true,
  Nor Mungo's, Rigby's, Bradshaw's friendship vain,
Far better scenes than these had blest our view,
  And realized the beauties which we feign:

Purged by the sword, and purified by fire,
  Then had we seen proud London's hated walls;
Owls would have hooted in St. Peter's choir,
  And foxes stunk and littered in St. Paul's.

QUESTIONS

Suppose the last line had read:
      And foxes slunk and whimpered in St. Paul's
   or
      And foxes lurked and flittered in St. Paul's.

Would either pair of verbs have suggested (a) as much *foxiness* as the original and (b) such utter desolation of all that London is?

Upon Julia's Clothes

Robert Herrick

Whenas in silks my Julia goes,

Then, then, methinks, how sweetly flows
      slip and rustle
The liquefaction of her clothes.
      soft cascading

Next when I cast mine eyes, and see
            disturbance
That brave vibration each way free,
      meander

O, how that glittering taketh me!

QUESTION

In what way do the alternate readings to either side of the original trouble the diction with unwelcome suggestions?

Simplex Munditiis
(In Simple Elegance)
Ben Jonson

Still to be neat, still to be dressed,
As you were going to a feast;
Still to be powdered, still perfumed:
Lady, it is to be presumed,
Though art's hid causes are not found,
All is not sweet, all is not sound.

Give me a look, give me a face,
   sweet innocence
That makes simplicity a grace;
   of naturalness

Robes loosely flowing, hair as free:

Such sweet neglect more taketh me
   counterfeits
Than all th' adulteries of art;
   appearances

They strike mine eyes, but not my heart.
  touch

QUESTION

In each case the original phrasing is that printed in the line itself. Compare the original with the alternate phrasings and attack or defend the original.

Elegy Written in a Country Churchyard
Thomas Gray

The curfew tolls the knell of parting day,
The lowing herd wind slowly o'er the lea,
The ploughman homeward plods his weary way,
And leaves the world to darkness and to me.

Now fades the glimmering landscape on the sight,
And all the air a solemn stillness holds,
Save where the beetle wheels his droning flight,
And drowsy tinklings lull the distant folds:

Save where from yonder ivy-mantled tower
The moping owl does to the moon complain
Of such as, wandering near her secret bower,
Molest her ancient solitary reign.

Beneath those rugged elms, that yew-tree's shade
Where heaves the turf in many a moldering heap,
Each in his narrow cell for ever laid,
The rude forefathers of the hamlet sleep.

The breezy call of incense-breathing morn,
The swallow twittering from the straw-built shed,
The cock's shrill clarion, or the echoing horn,
No more shall rouse them from their lowly bed.

For them no more the blazing hearth shall burn,
Or busy housewife ply her evening care:
No children run to lisp their sire's return,
Or climb his knees the envied kiss to share.

Oft did the harvest to their sickle yield,
Their furrow oft the stubborn glebe has broke;
How jocund did they drive their team afield!
How bowed the woods beneath their sturdy stroke!

Let not ambition mock their useful toil,
Their homely joys, and destiny obscure;
Nor grandeur hear with a disdainful smile
The short and simple annals of the poor.

The boast of heraldry, the pomp of power,
And all that beauty, all that wealth e'er gave
Awaits alike th' inevitable hour:—
The paths of glory lead but to the grave.

Nor you, ye proud, impute to these the fault,
If memory o'er their tomb no trophies raise,
Where through the long-drawn aisle and fretted vault
The pealing anthem swells the note of praise.

Can storied urn or animated bust
Back to its mansion call the fleeting breath?
Can honor's voice provoke the silent dust,
Or flattery soothe the dull, cold ear of death?

Perhaps in this neglected spot is laid
Some heart once pregnant with celestial fire,
Hands, that the rod of empire might have swayed,
Or waked to ecstasy the living lyre.

But knowledge to their eyes her ample page,
Rich with the spoils of time, did ne'er unroll;
Chill penury repressed their noble rage,
And froze the genial current of the soul.

Full many a gem of purest ray serene
The dark unfathomed caves of ocean bear:
Full many a flower is born to blush unseen,
And waste its sweetness on the desert air.

Some village-Hampden, that with dauntless breast
The little tyrant of his fields withstood;
Some mute inglorious Milton here may rest,
Some Cromwell, guiltless of his country's blood.

Th' applause of listening senates to command,
The threats of pain and ruin to despise,
To scatter plenty o'er a smiling land,
And read their history in a nation's eyes,

Their lot forbade: nor circumscribed alone
Their growing virtues, but their crimes confined;
Forbade to wade through slaughter to a throne,
And shut the gates of mercy on mankind;

The struggling pangs of conscious truth to hide,
To quench the blushes of ingenuous shame,
Or heap the shrine of luxury and pride
With incense kindled at the Muse's flame.

Far from the madding crowd's ignoble strife,
Their sober wishes never learned to stray;
Along the cool sequestered vale of life
They kept the noiseless tenor of their way.

Yet e'en these bones from insult to protect
Some frail memorial still erected nigh,
With uncouth rhymes and shapeless sculpture decked
Implores the passing tribute of a sigh.

Their name, their years, spelt by th' unlettered Muse,
The place of fame and elegy supply:
And many a holy text around she strews,
That teach the rustic moralist to die.

Hampden: soldier and statesman, a great leader in the English Civil War. **for thee:**
addressed to Richard West, a friend.

For who, to dumb forgetfulness a prey,
This pleasing anxious being e'er resigned,
Left the warm precincts of the cheerful day,
Nor cast one longing, lingering look behind?

On some fond breast the parting soul relies,
Some pious drops the closing eye requires;
E'en from the tomb the voice of Nature cries,
E'en in our ashes live their wonted fires.

For thee, who, mindful of th' unhonored dead,
Dost in these lines their artless tale relate;
If chance, by lonely contemplation led,
Some kindred spirit shall enquire thy fate,—

Haply some hoary-headed swain may say,
"Oft have we seen him at the peep of dawn
Brushing with hasty steps the dews away,
To meet the sun upon the upland lawn;

"There at the foot of yonder nodding beech
That wreathe its old fantastic roots so high,
His listless length at noon-tide would he stretch,
And pore upon the brook that babbles by.

"Hard by yon wood, now smiling as in scorn,
Muttering his wayward fancies he would rove;
Now drooping, woeful-wan, like one forlorn,
Or crazed with care, or crossed in hopeless love.

"One morn I missed him on the customed hill,
Along the heath, and near his favorite tree;
Another came; nor yet beside the rill,
Nor up the lawn, nor at the wood was he;

"The next, with dirges due in sad array
Slow through the church-way path we saw him borne—
Approach and read (for thou canst read) the lay
Graved on the stone beneath yon aged thorn."

THE EPITAPH

Here rests his head upon the lap of earth
A youth, to fortune and to fame unknown;
Fair science frowned not on his humble birth
And melancholy marked him for her own.

Large was his bounty, and his soul sincere;
Heaven did a recompense as largely send:
He gave to misery all he had, a tear;
He gained from heaven ('twas all he wished) a friend.

No farther seek his merits to disclose,
Or draw his frailties from their dread abode
(There they alike in trembling hope repose),
The bosom of his Father and his God.

Chapter Five

THE
SYMPATHETIC CONTRACT

Every poem makes some demand upon the reader's sympathies. In addressing his subject, the poet takes an attitude toward it and adopts a tone he believes to be appropriate. His sense of what is appropriate, either in tone or in attitude, is of course a question of values. As such, it is obviously basic to the effect of the poem upon the reader. The reader may be right or wrong in disagreeing with the poet's values, but once such disagreement has occurred, that poem has failed for that reader. It is a question, as Robert Frost once put it, of "the way the poet takes himself and the way the poet takes his subject."

That demand upon the reader's sympathies may be made implicitly or explicitly, but there can be no poem without some sort of sympathetic contract between poet and reader. If a poet writes, "O weep for me, for I am sick with love," he is clearly taking love as a matter of major consequence (so taking it, or pretending so to take it) and he is clearly taking himself (or pretending to) with a good round measure of self-pity. If the poem is to succeed with any given reader, that reader must be willing to sympathize with that attitude toward love and with that tone of self-pity.

But what of the reader who, far from being moved to weep, is inclined to think the poet silly and pretentious? For that reader at least, all is lost. It may be, of course, that "O weep for me" is simply a *convention*, which is to say, *a traditional form of poetic pretense.* In this case the "O weep for me" poet may be adopting the pastoral convention, common enough in English poetry, in which the poet pretends to the attitudes of an imaginary Greek shepherd. One must be careful to allow the poet his right to pretend an emotion for second purposes. Clearly, however, it can happen that a poet takes an attitude and strikes off on a tone with which the reader cannot sympathize.

Lewis Carroll's parodies of Southey (page 680) and of Watt (page 682) certainly began with Carroll's refusal to take seriously what these poets had asked him to take seriously. Carroll would have felt a fool had he allowed himself to agree with that request. Finding himself compelled to refuse it, he inevitably felt that the poets who made it were the fools, and pompous and hypocritical fools at that. Another reader might have stopped there, but happily Carroll was moved to deflate their pretentiousness. He did so by pretending to preserve the heavily moral tone and by pretending to take seriously the patly moral subject while rearranging the details of the subject into an obvious absurdity. Carroll clearly felt that he was dealing with bad poetry. It should be obvious, however, that there is nothing technically bad about either of the parodied poems: Carroll, in fact, preserves intact the technical standards of the poems he is lampooning.

The badness of bad poetry can always and only be located in the quality of the sympathetic contract. A bad poem is, finally, a failure of aesthetic character. True, a poem may strike the reader as technically inadequate to its own aims. Yet it is impossible to demonstrate with any final conviction that any poem is bad for specific technical reasons. "This poem," one says, "is bad because the rhymes are forced," and it is true that forced rhymes are one sign of bad poetic practice, but what is one to say then of such a poet as Ogden Nash who deliberately uses forced rhymes and to excellent effect? "Well, it is bad because it is cliché-studded," one says. But what of such a poem as Lawrence's 'Snake" (page 799) which falls into cliché after cliché and still remains memorable though flawed? "Well, then, it is bad because the images scatter all over the place and because the meter is uncertain." But what of John Donne's "Valediction Forbidding Mourning" (page 872) with its widely ranging images and with that typical metric that led Johnson to declare that Donne should have been hanged for "not keeping of accent"?

The fact is that no critic can find in any poem he means to condemn, a technical device he could not also find in a poem he would have to praise. Nor need that fact subvert all attention from technical detail. An obviously derivative, cliché-studded, rhyme-forced poem in which the poet mangles his metaphors *without seeming to know what he is doing* may still be flatly declared to be a bad poem. But to say *without seeming to know what he is doing* is at once to raise the question of tone and attitude. To handle technical elements ineptly is to take an incompetent attitude toward the poem: the serious poet will have studied his form harder and will have learned to master his techniques.

It is still true, however, that the badness of bad poetry cannot conclusively be shown to exist in the technical handling alone. And there are, moreover, any number of technically flawless poems that are certainly bad.

Invictus

William Ernest Henley

Out of the night that covers me,
    Black as the pit from pole to pole,
I thank whatever gods may be
    For my unconquerable soul.

In the fell clutch of circumstance
    I have not winced nor cried aloud.

Under the blugeoning of Chance
My head is bloody but unbowed.

Beyond this place of wrath and tears
Looms but the Horror of the shade,
And yet the menace of the years
Finds, and shall find, me unafraid.

It matters not how strait the gate,
How charged with punishment the scroll.
I am the master of my fate;
I am the captain of my soul.

"Invictus" (*i.e.,* "Unconquered") is perhaps the most widely known bad poem in English, and certainly there is no trace in it of a technical flaw on which its badness could be blamed. Nor is the poem bad because of its subject matter. Hardy and Housman, among others, have written many poems that take as bleakly pessimistic an attitude toward life as does "Invictus." The success of many such poems is sufficient evidence that English and American readers can enter into a sympathetic contract to consider the world as some sort of unhappy pit. It is not in the way Henley takes his subject, but in the way he takes himself that the reader parts company with the poet. To take the world as one's subject and to take the attitude that it is nothing but a place of suffering is one thing; but to react by taking onself with such chest-thumping heroics, is very much another. One feels that Henley is not really reacting from his own profoundest depths but that he is making some sort of over-dramatic speech about pessimism. There is a failure of character in the tone he has assumed. The poet has presented himself as unflinchingly valiant. The reader cannot help but find him merely inflated and self-dramatizing.

Inevitably, therefore, the reader finds that he does not believe what the poet is saying. The reader tends to frown upon the poet, moreover, for pinning too many medals for moral valor on his own chest. Were the reader in charge of the presentation ceremony, the chances are that Henley would not emerge with quite so many citations for nobility of purpose. The poem has generated distrust and a touch of scorn, whereas it clearly intended to persuade the reader of the validity of Henley's moral pose. The reader must feel that there is something wrong with the values of a man who cannot distinguish between the truly persuasive and the merely mock-heroic.

Thus, instead of being moved by the poem, one simply refuses to believe it. Does Henley honestly believe such a phrase as "this place of wrath and tears"? Isn't he, rather, being merely self-indulgent? One shrugs and turns the page, and there he finds this poem, by the same author and written within a year of "Invictus":

To A. D.

The nightingale has a lyre of gold,
　The lark's is a clarion call;
And the blackbird plays but a boxwood flute,
　But I love him best of all.

For his song is all of the joy of life,
　And we in the mad, spring weather,
We two have listened till he sang
　Our hearts and lips together.

Despite the great, roaring rhetoric of "Invictus" there is after all, just as one suspected, something more than "wrath and tears" in "this place." The poet does, of course, have every right to change his attitude and his tone from poem to poem. But "Invictus" has given itself to absolute statements, and does one have the right to change his absolutes that readily? One ends by confirming what he had suspected from the first: that what "Invictus" offered as absolutes were not absolutes at all.

Interestingly, one is less inclined to call "To A. D." a bad poem, though it is technically inferior to "Invictus." Note that the grammar of the first two lines of "To A. D." has run away from Henley and has left him speaking of the "lark's lyre" having a "clarion [trumpet] call." To be sure, there is a sense in which "clarion" may be taken to mean "loud and shrill" and possibly there may be such a thing as a "loud, shrill lyre," but certainly "clarion" cannot help but suggest "trumpet" as its first meaning, and how can one permit a poet the idea of a lyre-with-a-trumpet-call? "To A. D." is a flawed poem, therefore, but it remains a happily—turned little poem. It does not, at least, call Henley's character into doubt.

But what is a reader doing when he asks this sort of question of the poem? Must one conclude, for example, that one must be a Roman Catholic in order to read Dante with pleasure? Or that he must agree with Milton's theology in order to read Milton's poetry? Not at all. One must pause to recognize that subject and attitude are not the same thing. Attitude is the way one takes the subject, not the subject itself. The stature of such a poet as Dante, for example, is set in part by the fact that though he saw his subject as profoundly a matter of Roman Catholic doctrine, one may yet find his attitude and his tone valid in terms very different from those of Roman Catholicism. Dante took the state of the souls in Hell as examples of sin. A psychologist has only to receive the same details of the state of the damned as examples of behavioral flaws: Dante's tone and attitude remain equally apt to either interpretation. Whatever differences one may feel between himself and the poet in matters of detail, a good poem leaves us no quarrel with its sympathetic contract.

But assuming that the reader does refuse the sympathetic contract: is he within his rights in attacking the author's character? Let the question be asked in other terms: assume that Shakespeare had introduced into some play two characters, one of whom spoke the lines of "Invictus" and one of whom spoke the lines of "To A. D." Can one doubt that Shakespeare would have intended the first as a ridiculous figure? in somewhat the same way perhaps that Polonius is presented as a ridiculously pompous figure? (And what then, by the way, of the aesthetic situation of those very earnest student orators who annually declaim, as if it were high moral perception, Polonius's advice to Laertes—that passage ending "This above all to thine own self be true, etc."—a passage Shakespeare certainly intended to document the narrowness and sententiousness of Polonius's character?)

The reader has every bit as much right to judge the character the poet invents for his poems as Shakespeare had to judge the characters he invented for his plays. For the character is, in fact, invented. The declaimer on the cosmic soap box of "Invictus" is no more William Ernest Henley than is the sweetly nostalgic lover with the slightly confused grammar: each poem is founded upon a role Henley tried on for himself. Every poem, that is to say, by its choice of tone and attitude is a mask the poet assumes. In one mask he may present himself as heroic. In another as flightily gay. In another as philosophically detached, or as wistful, or as torn-two-ways.

But whatever the mask, the poet must make the role resound winningly within the reader. Poetry is not an ornamental exercise. It is man's best means of perceiving most profoundly the action and the consequence of his own emotions. Every poem addresses in some way, however slight, the question: "What is a man?" The reader tries on the mask through which the poet addresses that question and wills himself vicariously into the role the poet is playing; but he must then feel that the role is well and meaningfully played, and he must resist any effort by the poet to win him to shoddy emotions. Such identification is the essence of the sympathetic contract. The poem asks the reader to "be someone," but it must be someone the reader can reach to by an ideal extension of his own sympathies. "Yes," he must conclude, "on these premises I can accept this way of taking the subject and myself as meaningful."

When, on the other hand, the poet becomes untrustworthy within his mask (and let "mask" be taken to mean "the total complex of tone and attitude"), then the reader has no choice but to look down on the poet.

Thus the badness of a bad poem must always be located in the fact that it misplaces its human sympathies; or in the case of gross technical incompetence, in the fact that the poet has not given enough devoted attention to the demands of his own form, a failure that is in itself a failure of character.

But if tone and attitude are the one certain location of poetic badness, they are also the everlasting charm of poetry's variety and richness. Whatever the subject, one can never exhaust its poetry because there is never an end to the ways in which a poet can take that subject, and to the ways in which he can take himself in speaking of it.

QUESTIONS

The poems that follow are all, in one way or another, about love. Read each poem with special attention to the way the poet takes his subject (attitude) and the way he takes himself (tone). Try to state as accurately as possible the quality of each poem's tone and attitude. The following question should be asked of each poem:

1. Are the tone and attitude describable in the same terms, or does the poet take his subject more or less seriously than he takes himself?

2. Are the tone and attitude exactly what they profess to be or are they pretended for some second purpose?

3. Are the tone and attitude constant or does one or the other, or both, change in the course of the poem?

4. Are the tone and attitude single or does the author feel more than one way at the same time (ambivalence) about his subject and his relation to it?

5. What is the sympathetic contract? (*I.e.*, what does the poet ask the reader to agree with emotionally? to disagree with? which of his own details is the poet "for"? which, if any, is he "against"?) How willing should a good reader be to extend the sympathies the poet asks for? (The same question may be put as follows: To what extent should a good reader be willing to be "for" what the poet is "for" and "against" what the poet is "against"?)

NOTE. Many poems that appear elsewhere in this volume are about love and may well be compared with those that immediately follow.

Poems for Study

The Good-Morrow

John Donne

I wonder by my troth, what thou, and I
Did, till we lov'd? were we not wean'd till then?
But suck'd on countrey pleasures, childishly?
Or snorted we in the seaven sleepers den?
T'was so; But this, all pleasures fancies bee.
If ever any beauty I did see,
Which I desir'd, and got, t'was but a dreame of thee.

And now good morrow to our waking soules,
Which watch not one another out of feare;
For love, all love of other sights controules,
And makes one little roome, an every where.
Let sea-discoverers to new worlds have gone,
Let Maps to other, worlds on worlds have showne,
Let us possesse one world, each hath one, and is one.

My face in thine eye, thine in mine appeares,
And true plaine hearts doe in the faces rest,
Where can we finde two better hemispheares
Without sharpe North, without declining West?
What ever dyes, was not mixt equally;
If our two loves be one, or, thou and I
Love so alike, that none doe slacken, none can die.

Song

John Donne

Goe, and catche a falling starre,
   Get with child a mandrake roote,
Tell me, where all past yeares are,
   Or who cleft the Divels foot,
Teach me to heare Mermaides singing,
   Or to keep off envies stinging,
        And finde
        What winde
Serves to advance an honest minde.

If thou beest borne to strange sights,
   Things invisible to see,
Ride ten thousand daies and nights,
   Till age snow white haires on thee;
Thou, when thou retorn'st wilt tell mee
All strange wonders that befell thee,
        And sweare
        No where
Lives a woman true, and faire.

If thou findst one, let mee know,
   Such a Pilgrimage were sweet;
Yet doe not, I would not goe,
   Though at next doore wee might meet,
Though shee were true, when you met her,
And last, till you write your letter,
        Yet shee
        Will bee
False, ere I come, to two, or three.

When He Who Adores Thee

Thomas Moore

When he who adores thee has left but the name
    Of his fault and his sorrows behind,
Oh! say wilt thou weep, when they darken the fame
    Of a life that for thee was resign'd?
Yes, weep, and however my foes may condemn,
    Thy tears shall efface their decree;
For Heaven can witness, though guilty to them,
    I have been but too faithful to thee.

With thee were the dreams of my earliest love;
    Every thought of my reason was thine;
In my last humble prayer to the Spirit above,
    Thy name shall be mingled with mine.
Oh! blest are the lovers and friends who shall live
    The days of thy glory to see;
But the next dearest blessing that Heaven can give
    Is the pride of thus dying for thee.

The Time I've Lost in Wooing

Thomas Moore

The time I've lost in wooing,
In watching and pursuing
    The light that lies
    In woman's eyes,
Has been my heart's undoing.
Though Wisdom oft has sought me,
I scorn'd the lore she brought me,
    My only books
    Were woman's looks,
And folly's all they've taught me.

Her smile when Beauty granted,
I hung with gaze enchanted,
    Like him, the Sprite,
    Whom maids by night
Oft meet in glen that's haunted.
Like him, too, Beauty won me,
But while her eyes were on me:
    If once their ray
    Was turn'd away,
Oh, winds could not outrun me.

And are those follies going?
And is my proud heart growing
    Too cold or too wise
    For brilliant eyes
Again to set it glowing?
No, vain, alas! th' endeavor
From bonds so sweet to sever;
    Poor Wisdom's chance
    Against a glance
Is now as weak as ever.

Bright Be the Place of Thy Soul!

Lord Byron

Bright be the place of thy soul!
    No lovelier spirit than thine
E'er burst from its mortal control,
    In the orbs of the blessed to shine.

On earth thou wert all but divine,
    As thy soul shall immortally be;
And our sorrow may cease to repine
    When we know that thy God is with thee.

Light be the turf of thy tomb!
    May its verdure like emeralds be!
There should not be the shadow of gloom
    In aught that reminds us of thee.

Young flowers and an evergreen tree
    May spring from the spot of thy rest:
But nor cypress nor yew let us see;
    For why should we mourn for the blest?

When We Two Parted

Lord Byron

When we two parted
    In silence and tears,
Half broken-hearted
    To sever for years,
Pale grew thy cheek and cold,
    Colder thy kiss;
Truly that hour foretold
    Sorrow to this.

The dew of the morning
    Sunk chill on my brow—
It felt like the warning
    Of what I feel now.
Thy vows are all broken,
    And light is thy fame:
I hear thy name spoken,
    And share in its shame.

They name thee before me,
    A knell to mine ear;
A shudder comes o'er me—
    Why wert thou so dear?
They know not I knew thee,
    Who knew thee too well:—
Long, long shall I rue thee,
    Too deeply to tell.

In secret we met—
    In silence I grieve,
That thy heart could forget,
    Thy spirit deceive.
If I should meet thee
    After long years,
How should I greet thee?—
    With silence and tears.

She Walks in Beauty

Lord Byron

She walks in beauty, like the night
    Of cloudless climes and starry skies;
And all that's best of dark and bright
    Meet in her aspect and her eyes:
Thus mellow'd to that tender light
    Which heaven to gaudy day denies.

One shade the more, one ray the less,
    Had half impaired the nameless grace
Which waves in every raven tress,
    Or softly lightens o'er her face;
Where thoughts serenely sweet express
    How pure, how dear their dwelling-place.

And on that cheek, and o'er that brow,
So soft, so calm, yet eloquent,

The smiles that win, the tints that glow,
    But tell of days in goodness spent,
A mind at peace with all below,
    A heart whose love is innocent!

So, We'll Go No More A-Roving

Lord Byron

So, we'll go no more a-roving
    So late into the night,
Though the heart be still as loving,
    And the moon be still as bright.

For the sword outwears its sheath,
    And the soul outwears the breast,
And the heart must pause to breathe,
    And love itself have rest.

Though the night was made for loving,
    And the day returns too soon,
Yet we'll go no more a-roving
    By the light of the moon.

The Indian Serenade

Percy Bysshe Shelley

I arise from dreams of thee
    In the first sweet sleep of night,
When the winds are breathing low,
    And the stars are shining bright:
I arise from dreams of thee,
    And a spirit in my feet
Hath led me—who knows how?
    To thy chamber window, sweet!

The wandering airs, they faint
    On the dark, the silent stream;
The champak odors fail
    Like sweet thoughts in a dream;
The nightingale's complaint
    It dies upon her heart,
As I must die on thine,
    Oh, belovèd as thou art!

Oh, lift me from the grass!
  I die! I faint! I fail!
Let thy love in kisses rain
  On my lips and eyelids pale.
My cheek is cold and white, alas!
  My heart beats loud and fast;—
Oh! press it close to thine again,
  Where it will break at last.

Love's Philosophy

Percy Bysshe Shelley

The fountains mingle with the river
  And the rivers with the ocean;
The winds of heaven mix forever
  With a sweet emotion;
Nothing in the world is single;
  All things by a law divine
In one spirit meet and mingle.
  Why not I with thine?

See the mountains kiss high heaven,
  And the waves clasp one another;
No sister-flower would be forgiven
  If it disdained its brother;
And the sunlight clasps the earth,
  And the moonbeams kiss the sea:
What are all these kissings worth
  If thou kiss not me?

Rondeau

Leigh Hunt

Jenny kissed me when we met,
  Jumping from the chair she sat in;
Time, you thief, who love to get
  Sweets into your list, put that in:
Say I'm weary, say I'm sad,
  Say that health and wealth have missed me,
Say I'm growing old, but add,
  Jenny kissed me.

Rose Aylmer

Walter Savage Landor

Ah, what avails the sceptred race,
  Ah, what the form divine!
What every virtue, every grace!
  Rose Aylmer, all were thine.
Rose Aylmer, whom these wakeful eyes
  May weep, but never see,
A night of memories and of sighs
  I consecrate to thee.

Lady, Was It Fair of Thee

Thomas Lovell Beddoes

Lady, was it fair of thee
To seem so passing fair to me?
  Not every star to every eye
    Is fair; and why
Art thou another's share?
  Did thine eyes shed brighter glances,
Thine unkissed bosom heave more fair,
    To his than to my fancies?
      But I'll forgive thee still;
      Thou'rt fair without thy will.
      So be: but never know,
      That 'tis the hue of woe.

Lady, was it fair of thee
To be so gentle still to me?
  Not every lip to every eye
    Should let smiles fly.
Why didst thou never frown,
  To frighten from my pillow
Love's head, round which Hope wove a crown,
    And saw not 'twas of willow?
      But I'll forgive thee still,
      Thou knew'st not smiles could kill.
      Smile on: but never know,
      I die, nor of what woe.

Song

Thomas Hood

O lady, leave thy silken thread
And flowery tapestrie,
There's living roses on the bush,
And blossoms on the tree;
Stoop where thou wilt, thy careless hand
Some random bud will meet;
Thou canst not tread but thou wilt find
The daisy at thy feet.

'Tis like the birthday of the world,
When earth was born in bloom;
The light is made of many dyes,
The air is all perfume;
There's crimson buds, and white and blue—
The very rainbow show'rs
Have turn'd to blossoms where they fell,
And sown the earth with flow'rs.

There's fairy tulips in the East,
The garden of the sun;
The very streams reflect the hues,
And blossom as they run:
While morn opes like a crimson rose,
Still wet with pearly showers;
Then, lady, leave the silken thread
Thou twinest into flow'rs!

The Parting

Michael Drayton

Since there's no help, come let us kiss and part—
Nay, I have done, you get no more of me;
And I am glad, yea, glad with all my heart,
That thus so cleanly I myself can free.
Shake hands for ever, cancel all our vows,
And when we meet at any time again,
Be it not seen in either of our brows
That we one jot of former love retain.
Now at the last gasp of Love's latest breath,
When, his pulse failing, Passion speechless lies,

When Faith is kneeling by his bed of death,
And Innocence is closing up his eyes,
   —Now if thou wouldst, when all have given him over,
From death to life thou might'st him yet recover.

Beauty Clear and Fair

John Fletcher

Beauty clear and fair,
   Where the air
Rather like a perfume dwells;
   Where the violet and the rose
   Their blue veins and blush disclose,
And come to honour nothing else:

   Where to live near
   And planted there
Is to live, and still live new;
   Where to gain a favour is
   More than light, perpetual bliss—
Make me live by serving you!

Dear, again back recall
   To this light,
A stranger to himself and all!
   Both the wonder and the story
   Shall be yours, and eke the glory;
I am your servant, and your thrall.

To Electra

Robert Herrick

I dare not ask a kiss,
   I dare not beg a smile,
Lest having that, or this,
   I might grow proud the while.

No, no, the utmost share
   Of my desire shall be
Only to kiss that air
   That lately kissèd thee.

The Unfading Beauty

Thomas Carew

He that loves a rosy cheek,
   Or a coral lip admires,
Or from star-like eyes doth seek
   Fuel to maintain his fires:
As old Time makes these decay,
So his flames must waste away.

But a smooth and steadfast mind,
   Gentle thoughts and calm desires,
Hearts with equal love combined,
   Kindle never-dying fires.
Where these are not, I despise
Lovely cheeks or lips or eyes.

A Devout Lover

Thomas Randolph

I have a mistress, for perfections rare
In every eye, but in my thoughts most fair.
Like tapers on the altar shine her eyes;
Her breath is the perfume of sacrifice;
And wheresoe'er my fancy would begin,
Still her perfection lets religion in.
We sit and talk, and kiss away the hours
As chastely as the morning dews kiss flowers:
I touch her, like my beads, with devout care,
And come unto my courtship as my prayer.

To Amarantha, that She Would Dishevel Her Hair

Richard Lovelace

Amarantha sweet and fair,
Ah, braid no more that shining hair!
As my curious hand or eye
Hovering round thee, let it fly!

Let it fly as unconfined
As its calm ravisher, the wind,
Who hath left his darling, th' East,
To wanton o'er that spicy nest.

Every tress must be confest,
But neatly tangled at the best;
Like a clew of golden thread
Most excellently ravellèd.

Do not then wind up that light
In ribbands, and o'ercloud in night,
Like the Sun in's early ray;
But shake your head, and scatter day!

Ah, How Sweet It Is to Love!

John Dryden

Ah, how sweet it is to love!
  Ah, how gay is young Desire!
And what pleasing pains we prove
  When we first approach Love's fire!
Pains of love be sweeter far
Than all other pleasures are.

Sighs which are from lovers blown
  Do but gently heave the heart:
Ev'n the tears they shed alone
  Cure, like trickling balm, their smart:
Lovers, when they lose their breath,
Bleed away in easy death.

Love and Time with reverence use,
  Treat them like a parting friend;
Nor the golden gifts refuse
  Which in youth sincere they send:
For each year their price is more,
And they less simple than before.

Love, like spring-tides full and high,
  Swells in every youthful vein;
But each tide does less supply,
  Till they quite shrink in again:
If a flow in age appear,
'Tis but rain and runs not clear.

O That 'Twere Possible

Alfred, Lord Tennyson

O that 'twere possible
After long grief and pain
To find the arms of my true love
Round me once again! . . .

A shadow flits before me,
Not thou, but like to thee:
Ah, Christ, that it were possible
For one short hour to see
The souls we loved, that they might tell us
What and where they be!

You'll Love Me Yet

Robert Browning

You'll love me yet!—and I can tarry
   Your love's protracted growing:
June rear'd that bunch of flowers you carry,
   From seeds of April sowing.

I plant a heartful now: some seed
   At least is sure to strike,
And yield—what you'll not pluck indeed,
   Not love, but, may be, like.

You'll look at least on love's remains,
   A grave's one violet:
Your look?—that pays a thousand pains.
   What's death? You'll love me yet!

Chapter Six

THE IMAGE
AND THE POEM

"Man," said the critic Kenneth Burke, "is the symbol using animal." He might as well have said "Man is the metaphoric animal," for symbolism is simply a special case of metaphor. Carried a step further, the statement might have been, "Thoughts are made of pictures."

For though there seems to be a general illusion that man "thinks in words," it should be obvious that "thoughts" go through our minds much more rapidly than we can phrase them. Many a writer has filled pages in trying to verbalize what went through his mind in a split second of heightened perception, a span of time in which he could not possibly have "thought" that many words.

One may readily experiment for himself. He has only to pause, make an effort to clear his mind, and then "think" some such central experience as "Home for Christmas." Instantly many "thoughts" flash through one's mind. And clearly those thoughts are not words but "pictures" (and recollections of other sensory impressions such as sounds, smells, tastes). The "thought" in such a case is in fact many fragments of such images. Our consciousness may perhaps be best visualized as a kind of movie-strip photo-montage, a sequence of many simultaneous impressions, mostly visual.

When the poet comes to verbalize that consciousness (as distinct from his original experience of it) he tends inevitably to metaphor. That is to say, he offers pictures to represent thoughts. When Archibald MacLeish writes in "Ars Poetica" (p. 909)

> For all the history of grief
> An empty doorway and a maple leaf

the concept "all the history of grief" is made equal to the picture "an empty doorway and a maple leaf."

The fact that such a "picture" can be offered as the equivalent of so large a concept is fundamental not only to the poetic method but to all thought. The fact that such a picture is conceptual rather than actually drawn can only serve to underline the power of such pictorial suggestion. It would seem to be impossible for man to think in any depth were he not able to "see pictures" in his mind's eye. The very words of human languages are images at root, and all written languages seem to have evolved from some form of drawing.

A process so fundamental to human thinking could provide material for endless analysis but the present discussion of imagery can be relatively brief. It can be so because the earlier discussion of symbolism has already introduced one special case of imagery. And it can be so even more because the basically pictorial nature of language makes it possible for much of what has been said about the words of poetry to be applied without significant change to the discussion of imagery.

Like words, images possess both denotation and connotation: they denote certain sensory (usually visual) identifications and they connote an emotional aura. Like words, therefore, images in a poem tend to fall into overtone themes united by either their denotations or their connotations. Thus, all images related to the sea may be taken as denotatively united, whereas all images suggesting a given emotional quality (as for example the harshness of such a chain of images as "rasp, thong, gnarled granite, clawing winds") may be taken to be connotatively united.

Like words, too, images have histories. Images lacking the philological histories of words whereby submerged former meanings can be played against more recently evolved meanings, as for example a poet may speak of "the aberration of the sea" and mean to imply to the sea both the evolved meaning of "derangement" (the sea as a madness of nature) and the root meaning of *ab* plus *errare*, "to wander away from," as the sea wanders off into distance. But though images lack this quality of words, they are like words in that they can become so possessed by the way they have been used in the past that they become stereotyped and degenerate into forceless clichés. Images, moreover, can become stereotyped quite apart from the way in which they are phrased.

The image of the "lance of Achilles" is an excellent example of how a fresh image can become dead. Achilles inherited from his father a lance that possessed magic qualities. A touch of its sharp end never failed to wound and a touch of the other end never failed to heal. Early in the thirteenth century an Italian poet writing a sonnet of courtly love to his lady came on an inspired moment and compared her eyes to the lance of Achilles: with one sharp look she never failed to wound, and with one soft look she never failed to heal.

The comparison was marvelously right for the mood of the courtly sonnet. It was learned, it was gallant, it was touched with the romantic suggestion of the golden past, and it implied that the lady possessed magical (hence more than earthly) powers: an extremely apt extravagance. It was so apt, in fact, that it was doomed. Before long, every eligible grocer's daughter in Italy had become the subject of a sonnet in which her eyes were compared to Achilles' lance. Or if not her eyes, then her lips (wounding with a frown, healing with a smile), or her tongue (wounding with a sharp word, healing with a soft one). Inevitably, the image lost all force, however elegantly it may have been re-phrased. The first lady to be offered so gracious a comparison might well have been moved by it. The thousandth had every reason to feel that she was being offered shopworn daisies.

The reader, too, must be courted, and the good reader will be more demanding than the lady of the sonnets. He is ever-willing to receive a true poetic effect into his feelings, but he must resist cheapening his feelings. He cannot allow himself to be moved by lifeless imitation, just as Shakespeare refused, in Sonnet CXXX to cheapen his feelings by "false compare."

But though words and images have so much in common, there are a number of important ways in which images must be discussed in their own terms. Whether stereotyped or not, the image of Achilles' lance works exactly as does MacLeish's "empty doorway and a maple leaf." Both speak of one thing in terms of another.

But are they both, then, symbols? The distinction between a symbol and a metaphor can not be rigidly drawn, but a symbol tends to stand for a more formal and more expansive area of meaning or of experience (the image of ripples on a pool again) whereas a metaphor tends to be more specific and rather more sensory than conceptual. What is basic to both is *the metaphoric sense*.

Nothing is more characteristic of poetry than this metaphoric sense. When the poet says, "Gather ye rosebuds while ye may," he is not telling the reader to go into the garden to cut roses. And when the poet says, "Make hay while the sun shines," he is not issuing a directive to get the hay in before it rains. Nor do the two statements mean the same thing. True, they have something in common. Both could be categorized as examples of the idea "Seize the day for it is fleeting." But to assume that because the two statements could be placed in the same category, they therefore are "the same thing" is to ignore all the connotative differences between the romantic delicacy of "rosebuds" and the more walloping lustiness of "make hay." The fact is that a man "making hay" is involved in a psychic state vastly different from that of a man "gathering rosebuds."

Literal-minded readers, the Gradgrinds of the world, are forever in difficulty with the metaphoric sense of poetic language. They want to know "what the poem is *about*," and they resist the essential duplicity whereby the poem is never entirely about what it *seems* to be about. Rupert Brooke's "Heaven" (page 877), for example purports to be about fish and is, of course, a satire on certain religious attitudes. Richard Moore's "A Deep Discussion" (page 878), purports to be an argument between a sperm whale and a squid, but is actually a presentation of certain attitudes toward life. One must note, however, that both Brooke and Moore are doubly engaged: both are concerned for the second meanings of their poems, and both are obviously relishing the fun of playing with their purported meanings. As one might expect of poetry, more than one thing is happening at once, and the good reader must be prepared to respond at all levels simultaneously.

The essential doubleness of what is happening in these two poems involves the nature of *the metaphoric contract.*

All metaphor is basically a way of speaking of the unknown in terms of the known. The metaphoric formula may thus be stated:

$$X \text{ (unknown)} = Y \text{ (known)}$$

"My luve is like a red red rose," says Burns. The reader knows what a red red rose is, but he does not know what "my luve" is in Burns' way of thinking. By applying his known feelings for "red red rose" to his unformed sense of "my luve," however, the reader finds a sense of how Burns feels about his love.

Rarely, however, is X truly equal to Y in any literal sense. If one says, "Richard's eyes are like Peter's," then the unknown (Richard's eyes) may reasonably be taken as exactly equal to the known (Peter's eyes), but such a pure case rarely occurs in poetry. Even in responding richly to Burns' line, one knows very well that "my luve" is substantially unlike a "red red rose." One hopes, for example, that her complexion is not entirely that vivid, that her body is not green and thorny, and that she is not wholly vegetable. The point of similarity, that is to say, is nowhere in the denotation, and in fact must work *in spite of* the denotation. A semantically accurate statement of the case might be: "The connotations released by the concept 'red red rose' may be taken as equivalent to those released by the concept 'my luve.'" The metaphoric formula may better be stated, therefore, as "X does and does not equal Y." The poet, nevertheless, brushes aside such clinical considerations and goes joyously about making metaphors *as if* X did in fact equal Y. His contract is simple: if the reader will bring a fluent and a supple mind to play upon the Y of the metaphor, the poet will engage to give him an experience of the X.

But he will also undertake to give him an experience of the pleasurable interplay of X upon Y. So for both Rupert Brooke and Richard Moore. They are concerned for both X and Y, and they are further concerned for the happy duplicity of playing one against the other.

For the poet must engage himself to both sides of the metaphor at once. Having undertaken to speak of religion in terms of fish, or of certain attitudes in terms of whale and squid, everything he then says must be as true of his X as it is of his Y. If one begins to speak, for example, of "the ship of state," everything he says must be *equally applicable* to both a ship and the state. He may speak of the captain, of the voyage, of the wheelhouse, and depending upon his manipulation, the reader will understand these images as metaphorically apt to a discussion of the state (though they are, of course, clichés by now). But let one begin by speaking of "the ship of state" and of "the captain" and then refer to "the house of representatives," and all is lost. There has occurred a breach of metaphoric contract. It is as if an actor had undertaken to play the role of, let us say, Hamlet; had found himself incapable of projecting the role; and had stepped out of character to *tell* the audience what his acting was intended to be about. In any theatre seriously taken, such an action can call for nothing but tomatoes.

A related violation is the *mixed metaphor*, the situation in which the writer does not abandon metaphor but slides unwittingly from one metaphor to another. "We must put our noses to the grindstone and lift our eyes to the great vision of tomorrow if we truly mean to escape from the quicksands of confusion." There is always likely to be an element of the grotesque in such admixture. And as in all matters of poetry, mixed metaphor can be used for special effects. Any such instance of a special effect does not, however, cancel the force of the metaphoric contract. Rather, the special effect is possible only because it is a violation of a contract that is in force.

Grammatically, "metaphor" signifies an indirect, and "simile" a direct comparison. Thus to say "Richard has a heart like a lion's" is a simile, and to say "Richard the lion-hearted" is a metaphor. The distinction between such direct and indirect comparison has little meaningful application to poetic practice, and since "metaphor" can readily be made into an adjective, whereas "simile" would require the awkward adjectival form "similitudinous," the terms "metaphor" and "metaphoric" serve for all figurative comparisons in poetry.

"Imagery," however, is a wider term than "metaphor." Imagery is best defined as "the total sensory suggestion of poetry." Most of that sensory suggestion is, of course, visual, but metaphoric language can as readily suggest sound, as in Keats' "The silver snarling trumpets 'gan to chide"; or tactile sensation, as in MacLeish's "Dumb / As old medallions to the thumb"; or taste, as in Coleridge's "For she on honey dew has fed/ And drunk the milk of Paradise"; or even interior bodily sensation as in Emily Dickinson's "Without a tighter breathing,/ And Zero at the Bone."

Clearly, however, some of the sensory suggestion of poetry is involved in metaphoric comparisons, and some is not. Simple statements of fact, and even the simple names of things, convey sensory suggestion. One very definite sort of effect can be achieved in poetry by the device called the catalogue which consists simply of a list of names of things, or of sensory impressions, though in practice the catalogue tends to become a mixture of both names and metaphors. Walt Whitman has used the catalogue more extensively than any poet writing in English. The following passage from "Song of Myself" will illustrate both the basic quality of the catalogue as a simple listing of things, and the tendency for some metaphoric comparison to become involved in the list. As a first exercise, one might do well to underline every element in the catalogue that is simply the name of a thing, and to circle every element that involves some sort of metaphoric comparison.

Song of Myself (26)

Walt Whitman

Now I will do nothing but listen,
To accrue what I hear into this song, to let sounds contribute toward it.

I hear the bravuras of birds, bustle of growing wheat, gossip of flames,
    clack of sticks cooking my meals,
I hear the sound I love, the sound of the human voice,
I hear all sounds running together, combined, fused or following,
Sounds of the city and sounds out of the city, sounds of the day and night,
Talkative young ones to those that like them, the loud laugh of work-
    people at their meals,
The angry bass of disjointed friendship, the faint tones of the sick,
The judge with hands tight to the desk, his pallid lips pronouncing a
    death-sentence,
The heave'e'yo of stevedores unlading ships by the wharves, the refrain of
    the anchor-lifters,
The ring of alarm-bells, the cry of fire, the whirr of swift-streaking engines
    and hose-carts with premonitory tinkles and color'd lights,
The steam-whistle, the solid roll of the train of approaching cars,
The slow march play'd at the head of the association marching two and
    two,
(They go to guard some corpse, the flag-tops are draped with black
    muslin.)

I hear the violincello, ('tis the young man's heart's complaint,)
I hear the key'd cornet, it glides quickly through my ears,
It shakes mad-sweet pangs through my belly and breast.

I hear the chorus, it is a grand opera,
Ah this indeed is music—this suits me.

A tenor large and fresh as the creation fills me,
The orbic flex of his mouth is pouring and filling me full.

I hear the train'd soprano (what work with hers is this?)
The orchestra whirls me wider than Uranus flies,
It wrenches such ardors from me I did not know I possessed them,
It sails me, I dab with bare feet, they are licked by the indolent waves,
I am cut by bitter and angry hail, I lose my breath,
Steep'd amid honey'd morphine, my windpipe throttled in fakes of death,
At length let up again to feel the puzzle of puzzles,
And that we call Being.

For purposes of more convenient discussion, therefore, one may dis-
tinguish between *metaphors* and *properties* as the two sorts of imagery.

The term *property* is used in the same sense one has in mind when speaking of a theatrical prop-room.

Whitman fathered a large pretense that his catalogues were all-inclusive, that every sort of detail was equally welcome to his mind. Obviously, however, certain kinds of images were more welcome to his sensibilities than were others. Whitman tended to welcome without reserve, all images of industrial expansion, of fruitful nature, of the brotherhood of man, of astronomy, of the bustle of urban life, and of physical strength, for example, but one will not find anywhere in his catalogues such Satanic images as one may find in Poe or in Baudelaire. One has only to turn to "Prufrock" (page 757) or to "Dirge" (page 917) to see two catalogues of properties that would never occur in Whitman, despite his pretense to all-inclusiveness.

There is, that is to say, some *principle of selection* at work. One can see certain kinds of images that occurred readily to Whitman's mind and were welcomed into his poems. And one can locate other sorts of images that not only were pushed away from the poems, but that probably never occurred to the poet's mind.

It follows that a simple tabulation of the kind of image that appears in a man's poetry is one index to his mind. The contents of a prop-room can suggest, to some extent at least, what sort of play is being produced. The contents of the poetic catalogue can tell one much more accurately the nature of the poet's mind.

In a sense, moreover, the collected works of any poet are always a catalogue of a sort. There is a kind of image that is natural to one poet and not to another. The frequency with which certain kinds of images occur will say a great deal about the poet. Were one to compile a list of the most common images of such a poet as John Donne, for example, he would end with a listing that would certainly include the following:

> knots
> anchors
> royal crowns
> the king's face
> coins
> the king's image on a coin
> candles in darkness

There is no present need to make such a list complete. It is enough to note that this sort of image seems to occur frequently in Donne's poetry. Its very frequency would suggest that it answers the need of something the poet feels and is attempting to express. All these images, moreover, have a common quality: all of them are images that concentrate power in a small space. The knot is the point that concentrates the whole power of the rope. The anchor is the point that concentrates all those forces that keep a ship fast. The royal crown is the symbol of the total power of the sovereign, as is his face, and his image on a coin. The coin is a concentrated image of all wealth. The candle in darkness is the focus of all vision.

One might go through John Donne's poetry and find many more examples of this sort of imagery. Scattered as it is denotatively, all of it has a connotative area in common. And the consistency of that connotation will serve immediately to identify one of the psychic forces of John Donne's vision. He was a man who strained all of his life to concentrate emotional forces, to reach one intense experience that would summarize all of his life's meaning.

Imagery can, therefore, be taken as a language of its own, and one way to establish a first communication with a poet can be reduced to the mechanical exercise of tabulating the images a poet uses in a representative number of poems, noting the frequency with which each image occurs, the area of experience from which the image is drawn (as, for example, war, sports, nature, law), the denotation, the connotation, and whether the image is used metaphorically or as a property.

Some critics have made very elaborate tabulations of this sort, with even more elaborate cross-references. Needless to say the over-elaboration of any mechanical method of analysis, when applied to poetry, can very soon run into the law of diminishing returns. Any careful reader, on the other hand, will come to recognize at least those images a given poet tends to use most frequently.

The fact seems to be that in locating the image-making quality of a given poet, one comes close to identifying the center of his character as a poet. Even a relatively simple tabulation may provide clues to a true insight. If, for example, one does no more than to note that in a thousand lines of Poet A, flower images occur twenty-two times but that the flowers are seldom (except for, say, roses and daisies) given their particular names, whereas in a thousand lines of Poet B, flower images occur one hundred thirty-two times and almost invariably with such specific names as orchis, hyacinth, anemone, sweet william, arrowroot, and so on—if one notes no more than that, he will already have a reasonable measure of the importance of actual contact with nature in Poet A and Poet B. Clearly, whatever these two poets may profess of interest in nature, B is the one who has gone more observantly and more often into the fields and woods.

A simple way of making such tabulations is to comb through a representative number of lines by a given poet and to jot each image on a filing card, adding notes at one's own pleasure on the denotation, connotation, area of experience, and whether the image is used metaphorically or as a property. Such cards may then be sorted into many different categories. If for example "flowers" seems a natural category for the given poet, then the image "daisy" would be so classified. It may be, however, that as one sorts the filing cards, a more basic category for this poet seems to be "whiteness." In that case, daisy might be classified with snow, swans, albino rabbits, and cumulus clouds. Or it may well be that both "flowers" and "whiteness" are basic to that poet's mind and that "daisy" must be entered in both categories.

The point is that such categories cannot be set in advance. Each poet must suggest his own natural groupings to each reader. It is most precisely in finding those categories that seem most native to the imagery of a given poet that one comes closest to locating the emotional center of his poetic character. The mechanical business of jotting images on filing cards is simply a way of directing one's attention to the possible categories suggested by a given poet. The business must not become an end in itself, for poetry will not yield to such book-keeper analysis. Undertaken simply as an exercise in increasing one's perception of a single (and very central) quality of the poetry, however, such detailed image-analysis can prepare one to encounter the poet's work more meaningfully.

A more direct, and perhaps more rewarding, way of analyzing imagery is to take careful note of the overtone themes of the images within a single poem, in exactly the same way one may note the overtone themes of the diction of the poem.

When the images of a given poem, or of a given passage, are related by their denotations, that poem or that passage is said to be constructed on a *dominant image.* When the images are related by their connotations but range widely in their denotations, that poem or passage is said to make use of *scattered imagery.* John Donne's "Valediction Forbidding Mourning" may be taken as one of the great masterpieces of imagery in English poetry. Its first six stanzas are constructed on scattered images, its last three stanzas develop one of the most memorable dominant metaphors to be found in English literature.

A word on the situation of the poem will make it more meaningful to the reader not well acquainted with Donne's other poems. John Donne wrote the "Valediction Forbidding Mourning" as a farewell to his wife on the occasion of embarking for a diplomatic mission to France. He tells her not to mourn because mourning would belittle their love. Donne believed fervently in the union of souls in true love. Thus, since their souls remain united no matter what distance separates their bodies, true lovers suffer no real absence.

A Valediction Forbidding Mourning

John Donne

As virtuous men pass mildly away
  And whisper to their souls to go,
Whilst some of their sad friends do say,
  "The breath goes now," and some say, "No:"

So let us melt, and make no noise,
  No tear-floods, nor sigh-tempests move;

'Twere profanation of our joys
　To tell the laity our love.

Moving of th'earth brings harms and fears;
　Men reckon what it did, and meant.
But trepidation of the spheres,
　Though greater far, is innocent.

Dull sublunary lovers' love—
　Whose soul is sense—cannot admit
Absence, because it doth remove
　Those things which elemented it.

But we by a love so much refined
　That ourselves know not what it is,
Inter-assured of the mind,
　Care less eyes, lips, and hands to miss.

Our two souls, therefore, which are one,
　Though I must go, endure not yet
A breach, but an expansion,
　Like gold to airy thinness beat.

If they be two, they are two so
　As stiff twin compasses are two;
Thy soul, the fixed foot, makes no show
To move, but doth, if th'other do.

And though it in the center sit,
　Yet, when the other far doth roam,
It leans and harkens after it,
　And grows erect, as that comes home.

Such wilt thou be to me, who must,
　Like th'other foot, obliquely run;
Thy firmness makes my circle just,
　And makes me end where I begun.

moving of the earth: earth quake. **trepidation of the spheres:** the vibration of the spheres as conceived in the Ptolemaic system. It is the vibration of the spheres that produces Heavenly harmony. Thus, though the motion of the Heavenly spheres (here equated to the love of true lovers) is vastly greater than that of an earthquake (here equated to the sensuality of merely physical lovers) the higher motion produces no bad consequences. **sublunary:** below the circle of the moon, *i.e.*, on earth, *i.e.*, earthbound. **elemented it:** made up its elements, *i.e.*, those simply physical elements of which such love consists.

The denotations of the images in the first six stanzas scatter over many areas. The poet summons to his image-structure (1) the deathbed of a virtuous man, (2) the physical phenomena of melting, making noise, floods, and tempests, (3) church hierarchy, (4) earthquake and the vibration of the Ptolemaic spheres, (5) the process of refining what one suspects to be gold, and (6) the process of beating gold into gold leaf. The poet's mind seems to have reached in all directions and to have ranged widely in the search for images that will give force to the experience of the poem.

One is well justified, therefore, in waiving denotation as the unifying principle of selection here, and in concluding that Donne was willing to accept any illustration that carried the emotional connotation he sought. The kind of human behaviour that produces a poem, however, is seldom quite that simple. A closer student of Donne could argue with true point and insight, that all these images are from areas of learning that would naturally attract a speculative intellect of Donne's time. The deathbed of a virtuous man is an image suggesting many speculations on the meaning of life and of its relation to the idea of a hereafter. Physical phenomena of every sort suggest speculations into the nature of the world. The comparison between earthquake and the vibration of the Ptolemaic spheres suggests speculations into the nature of the universe. The processes of gold refining and gold-beating suggest speculations into the nature of man's technological grip upon the planet. These are all in some sense *metaphysical* concerns, and it is for this quality of his work that Donne is referred to as a "metaphysical poet."

But though one may be tempted to argue that the images of the first six stanzas are united by their metaphysical denotation, one has only to compare them to the single sustained comparison of the last three stanzas to see that they are indeed organized on a different principle. However widely their denotations range, all of these scattered images are connotatively associated in two overtone themes that might, for convenience, be labeled the *true-love* and the *merely-physical-love* themes. Throughout, the poet is clearly in favor of one set of his images, and clearly opposed to another. Those themes may be tabulated thus:

images of true love (approved)	images of merely physical love (disapproved)
virtuous men	
pass mildly away (having no fear)	
the undemonstrative nature of the passing from one state to the other	
melt (imperceptible change)	noise (violent change)
	tear-floods (violence)
	sigh-tempests (violence)
our joys (high)	profanation (low)
our love (high)	laity (low)

trepidation of the spheres (high and serene)	earthquake (low and violent)
refined love (high, serene)	dull sublunary lovers (low, coarse)
expansion (imperceptible change; high, as gold is a symbol of merit; serene)	breach (violent change, low, coarse as opposed to "airy thinness")
airy thinness (high, serene)	

One may see at once, even from so crude a list of jottings, that a development like that of theme and counter-theme in music is taking place. The images are entering the poem not only for their own sakes but in response to the images that have preceded them, both those images whose overtones they reinforce, and those whose overtones they oppose. Such imagery, as noted, is "scattered" only in the sense that its denotations range widely. Its connotations are intricately and meaningfully related.

In the last three stanzas, on the other hand, the single image of a compass is sustained and developed in great detail, and every detail is directly related to the way in which a compass draws a circle. The pleasure of such imagery arises not from the way the connotations are musically united into themes, but in the inventiveness and the aptness with which the poet works his image structure for more and more points of fitting comparison. One ends by feeling that the possibilities of the image have been wholly evoked. Certainly, too, one must note that the circle has long been a metaphysical symbol of unity and perfection. That perfect rounding serves to close the metaphysical implications of the whole poem in exactly the way a tonic chord rounds out and resolves a piece of music.

Poems for Study—Metaphor and Statement

Departmental

Robert Frost

An ant on the table cloth
Ran into a dormant moth
Of many times his size.
He showed not the least surprise.

His business wasn't with such.
He gave it scarcely a touch,
And was off on his duty run.
Yet if he encountered one
Of the hive's enquiry squad
Whose work is to find out God
And the nature of time and space,
He would put him onto the case.
Ants are a curious race;
One crossing with hurried tread
The body of one of their dead
Isn't given a moment's arrest—
Seems not even impressed.
But he no doubt reports to any
With whom he crosses antennae,
And they no doubt report
To the higher up at court.
Then word goes forth in Formic:
"Death's come to Jerry McCormic,
Our selfless forager Jerry.
Will the special Janizary
Whose office it is to bury
The dead of the commissary
Go bring him home to his people.
Lay him in state on a sepal.
Wrap him for shroud in a petal.
Embalm him with ichor of nettle.
This is the word of your Queen."
And presently on the scene
Appears a solemn mortician;
And taking formal position
With feelers calmly atwiddle,
Seizes the dead by the middle,
And heaving him high in air,
Carries him out of there.
No one stands round to stare.
It is nobody else's affair.

It couldn't be called ungentle.
But how thoroughly departmental.

QUESTIONS

1. Check the exact meaning of *Formic, Janizary, ichor, nettle,* and *sepal.*
2. Frost has written what purports to be a ritual of the society of ants.
That ritual seems clearly enough aimed at dramatizing the ant conception
of the relation of the individual to society. How does Frost feel about the
ants for being so "thoroughly departmental"? By human standards what is
lacking from a "thoroughly departmental" society?

3. If ant-society is the Metaphoric *X*, what is the metaphoric *Y*? (Do not be in a hurry to make *Y* equal one thing only.)

4. At what points does Frost seem to be having most fun in playing *X* against *Y*?

5. As a matter of the metaphoric contract, is the *hive's* enquiry squad (line 9) defensible? Do ants live in hives? Or should the phrase have been "the *hill's* enquiry squad"?

Heaven

Rupert Brooke

Fish (fly-replete, in depth of June
Dawdling away their wat'ry noon)
Ponder deep wisdom, dark or clear,
Each secret fishy hope or fear.
Fish say, they have their Stream and Pond;
But is there anything Beyond?
This life cannot be All, they swear,
For how unpleasant, if it were!
One may not doubt that, somehow, good
Shall come of Water and of Mud;
And, sure, the reverent eye must see
A Purpose in Liquidity.
We darkly know, by Faith we cry,
The future is not Wholly Dry.
Mud unto Mud!—Death eddies near—
Not here the appointed End, not here!
But somewhere, beyond Space and Time,
Is wetter water, slimier slime!
And there (they trust) there swimmeth One
Who swam ere rivers were begun,
Immense, of fishy form and mind,
Squamous, omnipotent and kind;
And under that Almighty Fin
The littlest fish may enter in.
Oh! never fly conceals a hook,
Fish say, in the Eternal Brook,
But more than mundane weeds are there,
And mud, celestially fair;
Fat caterpillars drift around,
And Paradisal grubs are found;
Unfading moths, immortal flies,
And the worm that never dies.
And in that Heaven of all their wish,
There shall be no more land, say fish.

QUESTIONS

1. Check the exact meaning of *squamous.*

2. As already noted, this poem purports to be about fish but is obviously enough about certain religious attitudes. In conceiving God and Heaven in their own image, the fish are illustrating the concept of religious anthropomorphism. Anthropomorphism is that concept which attributes human forms and desires to God. One critic has gone so far as to attack this poem as sacrilegious. What in the poem might have moved him to that opinion?

3. The *X* and the *Y* of Brooke's metaphor are clear enough but one should not fail to note that Brooke is obviously enjoying the process of working out his idea in "fishy" terms. Does Brooke persuade the reader that these are indeed the terms in which a reflective fish might conceive heaven? Does he violate his metaphor at any point by introducing "thoughts" that are inappropriate to a fish?

4. What is the effect of describing the rewards of faith in terms of "slimier slime," "Paradisal grubs," and "fat caterpillars"?

A Deep Discussion

Richard Moore

"That's a detestable thing you did!"
Said Mr. Sperm to Mr. Squid.

Said Mr. Squid to Mr. Sperm,
"It's done to save the epiderm."

Said Sperm, "Only a squid could think
Of squirting enemies with ink.
It's clear you literary sort
Have no respect for decent sport,
Producing fogs to hide beneath,
Fighting with glands instead of teeth.
I'm sure it makes you gay and proud
To make great whales address a cloud . . .
But think what fellowship you've missed
By being so obscurantist
And hiding in that murky stuff.
Come now, you've dallied long enough.
Come out of there . . . and don't delay . . .
Hunger disturbs me much today."

Said Squid, "Your appetite's to blame.
I shall return from where I came
Because you came to where I went.

REPRINTED by permission of *The Saturday Review* and of the author.

Can't you find tastier nourishment?
Go look for flounders, sharks, or smelts;
Go and be hungry somewhere else.
What's to be seen to be eaten here?"

Said Sperm, "You, when this water's clear.
I'll wait until your ink is thinner,
And then I'll have you for my dinner;
For you're a most unsocial kind
To stay down here so hard to find.
It irks us how you hide away
In sullen depths from light of day,
Heedless how other fishes swim,
Wandering where it's cold and dim.
No wonder squids are so resented,
When they're so obviously demented!"

"Hear what this lump-of-action hollers,"
Said Squid, "at dedicated scholars:
As if he'd no respect concerning
The civilized pursuits of Learning."

Said Sperm, "I was a student once . . ."

Said Squid, "You must have been a dunce."

Said the whale in rage, "I *led* my school!
But Learning's nothing but a tool,
And by itself stale tommyrot
That, once it's learned, is best forgot.
That fish is capable, I've found,
Who's seen the world and been around.
The Whale, who travels, is at ease
In tropical or polar seas.
When he intrepidly explores
Splendors of tropic island shores
Or tours with icebergs at the poles,
You squids hide in your murky holes.
You lack ambition such as mine
Because you're born without a spine."

"Perhaps," said Squid, "you may recall:
Most creatures are not born at all,
But come to life by various means.
I find it strange these splendid scenes
You have observed while traveling
Should fail to teach this simple thing."

"Teach?" cried Sperm, "Inky, spineless creatures!
Do-nothing squids! Let *them* be teachers!
Worthwhile experience has shown
There's nothing like a spine of bone."

"Nor like a skull," said Squid, "that's bony.
What's *in* the skull of such a phony?
Stupidity, whose sole defense
Is superficial arrogance.
Lost at my depths, you'll soon declare
It's masterful to rise for air.
Snails are more capable, that creep."

"Than whales," cried Sperm, "ruling the Deep?"

Said Squid, "You were not here, you know,
Scarcely a billion years ago:
The age when reptiles swam the ocean."

Said Sperm, "What a preposterous notion."

"Dear me," said Squid, "Not in the least.
The greatest gluttons at *this* feast
The soonest grow sick, bloat, and crawl
With slow convulsions to the wall.
Then their companions in the cup
As fossil trophies hang them up:
We are surrounded by these dead
(Daily one meets some bony head)
All stuffed! . . . How stupidly they stare
At stuffers in the glutton's chair!
The lowly scavenge as before.
Thus do I swim the ocean floor,
Ignoring savage insolence
Of those seeking preeminence,
Flashing their teeth, stuffing their cheeks:
Hubris it's called, among the Greeks.
I shun the harsh dichotomies
That splash and roil these endless seas:
Endless debates that but reveal
Which side shall be the other's meal.
In unsearched caverns of the sea
I seek a lost reality:
The secret that enables one
To feed on brilliance of the sun,
The mystic counterpoise that knits
Together clashing opposites,
The tertiary entity

That, century after century,
Endures you plunderers and mocks."
Said Sperm, "I'm from my school's hard knocks.
The thing you think so wonderful
Is nothing but a vegetable.
If once you'd leave your dismal murks,
You'd see how the world actually works."

The Squid resumed, not having heard,
"The Ancients gave this thing a word:
Called it, I think, the *Tertium Quid*—
But I am but an humble squid. . . .
Whales, I suspect, are seldom humble."

Sperm snorted and began to rumble,
"O I admire your wisdom greatly,
But I suspect you've eaten lately:
This is your after-dinner mood
In which you float, digest, and brood.
Your aim is obvious, I think:
Now that you've squirted all your ink,
You squirt your talk, and hide behind
Delusions of your murky mind.
There's only *one* reality:
All creatures who'd succeed at sea
Must murder for their daily meal.
What else can all your thoughts reveal?
Enough of this, you flabby one,
You'll never feed upon the sun,
For I propose to feed on you."

"That's an uncivil thing to do,"
Said Squid, "Do reconsider . . . wait!
You say I'm flabby—evil fate!
Flabby you say? I'm old and stale."

He spoke and dodged the lumbering whale.

Sperm cried, elated, "Happy fate
That I'm a spiney vertebrate!
Surely it's plain that no one trammels
Prerogatives of mighty mammals
And obvious that every squid
Should do as greater creatures bid.
So reconcile yourself to fate
And be like other squids I ate.
But stop this talk—bores me to death—
Stop it at once—I'm out of breath."

Squid cried, "You're out . . .? You're out of . . .? **Out**
With you, blundering, blubbered lout!
With all your brags and bluff commands!
I'll crack your spine with my ten hands,
I'll catch you in my clutching snare,
I'll snag you from your vital air,
I'll clasp you till you gasp and choke,
Grow bilious, or have a stroke,
Or anything you Rulers do
When your ruled ocean smothers you."

Sperm churned the depths with his angry tail
And cried, "You brother to the snail!
Flimsy and fat, soft as a worm.
Obviously made to feed the Sperm.
I tell you it's cruel, ugh! most unfair
To mock at me, gasping for air.
Ha! Dodged again! O whale of trouble!
I must . . . the surface . . . blow a bubble!"

And, having missed his entree there,
Sperm rose to gulp desserts of air.

QUESTIONS

1. Moore writes of a sperm whale and a squid (the metaphoric *X*) as if they were human beings (the metaphoric *Y*). To reinforce that second sense he even calls them *Mr.* Sperm and *Mr.* Squid. In how many ways can the *Y* be interpreted?

2. How many of Mr. Squid's characteristics flow from the fact that he is associated with ink? How many of Mr. Sperm's from the fact that he roams the whole world over? At what points does Moore seem to be having the most fun in elaborating the play of *X* against *Y*?

3. In the passage beginning " 'Dear me,' said Squid" Moore has the Squid speak of "the glutton's chair." Would a squid know anything about chairs? Might it have been more appropriate for the squid to have said "the glutton's lair"? Does "chair" violate the metaphoric contract (the pretence of putting every statement into "squiddic" without the interjection of "humanese")? Are there any points in the poem, here or elsewhere, at which human rather than squid-like terms seem to be forced upon Mr. Squid?

Ode on the Death of a Favorite Cat, Drowned in a Tub of Gold Fishes

Thomas Gray

'Twas on a lofty vase's side,
Where China's gayest art had dy'd
   The azure flowers, that blow;
Demurest of the tabby kind,
The pensive Selima reclin'd,
   Gazed on the lake below.

Her conscious tail her joy declar'd;
The fair round face, the snowy beard,
   The velvet of her paws,
Her coat, that with the tortoise vies,
Her ears of jet, and emerald eyes,
   She saw; and purr'd applause.

Still had she gaz'd; but 'midst the tide
Two angel forms were seen to glide,
   The Genii of the stream:
Their scaly armour's Tyrian hue
Thro' richest purple to the view
   Betray'd a golden gleam.

The hapless Nymph with wonder saw:
A whisker first and then a claw,
   With many an ardent wish,
She stretch'd in vain to reach the prize,
What female heart can gold despise?
   What Cat's averse to fish?

Presumptuous Maid! with looks intent
Again she stretch'd, again she bent,
   Nor knew the gulf between.
(Malignant Fate sat by, and smil'd)
The slipp'ry verge her feet beguil'd.
   She tumbled headlong in.

Eight times emerging from the flood
She mew'd to ev'ry watry God,
   Some speedy aid to send.
No Dolphin came, no Nereid stirr'd:
Nor cruel *Tom*, nor *Susan* heard.
   A Fav'rite has no friend!

From hence, ye Beauties, undeceiv'd,
Know, one false step is ne'er retriev'd,
   And be with caution bold.
Not all that tempts your wand'ring eyes
And heedless hearts, is lawful prize;
   Nor all, that glistens, gold.

QUESTIONS

1. Check the exact meaning of *Genii, Tyrian, Nymph,* and *Nereid.* What tone do such words set for the poem?

2. Identify the metaphoric *X* and *Y*.

3. Selima, the cat, reclined and looked into the "lake" below. Why does Gray call the goldfish bowl a "lake"?

4. What is the force (in stanza four) of placing as equal statements: "What female heart can gold despise?" and "What Cat's averse to fish?"

5. How many of the metaphoric implications of the poem flow from the "goldness" of the goldfish? What metaphoric points, that is, would have been lost, or would at least have been much harder to make, had the bowl contained black tropical fish? What was the cat's folly? If that folly is the metaphoric *X*, what is the metaphoric *Y*?

6. Note that Gray abandons his metaphoric pretense from time to time to interject a non-metaphoric statement, and that he adds a final injunction that might be thought of as altogether (though actually not quite) abandoning the metaphor. Frost, Brooke, and Moore were much more insistent on keeping their poems entirely within the metaphoric pretense. What is the difference in effect of these two methods?

To a Fair Lady Playing with a Snake

Edmund Waller

Strange that such Horror and such Grace
Should dwell together in one place,
A Fury's Arm, an Angel's Face.

'Tis innocence and youth which makes
In *Chloris's* fancy such mistakes,
To start at Love, and play with Snakes.

By this and by her coldness barr'd,
Her servants have a task too hard,
The Tyrant has a double guard.

Thrice happy Snake, that in her sleeve
May boldly creep, we dare not give
Our thoughts so unconfin'd a leave:

Contented in that nest of Snow
He lies, as he his bliss did know,
And to the wood no more would go.

Take heed, (fair *Eve*) you do not make
Another Tempter of this Snake,
A marble one so warm'd would speak.

QUESTIONS

1. Waller purports to describe a strange incident he has observed. Does he in all ways intend the incident to be taken as a strange one, or might he intend that, in one sense at least, all "Fair Lady's" play with some sort of metaphoric snake?

2. What differences of interpretation might have been stressed had the poem been titled "The Fall of Man"? Or "Beauty and the Beast"? Or " 'Twas Ever Thus"?

3. Note the proportion of metaphors to statements.

It is relatively rare for poems to sustain their metaphoric pretense as faithfully as do "Departmental," "Heaven," and "A Deep Discussion." Poems of the order of these three may be thought of as *parables* and in them the author's intent is clearly to state his poem *entirely within the metaphor*. The more usual tendency, as demonstrated by Waller's poem, is to allow a certain amount of plain (single) statement into the metaphoric (double) statement.

At the other extreme there are some poems and even some poets who make practically no use of metaphor. The following poem consists of thirty-two lines and only two of the statements that occur in it contain metaphoric elements. Mark them in the course of the reading.

A Satirical Elegy on the Death of a Late Famous General

Jonathan Swift

His Grace! impossible! what dead!
Of old age too, and in his bed!
And could that Mighty Warrior fall?
And so inglorious, after all!
Well, since he's gone, no matter how,
The last loud trump must wake him now:
And, trust me, as the noise grows stronger,
He'd wish to sleep a little longer.
And could he be indeed so old
As by the news-papers we're told?

Threescore, I think, is pretty high;
'Twas time in conscience he should die.
This world he cumber'd long enough;
He burnt his candle to the snuff;
And that's the reason some folks think,
He left behind *so great a s...k.*
Behold his funeral appears,
Nor widow's sighs, nor orphan's tears,
Wont at such times each heart to pierce,
Attend the progress of his herse.
But what of that, his friends may say,
He had those honours in his day.
True to his profit and his pride,
He made them weep before he dy'd.

Come hither, all ye empty things,
Ye bubbles rais'd by breath of Kings;
Who float upon the tide of state,
Come hither, and behold your fate.
Let pride be taught by this rebuke,
How very mean a thing's a Duke;
From all his ill-got honours flung,
Turn'd to that dirt from whence he sprung.

QUESTIONS

What differences of effect may be located between Swift's "Satirical Elegy" and Frost's "Departmental"? Both poems are clearly enough satirical. Frost keeps his satire interesting by a careful elaboration of metaphor. How does Swift keep his satire interesting? What does he use in place of metaphor? At what points in the poem does he seem to be having the most fun?

The Latest Decalogue

Arthur Hugh Clough

Thou shalt have one God only; who
Would be at the expense of two?
No graven images may be
Worshipped, except the currency.
Swear not at all; for, for thy curse
Thine enemy is none the worse.
At church on Sunday to attend
Will serve to keep the world thy friend.
Honor thy parents; that is, all
From whom advancement may befall.
Thou shalt not kill; but need'st not strive
Officiously to keep alive.

Do not adultery commit;
Advantage rarely comes of it.
Thou shalt not steal; an empty feat,
When it's so lucrative to cheat.
Bear not false witness; let the lie
Have time on its own wings to fly.
Thou shalt not covet, but tradition
Approves all forms of competition.

QUESTIONS

1. Clough has written a clear enough poem but there are, unfortunately, American readers who will miss some of the turns of his language. "who/ Would be at the expense of two?": who would put himself to the expense of supporting two Gods. "but need'st not strive/ Officiously to keep alive": Though we are forbidden to kill a man we certainly are not required to take on the burden of helping him to stay alive.

2. There is only one metaphor in this poem. Locate it.

3. What is the structure of each of the ten couplets? One must note at once that each statement is divided into two parts. What is there in the working out of that pattern of statement that can serve to take the place of metaphor?

Three Poems from the Japanese

Yamabe No Akahito

Translated by Kenneth Rexroth

I

I passed by the beach
At Tago and saw
The snow falling, pure white,
High on the peak of Fuji.

II

The mists rise over
The still pools at Asuka.
Memory does not
Pass away so easily.

III

I wish I were close
To you as the wet skirt of
A salt girl to her body.
I think of you always.

FROM *100 Poems from the Japanese,* by Kenneth Rexroth. All Rights Reserved. Reprinted by permission of New Directions.

Compare the method and the effect of these poems to the following translations from the Chinese.

Written on the Wall at Chang's Hermitage

Tu Fu

Translated by Kenneth Rexroth

It is Spring in the mountains.
I come alone seeking you.
The sound of chopping wood echoes
Between the silent peaks.
The streams are still icy.
There is snow on the trail.
At sunset I reach your grove
In the stony mountain pass.
You want nothing, although at night
You can see the aura of gold
And silver ore all around you.
You have learned to be gentle
As the mountain deer you have tamed.
The way back forgotten, hidden
Away, I become like you,
An empty boat, floating, adrift.

QUESTIONS

The last two lines of this poem obviously contain a metaphor. Is there a metaphor contained in the statement:

> although at night
> You can see the aura of gold
> And silver ore all around you?

Does the poet seem to intend the reader to take "the aura of gold and silver ore" literally? as perhaps a quality of the moonlight? as perhaps a spiritual quality?

FROM *100 Poems from the Chinese,* by Kenneth Rexroth. All Rights Reserved. Reprinted by permission of New Directions.

A Friend Advises Me to Stop Drinking

Mei Yao Ch'en

Translated by Kenneth Rexroth

In my young days I drank a
Lot of wine. There is nothing
Wrong with the love of drink. Now
I am old and my teeth and
Hairs are few and far between.
I still love to drink, but I
Can't do it as I used to.
Now when I drink it upsets
My stomach. There is not much
Pleasure in it. Today I
Got drunk and could not hold up
My head. The room turned round and round.
Seeking pleasure, I find only
Sickness. This is certainly
Not the way to care for my health.
Maybe I should give it up
Altogether. I am afraid
People will laugh at me. Still,
You say it would be a good
Idea. There is not much pleasure
In a sour stomach and
Bad breath. I really know that I
Ought to stop it. If I don't do it,
I don't know what will happen to me.

QUESTIONS

Is there anything in the tone and attitude of this poem that seems well
suited to the sparse and entirely unmetaphoric quality of the language?
In one sense, that is to say, metaphor is decorative. What is there about
this sort of statement that is best served by removing all decoration?

FROM *100 Poems from the Chinese*, by Kenneth Rexroth. All Rights Reserved. Reprinted by permission of New Directions.

To a Traveler

Su Tung P'o
Translated by Kenneth Rexroth

Last year when I accompanied you
As far as the Yang Chou Gate,
The snow was flying, like white willow cotton.
This year, Spring has come again,
And the willow cotton is like snow.
But you have not come back.
Alone before the open window,
I raise my wine cup to the shining moon.
The wind, moist with evening dew,
Blows the gauze curtains.
Maybe Chang-O the moon goddess,
Will pity this single swallow
And join us together with the chord of light
That reaches beneath the painted eaves of your home.

QUESTIONS

1. Will pity this single swallow: In Chinese convention, joined swallows, flying with one wing in common, are a symbol of steadfast love.

2. What is the significance of the fact that the language becomes metaphoric when the poet is most thinking of the past, and that metaphor disappears when he is most thinking of the present?

from A Bestiary

Kenneth Rexroth

DEER

Deer are gentle and graceful
And they have beautiful eyes.
They hurt no one but themselves,
The males, and only for love.
Men have invented several
Thousand ways of killing them.

HERRING

The herring is prolific.
There are plenty of herrings.
Some herrings are eaten raw.

FROM *100 Poems from the Chinese,* by Kenneth Rexroth. All Rights Reserved. Reprinted by permission of New Directions.

FROM *In Defense of the Earth,* by Kenneth Rexroth. Copyright 1956 by New Directions.

Many are dried and pickled.
But most are used for manure.
See if you can apply this
To your history lessons.

LION

The lion is called the king
Of beasts. Nowadays there are
Almost as many lions
In cages as out of them.
If offered a crown, refuse.

YOU

Let Y stand for you who says,
"Very clever, but surely
These were not written for you
Children?" Let Y stand for yes.

QUESTIONS

1. Rexroth's method in his "Bestiary" is obviously influenced by his interest in Japanese and Chinese poetry. Does it seem apt to say that Rexroth makes the dramatic (and often ironic) juxtaposition of statements serve as a substitute for metaphor?

2. The LION contains no phrase that may be identified as a metaphor, yet it is clearly possible to argue that the whole poem is a single metaphor. Discuss. (What, for example, would the effect have been if the last line had read: "If offered a crown, do not be like the lion, but refuse it or you, too, may end up in a cage"?)

Rexroth is not by any means the only English poet to have been powerfully influenced by Chinese and Japanese poetry. The poetic movement that began just before World War I and which was labeled Imagism, was deeply indebted to the Japanese and Chinese poets. The work of Amy Lowell, of H.D., and of John Gould Fletcher is characteristic of this movement, as is some of the work of Ezra Pound and of William Carlos Williams. The two following poems by Williams will illustrate.

The Red Wheelbarrow

William Carlos Williams

so much depends
upon

a red wheel
barrow

glazed with rain
water

beside the white
chickens.

QUESTION

Is "glazed" a metaphor?

This is Just to Say

William Carlos Williams

I have eaten
the plums
that were in
the icebox

and which
you were probably
saving
for breakfast

Forgive me
they were delicious
so sweet
and so cold.

The Chinese and Japanese are not the only sources for this sort of poetry. Stephen Crane, an American poet who died in 1900, had developed a similar sort of poem on his own impulse, and certainly was a native influence upon the imagists and on the kind of sparse unmetaphoric poem that developed in part from Imagism.

I Saw a Man

Stephen Crane

I saw a man pursuing the horizon;
Round and round they sped.
I was disturbed at this;
I accosted the man.
"It is futile," I said,
"You can never—"
"You lie," he cried.
And ran on.

The Book of Wisdom

Stephen Crane

I met a seer.
He held a book in his hands,
The book of wisdom.
"Sir," I addressed him,
"Let me read."
"Child—" he began.
"Sir," I said,
"Think not that I am a child,
For already I know much
Of that which you hold;
Aye, much."

He smiled.
Then he opened the book
And held it before me.
Strange that I should have grown
     so suddenly blind.

The Heart

Stephen Crane

In the desert
I saw a creature, naked, bestial,
Who, squatting upon the ground,
Held his heart in his hands,
And ate of it.
I said, "Is it good, friend?"
"It is bitter—bitter," he answered;
"But I like it
Because it is bitter,
And because it is my heart."

QUESTIONS

1. Has Crane allowed any metaphors into these poems?

2. Is it possible to think of each poem as itself constituting a dramatic metaphor? *I.e.,* Is the man pursuing the horizon, to be taken literally or does the whole incident "stand for" something else? If each of these meetings is taken as a metaphoric *X*, what might be the metaphoric *Y*? Is the metaphoric *Y* specific or is it better taken as standing for a whole area of experience? May one, that is to say, take each of these meetings—metaphorically sparse as they are in the way they are stated—as symbols?

3. See page 866. There an effort was made to distinguish between metaphor and symbol. Both involve a metaphoric X which stands for a metaphoric Y. If each of these poems by Crane is taken to be a symbol, what qualities of the symbolic X and symbolic Y do they suggest as distinct from the metaphoric X and metaphoric Y?

4. Apply the same criteria to the Japanese and Chinese poems.

5. Compare the qualities of Crane's poems as symbols with the qualities of the two metaphors that occur in Swift's "Satirical Elegy."

All the following poems are mixtures of *metaphor* and *statement*. Metaphor is of course the language of double meaning, it speaks of X in terms of Y. Statement, on the other hand, is single; it speaks of X as X. In each of the poems below underline every statement and bracket every metaphor. The following questions may then be asked of each poem:

1. How much statement does each poet employ as compared to how much metaphor?

2. A good paragraph tends to have a topic assertion followed by evidence or analysis in support of that assertion, or it tends to present a chain of evidence or analysis which is then summarized in a generalizing statement. In certain kinds of more sophisticated writing those opening assertions or closing summaries are omitted, or not so much omitted as left implicit. In all good writing there still tends to be present a relation of assertion (or summary) to evidence.

In each of these poems, does the poet tend to make his assertions or summaries as statements which are supported by metaphors, or does he make his assertions or summaries as metaphors which are supported by statements?

3. Does the change from statement to metaphor or from metaphor to statement bear any relation to changes in the poet's tone or attitude?

4. Distinguish, wherever possible, between symbols and metaphors.

The World is Too Much With Us; Late and Soon

William Wordsworth

The world is too much with us; late and soon
Getting and spending, we lay waste our powers:
Little we see in Nature that is ours;
We have given our hearts away, a sordid boon!
The Sea that bares her bosom to the moon;
The winds that will be howling at all hours,
And are up-gathered now like sleeping flowers;
For this, for everything, we are out of tune;
It moves us not.—Great God! I'd rather be
A Pagan suckled in a creed outworn;
So might I, standing on this pleasant lea,

Have glimpses that would make me less forlorn;
Have sight of Proteus rising from the sea;
Or hear old Triton blow his wreathèd horn.

QUESTIONS

"The Sea that bares her bosom to the moon" may, on one level, be taken simply as a visual image of the sea as a great breast. The metaphor, however, imputes certain qualities to the sea, suggesting that it is a Great Mother from which the Moon sucks its life-force. How does that suggestion relate to Wordsworth's assertion that we are losing our life-force? And how does it relate to the Pagan who sees Proteus and Triton (other life-force symbols) rising from the sea? Note that Wordsworth would not only prefer an outworn creed to ignorance of the life-force, but that he would rather be "suckled" in it. Thus the whole poem is animated by the suggestion of the infant (the individual) drawing the life substance from the Great Mother (Nature).

Sonnet LXXIII

William Shakespeare

That time of year thou mayst in me behold
When yellow leaves, or none, or few, do hang
Upon those boughs which shake against the cold,
Bare ruined choirs, where late the sweet birds sang;
In me thou see'st the twilight of such day
As after sunset fadeth in the west,
Which by and by black night doth take away,
Death's second self, that seals up all in rest.
In me thou see'st the glowing of such fire
That on the ashes of its youth doth lie,
As the death-bed whereon it must expire,
Consumed with that which it was nourished by.
This thou perceiv'st, which makes thy love more strong,
To love that well which thou must leave ere long.

QUESTIONS

Sonnet LXXIII consists of three metaphoric comparisons, each of which is stated in four lines, and all of which are summarized in two lines of statement. What is the progression of the metaphors from winter-of-the-year, through twilight-of-the-day, to last-glow-of-the-fire? How does that progression relate to the summarizing statement?

On First Looking Into Chapman's Homer

John Keats

Much have I travelled in the realms of gold,
 And many goodly states and kingdoms seen;
 Round many western islands have I been
Which bards in fealty to Apollo hold.
Oft of one wide expanse had I been told
 That deep-browed Homer ruled as his demesne:
 Yet never did I breathe its pure serene
Till I heard Chapman speak out loud and bold.
Then felt I like some watcher of the skies
 When a new planet swims into his ken;
Or like stout Cortez when with eagle eyes
 He stared at the Pacific—and all his men
Looked at each other with a wild surmise—
 Silent, upon a peak in Darien.

QUESTION

"Till I heard Chapman speak out loud and bold" is the only statement
in this poem, and even that may be argued to contain metaphoric ele-
ments. The rest of the poem consists of three metaphors: of traveling in
"realms of gold," of an astronomer discovering a new planet, and of
Cortez (Balboa, of course) discovering the Pacific. What do these scat-
tered images have in common and how do they relate to the statement?

Sonnet

Samuel Daniel

Fair is my Love, and cruel as she is fair;
 Her brow shades frowns, although her eyes are sunny,
 Her smiles are lightning, though her pride despair;
 And her disdains are Gall, her favors Honey.
A modest maid, deckt with a blush of honor,
 Whose feet do tread green paths of youth and love,
 The wonder of all eyes that look upon her:
 Sacred on earth, design'd a Saint above.
Chastity and Beauty, which were deadly foes,
 Live reconcilèd friends within her brow:
 And had she pity to conjoin with those,

---

design'd a Saint above: Designed (*i.e.*, so made as) to be a Saint in Heaven after she
departs from this world. Sense of the final couplet: "Had she not been beautiful and
at the same time as unkind as I have shown her to be, nothing would have compelled
me to write this lament, and thus no one would have known about her."

Then who had heard the plaint I utter now?
For had she not been fair, and thus unkind,
My Muse had slept, and none had known my mind.

QUESTION

Compare the quality of Daniel's metaphors with those of Keats.

Young Reynard

George Meredith

Gracefullest leaper, the dappled fox-cub
Curves over brambles with berries and buds,
Light as a bubble that flies from the tub,
Whisked by the laundry-wife out of her suds.
Wavy he comes, wooly, all at his ease,
Elegant, fashioned to foot with the deuce;
Nature's own prince of the dance: then he sees
Me, and retires as if making excuse.

Never closed minuet courtlier! Soon
Cub-hunting troops were abroad, and a yelp
Told of sure scent: ere the stroke upon noon
Reynard the younger lay far beyond help.
Wild, my poor friend, has the fate to be chased;
Civil will conquer: were 't other 'twere worse;
Fair, by the flushed early morning embraced,
Haply you live a day longer in verse.

Sense of lines 5 and 6 of stanza 2: "What is wild (the fox) is fated to be chased by what is man-controlled (the dogs) and what is man-controlled (civil) will conquer. Were it the other way around, that would be worse."

QUESTION

Note that Meredith's metaphors are almost exclusively descriptive and that all his larger implications are made as statements. Contrast this order of metaphor with that of Keat's in "On First Looking into Chapman's Homer."

To a Waterfowl

William Cullen Bryant

Whither, midst falling dew,
While glow the heavens with the last steps of day,
Far, through their rosy depths, does thou pursue
    Thy solitary way?

Vainly the fowler's eye
Might mark thy distant flight to do thee wrong,
As, darkly seen against the crimson sky,
    Thy figure floats along.

Seek'st thou the plashy brink
Of weedy lake, or marge of river wide,
Or where the rocking billows rise and sink
    On the chafed ocean-side?

There is a Power whose care
Teaches thy way along that pathless coast—
The desert and illimitable air—
    Lone wandering but not lost.
    All day thy wings have fanned,
At that far height, the cold, thin atmosphere,
Yet stoop not, weary, to the welcome land,
    Though the dark night is near.

And soon that toil shall end;
Soon shalt thou find a summer home, and rest,
And scream among thy fellows; reeds shall bend,
    Soon, o'er thy sheltered nest.

Thou'rt gone, the abyss of heaven
Hath swallowed up thy form; yet, on my heart
Deeply has sunk the lesson thou hast given,
    And shall not soon depart.

He who, from zone to zone,
Guides through the boundless sky thy certain flight,
In the long way that I must tread alone,
    Will lead my steps aright.

QUESTION

Compare the metaphoric method of "To a Waterfowl" to that of the following poem by Peter Viereck.

Poet

Peter Viereck

"Toute forme créée, même par l'homme, est immortelle.
Car la forme est indépendante de la matière, et ce ne sont pas les molécules qui
constituent la forme."

Baudelaire, "Mon Coeur Mis a Nu"

1

The night he died, earth's images all came
To gloat in liberation round his tomb.
Now vengeful colors, stones, and faces dare
    To argue with his metaphor;
And stars his fancy painted on the skies
Drop down like swords
                  to pierce his too wide eyes.

2

Words that begged favor at his court in vain—
Lush adverbs, senile rhymes in tattered gowns—
    Send notes to certain exiled nouns
And mutter openly against his reign.
While rouged clichés hang out red lights again,
Hoarse refugees report from far-flung towns
That exclamation-marks are running wild
And prowling half-truths carried off a child.

3

But he lives on in Form, and Form shall shatter
    This tuneless mutiny of Matter.
His bones are dead; his voice is horribly strong.
Those famed vibrations of life's dancing dust,
Whose thrice-named pangs are "birth" and "death" and "lust,"
Are but the split iambics of his song.
Scansion of flesh in endless ebb and flow,
The drums of duty and renown's great gong—
Mere grace-notes of that living thousand-year
Tyrannic metronome whose every gear
Is some shy craftsman buried long ago.
What terror crowns the sweetness of all song?

4

What hardness leaps at us from each soft tune,
And hammers us to shapes we never planned?
This was a different dying from our own.

Call every wizard in the land—
Bell, book, and test tube; let the dark be rife
With every exorcism we command.
In vain. This death is stronger than our life.

5

In vain we drive our stakes through such a haunter
Or woo with spiced applaudings such a heart.
His news of April do but mock our Winter
Like maps of heaven breathed on window-frost
By cruel clowns in codes whose key is lost.
Yet some sereneness in our rage has guessed
That we are being blessed and blessed and blessed
When least we know it and when coldest art
    Seems hostile,

               useless,

                     or apart.

6

Not worms, not worms in such a skull
But rhythms, rhythms writhe and sting and crawl.
He sings the seasons round, from bud to snow.
And all things are because he willed them so.

Poems for Study—Single and Multiple Imagery

THE SINGLE IMAGE

The poems that immediately follow all develop a central theme in terms of a single sustained comparison. They are constructed, that is to say, on a dominant metaphor.

As in the case of John Donne's great compass-image in the last three stanzas of "A Valediction Forbidding Mourning," the pleasure of such sustained comparisons must lie in (a) their aptness to the subject and to the poet's tone and attitude, (b) the inventiveness with which the poet draws more and more points of meaningful comparison from his basic metaphor, and (c) the management of the poet in making his inventions seem natural, unstrained, and inevitable. If at any point in a poem constructed on a single dominant metaphor, the poet must violate his metaphoric structure in order to make his point, that is bound to seem a breach of metaphoric contract.

Compare the following sonnet by Shakespeare with the rewritten version that follows it. The rewritten version contains many points at which the basic comparison of love to a fever is either violated or loosened. Discuss the effect of those changes.

Sonnet CXLVII

William Shakespeare

My love is as a fever, longing still
For that which longer nurseth the disease,
Feeding on that which doth preserve the ill,
The uncertain sickly appetite to please.
My reason, the physician to my love,
Angry that his prescriptions are not kept,
Hath left me, and I desperate now approve
Desire is death, which physic did except.
Past cure I am, now reason is past care,
And frantic-mad with evermore unrest;
My thoughts and my discourse as madmen's are,
At random from the truth vainly expressed:
For I have sworn thee fair, and thought thee bright,
Who art as black as hell, as dark as night.

ll. 1-4. Shakespeare compares his love to a fever that seeks to continue itself, thus to preserve the disease rather than to take the prescription of reason. **approve:** prove. Sense: Thus in my desperation I prove (demonstrate) that that desire which refuses medicine ("physic did except, *i.e.*, "take exception to"") is death.

Sonnet CXLVII

(rewritten in order to weaken the dominant metaphor)

My love is as a fever, longing still
For that which longer strengthens the disease,
Lusting for that which doth confirm the ill,
The uncertain fickle passion to appease.
My reason, the inspirer of my love,
Angry that his sage counsels are not kept,
Berates me, and I desperate now approve
Desire is mad, which wisdom did except.
Past hope I am, now all is in despair,
And robbed and stripped of every rag of rest.
My thoughts and my discourse as gossips' are,
At random from the truth vainly expressed:
For I have sworn thee fair, and thought thee bright,
Who are as black as hell, as dark as night.

Note that Shakespeare's sonnet develops the basic metaphor of love as a delirious fever without interruption. The single comparison flows on for twelve lines. It is then abandoned and a final couplet states Shakespeare's reasons for thinking of love in such terms.

Eliot's "The Hippopotamus" also develops a single comparison but in a different way, the poet constantly interrupting his metaphor in order to apply it. Thus the first two lines of each stanza make a statement about the hippopotamus, and the last two lines comment on that statement, usually by making that statement into a direct comparison with the Church.

Stanzas seven and eight vary that pattern. What is the effect of changing the pattern at that point in the poem?

The Hippopotamus

T. S. Eliot

Similiter et omnes revereantur Diaconos, ut mandatum Jesu Christi; et Episcopum, ut Jesum Christum, existentem filium Patris; Presbyteros autem, ut concilium Dei et conjunctionem Apostolorum. Sine his Ecclesia non vocatur; de quibis suadeo vos sic habeo.[1]

S. IGNATII AD TRALLIANOS

And when this epistle is read among you, cause that it be read also in the church of the Laodiceans.

> The broad-backed hippopotamus
> Rests on his belly in the mud;
> Although he seems so firm to us
> He is merely flesh and blood.
>
> Flesh and blood is weak and frail,
> Susceptible to nervous shock;
> While the True Church can never fail
> For it is based upon a rock.
>
> The hippo's feeble steps may err
> In compassing material ends,
> While the True Church need never stir
> To gather in its dividends.
>
> The 'potamus can never reach
> The mango on the mango-tree;
> But fruits of pomegranate and peach
> Refresh the Church from over sea.

FROM *Collected Poems 1909–1935* by T. S. Eliot, copyright, 1936, by Harcourt, Brace and Company, Inc.

[1]And likewise let all the deacons be reverenced, as commanded by Jesus Christ; and let the bishop be reverenced, as Jesus Christ, the living son of the Father; also let the presbyters be reverenced, as the council of God and the assembly of the apostles. Without these there can be no church; of these things I persuade you as I can.

Saint Ignatius' third epistle to
the Traillians

At mating time the hippo's voice
Betrays inflexions hoarse and odd,
But every week we hear rejoice
The Church, at being one with God.

The hippopotamus's day
Is passed in sleep; at night he hunts;
God works in a mysterious way—
The Church can sleep and feed at once.

I saw the 'potamus take wing
Ascending from the damp savannas,
And quiring angels round him sing
The praise of God, in loud hosannas.

Blood of the Lamb shall wash him clean
And him shall heavenly arms enfold,
Among the saints he shall be seen
Performing on a harp of gold.

He shall be washed as white as snow,
By all the martyr'd virgins kist,
While the True Church remains below
Wrapt in the old miasmal mist.

QUESTIONS

1. "The Hippopotamus" is obviously written as a satire of what Eliot labels "The True Church." What in the quality of the comparison makes for satire? (Cf. Goldsmith's remarks on Homer, page 780, as one clue.)

2. Savannas are the tropical grasslands where the hippo roams, the miasmal mist is the mist from the rivers and marshes the hippo inhabits. Why does Eliot say that the hippo will ascend to Heaven while the Church takes his place in the animal mists?

3. What is there in the tone of Saint Ignatius' epistle to the Traillians that connects with Eliot's tone in satirizing the True Church as a great ungainly beast?

The Burning Babe

Robert Southwell

As I in hoarie Winters night
   Stood shivering in the snow,
Surpriz'd I was with sudden heat,
   Which made my heart to glow;
And lifting up a fearefull eye
   To view what fire was neere,

A pretty Babe all burning bright
   Did in the aire appeare;
Who, scorchèd with excessive heat,
   Such floods of teares did shed,
As though his floods should quench his flames,
   With which his teares were bred:
Alas, (quoth he) but newly borne,
   In fiery heats I fry,
Yet none approach to warme their hearts,
   Or feel my fire but I;
My faultless breast the furnace is,
   The fuel wounding thorns:
Love is the fire, and sighs the smoke,
   The ashes shames and scorns;
The fuel justice layeth on,
   And mercy blows the coals,
The metal in this Furnace wrought,
   Are men's defilèd souls:
For which, as now on fire I am,
   To worke them to their good,
So will I melt into a bath
   To wash them in my blood.
With this he vanished out of sight,
   And swiftly shrunk away,
And straight I callèd unto mind
   That it was Christmas day.

QUESTIONS

1. What is Southwell's purpose in detailing the quality of the fire? Why does he develop the fire-image so long in order to tell us it is Christmas day?

2. Note that the poet stood *shivering* at the start of the poem. Mark each progression from shivering-cold to more and more intense heat and discuss the ways in which Southwell accomplishes that effect. If this heat-theme is taken as a symbol, what is it a symbol of?

The poems that follow are all in one way or another built on a single basic image. They are presented without comment as an opportunity for the reader to apply in his own way the criteria that have been developed.

The Flea

John Donne

Marke but this flea, and marke in this,
How little that which thou deny'st me is;
It suck'd me first, and now sucks thee,
And in this flea, our two bloods mingled bee;

Thou know'st that this cannot be said
A sinne, nor shame, nor losse of maidenhead,
   Yet this enjoyes before it wooe,
   And pamper'd swells with one blood made of two,
   And this, alas, is more than we would doe.

Oh stay, three lives in one flea spare,
Where wee almost, yea more than married are.
This flea is you and I, and this
Our marriage bed, and marriage temple is;
Though parents grudge, and you, w'are met,
And cloysterd in these living walls of Jet.
   Though use make you apt to kill mee,
   Let not to that, selfe murder added bee,
   And sacrilege, three sinnes in killing three.

Cruell and sodaine, has thou since
Purpled thy naile, in blood of innocence?
Wherein could this flea guilty bee,
Except in that drop which it suckt from thee?
Yet thou triumph'st and saist that thou
Find'st not thy selfe, nor mee the weaker now;
   'Tis true, then learne how false, feares bee;
   Just so much honor, when thou yeeld's to mee,
   Will wast, as this flea's death took life from thee.

A Simile for Her Smile

Richard Wilbur

Your smiling, or the hope, the thought of it,
Makes in my mind such pause and abrupt ease
As when the highway bridgegates fall,
Balking the hasty traffic, which must sit
On each side massed and staring, while
Deliberately the drawbridge starts to rise:

Then horns are hushed, the oilsmoke rarefies,
Above the idling motors one can tell
The packet's smooth approach, the slip,
Slip of the silken river past the sides,
The ringing of clear bells, the dip
And slow cascading of the paddle wheel.

Love at Large

Coventry Patmore

Whene'er I come where ladies are,
   How sad soever I was before,
Though like a ship frost-bound and far
   Withheld in ice from ocean's roar,
Third-winter'd in that dreadful dock,
   With stiffen'd cordage, sails decayed,
And crew that care for calm and shock
   Alike, too dull to be dismay'd,
Yet, if I come where ladies are
   How sad soever I was before,
Then is my sadness banish'd far,
   And I am like that ship no more;
Or like that ship if the ice-field splits,
   Burst by the sudden polar spring,
And all thank God with their warming wits,
   And kiss each other and dance and sing,
And hoist fresh sails, and make the breeze
   Blow them along the liquid sea,
Out of the North, where life did freeze,
   Into the heaven where they would be.

A Subterranean City

Thomas Lovell Beddoes

I followed once a fleet and mighty serpent
Into a cavern in a mountain's side;
And, wading many lakes, descending gulphs,
At last I reached the ruins of a city,
Built not like ours but of another world,
As if the aged earth had loved in youth
The mightiest city of a perished planet,
And kept the image of it in her heart,
So dream-like, shadowy, and spectral was it.
Nought seemed alive there, and the very dead
Were of another world the skeletons.
The mammoth, ribbed like to an arched cathedral,
Lay there, and ruins of great creatures else
More like a shipwrecked fleet, too great they seemed
For all the life that is to animate:
And vegetable rocks, tall, sculptured palms,
Pine grown, not hewn, in stone; and giant ferns
Whose earthquake-shaken leaves bore graves for nests.

A Poison Tree

William Blake

I was angry with my friend:
I told my wrath, my wrath did end.
I was angry with my foe:
I told it not, my wrath did grow.

And I water'd it in fears,
Night and morning with my tears:
And I sunnèd it with smiles,
And with soft deceitful wiles.

And it grew both day and night,
Till it bore an apple bright;
And my foe beheld it shine,
And he knew that it was mine,

And into my garden stole
When the night had veil'd the pole:
In the morning glad I see
My foe outstretch'd beneath the tree.

MULTIPLE IMAGES

All the poems that immediately follow are built of many images rather than on a single basic comparison. All of them are in some sense catalogues, though in some cases the catalogue is more formal than in others.

Since poems constructed of multiple images lack the denotative unity of poems built on a single image, the unity of their images must be found —if at all—in the connotations (overtones) exactly as in the analysis of overtone themes in the diction of the poem. *Any reasonable analysis of poetic overtones, in fact, must combine the overtone themes of the words and the images into a single unity.* In fact, nothing but confusion could follow were one to think in terms of one set of overtones for the diction and of another for the images. Word and image are forever closely related, and they are usually inseparable. These overtones may gather into a single *overtone theme,* or into combinations of theme and counter-theme, as in the first six stanzas of Donne's "Valediction."

A *catalogue* is a more or less deliberate listing of metaphors and properties. Theoretically, a catalogue might be based on a single metaphor, as would be the case were one to write a poem called "The House of Love" in which he compiled a list of all the furnishings of the house as metaphoric equivalents of love. Yet within that single image the catalogue would have to reach in many directions to bring together such disparate elements as roof, fireplace, store-house, and foundation. Even more importantly, the basic impulse of the catalogue is akin to name-magic: the poet writing a catalogue tends simply to *list* his properties without any such metaphoric development and connection of image to image as one finds in Donne's "Valediction."

A catalogue, then, may be taken to be a *list* of properties under a single topic. The impulse of the poet in making such a list is primarily to *name*. That topic, moreover, is almost always a *statement* rather than a metaphor. "I hear America singing," states Whitman: he then proceeds to *name* the many ways in which he hears that singing. So Mrs. Browning asks, "How do I love thee?" and then lists the ways. So Rupert Brooke states "These I have loved," and compiles, without much metaphoric development of any one item, the list of his most enduring pleasures.

When, on the other hand, there is no deliberate assertion of a topic, but rather a development from image to image, each succeeding image called into being not by a single original assertion, but by the suggestion of what has gone before it (once again, as in the first six stanzas of Donne's "Valediction")—that method is better taken to be the development of an overtone theme.

The following questions may be asked of all these poems:

1. How many overtone themes are identifiable? What is the connotative quality of each overtone theme? (What is the principle of selection of each overtone theme?)

2. What progression is observable in the development of each overtone theme? (Do the images go from large to small? from less-intense to more-intense? by some sort of parallelism? by a series of balanced antitheses? from near to far? from relatively concrete to relatively abstract? etc.)

3. If there is more than one overtone theme, are there any image-elements which are common to both themes and, if so, how do they serve to bring the two themes together?

4. Within each theme what relative proportion of the images are metaphors? properties? How many of the metaphors are basically sensory and how many tend to be symbols?

5. What is the proportion of statement to metaphor, and how are the two related?

6. If the poem is a catalogue, what is its topic assertion? What is the proportion of properties to metaphors? Are any of the metaphors elaborated or is the poet satisfied simply to *name* his elements? Is there any order of development in the listing or are the details listed at random?

7. In "Ars Poetica," MacLeish makes a statement that has become famous in literary discussion:

> A poem should not mean
> But be.

That statement concludes three catalogues of images detailing what a poem is. How are the images of each of these following poems related to the "being" (which is to say, the performance) of the poem?

Ars Poetica

Archibald MacLeish

A poem should be palpable and mute
As a globed fruit,

Dumb
As old medallions to the thumb,

Silent as the sleeve-worn stone
Of casement ledges where the moss has grown—

A poem should be wordless
As the flight of birds.

      ✿   ✿   ✿

A poem should be motionless in time
As the moon climbs,

Leaving, as the moon releases
Twig by twig the night-entangled trees,

Leaving, as the moon behind the winter leaves,
Memory by memory the mind—

A poem should be motionless in time
As the moon climbs.

      ✿   ✿   ✿

A poem should be equal to:
Not true.

For all the history of grief
An empty doorway and a maple leaf.

For love
The leaning grasses and two lights above the sea—

A poem should not mean
But be.

QUESTION

Assume that "Ars Poetica" had been written without images and that the following is what is left:

FROM *Collected Poems 1917–1952* by Archibald MacLeish. Reprinted by permission of Houghton Mifflin Company.

A poem should be palpable, mute,
Dumb,
Silent,
And wordless.

It should be motionless
In a single illuminated
Moment of time.

It should be equal to:
Not true,
Expressing each concept
In a single telling symbol.
Thus
A poem should not mean
But be.

Ignoring the debauchery of the rhythm incident to such manhandling, what part of the poem's "being" has been removed from it?

How do I Love Thee?

Elizabeth Barrett Browning

How do I love thee? Let me count the ways.
I love thee to the depth and breadth and height
My soul can reach, when feeling out of sight
For the ends of Being and ideal Grace.
I love thee to the level of everyday's
Most quiet need, by sun and candle-light.
I love thee freely, as men strive for Right;
I love thee purely, as they turn from Praise.
I love thee with the passion put to use
In my old griefs, and with my childhood's faith.
I love thee with a love I seemed to lose
With my lost saints—I love thee with the breath,
Smiles, tears, of all my life!—and, if God choose,
I shall but love thee better after death.

QUESTION

Lines 12–13 seem to be offered as a summary of the ways in which the poet loves. Do all the elements in the preceding catalogue fit that summary (*i.e.*, does the summary state the unifying principle of the catalogue)?

What the Sonnet Is

Eugene Lee Hamilton

Fourteen small broidered berries on the hem
Of Circe's mantle, each of magic gold;
Fourteen of lone Calypso's tears that rolled
Into the sea, for pearls to come of them;
Fourteen clear signs of omen in the gem
With which Medea human fate foretold;
Fourteen small drops, which Faustus, growing old,
Craved of the Fiend, to water Life's dry stem.
It is the pure white diamond Dante brought
To Beatrice, the sapphire Laura wore
When Petrarch cut it sparkling out of thought;
The ruby Shakespeare hewed from his heart's core;
The dark deep emerald that Rossetti wrought
For his own soul, to wear for ever more.

QUESTION

Hamilton's sonnet is a catalogue of eight things to which the sonnet is equated. What have the elements of this catalogue in common in their denotations? in their connotations?

The Great Lover

Rupert Brooke

I have been so great a lover: filled my days
So proudly with the splendor of Love's praise,
The pain, the calm, and the astonishment,
Desire illimitable, and still content,
And all dear names men use, to cheat despair,
For the perplexed and viewless streams that bear
Our hearts at random down the dark of life.
Now, ere the unthinking silence on that strife
Steals down, I would cheat drowsy Death so far,

Circe: The enchantress of the Odyssey who changed men into beasts. **Calypso:** The nymph who detained Odysseus for seven years on her island. **Medea:** The enchantress who helped Jason win the Golden Fleece of Colchis. **drops . . . to water Life's dry stem:** The blood of Christ. One drop would serve to win Faustus' redemption but the Devil (in Marlowe's *Faustus*) would not allow Faustus that drop. **Beatrice:** Dante's symbol of Divine Love. **Laura:** The Lady of Petrarch's sonnets.

REPRINTED by permission of Dodd, Mead & Company from *The Collected Poems of Rupert Brooke.* Copyright 1915 by Dodd, Mead & Company, Inc. Copyright 1943 by Edward Marsh.

My night shall be remembered for a star
That outshone all the suns of all men's days.
Shall I not crown them with immortal praise
Whom I have loved, who have given, dared with me
High secrets, and in darkness knelt to see
The inenarrable godhead of delight?
Love is a flame:—we have beaconed the world's night.
A city:—we have built it, these and I.
An emperor:—we have taught the world to die.
So, for their sakes I loved, ere I go hence,
And the high cause of Love's magnificence,
And to keep loyalties young, I'll write those names
Golden for ever, eagles, crying flames,
And set them as a banner, that men may know,
To dare the generations, burn, and blow
Out on the wind of Time, shining and streaming . . .
These I have loved:
    White plates and cups, clean-gleaming,
Ringed with blue lines; and feathery, faery dust;
Wet roofs, beneath the lamp-light; the strong crust
Of friendly bread; and many-tasting food;
Rainbows; and the blue bitter smoke of wood;
And radiant raindrops couching in cool flowers,
And flowers themselves, that sway through sunny hours,
Dreaming of moths that drink them under the moon;
Then, the cool kindliness of sheets, that soon
Smooth away trouble; and the rough male kiss
Of blankets; grainy wood; live hair that is
Shining and free; blue-massing clouds; the keen
Unpassioned beauty of a great machine;
The benison of hot water; furs to touch;
The good smell of old clothes; and other such—
The comfortable smell of friendly fingers,
Hair's fragrance, and the musty reek that lingers
About dead leaves and last year's ferns. . . .
                                        Dear names,
And thousand others throng me! Royal flames;
Sweet water's dimpling laugh from tap or spring;
Holes in the ground; and voices that do sing:
Voices in laughter, too; and body's pain,
Soon turned to peace; and the deep-panting train;
Firm sands; the little dulling edge of foam
That browns and dwindles as the wave goes home;
And washen stones, gay for an hour; the cold
Graveness of iron; moist black earthen mold;
Sleep; and high places; footprints in the dew;
And oaks; and brown horse-chestnuts, glossy-new;
And new-peeled sticks and shining pools on grass;—

All these have been my loves. And these shall pass,
Whatever passes not, in the great hour,
Nor all my passion, all my prayers, have power
To hold me with them through the gate of Death.
They'll play deserter, turn with traitor breath,
Break the high bond we made, and sell Love's trust
And sacramental covenant to the dust.
—Oh, never a doubt but, somewhere, I shall wake,
And give what's left of love again, and make
New friends now strangers. . . .
                              But the best I've known
Stays here, and changes, breaks, grows old, is blown
About the winds of the world, and fades from brains
Of living men, and dies.
                              Nothing remains.

O dear my loves, O faithless, once again
This one last gift I give: that after men
Shall know, and later lovers, far-removed
Praise you, "All these were lovely"; say, "He loved."

QUESTIONS

1. "The Great Lover" centers on the catalogue beginning "These I have
loved." Before and after the catalogue the poet explains its importance
to him.
   At the end he points out that all the things he has loved are temporary.
There are, for example, no angels, eternal verities, cosmic laws, geometric
theorems, or unfading essences among the items of his catalogue. Have
those items anything else in common? *I.e.,* what principle of selection
chooses the items for Brooke's catalogue?

2. Some of those items are metaphoric and some are properties. What
is the connotative force of the metaphoric items? Do the connotations of
the properties harmonize with the connotations of the metaphors?

3. Is the catalogue more interesting in itself than is Brooke's comment
on it, before and after?

Compare Brooke's catalogue with that of the following poem by Karl
Shapiro. Scyros, it is interesting to note, is the island on which Brooke met
his death, and the motto, "snuffle and sniff and handkerchief" is from one
of Brooke's letters.

Scyros

Karl Shapiro

snuffle and sniff and handkerchief

The doctor punched my vein
The Captain called me Cain
Upon my belly sat the sow of fear
  With coins on either eye
  The President came by
And whispered to the braids what none could hear

  High over where the storm
  Stood steadfast cruciform
The golden eagle sank in wounded wheels
  White negroes laughing still
  Crept fiercely on Brazil
Turning the navies upward on their keels

  Now one by one the trees
  Stripped to their naked knees
To dance upon the heaps of shrunken dead
  The roof of England fell
  Great Paris tolled her bell
And China staunched her milk and wept for bread

  No island singly lay
  But lost its name that day
The Ainu dived across the plunging sands
  From dawn to dawn to dawn
  King George's birds came on
Strafing the tulips from his children's hands

  Thus in the classic sea
  Southeast from Thessaly
The dynamited mermen washed ashore
  And tritons dressed in steel
  Trolled heads with rod and reel
And dredged potatoes from the Aegean floor

  Hot is the sky and green
  Where Germans have been seen
The moon leaks metal on the Atlantic fields
  Pink boys in birthday shrouds
  Look lightly through the clouds
Or coast the peaks of Finland on their shields

That prophet year by year
Lay still but could not hear
Where scholars tapped to find his new remains
Gog and Magog ate pork
In vertical New York
And war began next Monday on the Danes.

It is clear enough that Shapiro's images were chosen by a principle of selection and for a purpose markedly different from those that chose the images of "The Great Lover." Note that Shapiro gives no explanation for his catalogue but leaves it to stand as itself.

The careful reader will have no difficulty in seeing that Shapiro has reached in many directions for images whose force will express his sense of modern war. Certainly the opening three lines can describe nothing but the scene of a man's induction into the army; and the following three, nothing but a glimpse of the President discussing matters of war policy with the ranking brass. Thereafter all seems to be made of scattered glimpses of destruction flung meaninglessly all over the globe. To emphasize that sense of meaninglessness, Shapiro has built many of his images upon paradoxes and has left out all inter-relating statements, even omitting all punctuation except for the final period.

QUESTION

Can Shapiro's images be taken as a simple catalogue illustrating the inhumanity of mechanical war, or should one identify two themes in this poem, one working against the other?

Gee I Like to Think of Dead

E. E. Cummings

gee I like to think of dead it means nearer because deeper
firmer since darker than little round water at one end of
the well   it's too cool to be crooked and it's too firm
to be hard but it's sharp and thick and it loves,   every
old thing falls in rosebugs and jacknives and kittens and
pennies they all sit there looking at each other having the
fastest time because they've never met before

dead's more even than how many ways of sitting on
your head your unnatural hair has in the morning

FROM *Poems 1923–1954*. Harcourt, Brace and Company. Copyright 1925, 1953 by E. E. Cummings.

dead's clever too like POF goes the alarm off and the
little striker having the best time tickling away every-
body's brain so everybody just puts out their finger
and they stuff the poor thing all full of fingers

dead has a smile like the nicest man you've never met
who maybe winks at you in a streetcar and you pretend
you don't but really you do see and you are My how
glad he winked and hope he'll do it again

or if it talks about you somewhere behind your back it
makes your neck feel pleasant and stoopid   and if
dead says may i have this one and was never intro-
duced you say Yes because you know you want it to
dance with you and it wants to and it can dance and
Whocares

dead's fine like hands do you see that water flowerpots
in windows but they live higher in their house than
you so that's all you see but you don't want to

dead's happy like the way underclothes All so differ-
ently solemn and inti and sitting on one string

dead never says my dear, Time for your musiclesson
and you like music and to have somebody play who
can but you know you never can and why have to?

dead's nice like a dance where you danced simple hours
and you take all your prickly-clothes off and squeeze-
into-largeness without one word   and you lie still as
anything   in largeness and this largeness begins to
give you, the dance all over again and you, feel all again
all over the way men you liked made you feel when they
touched you(but that's not all)because largeness tells
you so you can feel what you made, men feel when, you
touched, them

dead's sorry like a thistlefluff-thing which goes land-
ing away all by himself on somebody's roof or some-
thing where who-ever-heard-of-growing and nobody
expects you to anyway

dead says come with me he says(and whyevernot)into
the round well and see the kitten and the penny and
the jacknife and the rosebug

                       and you say Sure you
say (like that) sure i'll come with you you say for i
like kittens i do and jacknives i do and pennies i do
and rosebugs i do

QUESTIONS

1. E. E. Cummings has often been held up for attack as the figure of the "unintelligible modern poet." "Gee I Like to Think of Dead" is a reasonably representative Cummings poem, though it makes no use of the typographical devices that have become one of Cummings' trademarks. Is this poem unintelligible?

2. "The poem is a catalogue of the fantasies that go through a young girl's head when she thinks of death, an idea strongly connected in her mind with the idea of sex. The girl, by the very terms in which she thinks, can be identified as living in some large city—almost certainly New York—but it is clear that she has come there from a rural childhood." Discuss this comment.

3. Is this catalogue connotatively united?

4. What is the tone of the girl's thinking? Is the tone constant or does it change at any point?

Dirge

Kenneth Fearing

1-2-3 was the number he played but today the number came
  3-2-1;
    bought his Carbide at 30 but it went to 29; had the
    favorite at Bowie but the track was slow—

O, executive type, would you like to drive a floating power,
  knee action, silk-upholstered six? Wed a Hollywood star?
  Shoot the course in 58? Draw to the ace, king, jack?
O, fellow with a will who won't take no, watch out for three
  cigarettes on the same, single match; O democratic voter
  born in August under Mars, beware of liquidated rails—

Dénouement to dénouement, he took a personal pride in the
  certain, certain way he lived his own, private life,
  but nevertheless, they shut off his gas; nevertheless,
  the bank foreclosed; nevertheless, the landlord called;
  nevertheless, the radio broke,

And twelve o'clock arrived just once too often,
  just the same he wore one gray tweed suit, bought one
    straw hat, drank one straight Scotch, walked one short
    step, took one long look, drew one deep breath,
  just one too many,

FROM *New and Selected Poems*, by Kenneth Fearing. Reprinted by permission of Indiana University Press.

And wow he died as wow he lived,
  going whop to the office and blooie home to sleep and
    biff got married and bam had children and oof got fired,
  zowie did he live and zowie did he die,

With who the hell are you at the corner of his casket,
  and where the hell we going on the right hand silver
  knob, and who the hell cares walking second from the
  end with an American Beauty wreath from why the hell
  not.

Very much missed by the circulation staff of the New York
  Evening Post; deeply, deeply mourned by the B.M.T.,

Wham, Mr. Roosevelt; pow, Sears Roebuck; awk, big dipper;
  bop, summer rain;
  bong, Mr., bong, Mr., bong, Mr., bong.

QUESTIONS

1. Assume "Dirge" to be a catalogue. Compare its images, both properties and metaphors, with those of Whitman's catalogue in "Song of Myself (26)." Both catalogues are drawn largely from city life, but quite obviously the similarity ends there. Fearing's images are obviously not of things that Whitman would welcome into his poem. What is the difference in the two principles of selection? (If in doubt make parallel listings of the items in Whitman's and Fearing's catalogues. What would two such lists tell one of the way each poet conceived city life?)

2. On careful reading one cannot fail to note that there are at least two overtone themes in "Dirge." "Bought his Carbide at 30 but it went to 29," for example, is vastly different in connotation from "O democratic voter born in August under Mars." Make a list of everything in the poem that immediately relates to the order of life suggested by "bought his Carbide at 30 but it went to 29"; and another list of everything that immediately relates to "born in August under Mars." Are there any images that seem to fall into an in-between theme? If "buying Carbide" is thought of as "mundane" and "born in August under Mars" as "human aspiration," is there a third theme that might be labeled "aspirations of the mundane"? Note that all the mundane images are images of loss. Are all the aspiration images also of loss?

from Hero and Leander

Christopher Marlowe

Her veil was artificial flowers and leaves,
Whose workmanship both man and beast deceives.
Many would praise the sweet smell as she passed,
When 'twas the odor which her breath forth cast;

And therefor honey bees have sought in vain,
And, beat from thence, have lighted there again.
About her neck hung chains of pebble-stone,
Which, lightened by her neck, like diamonds shone. **. . .**

. . . Buskins of shell all silvered, used she,
And branched with blushing coral to the knee,
Where sparrows perched, of hollow pearl and gold,
Such as the world would wonder to behold;
Those with sweet water oft her handmaid fills,
Which, as she went, would chirrup through the bills.
Some say, for her the fairest cupid pined,
And, looking in her face, was strooken blind.

QUESTION

Marlowe piles up a great deal of very peculiar ornamentation in his description of Hero's dress. Shell boots ornamented with branches of coral on which are perched jeweled metal birds hardly make for comfort, but Marlowe goes further: a serving maid keeps filling the metal birds with water that makes a sound of chirruping as it passes through their bills. Strange regalia; do the details of that regalia have anything in common? Denotatively? Connotatively? Has the catalogue of Hero's dress anything in common with the description of her physical presence?

buskins: boots. **strooken:** stricken.

Chapter Seven

THE POEM IN MOTION

Buick

Karl Shapiro

As a sloop with a sweep of immaculate wings on her delicate spine
And a keel as steel as a root that holds in the sea as she leans,
Leaning and laughing, my warm hearted beauty, you ride, you ride,
You tack on the curves with parabola speed and a kiss of goodbye,
Like a thoroughbred sloop, my new high-spirited spirit, my kiss.

As my foot suggests that you leap in the air with your hips of a girl,
My finger that praises your wheel and announces your voices of song,
Flouncing your skirts, you blueness of joy, you flirt of politeness,
You leap, you intelligence, essence of wheelness with silvery nose,
And your platinum clocks of excitement stir like the hairs of a fern.

But now with your eyes that enter the future of roads you forget;
Where you turned on the stinging lathes of Detroit and Lansing at night
And shrieked at the torch in your secret parts and the amorous tests,
But now with your eyes that enter the future of roads you forget;
You are all instinct with your phosphorous glow and your streaking hair.

And now when we stop it is not as the bird from the shell that I leave
Or the leathery pilot who steps from his bird with a sneer of delight,
And not as the ignorant beast do you squat and watch me depart,
But with exquisite breathing you smile, with satisfaction of love,
And I touch you again as you tick in the silence and settle in sleep.

No one who reads this poem can miss the fact that the poet is lovingly
concerned with the motion of his saying. A poem exists in time. The first
line comes first, the others follow in their order to the last line, and there
is no other order in which the lines can be read.

And since a poem has duration, it also has pace. One poem may ob-
viously urge the voice at a faster pace than does another. Within the same
poem, morever, one part may urge itself much more rapidly than another.
Even within an individual line, one phrase may clearly be indicated as
moving more rapidly or more slowly than another. For just as music carries
with it a notation that tells the musician at what rate and with what feel-

ing to play a given passage, so every good piece of writing, and poetry in particular, carries within it a series of unmistakable notations that tell the good reader how any given passage should be read. One of the poet's chief delights is in the manipulation of his pace and its changes. He is deeply involved in the *feeling of his motion*. Since a poem is always about something felt, its motion is certainly part of what it is about, part of what it feels, and, therefore, part of what it "means." Even more importantly, the motion is fundamental to *how* the poem means.

All writing has pace. Poetry has all the notation for pace that one may find in other writing, and it has the additional notation of metrics. "Pace" must be understood to be the more inclusive term, but since metric is the peculiar characteristic of poetry, an understanding of the poem's pace must begin with some understanding of metrics. What follows is in no sense a complete survey of English metrics, but simply a first look at some basic metrical phenomena.

As a working simplification, the basic line of English poetry may be taken to be *iambic pentameter*. "Iambic" indicates the "beat" of the rhythm, "pentameter" indicates the length of the line. English line lengths in progression from one-foot to eight-foot are labeled: *monometer, dimeter, trimeter, tetrameter, pentameter, hexameter, septameter,* and *octameter.* The basic English metric feet are *iambic, trochaic, anapestic, dactylic, amphibrachic, pyrrhic, spondaic,* and *monosyllabic.*

The *iamb* (iambic) is a two-syllable foot consisting of an unaccented syllable followed by an accented syllable: ta-*tum*. It is the basic English foot for the idiomatic reason that most English words of two syllables (many exceptions are, of course, to be noted) are accented on the second syllable (re-fér, a-bóut, des-tróy). English, moreover, contains many monosyllabic words which when preceded by a monosyllabic article or preposition fall into a natural iambic rhythm. Metric principle does not exist in a vacuum. Iambic has become the basic beat of English poetry and pentameter the basic line length because these measures are most responsive to the qualities of English speech. A great deal of the poetic energy of the sixteenth century in England went into testing the iambic pentameter line (among others) as a vehicle for poetry in English. Some poets, for example, tried to tune English speech to the measures of Latin hexameters, basing their metric on *quantitative* measure (the succession of long and short syllables) rather than on *qualitative* (the succession of accented and unaccented) syllables. Quantitative measure failed in English poetry because it is not adapted to the nature of English speech. By the last quarter of the sixteenth century iambic pentameter was firmly established. One important reason for the great flowering of poetry in Shakespeare's time lay in the fact that such a basic line had been established and that it proved itself capable of such great range and flexibility.

The *trochee* (trochaic) is a two-syllable foot consisting of an accented syllable followed by an unaccented syllable: *tum*-ta, a reversed iambic. The trochee is inevitable in English because so many two-syllable words, despite the general iambic nature of the language, are stressed on the first syllable (wáit-ing, áp-ple, sín-gle). Note that when such words are preceded by an article or by a monosyllabic preposition, a light-heavy or iambic sequence happens. There is a general tendency in southern midwestern American speech to move the accent forward in the word, that is, toward a trochaic accentuation. If such speech habits continue to spread as they (unfortunately) seem to be doing, the basic meter of American poetry will undergo considerable change. In Món-roe, Loó z'ana, which is locally known as part of the Ú-nited States, the pó-lice station is near the thé-ay-ta. Get the í-dee?

The *anapest* (anapestic) is a three-syllable foot consisting of two unaccented syllables followed by an accented syllable: ta-ta-*tum*. If the iamb is conceived, by a musical analogy, to be in three-eighths time, then the unstressed syllable is an eighth note and the stressed is a quarter note. If the eighth comes before the quarter and is changed to two sixteenths, the result can be taken as analagous to anapestic meter (of the dáy, in a while, lem-on-áde). There are very few naturally anapestic words in English but many combinations of preposition-article-noun that demand the anapestic beat.

The *dactyl* (dactylic) is, simply enough, a reversed anapest: *tum*-ta-ta. Obviously it bears the same relation to the trochee that the anapest bears to the iamb.

The *amphibrach* is a three-syllable foot consisting of unstressed-stressed-unstressed syllables: ta-*tum*-ta, as in the word re-bút-tal. The amphibrach may be thought of as a feminine iamb. (See below for the terms *feminine* and *masculine*.)

The *pyrrhic* is a foot consisting of two unstressed syllables. It is possible to construct a theory of metrics in which the pyrrhic does not exist. In conventional metrics, however, it is impossible to scan certain lines without resort to the pyrrhic. A famous example occurs in Shakespeare's much quoted line:

> To mó/rrow and / to mó/rrow and / to mó rrow

So scanned, the line is seen to consist of iamb-pyrrhic-iamb-pyrrhic-amphibrach (or feminine iamb).

The *spondee* (spondaic) is a two-syllable foot consisting of two stressed syllables: *tum*-*tum*. In such a line as "Blow, blow, ye wintry winds!" it should be obvious that the first two syllables cannot meaningfully be read either as blow-BLOW or as BLOW-blow: they must be given equal and heavy stress.

The *monosyllabic* foot consists of a single stressed syllable. The uncorrupted version of Lady Macbeth's famous lines, display richly the dramatic effect that may be achieved by the use of the monosyllabic foot:

Óut,// dámn ēd/ spót!// óut// Í sáy!
Whát,// wíll thēse/ hánds/ né vēr/ bē cléan?

It is possible to interpret these lines with a somewhat different emphasis and hence with some variation in the scansion. But it should be clear that Shakespeare deliberately used the monosyllabic foot in combination with a basically trochaic meter to indicate more than usual passion (hence a speech rhythm far from normal). Note, too, that the monosyllabic foot falls, in each case, before a double-line, the notation for the caesura.

Caesura is an essential term in metrics and labels the internal pauses in a passage. It corresponds to a rest in music. A pause, one must remember, also consumes time, and as one may imagine by analogy to music, can also compensate for missing measures either accented or unaccented.

When caesura occurs at the end of the line, the line is said to be *end-stopped*. When the voice must continue to the next line without pause, the line is said to be *run-on*, or *enjambed*.

Feminine and *masculine* are terms that may be used to describe poetic lines, feet, or rhymes. These elements are feminine if they end on an unaccented syllable; masculine if they end on an accented syllable.

Hē cáme/ tō mé/ and tóld/ me hé/ must leáve me

is a feminine line (ending in the unaccented "me"). With a slight change it can become the masculine line:

Hē cáme/ tō mé/ and tóld/ me hé/ must leáve.

English not only tolerates but welcomes such extra light beats, especially before an end-stop or a caesura.

These are the most common elements of English metrics, but the practice of individual poets varies widely. It seems best, however, to establish these basic measures and to note variations as they occur.

A mechanically flawless iambic pentameter would read: ta-*tum* ta-*tum*, ta-*tum*, ta-*tum*, ta-*tum*. English poetry, however, is capable of far more interesting effects than such mechanical regularity. It is useful to think of the pattern of mechanical iambic pentameter as roughly corresponding to the squares on graph paper: the variations of the drawn graph are meaningful only as they work against the fixed norm of the squares. In poetry the mechanical pattern may be thought of as an *expectation*. The metric performance of any line happens in the way it works its variations against the established expectation.

Good poets, moreover, do not work by rule but by ear (their own strictest rule), by feel rather than by meticulous observance of generalizations about metrics. As a starting generalization, however, one may safely say that all poets work against a pattern of expectation (a norm) and vary its dead regularity by (1) slipping in extra unaccented syllables,

(2) by displacing an expected accent, as in the reversed foot, (3) by increasing the number of stresses, primarily by the use of spondees and monosyllabic feet, (4) by grouping stressed or unstressed syllables, and (5) by the manipulation of internal pauses (caesura), end-stops, and run-ons. These are the basic metric devices that speed up or slow down the line and change its voice emphases. A number of non-metrical devices that serve the same function of speeding-up or slowing-down the line will be considered as they occur. But for poets, the rule-of-thumb is still the law of practice.

Alexander Pope's *Essay on Criticism* (an extended poem in rhymed iambic pentameter couplets) offers, among other things, a number of such useful rules-of-thumb. In one famous passage Pope discusses a number of poetic faults and graces, illustrating each by the line in which he mentions it. He points out, for example, that if all the vowels in a given passage are open, the effect is laborious (hence a non-metric device for slowing-down the line); and in saying so he piles up a succession of open vowels, all of equal duration. Pope's "these" refers to a class of critics he is satirizing:

> These equal syllables alone require,
> Though oft the ear the open vowel tire.

Pope goes on to condemn the pointless expletive *do,* run into a line without grammatical integrity but simply to pad out the syllabic count. Thus instead of writing the normal English "while expletives join (then pronounced 'jine') their feeble aid," Pope illustrates:

> While expletives their feeble aid *do* join.

And he concludes the couplet with an example of the general lifelessness of a line that consists of ten equal monosyllables:

> And ten low words oft creep in one dull line.

Later in the same passage he discusses and illustrates the necessity for meaningful change of pace:

> When Ajax strives some rocks vast weight to throw,
> The line, too, labors, and the words move slow:
> Not so when swift Camilla scours the plain,
> Flies o'er the unbending corn, and skims along the main.

Clearly the first line of this passage is *impeded* (slowed-down) by the effort required to wrestle through the consonantal cluster of "When Ajax strives some rocks." And clearly the fourth line is *accelerated* (speeded-up) by the meter. But slowed down and speeded up from what? Pope's own "dull line" will serve to establish a norm:

> And ten low words oft creep in one dull line.

Nothing could be more regular, and hence more dull.

Pope must certainly have believed that the dullness of this line resulted from the combination of its two chief metrical characteristics: first, that all of the line moves at exactly the same pace, and second, that all of its stressed syllables are equal, as are all of its unstressed syllables. Such lack of variation, however, is not final evidence that any given line is a bad one. Pope, for example, uses its monotony brilliantly to illustrate monotony. The last line of the following poem makes use of ten monosyllables for a tremendous special emphasis. The poet, moved by the mystical quality of El Greco's painting in which the human body is elongated and distorted into flame-like shapes suggesting the enormous upward tug of the spirit, is driven to ask a question of those other-worldly men. If they so yearn to enter the houses of eternity (whose doorway is the tomb) and if that eternity is full of such radiance as they envision, then—and each syllable of the line pounds the question—WHY, DOES, NO, LIGHT, COME, THROUGH, AS, THOSE, DOORS, CLOSE?

El Greco

E. L. Mayo

See how the sun has somewhat not of light
Falling upon those men who stand so tall;
See how their eyes observe some inward sight
And how their living takes no room at all, —
Their passing stirs no air, so thin they are;
Behind them see small houses with small doors;
The light comes from an unfamiliar star
That lights their walls and falls across their floors.

What shall we say when one of those men goes
Into his house and we no longer see
His eyes observing something that he knows.
And if those houses brim with radiancy
Why does no light come through as those doors close?

Any poetic device can be used triumphantly for special effects, and one should be cautious of making categoric assertions about poetry. With that much understood, it is still possible to say that any passage of poetry in which line after line is made up of equally measured monosyllables, or nearly, will tend to montony. A pianist playing to strict metronomic beat is painful to listen to. One needs the felt variations and compensation of a more human response. So in poetry.

I put my hat upon my head
And strolled into the Strand,
And there I met another man
Whose hat was in his hand.

REPRINTED by permission of the author and of *The New York Times.*

The lines are metrically perfect, but as lifeless as the metronome. One
need hardly be told that the passage is deliberate parody.

Yet part of the insipidity of those lines is certainly due to the in-
sipidity of what they are saying. The following poem is nearly as mono-
syllabic as the parody above, but it may well be cited as a masterpiece of
one sort of pure English lyricism:

With Rue My Heart Is Laden

A. E. Housman

> With rue my heart is laden
> For laughing friends I had,
> For many a rose-lipt maiden
> And many a light-foot lad.
>
> By brooks too broad for leaping
> The light-foot lads are laid.
> And rose-lipt girls are sleeping
> In fields where roses fade.

The very monosyllabic understatement of the poem is important to its
lyrical restraint and success. Yet certainly the gracious variety provided
by the adjectives (most of them compounded monosyllables) and by the
delicate interplay of feminine and masculine rhymes, is inseparable from
the poem's success. It is not necessary to have great variation, but some
variation there must certainly be. One need only convert Housman's
feminine rhymes into masculine counterparts to see how much the little
upward flip of the extra feminine syllable at the ends of alternate lines
enriches the total effect, and how leaden the effect becomes without such
enrichment:

> With rue my heart is laid
> For laughing friends I had,
> For many a rose-lipt maid
> And many a light-foot lad.
>
> By brooks too broad to leap
> The light-foot lads are laid.
> And rose-lipt girls now sleep
> In fields where roses fade.

Pope's Ajax, as noted, moves more slowly than does his Camilla. The
slowness of the Ajax line is due to non-metrical impedance caused by the

clustering of consonants. Metrically, two causes combine to give the little tripping speed-up to the last line of that passage. The line, it must be noted, is an *Alexandrine, i.e.*, a hexameter used as a final variation in a passage of pentameter lines. Normally the Alexandrine, by drawing the line out an extra foot, tends to slow it down. Pope himself has satirized the over-reliance of some poets on Alexandrines:

> A needless Alexandrine ends the song,
> That, like a wounded snake, drags its slow length along.

Despite the Alexandrine's tendency to slow down the line, however (especially when impeded by caesuras), Pope accelerates the last line of his Ajax-Camilla passage:

> Flíes o'ēr / thē ūn bénd/ ĭng córn// ānd skíms/ ā lóng/
> thē maín

The first foot of this line has sometimes been scanned as an iamb rather than as a trochee. The present scansion takes the grammatical force of the parallelism in this passage to play *flies* against *skims*: Camilla *flies* over the corn and *skims* across the sea. If the first foot is taken as an iamb, then one must argue that she flies *o'er* and skims *along*—a reading one may not be able to defend. The first cause of the acceleration is obviously in the anapest of the second foot. Just as sixteenth notes must be played more rapidly than eighths, so the two unaccented syllables of the anapest must be read more rapidly than would be a single unaccented syllable. This first cause is assisted, moreover, by the reversal of the first foot, since that reversal puts three rather than two unstressed syllables in a row. The fundamental basis of all metrical acceleration should be apparent: *the more unstressed syllables are brought together between accents, the faster the line will tend to move.*

The two basic metric devices for impeding the line are the caesura and the grouping of heavily accented syllables. *The more caesuras and the more stressed syllables that occur in a given passage, the slower its pace will tend to be.*

Caesura, by definition, could hardly serve any other purpose than to slow down a passage. One need only observe how it functions in such a passage as the speech in which Macbeth pours out his grief and his death wish:

> I have lived long enough// my way of life
> Is fallen into the sere,// the yellow leaf,//
> And that which should accompany old age//
> As honor,// love,// obedience,// troops of friends,//
> I must not look to have// but, // in their stead//
> Curses,// not loud but deep,// mouth honour,// breath,//
> Which the poor heart would fain deny// and dare not.

One may interpret this passage also in slightly different ways, and argue for the removal of the caesuras after "old age" in line three, after "but" in line five, and after "stead" at the end of line five; but even so interpreted, the passage clearly derives its pace primarily from the heavy incidence of caesura.

One should note also that as caesuras grow closer and closer together, there must inevitably be less language between them. Since it is the unstressed syllables that tend to be squeezed out (partly compensated for by the pauses), such passages tend to cluster accents, with a consequent greater likelihood of more monosyllabic feet. Since stressed syllables are obviously more emphatic than unstressed, caesural pause is closely linked with especially powerful voice emphasis.

John Donne, one of the most metrically skilled of English poets, was also one of the most passionately religious. Many of his later poems burn with desire for a direct physical experience of God. In the urgency of that desire, Donne pounds and beats his language. In one of his *Holy Numbers* he calls upon God to ravish him. The metrics of that passage, in seeking to find a motion equal to the emotion, makes extraordinary use of the caesura combined with many monosyllabic feet.

> Batt er/ my heart/ three per/ soned God,// for you
> As yet/ but knock// breathe // shine// and seek/ to mend.//
> That I/ may rise,/ and stand// o'er throw me// and bend
> Your powers/ to break// blow// burn// and make/ me new.

The passage is exquisitely controlled and emphasized from the first reversed (trochaic) foot that plunges the voice in with a sharp thrust on the hard *bat* sound, to the final clustering of accents in the iamb-and-spondee combination at the end of line four.

But if this introduction is not to become a treatise, it will be necessary to pass over many fine points. Metrics, as noted, tends to go by practice rather than by rule. No one has ever compiled a wholly satisfactory set of metric rules. There seem in fact to be many systems of metrics at work in various periods of English poetry. The best way to familiarize oneself with the resources of English metrics is by specific example. Let the poem illustrate the poem.

A Metrical Exercise

To Lucasta, On Going to the Wars

Richard Lovelace

Tell me not, Sweet, I am unkind
    That from the nunnery
Of thy chaste breast and quiet mind
    To war and arms I fly.

True, a new mistress now I chase,
    The first foe in the field;
And with a stronger faith embrace
    A sword, a horse, a shield.

Yet this inconstancy is such
    As you, too, shall adore;
I could not love you, dear, so much,
    Loved I not honour more.

A glance at Lovelace's poem should be enough to make it clear that the poem is built metrically on an iambic norm and consists of alternate tetrameters and trimeters. The complications that Lovelace has worked into his metric pattern may tend momentarily to obscure the essentially iambic base, but one has only to read the last line of the first two stanzas to be reassured that the meter is in fact iambic. Nothing could be more mechanically correct than the iambic trimeter of those lines, and one will do well to note that almost all good poets who use complicated metrics provide such "rest" lines at intervals. Whether or not they do so consciously is more or less irrelevant. The fact seems to be that few good poets actually scan their lines. And why should they?—their ears have been attuned by years of reading and writing, and it is the ear that decides.

The trouble is that the ear decides in ways too subtle for simple rules. The beginner, therefore, must approach metrics by means a bit simpler than the whole truth. If he is a good reader, he will assume the responsibility for carrying these simplifications further, toward a more valid metrical sense. But one must begin somewhere.

Were one to read the first stanza of the Lovelace poem mechanically, ignoring everything but the alternation of stressed and unstressed syllables, the stanza might be scanned so:

$$\text{Tell mé / nŏt Swéet / Ī am / ŭn kínd}$$
$$\text{Thăt fróm / thĕ núnn/ ĕr ý}$$

$$\bar{O}f\ th\acute{y}\ /\ ch\bar{a}ste\ br\acute{e}ast\ /\ and\ qu\bar{i}\ /\ et\ m\acute{i}nd$$
$$\bar{T}o\ w\acute{a}r\ /\ \bar{a}nd\ arm\acute{s}\ /\ \bar{I}\ fl\acute{y}.$$

Such scansion may be called *mechanical*.

Now let the lines be read in a more meaningful and more felt way. Let them be read as nearly as possible without attention to metrical principles, simply as an exercise in locating the voice emphasis of English speech, and let those syllables that must be stressed in such a meaningful rendering be indicated by a caret below the line. One will sense at once that certain syllables, though they are clearly stressed, are stressed more or less heavily than others. A large caret for more emphatically stressed syllables and a smaller one for those less heavily stressed will serve our present purposes. The same lines might then be *meaningfully* scanned as follows:

Tell me not, Sweet, I am unkind

That from the nunnery

Of thy chaste breast and quiet mind

To war and arms I fly.

Now if the same passage be marked for both the mechanical and the meaningful scansion, it will appear as follows:

$$\bar{T}ell\ me\ /\ n\acute{o}t,\ Sweet\ /\ \bar{I}\ am\ /\ \bar{u}n\ k\acute{i}nd$$

$$\bar{T}hat\ from\ /\ the\ n\acute{u}nn\ /\ \bar{e}r\ \acute{y}$$

$$\bar{O}f\ th\acute{y}\ /\ ch\bar{a}ste\ br\acute{e}ast\ /\ and\ qu\bar{i}\ /\ et\ m\acute{i}nd$$

$$\bar{T}o\ w\acute{a}r\ /\ \bar{a}nd\ arm\acute{s}\ /\ \bar{I}\ fl\acute{y}.$$

With these two scansions thus indicated, one may sense at once that all metric effect must result from the interplay of the mechanical and the meaningful beat. The mechanical beat corresponds roughly to those squares on the graph paper, and the meaningful beat to the variations of the drawn graph against the mechanical pattern.

Comparison of the two patterns shows that *a line may have more or fewer meaningful than mechanical stresses.* The second line, for example, has three mechanical stresses and two meaningful; the third has four mechanical and five meaningful. Such variation is more common than not in English metrics.

Moreover, *the stresses of the mechanical and of the meaningful scansions do not always coincide.* In the first line of the Lovelace passage, for example, three syllables unstressed in mechanical scansion receive meaningful stresses, and three syllables stressed in mechanical scansion receive no meaningful stresses. Such displacement will at once serve to indicate the presence of reversed feet—in this case, the presence of trochaic feet in an iambic line.

Further, *the mechanical and the meaningful stresses may coincide,* as in the fourth line. Such coincidence will serve to indicate a smooth or "rest" line. When a poem is metrically smooth for too long the effect will tend to monotony (an effect that can, of course, be sought deliberately as in part three of Auden's "In Memory of W. B. Yeats," page 830). Accomplished poets always tend to bring a metrically complicated poem "to rest" from time to time, but inept poets, by keeping the metrics too smooth for too long, tend to produce only a graceless and soporific tick-tock:

> O do not say that dreams are vain
> And love is not the goal of time.
> The soul of man was made to climb
> By love and dreams above the plain
> Where beasts do roam and must remain
> While man aspires to win that clime
> Where soul and soul are made to rhyme
> At home in bliss with Him again.

Once aware of these two patterns, one will be able to understand that conventional metric notation (itself not by any means an infallible measure) is an effort to indicate the interplay of meaningful and mechanical scansion in a single system of notation. He will see, further, that no one system of metrics is likely to serve all cases unless the notation becomes extremely conplicated.

The metric interpretation of the first word of Lovelace's poem is a case in point. Is there any sort of stress on "Tell"? One might reasonably argue that some slight stress should be indicated, though not as much as falls on "not"; but to indicate the degree of that stress would require a third size of caret, one smaller than the caret reserved for "not." The next step, obviously, is to evolve a system of caret sizes so complicated as to become more confusing than helpful.

In the case of unstressed syllables, on the other hand, conventional metrics has a useful measure in the very number of unstressed syllables per foot. If, as previously noted, iambic may be taken as corresponding to three-eighths time, then the unaccented syllable of the iambic foot corresponds to an eighth, and the unaccented syllables of an anapestic foot correspond to sixteenths. To keep the discussion within reasonable limits, nothing has been said of cases in which more than two unstressed syllables occur within a foot, though Richard Eberhart's "The Fury of Aerial Bombardment" (page 998) will demonstrate such a case. The poet Gerard Manley Hopkins evolved a metric of his own, largely on the premise that *there is no certain limit to the number of light sylla-*

bles that may be swallowed into a given foot. Thus the presence of three unstressed syllables within a foot would indicate thirty-seconds; of four, sixty-fourths, and so on.

Conventional metrics, however, does not generally admit a notation that distinguishes the relative emphases of stressed syllables, relying on a single vertical mark (ictus) to indicate stress. It will be well, however, by analogy to the carets of meaningful stress to use a double ictus to indicate exceptionally heavy stress. So indicated, Lovelace's poem may be scanned as follows:

> Tell me not// Sweet,// I am/ un kind
> That from/ the nunn/ er y
> Of thy / chaste breast / and qui / et mind
> To war / and arms / I fly.
>
> True,// a new mis / tress now / I chase,
> The first / foe in / the field;
> And with / a stron / ger faith / em brace
> A sword,/ a horse, / a shield.
>
> Yet this / in con / stan cy / is such
> As you/ too/ shall a dore;
> I could not / love you,/ dear,/ so much
> Loved I not/ hon our / more.

A study of this scansion should make clear that English metrics consists of a series of variations and compensations that are usually open to various interpretation. The first line of the second stanza, for example, might have been scanned in a less controversial way as follows:

> True, a / new mis / tress now / I chase

If, however, the obvious prose-rhythm of the phrasing (as further indicated by the comma) is to be honored, "True" must be a monosyllabic foot unless one wishes to admit the possibility of a caesura within the metric foot. That possibility can indeed be considered (see p. 948) but will not serve the present purpose. It is more apt to introduce the arrow, as in the first scansion, to indicate a special compensation whereby the unstressed syllable that would normally accompany the stressed "True" is shifted into the next measure.

One may reasonably argue, to take another example, that normal voice stress might put an accent on "And" at the beginning of the third line of the second stanza and that the first foot is, accordingly, a trochee rather than a pyrrhic.

It is the second line of this stanza, however, that deserves most particular attention. Shall it be indicated:

$$\text{Th}\bar{\text{e}} \text{ fi}\acute{\text{r}}\text{st} / \text{ f}\acute{\text{o}}\text{e } \bar{\text{in}} / \text{ th}\bar{\text{e}} \text{ fi}\acute{\text{e}}\text{ld}$$

or should it be:

$$\text{Th}\bar{\text{e}} \text{ fi}\acute{\text{r}}\text{st}/ \text{ f}\acute{\text{o}}\text{e}/ \bar{\text{in}} \text{ th}\bar{\text{e}} \text{ fi}\acute{\text{e}}\text{ld?}$$

Certainly the prose-rhythm force of the phrasing is such that "in the field" is clearly anapestic. Here is one more case in which an arrow would be useful to indicate a displacement, thus:

$$\text{Th}\bar{\text{e}} \text{ fi}\acute{\text{r}}\text{st } / \text{ f}\acute{\text{o}}\text{e}/ \text{ in th}\bar{\text{e}} \text{ fi}\acute{\text{e}}\text{ld.}$$

Such displacement may be taken as a principle of English metrics: *whenever a monosyllabic foot occurs, an unaccented syllable that would accompany the accent in a mechanical scansion may be displaced to the preceding or the following foot.* When the displaced unaccented syllable occurs in the preceding foot, that foot becomes feminine and no further notation is absolutely demanded, though the arrow may still be used as an indication. When the displaced unaccented syllable occurs in the following foot, it is well to indicate that displacement by an arrow.

The first line of Lovelace's poem will illustrate the further metric complication that *the same syllables cannot always be scanned in the same way.* "Tell me not, Sweet, I am unkind" has here been scanned with the first three syllables, "Tell me not," rendered as an anapestic foot. The same phrase in another context, however, might be emphatically trochaic:

$$\text{T}\acute{\text{e}}\text{ll m}\bar{\text{e}} / \text{ n}\acute{\text{o}}\text{t in} / \text{ m}\acute{\text{o}}\text{urn f}\bar{\text{ul}} / \text{ n}\acute{\text{u}}\text{m b}\bar{\text{e}}\text{rs.}$$

Or it might be iambic:

$$\text{T}\bar{\text{e}}\text{ll m}\acute{\text{e}} / \text{ n}\bar{\text{o}}\text{t h}\acute{\text{i}}\text{m. } // \text{ }\bar{\text{Is}} \text{ h}\acute{\text{e}}/ \text{ th}\bar{\text{e}} \text{ ju}\acute{\text{d}}\text{ge } / \text{ }\bar{\text{o}}\text{f l}\acute{\text{o}}\text{ve?}$$

The grammatical context, determining as it does the voice emphases of the spoken language (meaningful stress), is never entirely separable from metrics.

One further notation in the scansion of the Lovelace poem needs discussion. The first foot of the first line of the last stanza was marked: Yet this. Such notation indicates a *distributed stress*. The foot is not clearly spondaic in the sense that each syllable requires a distinct accent, yet the two syllables are clearly equal and not entirely unaccented. Whatever stress is to be allotted to that foot seems evenly divided between the two syllables.

Many other notations could be introduced into the discussion, but these will suffice for present purposes. One would do well to attempt detailed scansions of some of the following poems, or at least of some of their more interesting passages. Whether or not one undertakes such detailed scansions, he should at least apply the following measures to all of the poems:

QUESTIONS

1. If the poem is metrical—such a poem as H. D.'s "Socratic" (p. 975) for example, is not—identify the basic meter (i.e., as iambic pentameter, trochaic trimeter, etc.).

2. Place the notation for the mechanical scansion above the line and the carets for the meaningful stresses below the line.

3. To what extent do the mechanical and meaningful stresses coincide? (I.e., is the metrics smooth or rough?) Note that no matter how rough the metrics of some lines may be, the poet will introduce smooth or "rest" lines from time to time.

4. Mark the pattern of caesuras and end-stops.

5. Note any tendency for unstressed syllables to fall together.

6. Note any tendency for stressed syllables to fall together.

7. Note marginally any non-metrical devices that tend to accelerate or impede any part of the poem. A number of such non-metrical devices that contribute to acceleration or impedence will be discussed in connection with some of the poems that follow.

Poems for Guided Study—Acceleration and Impedance

Shapiro's "Buick" (p. 920) is written as a *tour de force* in anapestic hexameter, a rare meter in English. Sustained anapestic meter is much rarer in English poetry than sustained iambic, and good poets who use such a meter invariably introduce many little variations to keep the voice from being swept entirely away by the flow of the tripping unstressed syllables.

No poet in English has relied more heavily upon the anapest than has Swinburne. Long chains of anapests combined with the non-metrical acceleration produced by heavy alliteration became so characteristic of

Swinburne's style that he was moved to write a nonsense poem in self-parody. "Nephelidia" (Little Clouds) for the fun of it, carries both these devices to the point of absurdity, and as a pleasant gesture of recognizing one's own weaknesses. The meter is basically anapestic octameter, the eight-foot line serving to exaggerate further the anapestic abuse of the rhythm. The alliteration is beyond description. "Meaning" is nowhere to be found except in the fun of the trick itself.

In assessing what produces the extraordinary acceleration of this poem, the reader will do well to consider carefully before assigning the effect to any one cause. Metrically, the speed of the poem is certainly due to the anapestic structure and to the fact that Swinburne drags it out through an extraordinary eight-foot line. Non-metrically, the acceleration is certainly assisted by the heavy alliteration. It is important to bear in mind, however, that all these devices work together in producing the total effect.

Nephelidia

(an excerpt)

Algernon Charles Swinburne

From the depth of the dreamy decline of the dawn through a notable
    nimbus of nebulous noonshine,
    Pallid and pink as the palm of the flag-flower that flickers with fear of
        the flies as they float—
Are the looks of our lovers that lustrously lean from a marvel of mystic
    miraculous moonshine,
    These that we feel in the blood of our blushes that thicken and threaten
        with throbs through the throat?
Thicken and thrill as a theatre thronged at appeal of an actor's appalled
    agitation,
    Fainter with fear of the fires of the future than pale with the promise
        of pride in the past;
Flushed with the famishing fullness of fever that reddens with radiance of
    rathe recreation,
    Gaunt as the ghastliest of glimpses that gleam through the gloom of the
        gloaming when ghosts go aghast?
Nay, for the nick of the tick of the time is a tremulous touch on the
    temples of terror,
    Strained as the sinews yet strenuous with strife of the dead who is dumb
        as the dust-heaps of death:
Surely no soul is it, sweet as the spasm of erotic emotional exquisite error,
    Bathed in the balms of beatified bliss, beatific itself by beatitude's
        breath.
Surely no spirit or sense of a soul that was soft to the spirit and soul of our
    senses

Sweetens the stress of suspiring suspicion that sobs in the semblance
  and sound of a sigh;
Only this oracle opens Olympian, in mystical moods and triangular tenses—
  "Life is the lust of a lamp for the light that is dark till the dawn of the
  day that we die."

The last line of this excerpt is a triumph of fun. Note that it begins and
ends with stressed syllables. Since "Life" must obviously be stressed, one
may be tempted to read the line as that rare thing, a dactyllic octameter.
A second look, however, will make it clear that like others in the extract,
the line is anapestic with a monosyllabic first foot:

$$\text{Life/ is the lust/ of a lamp/ for the light/ etc.}$$

The first foot in such lines is *truncated*. In any art form *pattern* exerts
a powerful force. With a strong anapestic pattern established in the
first line, it becomes possible to omit some part of the pattern and still
to feel its force. Suppose, for example, that Swinburne had written the
first foot of every line in full conformity with the pattern: e.g., "As our
life." And suppose then that he struck out the first two syllables in
the course of revising the poem. In order to feel free to do so he must
certainly have relied on the fact that his pattern was so strongly estab-
lished that he could easily afford to swallow two syllables without dis-
rupting the reading. The truncation of those two syllables (whether or
not they ever existed on paper) may be indicated by commas if one
wishes, and the first foot may then be scanned:

$$\text{, , Life/}$$

Swinburne's self-parody will do as well as any passage in English to
demonstrate the dangers inherent in the sustained anapest. The meter
trips so fast that it tends to take over from the poet the management of
the poem. The poet is left nothing to do but to turn the crank for more
and more anapests, the meter becoming more and more mechanical.

Alliteration is, of course, inseparable from the total effect of "Nephe-
lidia." The three poems that follow will demonstrate a number of non-
metrical devices that affect the motion of the poem.

Sir Beelzebub

Edith Sitwell

WHEN
Sir
Beelzebub called for his syllabub in the hotel in Hell
  Where Proserpine first fell,
  Blue as the gendarmerie were the waves of the sea,

REPRINTED by permission of the publisher, The Vanguard Press, from *The Collected Poems of Edith Sitwell*. Copyright, 1954, by Edith Sitwell.

(Rocking and shocking the bar-maid.)

Nobody comes to give him his rum but the
Rim of the sky hippopotamus-glum
Enhances the chances to bless with a benison
Alfred Lord Tennyson crossing the bar laid
With cold vegetation from pale deputations
Of temperance workers (all signed In Memoriam)
Hoping with glory to trip up the Laureate's feet,

(Moving in classical meters). . . .

Like Balaclava, the lava came down from the
Roof, and the sea's blue wooden gendarmerie
Took them in charge while Beelzebub roared for his rum.

. . . None of them come!

The principal non-metrical devices for acceleration and impedance are:

(1) sound patterns: alliteration, vowel and consonant sequences, consonantal clusters, rhyme, internal rhyme, repetition of the same word or phrase.

(2) visual patterns: the isolation of words as single lines, the separation of words from one another by unusual spacings in the line, the breaking off of lines for special effect.

(3) punctuation: in one sense punctuation is a special case of visual pattern. Punctuation must be taken to include the capitalization of whole words or of their first letters, and the use of italics.

(4) grammatical structure: particularly parallel constructions and balanced antitheses as devices for controlling the voice emphases of the speech rhythms.

Of these devices, only the first will require special discussion here. The remaining three are obvious and can be cited as they occur in specific poems.

"Sir Beelzebub" makes notable use of sound patterns, but it depends on all the other elements as well for its effect. The isolation of single words in the first two lines, and the capitalization of WHEN in the first, cannot fail to instruct the voice to apply special emphases to these words: they lead into the poem like two slow drum beats. They are then immediately followed by an enormously accelerated passage. One should note also the special effect of the punctuation in varying the pace of the poem from passage to passage, the function of the two parentheses in varying the pace, and the unusual way in which some of the lines break off on "the."

Unlike the sound patterns of "Nephelidia," however, those of "Sir Beelzebub" run much more to internal rhyme than to alliteration, though some alliteration assists the total effect. The internal rhymes, moreover, tend to involve more than one syllable: "Beelzebub—syllabub," "enhances—chances," "benison—Tennyson." What would have been the difference of effect had those rhymes involved a single syllable only?

> WHEN
> Sir
> Glub called for his tub in the hotel in Hell . . .

Which of the non-metrical devices listed above work for acceleration in "Sir Beelzebub," and which work for impedance? How concerned is the poet for ringing the changes from impedance to acceleration?

Apply the same measures to the two poems that follow.

The Congo
(A Study of the Negro Race)
Vachel Lindsay

I. THEIR BASIC SAVAGERY

Fat black bucks in a wine-barrel room,	
Barrel-house kings, with feet unstable,	
Sagged and reeled and pounded on the table,	*A deep rolling*
Pounded on the table,	*bass.*
Beat an empty barrel with the handle of a broom,	
Hard as they were able,	
Boom, boom, BOOM,	
With a silk umbrella and the handle of a broom,	
Boomlay, boomlay, boomlay, BOOM.	

THEN I had *r*eligion, THEN I had a vision.	
I could not turn from their revel in derision.	
THEN I SAW THE CONGO, CREEPING THROUGH THE BLACK,	*More deliberate.*
CUTTING THROUGH THE JUNGLE WITH A GOLDEN TRACK.	*Solemnly chanted.*

Then along that riverbank	
A thousand miles	
Tattooed cannibals danced in files;	
Then I heard the boom of the blood-lust song	
And a thigh-bone beating on a tin-pan gong.	*A rapidly piling*
And "BLOOD" screamed the whistles and the fifes of the	*climax of speed*
warriors,	*and rocket.*

FROM *Collected Poems,* by Vachel Lindsay. Used with permission of The Macmillan Company.

"Blood" screamed the skull-faced, lean witch-doctors,
"Whirl ye the deadly voo-doo rattle,
Harry the uplands,
Steal all the cattle,
Rattle-rattle, rattle-rattle,
Bing!
Boomlay, boomlay, boomlay, Boom,"
A roaring, epic, rag-time tune   *With a philo-*
From the mouth of the Congo   *sophic pause.*
To the Mountains of the Moon.
Death is an Elephant,   *Shrilly and with a*
Torch-eyed and horrible,   *heavily accented*
Foam-flanked and terrible.   *meter.*
Boom, steal the pygmies,
Boom, kill the Arabs,
Boom, kill the white men,
Hoo, Hoo, Hoo.   *Like the wind in*
Listen to the yell of Leopold's ghost   *the chimney.*
Burning in Hell for his hand-maimed host.
Hear how the demons chuckle and yell
Cutting his hands off, down in Hell.
Listen to the creepy proclamation,
Blown through the lairs of the forest-nation,
Blown past the white-ants' hill of clay,
Blown past the marsh where the butterflies play:—
"Be careful what you do,
Or Mumbo-Jumbo, God of the Congo,   *All the o sounds*
And all of the other   *very golden.*
Gods of the Congo,   *Heavy accents*
     very heavy.
Mumbo-Jumbo will hoo-doo you,   *Light accents*
Mumbo-Jumbo will hoo-doo you,   *very light. Last*
Mumbo-Jumbo will hoo-doo you."   *line whispered.*

II. Their Irrepressible High Spirits

Wild crap-shooters with a whoop and a call   *Rather shrill*
Danced the juba in their gambling-hall   *and high.*
And laughed fit to kill, and shook the town,
And guyed the policemen and laughed them down
With a boomlay, boomlay, boomlay, Boom. . . .
Then I saw the Congo, creeping through the black,   *Read exactly as*
Cutting through the jungle with a golden track.   *in first section.*
A negro fairyland swung into view,   *Lay emphasis on*
A minstrel river   *the delicate ideas.*
Where dreams come true.   *Keep as light-*
     footed as possible.
The ebony palace soared on high
Through the blossoming trees to the evening sky,
The inlaid porches and casements shone

With gold and ivory and elephant-bone.
And the black crowd laughed till their sides were sore
At the baboon butler in the agate door,
And the well-known tunes of the parrot band
That trilled on the bushes of that magic land.
A troupe of skull-faced witch-men came   *With pomposity.*
Through the agate doorway in suits of flame,
Yes, long-tailed coats with a gold-leaf crust
And hats that were covered with diamond-dust.
And the crowd in the court gave a whoop and a call
And danced the juba from wall to wall.
But the witch-men suddenly stilled the throng   *With a great*
With a stern cold glare, and a stern old song:—   *deliberation and*
"Mumbo-Jumbo will hoo-doo you." . . .   *ghostliness.*
Just then from the doorway, as fat as shotes,   *With overwhelm-*
Came the cake-walk princes in their long red coats,   *ing assurance,*
Shoes with a patent leather shine,   *good cheer, and*
And tall silk hats that were red as wine.   *pomp.*
And they pranced with their butterfly partners there,   *With growing*
Coal-black maidens with pearls in their hair,   *speed and*
Knee-skirts trimmed with the jessamine sweet,   *sharply marked*
And bells on their ankles and little black feet.   *dance-rhythm.*
And the couples railed at the chant and the frown
Of the witch-men lean, and laughed them down.
(O rare was the revel, and well worth while
That made those glowering witch-men smile).

The cake-walk royalty then began
To walk for a cake that was tall as a man
To the tune of "Boomlay, boomlay, Boom,"
While the witch-men laughed, with a sinister air,   *With a touch of*
And sang with the scalawags prancing there:—   *negro dialect,*
"Walk with care, walk with care,   *and*
Or Mumbo-Jumbo, God of the Congo,   *as rapidly as*
And all of the other   *possible toward*
Gods of the Congo,   *the end.*
Mumbo-Jumbo will hoo-doo you.
Beware, beware, walk with care,
Boomlay, boomlay, boomlay, boom.
Boomlay, boomlay, boomlay, boom,
Boomlay, boomlay, boomlay, boom,
Boomlay, boomlay, boomlay,
Boom."
O rare was the revel, and well worth while   *Slow philo-*
That made those glowering witch-men smile.   *sophic calm.*

III. THE HOPE OF THEIR RELIGION

A good old negro in the slums of the town
Preached at a sister for her velvet gown.
Howled at a brother for his low-down ways,
His prowling, guzzling, sneak-thief days.
Beat on the Bible till he wore it out,
Starting the jubilee revival shout.
And some had visions, as they stood on chairs,
And sang of Jacob, and the golden stairs.
And they all repented, a thousand strong,
From their stupor and savagery and sin and wrong
And slammed their hymn books till they shook the room
With "Glory, glory, glory,"
And "Boom, boom, BOOM."

Heavy bass. With a literal imitation of camp-meeting racket, and trance.

THEN I SAW THE CONGO, CREEPING THROUGH THE BLACK,
CUTTING THROUGH THE JUNGLE WITH A GOLDEN TRACK.
And the gray sky opened like a new-rent veil
And showed the Apostles with their coats of mail.
In bright white steel they were seated round
And their fire-eyes watched where the Congo wound.
And the twelve Apostles, from their thrones on high,
Thrilled all the forest with their heavenly cry:—
"Mumbo-Jumbo will die in the jungle;
Never again will he hoo-doo you,
Never again will he hoo-doo you."

Exactly as in the first section.

Sung to the tune of "Hark, ten thousand harps and voices."

Then along that river, a thousand miles
The vine-snared trees fell down in files.
Pioneer angels cleared the way
For a Congo paradise, for babes at play,
For sacred capitals, for temples clean.
Gone were the skull-faced witch-men lean.
There, where the wild ghost-gods had wailed
A million boats of the angels sailed
With oars of silver, and prows of blue
And silken pennants that the sun shone through.
'Twas a land transfigured, 'twas a new creation.
Oh, a singing wind swept the negro nation
And on through the backwoods clearing flew:—
"Mumbo-Jumbo is dead in the jungle.
Never again will he hoo-doo you.
Never again will he hoo-doo you."

With growing deliberation and joy.

In a rather high key—as delicately as possible.

To the tune of "Hark, ten thousand harps and voices."

Redeemed were the forests, the beasts and the men,
And only the vulture dared again
By the far, lone mountains of the moon
To cry, in the silence, the Congo tune:—
"Mumbo-Jumbo will hoo-doo you,
Mumbo . . . Jumbo . . . will . . . hoo-doo . . . you."

Dying off into a penetrating, terrified whisper.

How Jack Found that Beans May Go Back on a Chap

Guy Wetmore Carryl

Without the slightest basis
For hypochondriasis
   A widow had forebodings which a cloud around her flung,
And with expression cynical
For half the day a clinical
   Thermometer she held beneath her tongue.

Whene'er she read the papers
She suffered from the vapors,
   At every tale of malady or accident she'd groan;
In every new and smart disease,
From housemaid's knee to heart disease,
   She recognized the symptoms as her own!

She had a yearning chronic
To try each novel tonic,
   Elixir, panacea, lotion, opiate, and balm;
And from a homeopathist
Would change to an hydropathist,
   And back again, with stupefying calm!

She was nervous, cataleptic,
And anemic, and dyspeptic:
   Though not convinced of apoplexy, yet she had her fears.
She dwelt with force fanatical
Upon a twinge rheumatical,
   And said she had a buzzing in her ears!

Now all of this bemoaning
And this grumbling and this groaning
   The mind of Jack, her son and heir, unconscionably bored.
His heart completely hardening,
He gave his time to gardening,
   For raising beans was something he adored.

Each hour in accents morbid
This limp maternal bore bid
   Her callous son affectionate and lachrymose good-bys.
She never granted Jack a day
Without some long "Alackaday!"
   Accompanied by rolling of the eyes.

But Jack, no panic showing,
Just watched his beanstalk growing,
   And twined with tender fingers the tendrils up the pole.

At all her words funereal
He smiled a smile ethereal,
   Or sighed an absent-minded "Bless my soul!"

That hollow-hearted creature
Would never change a feature:
   No tear bedimmed his eye, however touching was her talk.
She never fussed or flurried him,
The only thing that worried him
   Was when no bean-pods grew upon the stalk!

But then he wabbled loosely
His head, and wept profusely,
   And, taking out his handkerchief to mop away his tears,
Exclaimed: "It hasn't got any!"
He found this blow to botany
   Was sadder than were all his mother's fears.

The Moral is that gardeners pine
Whene'er no pods adorn the vine.
Of all sad words experience gleans
The saddest are: "It *might* have beans."
   (I did not make this up myself:
   'Twas in a book upon my shelf.
   It's witty, but I don't deny
   It's rather Whittier than I!)

To observe the effect of rhymes running to more than one syllable, compare the following lines with the first two stanzas of Carryl's poem:

Without the slightest need
For feeling off her feed
   A widow had forebodings which a cloud around her flung,
And with a look like brass
For half a day a glass
   Thermometer she held beneath the tongue.

Whene'er she read the news
She suffered from the blues,
   At every tale of malady or accident she'd groan;
In every new and smart ill
From housemaid's knees to flu-chill,
   She recognized the symptoms as her own.

Rhyme can function very importantly in affecting the motion of the poem. In general the heavier and more complicated the rhymes (whether internal or at the end of the line) the more they will tend to accelerate the pace. Poets, in fact, shun especially complicated rhymes in serious poems. They do so because the cleverness and the acceleration of such rhymes seems incompatible with *seriousness*. Such tricky rhyme sequences, therefore, remain the almost exclusive device of light verse writers.

While the discussion is on rhyme it seems pertinent to mention some of the devices introduced into English rhymes by more recent poets, even though those devices are not intimately connected with the pace of the poem. Traditional English rhyme is *syllabic*. That is, it rhymes the final syllable of each rhyme-word. Examples of syllabic rhyme are: dove—love, and—hand, clever—never, "intellectual—hen-pecked-you-all." Within English convention, and for reasons that need not be discussed here, a number of common rhymes are merely *visual*. Examples of such visual rhymes are: "love—move," "wind—mind," "has—was." Obviously, such rhymes are intended to function as syllabic.

English convention also has a certain tolerance, though bad poets are forever abusing that tolerance, for *false rhyme*. True rhyme pairs stressed syllable with stressed syllable. False rhyme offers an unstressed syllable as a rhyme for a stressed syllable. Examples of false rhymes are: apple—full, sea—eternity, widow—snow. Few poetic abuses can be drearier than the rhyming of a poet who keeps pairing such monosyllabic and simple rhymes as "sea" with such easy, large poeticisms as "ecstacy, infinity, inconstancy," and with such adverbs as "exultantly, mystically, imponderably."

But, as was observed in the discussion of Frost's "Stopping by Woods on a Snowy Evening," English is a rhyme-poor language. Inevitably certain rhymes tend to pair up, with a consequent sense of dull predictability. And inevitably the poets will cast about for ways of refreshing their rhymes.

One resort of the past and one still importantly current is to abandon rhyme altogether. When the poetry is metrically regular but unrhymed, it is referred to as *blank verse*. Almost all blank verse of the past was written in iambic pentameter, but many twentieth century poets and some of their forerunners have dropped not only rhyme but metrical regularity to write what has become known as *free verse*.

Rhyme, however, is too valuable a device to be abandoned permanently, and many more recent poets have worked to vary their rhyme methods rather than to eliminate rhyme altogether. The principal variations from syllabic rhyme are consonantal, assonantal, and approximate rhyme.

Of these variations, *consonantal rhyme* is perhaps the most immediately apt to the quality of English speech. It has the further advantage of being every bit as strict as syllabic rhyme. Consonantal rhyme, however, does not rhyme the syllable (which consists generally of a vowel-and-consonant sound group, though it may consist of a single vowel) but rhymes instead the consonants that enclose the last syllable while varying the vowel. Examples of consonantal rhyme are: "run—ran," "maid—mud," "hill—hall." Note especially, however, that consonantal rhymes tend to run in

readily available chords: "run—wren—ran—Rhine—rune—ruin," or "maid
—mid—Maud—mud—mad," or "hill—hale—heil—hall—hole—who'll," etc.
No poet as yet has systematically worked out the possibilities of such
chords as the rhymes for whole stanzas (Wilfred Owen, killed at twenty-
five in World War I, comes closest to having done so) but certainly they
make possible special stanzaic effects. Combined with syllabic rhymes,
consonantal rhymes make possible extended progressions of rhyme, as for
example, "rain—wren—when—wan—dawn—dine—mine—main—rain."
Consonantal rhyme is often used in combination with syllabic, assonantal,
or approximate rhyme.

Assonantal rhyme reverses the procedure of consonantal rhyme and
pairs simply the vowel sound without regard to the consonants. Examples
of such rhyme are: "hat—mad, shine—smile, gruff—dud," but more charac-
teristically: "shine—eye, heel—sea, grave—day"; the second rhyme of an
assonantal pairing, that is to say, seems to work best when the vowel is
not closed in by a final consonant. Assonance is native to French poetry
because of the number of words in French that lend themselves to such
treatment: it seems doubtful that assonance will ever become a major
device of English poetry though it can contribute certain grace notes to
the poetic structure.

Approximate rhyme is a more indeterminate name for all rhymes that
are not quite syllabic, not quite consonantal, and not quite assonantal, but
that obviously pair words of somewhat related sound. Approximate rhymes
tend to occur most naturally around such strong sounds as *x* as in: "depicts
—fix, lacks—fox, tax—tanks." They may, however, occur in combinations
of all other English sounds. Wilfred Owen made extensive use of approxi-
mate rhymes in combination with others. Here, for example, are the
rhyme sequences of the first twenty-one lines of one of Owen's war poems:
"escaped—scooped—groined—groaned—bestirred—stared—eyes—bless—
hall—Hell—grained—ground—moan—mourn—years—yours—wild—world
—hair—hour—here."

To return to the discussion of rhyme as it affects the pace of the poem, it
seems to be a general rule that heavy rhyme (*i.e.*, a sequence of more
than two rhymes), especially when it occurs in poems with short lines,
tends to produce acceleration and emphasis together, as in a rapid and
staccato liturgy. In such a poet as John Skelton, for example, the short
rough line that might have resulted in a heavily emphasized slowing of
the pace because of the natural tendency of the voice to pause at the end
of the line, is hurtled along by the heavy pounding of the rhyme. Skelton,
it must be borne in mind, died in 1529, and English pronunciation has
changed markedly since his time. Skelton's movement will be better
approximated if one reads joyoúsly, maidénly, womanly, demeaníng.
Thus part of the effect may be seen to reside in the fact that one must
swallow many light syllables *en route* to a heavy final accent.

To Mistress Margaret Hussey

John Skelton

Merry Margaret
As midsummer flower,
Gentle as falcon
Or hawk of the tower;
With solace and gladness,
Much mirth and no madness,
All good and no badness;
So joyously,
So maidenly,
So womanly,
Her demeaning,
In every thing
Far far passing
That I can indite
Or suffice to write
Of merry Margaret,
As midsummer flower,
Gentle as falcon
Or hawk of the tower.

As patient and as still,
And as full of good will,
As the fair Isyphill,
Coriander,
Sweet pomander,
Good Cassander,
Steadfast of thought,
Well made, well wrought.
Far may be sought
Ere that ye can find
So courteous, so kind,
As merry Margaret,
This midsummer flower,
Gentle as falcon
Or hawk of the tower.

That I can indite: That which I can write. **Isyphill:** Hypsipyle, a beautiful woman of Greek legend. **Coriander:** an aromatic herb. **pomander:** a sachet. **Cassander:** Cassandra, daughter of King Priam of Troy.

But rhyme may also function for emphasis or to slow down a passage. Yeats uses internal rhyme for stunning emphasis in the sixth line of the following poem. "Supreme theme" is clearly a climactic assertion. Yeats emphasizes it not only metrically but by the heavy rhyme sounds that occur with nothing between them.

After Long Silence

William Butler Yeats

Speech after long silence; it is right
All other lovers being estranged or dead,
Unfriendly lamplight hid under its shade,
The curtains drawn upon unfriendly night,
That we descant and yet again descant
Upon the supreme theme of Art and Song:
Bodily decrepitude is wisdom; young
We loved each other and were ignorant.

In "The Grindstone," Robert Frost uses an unusual final rhyme for emphasis. The poem concludes:

What if it wasn't all it should be? I'd
Be satisfied, if he'd be satisfied.

The reader is forced to punch down hard on the "I'd" rhyme, in part because it is an unusual rhyme, and in part because of the unusual placement of the word (visual pattern). Then, having been forced to emphasize "I'd," the reader must emphasize "he'd" in the next line, as demanded by the force of the parallel grammatical construction.

To these non-metrical devices for emphasis, one must add the metrical force of "I'd" as a monosyllabic foot. The metric situation of the monosyllabic foot is well worth a particular look. Note the following examples:

'Tis with/ our judg/ ments as/ our wa tches, // none
Go just / a like,// yet each/ be lieves/ his own.

> Alexander Pope

Bod' ly/ de crep/ i tude/ is wis dom;// young
We loved/ each o ther// and were ig/ nor ant.

> W. B. Yeats

What if/ it was/ n't all/ it should be?// I'd
Be sat/ is fied/ if he'd/ be sat/ is fied.

> Robert Frost

From *Collected Poems* by William Butler Yeats. Used with permission of The Macmillan Company.

The second line of the Yeats excerpt is metrically very complicated. One may also scan the line as follows:

$$\text{We lov\'ed/ each o/ ther//and / were ig/ nor ant}$$

with the third foot rendered as a pyrrhic containing a caesura within it. If the line must be brought to five feet at all costs it seems far more reasonable to take the caesura as a foot all by itself (a full measure rest) than to render a *split-pyrrhic*, whatever that might be. The fact is that Yeats' line (it is the last line of the poem) is constructed for a deliberately falling rhythm. And might almost be rendered:

$$\text{We lov\'ed/ each o ther//and were ig nor ant.}$$

Certainly the stress on the last syllable of "ignorant" is hardly more than formal as compared to the stress on the first syllable. Note, however, that despite all variation, the syllable count is full and the mechanical scansion presents no difficulties:

$$\text{We lov\'ed/ each o/ ther and/ were ig/ nor ant.}$$

In each of these passages the final monosyllabic foot at the end of the first line is used in exactly the same way. That metric pattern may be represented thus:

$$- / - // //$$

Note that in each case there is an extra unstressed (feminine) syllable immediately before the caesura. Obviously, a light syllable has been displaced from the last foot to the preceding foot, and one might use the arrow as the notation for such displacement, thus:

$$- / - \overset{\curvearrowright}{//} //$$

The need for such a light syllable preceding the caesura will be evident at once if one substitutes "clocks" for "watches," "wise" for "wisdom," and "I'd hoped" for "it should be." The result would not be increased emphasis but awkwardness. *The normal pattern for a final monosyllabic foot requires an unstressed syllable before the caesura that divides the foot from the line.*

The next to last line of the following passage will illustrate that *there will be an exception to this rule when the last two feet are both monosyllabic*:

Voice of the Studio Announcer
from *The Fall of the City*
Archibald MacLeish

Ladies and gentlemen:
This broadcast comes to you from the city.
Listeners over the curving air have heard
From furthest off frontiers of foreign hours
Mountain Time: Ocean Time: of the islands:
Of waters after the islands   some of them waking
Where noon here is night there: some
Where noon is the first few stars they see or the last one.

The next to last line may be scanned:

$$\overset{-}{\text{Where}} \overset{/}{\text{noon}}/ \overset{//}{\text{here}}/ \overset{-}{\text{is}} \overset{/}{\text{night}}/ \overset{//}{\text{there}}: // \overset{//}{\text{some}}$$

The extraordinary metrics of this line obviously reflects MacLeish's special concern for the staccato quality of the radio announcer's way of speaking. Note how important caesura is to the special effect of the entire passage.

Pause, whether achieved by metrical or non-metrical devices, is fundamental to the quality of any poetic line. The nature of the poetic line itself, however, must be considered. A poetic line is not simply a quantity of language. One might, for example, write in flawless syllabic count without remotely approaching poetry:

> I bought some shoes and then I put them on
> My feet and took a walk and they felt good.

The deadness of such lines results not only from the fact that they are metronomic, but that *they are not true units of phrase.* Compare the following individual lines from many sources:

> When in disgrace with fortune and men's eyes

> Yet once more, O ye laurels, and once more

> Since there's no help, come, let us kiss and part

> It is morning, Senlin says, and in the morning

> Full fathom five thy father lies

From *The Fall of the City*, by Archibald MacLeish. Copyright, 1937, by Archibald MacLeish. Reprinted by permission of Rinehart & Company, Inc., New York, Publishers.

Bid me to live and I will live

Bob Southey! You're a poet — Poet Laureate

Whenas in silks my Julia goes

The mellow ousel fluted in the elm

Such lines are not only metrical units but natural units of language. They are metrical units for reasons that should now be clear. They are units of language because they seem to fit naturally onto the tongue and the breath-groupings of English speaking people, and to fit as rounded phrases rather than as fragments of phrases. To resort once more to a musical analogy, the lines seem to be not simply quantities of notes, but discreet and sufficient musical phrases: stop them anywhere short of their own end and one has not a phrase but a fragment of a phrase. One may note also that the lines powerfully suggest how they should read, even as isolated lines.

One part of the suggestion of a true poetic line is its general tendency to bring the voice to rest at the line-ending. Such lines are referred to as *end-stopped*. Inevitably, however, there will be situations in which the poet finds it necessary to urge the voice on to the next line without an end-stop. A poet's way of handling end-stops and run-ons can have a great deal to do with the pace of his poem.

In the two following poems mark every end-stop and every run-on. (A down-curving arrow is a useful notation for a run-on line.)

Then, preferably with ink or pencil of a different color, mark all internal pauses. Which poem has more internal pause? Is there any observable relation between internal pauses and end-stops, or between internal pauses and run-ons? Which poem seems more colloquial in its speech rhythms and which more formal? Have the pauses (both internal and end-stop) and the run-ons any discernible relation to the differences of the speech rhythms?

My Last Duchess

Robert Browning

That's my last Duchess painted on the wall,
Looking as if she were alive. I call
That piece a wonder, now: Frà Pandolf's hands
Worked busily a day, and there she stands.
Will't please you sit and look at her? I said
"Frà Pandolf" by design, for never read
Strangers like you that pictured countenance,
The depth and passion of its earnest glance,

But to myself they turned (since none puts by
The curtain I have drawn for you, but I)
And seemed as they would ask me, if they durst,
How such a glance came there; so, not the first
Are you to turn and ask thus. Sir, 'twas not
Her husband's presence only, called that spot
Of joy into the Duchess' cheek: perhaps
Frà Pandolf chanced to say, "Her mantle laps
Over my Lady's wrist too much," or "Paint
Must never hope to reproduce the faint
Half-flush that dies along her throat"; such stuff
Was courtesy, she thought, and cause enough
For calling up that spot of joy. She had
A heart—how shall I say?—too soon made glad,
Too easily impressed; she liked whate'er
She looked on, and her looks went everywhere.
Sir, 'twas all one! My favor at her breast,
The dropping of the daylight in the West,
The bough of cherries some officious fool
Broke in the orchard for her, the white mule
She rode with round the terrace—all and each
Would draw from her alike the approving speech,
Or blush, at least. She thanked men,—good; but thanked
Somehow—I know not how—as if she ranked
My gift of a nine-hundred-years'-old name
With anybody's gift. Who'd stoop to blame
This sort of trifling? Even had you skill
In speech—(which I have not)—to make your will
Quite clear to such an one, and say, "Just this
Or that in you disgusts me; here you miss,
Or there exceed the mark"—and if she let
Herself be lessoned so, nor plainly set
Her wits to yours, forsooth, and made excuse,
—E'en then would be some stooping, and I choose
Never to stoop. Oh, sir, she smiled, no doubt,
Whene'er I passed her; but who passed without
Much the same smile? This grew; I gave commands;
Then all smiles stopped together. There she stands
As if alive. Will't please you rise? We'll meet
The company below, then. I repeat,
The Count your master's known munificence
Is ample warrant that no just pretence
Of mine for dowry will be disallowed;
Though his fair daughter's self, as I avowed
At starting, is my object. Nay, we'll go
Together down, sir! Notice Neptune, though,
Taming a sea-horse, thought a rarity,
Which Claus of Innsbruck cast in bronze for me!

from Crass Times Redeemed by Dignity of Souls

Peter Viereck

II

The tenderness of dignity of souls
Sweetens our cheated gusto and consoles.
It shades love's lidless eyes like parasols
And tames the earthquake licking at our soles.
Retunes the tensions of the flesh we wear.
Forgives the dissonance our triumphs blare.
And maps the burrows of heart's buried lair
Where furtive furry Wishes hide like moles.
O hear the kind voice, hear it everywhere
(It sings, it sings, it conjures and cajoles,
Prompting us shyly in our half-learnt rôles.
It sprouts the great chromatic vine that lolls
In small black petals on our music scrolls
(It flares, it flowers—it quickens yet controls).
It teaches dance-steps to this uncouth bear
Who hops and stumbles in our skin and howls.

The weight that tortures diamonds out of coals
Is lighter than the skimming hooves of foals
Compared to one old heaviness our souls
Hoist daily, each alone, and cannot share:
To-be-awake, to sense, to be aware.
Then even the dusty dreams that clog our skulls,
The rant and thunder of the storm we are,
The sunny silences our prophets hear,
The rainbow of the oil upon the shoals,
The crimes and Christmases of creature lives,
And all pride's barefoot tarantelle on knives
Are but the search for dignity of souls.

As always, one device tends to work with another. "Crass Times Re-
deemed by Dignity of Souls" is not so much a colloquially-spoken as an
incantatory poem. The poet wants the poem intoned in a mechanical,
litanized way. Such a reading requires a full stop at the end of each line
(and with that pause as the dominant voice punctuation, such a reading
requires little internal pause, since internal pause would make the end
pauses less emphatic). Especially in the second verse-paragraph of the ex-
cerpt, however, the meaning does not come to a rest at the end of each
line and normally the voice would run on to the next. Here the poet makes

the rhyme function as additional emphasis. Repetition, as already noted, is a natural means of emphasis.

Viereck, by picking up in his second paragraph the heavy sequence of strong "oles" rhymes which he established in the first, instructs the voice to pause at the end of the first three lines where it would normally run on. He also eliminates all internal pause in these lines. In the fourth, both the sense of the line and the final colon are pause enough, and he can accordingly change rhyme-scheme and allow caesuras in the line without losing his incantatory effect. The rhyme assistance is not needed in lines four to ten since the meaning comes to its own pause at the end of each, but note that after a variation into internal pause in lines four and five, the lines once more march straight to their end-stop, re-emphasizing the incantatory effect. Finally, there would be a normal tendency to run-on in the next to the last line were one to depend upon the meaning alone, and here Viereck once more returns to much heavier and closer rhyme than he has been using in the immediately preceding lines. "Knives-lives" are strong sounds and close together. As further instruction to the reader Viereck isolates the last line into a special sense by italicizing it. It is impossible to miss his voice-instruction (which is, of course, his control of pace) if one takes these clear indications into account. It is pertinent, however, to ask again how the poem could mean what it means without that incantatory insistence of the rhythm. A related question may be useful in locating this idea: Would a prayer "mean" what it "means" if, without changing any of its words, its normal intonations were syncopated into a jazz beat?

Poems for Individual Analysis: Acceleration and Impedance

The End of the World

Archibald MacLeish

Quite unexpectedly as Vasserot
The armless ambidextrian was lighting
A match between his great and second toe
And Ralph the lion was engaged in biting
The neck of Madame Sossman while the drum
Pointed, and Teeny was about to cough
In waltz-time swinging Jocko by the thumb—
Quite unexpectedly the top blew off.

FROM *Collected Poems 1917–1952* by Archibald MacLeish. Reprinted by permission of Houghton Mifflin Company.

And there, there overhead, there, there, hung over
Those thousands of white faces, those dazed eyes,
There in the starless dark, the poise, the hover,
There with vast wings across the canceled skies,
There in the sudden blackness, the black pall
Of nothing, nothing, nothing—nothing at all.

The Traveler's Curse after Misdirection
(*from the Welsh*)

Robert Graves

May they wander stage by stage
Of the same vain pilgrimage,
Stumbling on, age after age,
Night and day, mile after mile,
At each and every step, a stile;
At each and every stile, withal,
May they catch their feet and fall;
At each and every fall they take,
May a bone within them break;
And may the bones that break within
Not be, for variation's sake,
Now rib, now thigh, now arm, now shin,
But always, without fail, THE NECK.

The Rubáiyát of Omar Khayyám (excerpts)
—*translated by Edward Fitzgerald*

I.　A Book of Verses underneath the Bough,
A Jug of Wine, a Loaf of Bread—and Thou
　　Beside me singing in the Wilderness—
Ah, Wilderness were Paradise enow!

II.　I sometimes think that never blows so red
The Rose at where some buried Caesar bled;
　　That every Hyacinth the Garden wears
Dropt in her Lap from some once lovely Head.

III.　Think in this battered Caravanserai
Whose Portals are alternate Night and Day,
　　How Sultan after Sultan with his Pomp
Abode his destined Hour and went his way.

IV. Ah, my Beloved, fill the Cup that clears
Today of past Regret and future Fears:
    Tomorrow!—Why, Tomorrow I may be
Myself with Yesterday's Sev'n Thousand Years.

V. For some we loved, the loveliest and the best
That from his Vintage rolling Time hath prest,
    Have drunk their Cup a Round or two before,
And one by one crept solemnly to rest.

VI. Myself when young did eagerly frequent
Doctor and Saint, and heard great argument
    About it and about: but evermore
Came out by the same Door where in I went.

VII. With them the seed of Wisdom did I sow,
And with mine own hand wrought to make it grow;
    And this was all the Harvest that I reaped—
"I came like Water, and like Wind I go."

VIII. The Moving Finger writes; and, having writ,
Moves on: nor all your Piety nor Wit
    Shall lure it back to cancel half a Line,
Nor all your Tears wash out a Word of it.

IX. Ah Love! could you and I with Him conspire
To grasp this sorry Scheme of Things entire,
    Would we not shatter it to bits—and then
Remould it nearer to the Heart's Desire.

X. Come, fill the Cup, and in the fire of Spring
Your Winter-garment of Repentance fling:
    The Bird of Time has but a little way
To flutter—and the Bird is on the Wing.

XI. Some for the Glories of This World; and some
Sigh for the Prophet's Paradise to come;
    Ah, take the Cash and let the Credit go,
Nor heed the rumble of a distant Drum!

XII. The Worldly Hope men set their Hearts upon
Turns Ashes—or it prospers; and anon,
    Like Snow upon the Desert's dusty Face,
Lighting a little hour or two—is gone.

XIII. Why, all the Saints and Sages who discussed
Of the Two Worlds so wisely—they are thrust
    Like foolish Prophets forth; their Words to Scorn
Are scattered, and their Mouths are stopt with Dust.

XIV.   A Moment's Halt—a momentary taste
Of Being from the Well amid the Waste—
    And Lo!—the phantom Caravan has reached
The Nothing it set out from—Oh, make haste!

XV.   There was the Door to which I found no Key;
There was the Veil through which I might not see:
    Some little talk awhile of Me and Thee
There was—and then no more of Thee and Me.

Daffodils

William Wordsworth

I wandere'd lonely as a cloud
    That floats on high o'er vales and hills,
When all at once I saw a crowd,
    A host, of golden daffodils;
Beside the lake, beneath the trees,
Fluttering and dancing in the breeze.

Continuous as the stars that shine
    And twinkle on the Milky Way,
They stretch'd in never-ending line
    Along the margin of a bay:
Ten thousand say I at a glance,
Tossing their heads in sprightly dance.

The waves beside them danced, but they
    Out-did the sparkling waves in glee:
A poet could not but be gay,
    In such a jocund company:
I gazed—and gazed—but little thought
What wealth the show to me had brought:

For oft, when on my couch I lie
    In vacant or in pensive mood,
They flash upon that inward eye
    Which is the bliss of solitude;
And then my heart with pleasure fills,
And dances with the daffodils.

L'Allegro

John Milton

Hence, loathed Melancholy
   Of Cerberus and blackest Midnight born,
In Stygian cave forlorn
   'Mongst horrid shapes, and shrieks, and sights unholy!
Find out some uncouth cell
   Where brooding Darkness spreads his jealous wings
And the night-raven sings;
   There under ebon shades, and low-browed rocks
As ragged as thy locks,
   In dark Cimmerian desert ever dwell.
But come, thou goddess fair and free,
In heaven yclept Euphrosyne,
And by men, heart-easing Mirth,
Whom lovely Venus at a birth
With two sister Graces more
To ivy-crownéd Bacchus bore;
Or whether (as some sager sing)
The frolic wind that breathes the spring,
Zephyr, with Aurora playing,
As he met her once a-Maying—
There on beds of violets blue
And fresh-blown roses washed in dew
Filled her with thee, a daughter fair,
So buxom, blithe, and debonair.
   Haste thee, Nymph, and bring with thee
Jest and youthful Jollity,
Quips and Cranks and wanton Wiles,
Nods and Becks and wreathéd Smiles,
Such as hang on Hebe's cheek
And love to live in dimple sleek;
Sport that wrinkled Care derides,
And Laughter holding both his sides.
Come, and trip it as you go
On the light fantastic toe;
And in thy right hand lead with thee
The mountain-nymph, sweet Liberty;
And if I give thee honor due
Mirth, admit me of thy crew,
To live with her, and live with thee
In unreprovéd pleasures free;
To hear the lark begin his flight
And singing startle the dull night
From his watch-tower in the skies,

Till the dappled dawn doth rise;
Then to come, in spite of sorrow,
And at my window bid good-morrow
Through the sweetbriar, or the vine,
Or the twisted eglantine:
While the cock with lively din
Scatters the rear of darkness thin,
And to the stack, or the barn-door,
Stoutly struts his dames before:
Oft listening how the hounds and horn
Cheerly rouse the slumbering morn,
From the side of some hoar hill,
Through the high wood echoing shrill;
Sometime walking, not unseen,
By hedge-row elms, on hillocks green,
Right against the eastern gate
Where the great Sun begins his state,
Robed in flames and amber light,
The clouds in thousand liveries dight;
While the ploughman, near at hand,
Whistles o'er the furrowed land,
And the milkmaid singeth blithe,
And the mower whets his scythe,
And every shepherd tells his tale
Under the hawthorn in the dale.
    Straight mine eye hath caught new pleasures
Whilst the landscape round it measures:
Russet lawns, and fallows gray,
Where the nibbling flocks do stray;
Mountain, on whose barren breast
The laboring clouds do often rest;
Meadows trim with daisies pied,
Shallow brooks, and rivers wide.
Towers and battlements it sees
Bosomed high in tufted trees,
Where perhaps some beauty lies,
The cynosure of neighboring eyes.
Hard by, a cottage chimney smokes
From betwixt two aged oaks,
Where Corydon and Thyrsis met
Are at their savory dinner set
Of herbs, and other country messes
Which the neat-handed Phillis dresses;
And then in haste her bower she leaves,
With Thestylis to bind the sheaves;
Or, if the earlier season lead,
To the tanned haycock in the mead.
    Sometimes with secure delight

The upland hamlets will invite,
When the merry bells ring round,
And the jocund rebecks sound
To many a youth and many a maid,
Dancing in the chequered shade;
And young and old come forth to play
On a sunshine holy-day,
Till the livelong daylight fail:
Then to the spicy nut-brown ale,
With stories told of many a feat,
How faery Mab the junkets eat:—
She was pinched, and pulled, she said;
And he, by friar's lantern led,
Tells how the drudging Goblin sweat
To earn his cream-bowl duly set,
When in one night, ere glimpse of morn,
His shadowy flail hath threshed the corn
That ten day-laborers could not end;
Then lies him down the lubber fiend,
And, stretched out all the chimney's length,
Basks at the fire his hairy strength;
And crop-full out of doors he flings,
Ere the first cock his matin rings.
Thus done the tales, to bed they creep,
By whispering winds soon lulled asleep.
Towered cities please us then
And the busy hum of men,
Where throngs of knights and barons bold,
In weeds of peace, high triumphs hold,
With store of ladies, whose bright eyes
Rain influence, and judge the prize
Of wit or arms, while both contend
To win her grace, whom all commend.
There let Hymen oft appear
In saffron robe, with taper clear,
And pomp, and feast, and revelry,
With mask, and antique pageantry;
Such sights as youthful poets dream
On summer eves by haunted stream.
Then to the well-trod stage anon,
If Jonson's learnéd sock be on,
Or sweetest Shakespeare, Fancy's child,
Warble his native wood-notes wild.
　　And ever against eating cares
Lap me in soft Lydian airs,
Married to immortal verse,
Such as the meeting soul may pierce,

Friar's lantern: will-o'-the-wisp. **lubber:** oafish. **Sock:** the slipper worn by comic actors.

In notes with many a winding bout
Of linkéd sweetness long drawn out,
With wanton heed and giddy cunning,
The melting voice through mazes running,
Untwisting all the chains that tie
The hidden soul of harmony;
That Orpheus' self may heave his head
From golden slumber, on a bed
Of heaped Elysian flowers, and hear
Such strains as would have won the ear
Of Pluto, to have quite set free
His half-regained Eurydice.
  These delights if thou canst give,
Mirth, with thee I mean to live.

Il Penseroso

John Milton

Hence, vain deluding Joys,
  The brood of Folly without father bred!
How little you bested
  Or fill the fixéd mind with all your toys!
Dwell in some idle brain,
  And fancies fond with gaudy shapes possess
As thick and numberless
  As the gay motes that people the sunbeams,
Or likest hovering dreams,
  The fickle pensioners of Morpheus' train.
But hail, thou goddess sage and holy,
Hail, divinest Melancholy!
Whose saintly visage is too bright
To hit the sense of human sight,
And therefore to our weaker view
O'erlaid with black, staid Wisdom's hue;
Black, but such as in esteem
Prince Memnon's sister might beseem,
Or that starred Ethiop queen that strove
To set her beauty's praise above
The sea-nymphs, and their powers offended.
Yet thou are higher far descended:
Thee bright-haired Vesta long of yore
To solitary Saturn bore;
His daughter she; in Saturn's reign
Such mixture was not held a stain:
Oft in glimmering bowers and glades
He met her, and in secret shades

Of woody Ida's inmost grove,
While yet there was no fear of Jove.
   Come, pensive Nun, devout and pure,
Sober, steadfast, and demure,
All in a robe of darkest grain
Flowing with majestic train,
And sable stole of cypress lawn
Over thy decent shoulders drawn.
Come, but keep thy wonted state,
With even step, and musing gait,
And looks commercing with the skies,
Thy rapt soul sitting in thine eyes:
There, held in holy passion still,
Forget thyself to marble, till
With a sad leaden downward cast
Thou fix them on the earth as fast.
And join with thee calm Peace, and Quiet,
Spare Fast, that oft with gods doth diet,
And hears the Muses in a ring
Aye round about Jove's altar sing:
And add to these retired Leisure
That in trim gardens takes his pleasure:—
But first and chiefest, with thee bring
Him that yon soars on golden wing
Guiding the fiery-wheeléd throne,
The cherub Contemplatión;
And the mute Silence hist along,
'Less Philomel will deign a song
In her sweetest saddest plight,
Smoothing the rugged brow of Night,
While Cynthia checks her dragon yoke
Gently o'er the accustomed oak.
Sweet bird, that shunn'st the noise of folly,
Most musical, most melancholy!
Thee, chauntress, oft the woods among
I woo, to hear thy even-song;
And missing thee, I walk unseen
On the dry smooth-shaven green,
To behold the wandering Moon
Riding near her highest noon,
Like one that had been led astray
Through the heaven's wide pathless way,
And oft, as if her head she bowed,
Stooping through a fleecy cloud.
   Oft, on a plat of rising ground
I hear the far-off curfew sound
Over some wide-water'd shore,

Cynthia: the moon.

Swinging slow with sullen roar;
Or, if the air will not permit,
Some still removed place will fit,
Where glowing embers through the room
Teach light to counterfeit a gloom;
Far from all resort of mirth,
Save the cricket on the hearth,
Or the bellman's drowsy charm
To bless the doors from nightly harm.
   Or let my lamp at midnight hour
Be seen in some high lonely tower,
Where I may oft out-watch the Bear
With thrice-great Hermes, or unsphere
The spirit of Plato, to unfold
What worlds or what vast regions hold
The immortal mind that hath forsook
Her mansion in this fleshly nook;
And of those Daemons that are found
In fire, air, flood, or underground,
Whose power hath a true consent
With planet, or with element.
Sometime let gorgeous Tragedy
In sceptered pall come sweeping by,
Presenting Thebes, or Pelops' line,
Or the tale of Troy divine;
Or what (though rare) of later age
Ennobled hath the buskined stage.
   But, O sad Virgin, that thy power
Might raise Musaeus from his bower,
Or bid the soul of Orpheus sing
Such notes as, warbled to the string,
Drew iron tears down Pluto's cheek
And made Hell grant what Love did seek!
Or call up him that left half-told
The story of Cambuscan bold,
Of Camball, and of Algarsife,
And who had Canace to wife,
That owned the virtuous ring and glass,
And of the wondrous horse of brass,
On which the Tartar king did ride;
And if aught else great bards beside
In sage and solemn tunes have sung,
Of tourneys, and of trophies hung,
Of forests, and enchantments drear,
Where more is meant than meets the ear.
     Thus, Night, oft see me in thy pale career,

Unsphere: call down from the spheres of Heaven. **buskined:** wearing the heavy shoe
of tragic actors. **him:** Chaucer.

Till civil-suited Morn appear,
Not tricked and frounced as she was wont
With the Attic boy to hunt,
But kerchiefed in a comely cloud
While rocking winds are piping loud,
Or ushered with a shower still,
When the gust hath blown his fill,
Ending on the rustling leaves
With minute-drops from off the eaves.
And when the sun begins to fling
His flaring beams, me, goddess, bring
To arched walks of twilight groves,
And shadows brown, that Sylvan loves,
Of pine, or monumental oak,
Where the rude axe, with heavéd stroke,
Was never heard the nymphs to daunt
Or fright them from their hallowed haunt.
There in close covert by some brook
Where no profaner eye may look,
Hide me from day's garish eye,
While the bee with honeyed thigh,
That at her flowery work doth sing,
And the waters murmuring,
With such consort as they keep,
Entice the dewy-feathered Sleep;
And let some strange mysterious dream
Wave at his wings in airy stream
Of lively portraiture displayed,
Softly on my eyelids laid:
And, as I wake, sweet music breathe
Above, about, or underneath,
Sent by some spirit to mortals good,
Or the unseen Genius of the wood.
  But let my due feet never fail
To walk the studious cloister's pale
And love the high-embowéd roof,
With antique pillars massy proof
And storied windows richly dight,
Casting a dim religious light:
There let the pealing organ blow
To the full-voiced quire below
In service high and anthems clear,
As may with sweetness, through mine ear,
Dissolve me into ecstasies,
And bring all Heaven before mine eyes.
  And may at last my weary age
Find out the peaceful hermitage,
The hairy gown and mossy cell

Where I may sit and rightly spell
  Of every star that heaven doth shew,
And every herb that sips the dew;
  Till old experience do attain
To something like prophetic strain.
  These pleasures, Melancholy, give,
And I with thee will choose to live.

Tom O' Bedlam's Song

Anonymous

In England during the sixteenth and seventeenth centuries, it was the
custom to discharge the insane from the overcrowded and miserable
asylums and to let them roam the country begging. Most of the insane
so discharged were harmless, but under the pressures of overcrowding
some not-so-harmless patients were also released in chains. They were
given badges that permitted them to beg, but desperate as their condi-
tion already was, it was further complicated by the fact that various
impostors took to the roads with them, the felonies and sharp tricks of
the impostors tending to make all men suspicious of the authentic beg-
gars. Bedlam is the swallowed English pronunciation of Bethlehem. The
Hospital of Saint Mary in Bethlehem was located in London.

As the lunatic beggars roamed the streets, they developed various
chants and street-cries that would attract attention, and it is such
snatches that have been woven here into "Tom O' Bedlam's Song." The
song survives as anonymous, and it may possibly have developed by
authentic folk-methods, but many scholars believe it must at least have
been shaped into final form by some unknown poet. Whatever its origin,
its blend of fantasy and melody mark it as a lyric masterpiece.

From the hag and hungry goblin
  That into rags would rend ye,
And the spirit that stands by the naked man
  In the book of moons, defend ye,
That of your five sound senses
  You never be forsaken,
Nor wander from yourselves with Tom,
  Abroad to beg your bacon.

While I do sing: Any food,
  Any feeding, drink, or clothing?
Come, dame or maid, be not afraid,
  Poor Tom will injure nothing.

Of thirty bare years have I
  Twice twenty been enragèd,

And for forty been three times fifteen
   In durance soundly cagèd
On the lordly lofts of Bedlam,
   With stubble soft and dainty,
Brave bracelets strong, sweet whips, ding-dong,
   With wholesome hunger plenty.

      And now I sing: Any food, . . .

With a thought I took for Maudlin,
   And a cruse of cockle pottage,
With a thing thus tall, sky bless you all,
   I befell into this dotage.
I slept not since the Conquest,
   Till then I never wakèd,
Till the rougish boy of love where I lay
   Me found and stripped me naked.

      And now I sing: Any food, . . .

When I short have shorn my sour-face,
   And swigged my horny barrel,
In an oaken inn I pound my skin,
   As a suit of gilt apparel.
The moon's my constant mistress,
   And the lovely owl my morrow,
The flaming drake and the night-crow make
   Me music to my sorrow.

      And now I sing: Any food, . . .

The palsy plagues my pulses,
   When I prig your pigs or pullen,
Your culvers take, or matchless make
   Your chanticleer or sullen.
When I want provant, with Humphry
   I sup, and when benighted,
I repose in Powles with waking souls,
   Yet never am affrighted.

      But I do sing: Any food, . . .

I know more than Apollo,
   For oft when he lies sleeping,
I see the stars at bloody wars
   In the wounded welkin weeping,
The moon embrace her shepherd,
   And the queen of love her warrior,

While the first doth horn the star of morn,
    And the next the heavenly Farrier.

            While I do sing: Any food, . . .

The gypsy Snap and Pedro
    Are none of Tom's comradoes.
The punk I scorn, and the cutpurse sworn,
    And the roaring boys' bravadoes.
The meek, the white, the gentle,
    Me handle, touch, and spare not;
But those that cross Tom Rhinoceros
    Do what the panther dare not.

            Although I sing: Any food, . . .

With an host of furious fancies
    Whereof I am commander,
With a burning spear and a horse of air
    To the wilderness I wander.
By a knight of ghosts and shadows
    I summoned am to tourney
Ten leagues beyond the wide world's end,
    Methinks it is no journey.

            Yet will I sing: Any food, . . .

How They Brought the Good
News from Ghent to Aix

Robert Browning

I sprang to the stirrup, and Joris, and he;
I galloped, Dirck galloped, we galloped all three;
"Good speed!" cried the watch, as the gatebolts undrew;
"Speed!" echoed the wall to us galloping through;
Behind shut the postern, the lights sank to rest,
And into the midnight we galloped abreast.

Not a word to each other; we kept the great pace
Neck by neck, stride by stride, never changing our place;
I turned in my saddle and made its girths tight,
Then shortened each stirrup, and set the pique right,
Rebuckled the cheek-strap, chained slacker the bit,
Nor galloped less steadily Roland a whit.

'Twas moonset at starting; but while we drew near
Lokeren, the cocks crew and twilight dawned clear;
At Boom, a great yellow star came out to see;
At Duffeld, 'twas morning as plain as could be;
And from Mecheln church-steeple we heard the half-chime,
So Joris broke silence with, "Yet there is time!"

At Aershot, up leaped of a sudden the sun,
And against him the cattle stood black every one,
To stare through the midst at us galloping past,
And I saw my stout galloper Roland at last,
With resolute shoulders, each butting away
The haze, as some bluff river headland its spray;

And his low head and crest, just one sharp ear bent back
For my voice, and the other pricked out on his track;
And one eye's black intelligence—ever that glance
O'er its white edge at me, his own master, askance!
And the thick heavy spume-flakes which aye and anon
His fierce lips shook upwards in galloping on.

By Hasselt, Dirck groaned; and cried Joris, "Stay spur!
Your Roos galloped bravely, the fault's not in her,
We'll remember at Aix"—for one heard the quick wheeze
Of her chest, saw the stretched neck and staggering knees,
And sunk tail, and horrible heave of the flank,
As down on her haunches she shuddered and sank.

So we were left galloping, Jorris and I,
Past Looz and past Tongres, no cloud in the sky;
The broad sun above laughed a pitiless laugh,
'Neath our feet broke the brittle bright stubble like chaff;
Till over by Dalhem a dome-spire sprang white,
And "Gallop," gasped Joris, "for Aix is in sight!"

"How they'll greet us!"—and all in a moment his roan
Rolled neck and croup over, lay dead as a stone;
And there was my Roland to bear the whole weight
Of the news which alone could save Aix from her fate,
With his nostrils like pits full of blood to the brim,
And with circles of red for his eye-sockets' rim.

Then I cast loose my buffcoat, each holster let fall,
Shook off both my jack-boots, let go belt and all,
Stood up in the stirrup, leaned, patted his ear,
Called my Roland his pet-name, my horse without peer;
Clapped my hands, laughed and sang, any noise, bad or good,
Till at length into Aix Roland galloped and stood.

And all I remember is—friends flocking round
As I sat with his head 'twixt my knees on the ground;
And no voice but was praising this Roland of mine,
As I poured down his throat our last measure of wine,
Which (the burgesses voted by common consent)
Was no more than his due who brought good news from Ghent.

The Charge of the Light Brigade

Alfred, Lord Tennyson

Half a league, half a league,
Half a league onward,
All in the valley of Death
   Rode the six hundred.
"Forward the Light Brigade!
Charge for the gun!" he said.
Into the valley of Death
   Rode the six hundred.

"Forward, the Light Brigade!"
Was there a man dismayed?
Not though the soldier knew
   Someone had blundered.
Theirs not to make reply,
Theirs not to reason why,
Theirs but to do and die.
Into the valley of Death
   Rode the six hundred.

Flashed all their sabers bare,
Flashed as they turned in air
Sabring the gunners there,
Charging an army, while
   All the world wondered.
Plunged in the battery-smoke
Right through the line they broke;
Coasack and Russian
Reeled from the saber-stroke
   Shattered and sundered.
Then they rode back, but not,
   Not the six hundred.

Cannon to right of them,
Cannon to left of them,
Cannon behind them
   Volleyed and thundered;

Stormed at with shot and shell,
While horse and hero fell,
They that had fought so well
Came through the jaws of Death,
Back from the mouth of hell,
All that was left of them,
    Left of six hundred.

When can their glory fade?
O the wild charge they made!
    All the world wondered.
Honor the charge they made!
Honor the Light Brigade,
    Noble six hundred.

To Be, or Not to Be

William Shakespeare

To be, or not to be: that is the question:
Whether 'tis nobler in the mind to suffer
The slings and arrows of outrageous fortune,
Or to take arms against a sea of troubles,
And by opposing end them. To die: to sleep;
No more; and by a sleep to say we end
The heart-ache, and the thousand natural shocks
That flesh is heir to. 'Tis a consummation
Devoutly to be wish'd. To die, to sleep;
To sleep? Perchance to dream! aye, there's the rub;
For in that sleep of death what dreams may come,
When we have shuffled off this mortal coil,
Must give us pause: there's the respect
That makes calamity of so long life;
For who would bear the whips and scorns of time,
The oppressor's wrong, the proud man's contumely,
The pangs of despised love, the law's delay,
The insolence of office, and the spurns
That patient merit of the unworthy takes,
When he himself might his quietus make
With a bare bodkin? who would fardels bear,
To grunt and sweat under a weary life,
But that the dread of something after death,
The undiscovered country from whose bourn
No traveler returns, puzzles the will,
And makes us rather bear those ills we have
Than fly to others that we know not of?
Thus conscience does make cowards of us all,

And thus the native hue of resolution
Is sicklied o'er with the pale cast of thought,
And enterprises of great pitch and moment
With this regard their currents turn awry
And lose the name of action.

from *Hamlet*

For God's Sake, Let Us Sit upon the Ground

William Shakespeare

For God's sake, let us sit upon the ground,
And tell sad stories of the death of kings:
How some have been deposed; some slain in war;
Some haunted by the ghosts they have deposed;
Some poisoned by their wives; some sleeping killed;
All murdered:—for within the hollow crown
That rounds the mortal temples of a king
Keeps Death his court; and there the antick sits,
Scoffing his state, and grinning at his pomp;
Allowing him a breath, a little scene,
To monarchize, be feared, and kill with looks;
Infusing him with self and vain conceit—
As if this flesh, which walls about our life,
Were brass impregnable; and humored thus,
Comes at the last, and with a little pin
Bores through his castle-wall, and—farewell king!

from *King Richard the Second*

Under the Greenwood Tree

William Shakespeare

Under the greenwood tree
Who loves to lie with me,
And turn his merry note
Unto the sweet bird's throat—
Come hither, come hither, come hither!
Here shall he see
No enemy
But winter and rough weather.

Who doth ambition shun
And loves to live i' the sun,
Seeking the food he eats

And pleased with what he gets—
Come hither, come hither, come hither!
  Here shall he see
    No enemy
But winter and rough weather.

from As You Like It

Full Fathom Five

William Shakespeare

Full fathom five my father lies:
  Of his bones are coral made;
Those are pearls that were his eyes:
  Nothing of him that doth fade,
But doth suffer a sea-change
Into something rich and strange.
Sea-nymphs hourly ring his knell:
  Hark! now I hear them,—
    Ding, dong, Bell.

from The Tempest

In a Time of Pestilence

Thomas Nashe

Adieu, farewell earth's bliss.
This world uncertain is;
Fond are life's lustful joys,
Death proves them all but toys.
None from his darts can fly;
I am sick, I must die.
    Lord, have mercy on us!

Rich men, trust not in wealth,
Gold cannot buy your health;
Physic himself must fade;
All things to end are made;
The plague full swift goes by.
I am sick, I must die.
    Lord, have mercy on us!

Beauty is but a flower
Which wrinkles will devour;
Brightness falls from the air;
Queens have died young and fair;

Dust hath closed Helen's eye.
I am sick, I must die.
Lord, have mercy on us!

Strength stoops unto the grave,
Worms feed on Hector brave;
Swords may not fight with fate;
Earth still holds ope her gate;
Come, come! the bells do cry.
I am sick, I must die.
Lord, have mercy on us!

Wit with his wantonness
Tasteth death's bitterness;
Hell's executioner
Hath no ears for to hear
What vain art can reply.
I am sick, I must die.
Lord, have mercy on us!

Haste therefore each degree
To welcome destiny;
Heaven is our heritage,
Each but a player's stage.
Mount we unto the sky.
I am sick, I must die.
Lord, have mercy on us!

The "Revenge"

Alfred, Lord Tennyson

At Florés in the Azores Sir Richard Grenville lay,
And a pinnace, like a fluttered bird, came flying from far away:
"Spanish ships of war at sea! we have sighted fifty-three!"
Then sware Lord Thomas Howard: "'Fore God I am no coward;
But I cannot meet them here, for my ships are out of gear,
And the half my men are sick. I must fly, but follow quick.
We are six ships of the line; can we fight with fifty-three?"

Then spake Sir Richard Grenville: "I know you are no coward;
You fly them for a moment to fight with them again.
But I've ninety men and more that are lying sick ashore.
I should count myself the coward if I left them, my Lord Howard,
To these Inquisition dogs and the devildoms of Spain."

So Lord Howard passed away with five ships of war that day,
Till he melted like a cloud in the silent summer heaven;
But Sir Richard bore in hand all his sick men from the land
Very carefully and slow,
Men of Bideford in Devon,
And we laid them on the ballast down below;
For we brought them all aboard,
And they blessed him in their pain, that they were not left to Spain,
To the thumbscrew and the stake, for the glory of the Lord.

He had only a hundred seamen to work the ship and to fight,
And he sailed away from Florés till the Spaniard came in sight,
With his huge sea-castles heaving upon the weather bow.
"Shall we fight or shall we fly?
Good Sir Richard, tell us now,
For to fight is but to die!
There'll be little of us left by the time this sun be set."
And Sir Richard said again: "We be all good English men.
Let us bang these dogs of Seville, the children of the devil,
For I never turned my back upon Don or devil yet."

Sir Richard spoke and he laughed, and we roared a hurrah, and so
The little *Revenge* ran on sheer into the heart of the foe,
With her hundred fighters on deck, and her ninety sick below;
For half of their fleet to the right and half to the left were seen,
And the little *Revenge* ran on through the long sea-lane between.

Thousands of their soldiers looked down from their decks and laughed,
Thousands of their seamen made mock at the mad little craft
Running on and on, till delayed
By their mountain-like *San Philip* that, of fifteen hundred tons,
And up-shadowing high above us with her yawning tiers of guns,
Took the breath from our sails, and we stayed.

And while now the great *San Philip* hung above us like a cloud
Whence the thunderbolt will fall
Long and loud,
Four galleons drew away
From the Spanish fleet that day,
And two upon the larboard and two upon the starboard lay,
And the battle-thunder broke from them all.

But anon the great *San Philip*, she bethought herself and went,
Having that within her womb that had left her ill content;
And the rest they came aboard us, and they fought us hand to hand,
For a dozen times they came with their pikes and musqueteers,
And a dozen times we shook 'em off as a dog that shakes his ears
When he leaps from the water to the land.

And the sun went down, and the stars came out far over the summer sea,
But never a moment ceased the fight of the one and the fifty-three,
Ship after ship, the whole night long, their high-built galleons came,
Ship after ship, the whole night long, drew back with her dead
                                    and her shame.
For some were sunk and many were shattered, and so could fight us no
                                    more—
God of battles, was ever a battle like this in the world before?

For he said, "Fight on! fight on!"
Though his vessel was all but a wreck;
And it chanced that, when half of the short summer night was gone,
With a grisly wound to be dressed he had left the deck,
But a bullet struck him that was dressing it suddenly dead,
And himself he was wounded again in the side and the head,
And he said, "Fight on! fight on!"

And the night went down, and the sun smiled out far over the summer sea,
And the Spanish fleet with broken sides lay round us all in a ring;
But they dared not touch us again, for they feared that we still could
                                    sting,
So they watched what the end would be.
And we had not fought them in vain,
But in perilous plight were we,
Seeing forty of our poor hundred were slain,
And half of the rest of us maimed for life
In the crash of the cannonades and the desperate strife;
And the sick men down in the hold were most of them stark and cold,
And the pikes were all broken or bent, and the powder was all of it spent;

And the masts and the rigging were lying over the side;
But Sir Richard cried in his English pride,
"We have fought such a fight for a day and a night
As may never be fought again!
We have won great glory, my men!
And a day less or more
At sea or ashore,
We die—does it matter when?
Sink me the ship, Master Gunner—sink her, split her in twain!
Fall into the hands of God, not into the hands of Spain!"

And the gunner said, "Ay, ay," but the seamen made reply:
"We have children, we have wives,
And the Lord hath spared our lives.
We will make the Spaniard promise, if we yield, to let us go;
We shall live to fight again and to strike another blow."
And the lion there lay dying, and they yielded to the foe.

And the stately Spanish men to their flagship bore him then,
Where they laid him by the mast, old Sir Richard caught at last,
And they praised him to his face with their courtly foreign grace;
But he rose upon their decks, and he cried:
"I have fought for Queen and Faith like a valiant man and true;
I have only done my duty as a man is bound to do.
With a joyful spirit I Sir Richard Grenville die!"
And he fell upon their decks and he died.
And they stared at the dead that had been so valiant and true,
And had holden the power and glory of Spain so cheap
That he dared her with one little ship and his English few;
Was he devil or man? He was devil for aught they knew,
But they sank his body with honor down into the deep,
And they manned the *Revenge* with a swarthier alien crew,
And away she sailed with her loss and longed for her own;
When a wind from the lands they had ruined awoke from sleep,
And the water began to heave and the weather to moan,
And or ever that evening ended a great gale blew,
And a wave like the wave that is raised by an earthquake grew,
Till it smote on their hulls and their sails and their masts and their flags,
And the whole sea plunged and fell on the shot-shattered navy of Spain,
And the little *Revenge* herself went down by the island crags
To be lost evermore in the main.

Socratic

H. D.

"They cut it in squares,
sometimes it comes
in little jars—"

"O—?"

"Under the trees—"

"Where?"

"By his *sheep*-pen."

"Whose?"

"The man
who brings eggs:
he put it
in a basket with moss."

Reprinted by permission of Norman Holmes Pearson.

"What?"

"Why,
the little jar."

"What for?"

"Why,
to carry it over—"

"Over where?"

"The field to Io's house."

"Then?"

"*Her* mother took it out
of the moss,
opened it—"

"What?"

"The little jar."

"And then?"

"We each *had* some."

"What?"

"Why the thing
in the little jar
they got
from the straw huts."

"What huts?"

"Why,
the little huts
under the apple-trees,
where they live—"

"Who live?"

"Why,
the *bees*."

Annabel Lee

Edgar Allan Poe

It was many and many a year ago,
    In a kingdom by the sea,
That a maiden there lived whom you may know
    By the name of Annabel Lee.
And this maiden she lived with no other thought
    Than to love and be loved by me.

I was a child and she was a child
    In this kingdom by the sea:
But we loved with a love that was more than love—
    I and my Annabel Lee,
With a love that the wingèd seraphs of heaven
    Coveted her and me.

And this was the reason that, long ago,
    In this kingdom by the sea,
A wind blew out of a cloud, chilling
    My beautiful Annabel Lee,
So that her high-born kinsmen came
    And bore her away from me,
To shut her up in a sepulchre
    In this kingdom by the sea.

The angels, not half so happy in heaven,
    Went envying her and me—
Yes! that was the reason (as all men know,
    In this kingdom by the sea)
That the wind came out of the cloud one night,
    Chilling and killing my Annabel Lee.

But our love it was stronger by far than the love
    Of those who were older than we—
    Of many far wiser than we—
And neither the angels in heaven above,
    Nor the demons down under the sea,
Can ever dissever my soul from the soul
    Of the beautiful Annabel Lee:

For the moon never beams without bringing me dreams
    Of the beautiful Annabel Lee;
And the stars never rise, but I feel the bright eyes
    Of the beautiful Annabel Lee;
And so, all the night-tide, I lie down by the side
Of my darling—my darling—my life and my bride,
    In the sepulchre there by the sea,
    In her tomb by the sounding sea.

La Belle Dame sans Merci

John Keats

"O what can ail thee, knight-at-arms,
　　Alone and palely loitering?
The sedge is wither'd from the lake,
　　And no birds sing.

"O what can ail thee, knight-at-arms,
　　So haggard and so woe-begone?
The squirrel's granary is full,
　　And the harvest's done.

"I see a lily on thy brow
　　With anguish moist and fever dew;
And on thy cheek a fading rose
　　Fast withereth too."

"I met a lady in the meads,
　　Full beautiful—a faery's child,
Her hair was long, her foot was light,
　　And her eyes were wild.

"I made a garland for her head,
　　And bracelets too, and fragrant zone;
She look'd at me as she did love,
　　And made sweet moan.

"I set her on my pacing steed
　　And nothing else saw all day long,
For sideways would she lean, and sing
　　A faery's song.

"She found me roots of relish sweet,
　　And honey wild and manna dew,
And sure in language strange she said,
　　'I love thee true!'

"She took me to her elfin grot,
　　And there she wept and sigh'd full sore;
And there I shut her wild, wild eyes
　　With kisses four.

"And there she lullèd me asleep,
　　And there I dream'd—Ah! woe betide!
The latest dream I ever dream'd
　　On the cold hill's side.

"I saw pale kings and princes too,
  Pale warriors, death-pale were they all;
Who cried—'La belle Dame sans Merci
    Hath thee in thrall!'

"I saw their starved lips in the gloam
  With horrid warning gapèd wide,
And I awoke and found me here
    On the cold hill's side.

"And this is why I sojourn here
  Alone and palely loitering,
Though the sedge is wither'd from the lake,
    And no birds sing."

Kubla Khan

Samuel Taylor Coleridge

In Xanadu did Kubla Khan
  A stately pleasure-dome decree:
Where Alph, the sacred river, ran
Through caverns measureless to man
  Down to a sunless sea.
So twice five miles of fertile ground
With walls and towers were girdled round:
And here were gardens bright with sinuous rills,
Where blossomed many an incense-bearing tree,
And here were forests ancient as the hills,
Enfolding sunny spots of greenery.

But oh! that deep romantic chasm which slanted
Down the green hill athwart a cedarn cover!
A savage place; as holy and enchanted
As e'er beneath a waning moon was haunted
By woman wailing for her demon-lover!
And from this chasm, with ceaseless turmoil seething,
As if this earth in fast thick pants were breathing,
A mighty fountain momently was forced,
Amid whose swift half-intermitted burst
Huge fragments vaulted like rebounding hail,
Or chaffy grain beneath the thresher's flail:
And 'mid these dancing rocks at once and ever
It flung up momently the sacred river.
Five miles meandering with a mazy motion
Through wood and dale the sacred river ran,
Then reached the caverns measureless to man,

And sank in tumult to a lifeless ocean:
And 'mid this tumult Kubla heard from far
Ancestral voices prophesying war!

    The shadow of the dome of pleasure
    Floated midway on the waves;
    Where was heard the mingled measure
    From the fountain and the caves.
It was a miracle of rare device,
A sunny pleasure-dome with caves of ice!

    A damsel with a dulcimer
    In a vision once I saw:
    It was an Abyssinian maid,
    And on her dulcimer she played,
    Singing of Mount Abora.
    Could I revive within me
    Her symphony and song,
    To such a deep delight 'twould win me,
That with music loud and long,
I would build that dome in air,
That sunny dome! those caves of ice!
And all who heard should see them there,
And all should cry, Beware! Beware!
His flashing eyes, his floating hair!
Weave a circle round him thrice,
And close your eyes with holy dread,
For he on honey-dew hath fed,
And drunk the milk of Paradise.

Song

Thomas Carew

Ask me no more where Jove bestows,
When June is past, the fading rose;
For in your beauty's orient deep
These flowers, as in their causes, sleep.

Ask me no more whither do stray
The golden atoms of the day;
For in pure love heaven did prepare
Those powders to enrich your hair.

Ask me no more whither doth haste
The nightingale when May is past;
For in your sweet dividing throat
She winters and keeps warm her note.

Ask me no more where those stars 'light
That downwards fall in dead of night;
For in your eyes they sit, and there
Fixèd become as in their sphere.

Ask me no more if east or west
The Phœnix builds her spicy nest;
For unto you at last she flies,
And in your fragrant bosom dies.

Why so Pale and Wan?

Sir John Suckling

Why so pale and wan, fond lover?
   Prithee, why so pale?
Will, when looking well can't move her,
   Looking ill prevail?
   Prithee, why so pale?

Why so dull and mute, young sinner?
   Prithee, why so mute?
Will, when speaking well can't win her,
   Saying nothing do 't?
   Prithee, why so mute?

Quit, quit for shame! This will not move;
   This cannot take her.
If of herself she will not love,
   Nothing can make her:
   The devil take her!

The Bridge of Sighs

Thomas Hood

One more Unfortunate,
   Weary of breath,
Rashly importunate,
   Gone to her death!

Take her up tenderly,
   Lift her with care;
Fashion'd so slenderly
   Young, and so fair!

Look at her garments
Clinging like cerements;
Whilst the wave constantly
   Drips from her clothing;
Take her up instantly,
   Loving, not loathing.

Touch her not scornfully;
Think of her mournfully,
   Gently and humanly;
Not of the stains of her,
All that remains of her
   Now is pure womanly.

Make no deep scrutiny
Into her mutiny
   Rash and undutiful:
Past all dishonour,
Death has left on her
   Only the beautiful.

Still, for all slips of hers,
   One of Eve's family—
Wipe those poor lips of hers
   Oozing so clammily.

Loop up her tresses
   Escaped from the comb,
Her fair auburn tresses;
Whilst wonderment guesses
   Where was her home?

Who was her father?
   Who was her mother?
Had she a sister?
   Had she a brother?
Or was there a dearer one
Still, and a nearer one
   Yet, than all other?

Alas! for the rarity
Of Christian charity
   Under the sun!
O, it was pitiful!
Near a whole city full,
   Home she had none.

Sisterly, brotherly,
Fatherly, motherly

Feelings had changed:
Love, by harsh evidence,
Thrown from its eminence;
Even God's providence
   Seeming estranged.

Where the lamps quiver
So far in the river,
   With many a light
From window and casement,
From garret to basement,
She stood, with amazement,
   Houseless by night.

The bleak wind of March
   Made her tremble and shiver;
But not the dark arch,
Or the black flowing river:
Mad from life's history,
Glad to death's mystery,
   Swift to be hurl'd—
Anywhere, anywhere
   Out of the world!

In she plunged boldly—
No matter how coldly
   The rough river ran—
Over the brink of it,
Picture it—think of it,
   Dissolute Man!
Lave in it, drink of it,
   Then, if you can!

Take her up tenderly,
   Lift her with care;
Fashion'd so slenderly,
   Young, and so fair!

Ere her limbs frigidly
Stiffen too rigidly,
   Decently, kindly,
Smooth and compose them;
And her eyes, close them,
   Staring so blindly!

Dreadfully staring
   Thro' muddy impurity,

As when with the daring
Last look of despairing
   Fix'd on futurity.

Perishing gloomily,
Spurr'd by contumely,
Cold inhumanity,
Burning insanity,
   Into her rest.—
Cross her hands humbly
As if praying dumbly,
   Over her breast!

Owning her weakness,
   Her evil behaviour,
And leaving, with meekness,
   Her sins to her Saviour!

Early Evening Quarrel

Langston Hughes

Where is that sugar, Hammond?
I sent you this morning to buy?
I say, where is that sugar
I sent you this morning to buy?
Coffee without sugar
Makes a good woman cry.

   I ain't got no sugar, Hattie,
   I gambled your dime away.
   Ain't got no sugar, I
   Done gambled that dime away.
   But if you's a wise woman, Hattie,
   You ain't gonna have nothin to say.

I ain't no wise woman, Hammond.
I am evil and mad.
Ain't no sense in a good woman
Bein' treated so bad.

   I don't treat you bad, Hattie,
   Neither does I treat you good.
   But I reckon I could treat you
   Worser if I would.

Lawd, these things we women
Have to stand!
I wonder is there anywhere a
Do-right man?

from Essay on Criticism

Alexander Pope

A little learning is a dang'rous thing;
Drink deep, or taste not the Pierian spring:
There shallow draughts intoxicate the brain,
And drinking largely sobers us again.
Fir'd at first sight with what the Muse imparts,
In fearless youth we tempt the heights of arts,
While from the bounded level of our mind,
Short views we take, nor see the lengths behind;
But more advanc'd, behold with strange surprise
New distant scenes of endless science rise!
So pleas'd at first the tow'ring Alps we try,
Mount o'er the vales, and seem to tread the sky;
Th' eternal snows appear already past,
And the first clouds and mountains seem the last;
But, those attain'd, we tremble to survey
The growing labours of the lengthen'd way,
Th' increasing prospect tires our wand'ring eyes,
Hills peep o'er hills, and Alps on Alps arise!

from Epistle to Dr. Arbuthnot

Alexander Pope

Shut, shut the door, good John! fatigu'd, I said.
Tie up the knocker! say I'm sick, I'm dead.
The dog-star rages! nay, 'tis past a doubt,
All Bedlam, or Parnassus, is let out:
Fire in each eye, and papers in each hand,
They rave, recite, and madden round the land.
What walls can guard me, or what shades can hide?
They pierce my thickets, through my grot they glide.
By land, by water, they renew the charge,
They stop the chariot, and they board the barge.
No place is sacred, not the church is free,
Ev'n Sunday shines no Sabbath-day to me:
Then from the Mint walks forth the man of rhyme
Happy! to catch me just at dinner-time.

Is there a parson much be-mus'd in beer,
A maudlin poetess, a rhyming peer,
A clerk, foredoom'd his father's soul to cross,
Who pens a stanza when he should engross?
Is there, who, lock'd from ink and paper, scrawls
With desp'rate charcoal round his darken'd walls?
All fly to Twit'nam, and in humble strain
Apply to me, to keep them mad or vain.

Alexander Pope

What Riddle Asked the Sphinx

Archibald MacLeish

In my stone eyes I see
The saint upon his knee
Delve in the desert for eternity.

In my stone ears I hear
The night-lost traveller
Cry *When?* to the earth's shadow: *When?   Oh Where?*

Stone deaf and blind
I ponder in my mind
The bone that seeks, the flesh that cannot find.

Stone blind I see
The saint's eternity
Deep in the earth he digs in.   Cannot he?

Stone deaf I hear
The night say *Then!* say *There!*
Why cries the traveller still to the night air?

The one is not content
With silence, the day spent;
With earth the other. More, they think, was meant.

Stone that I am, can stone
Perceive what flesh and bone
Are blind and deaf to?
                    Or has hermit known,
Has traveller divined,
Some question there behind
I cannot come to, being stone and blind?

FROM *Collected Poems 1917–1952*, by Archibald MacLeish. Reprinted by permission of Houghton Mifflin Company.

To all who ken or can
I ask, since time began,
What riddle is it has for answer, Man?

The Anniversarie

John Donne

All Kings, and all their favorites,
  All glory of honors, beauties, wits,
The Sun itselfe, which makes times, as they passe,
Is elder by a yeare, now, than it was
When thou and I first one another saw:
All other things, to their destruction draw,
  Only our love hath no decay;
This, no to morrow hath, nor yesterday,
Running it never runs from us away,
But truly keepes his first, last, everlasting day.

Two graves must hide thine and my coarse,
  If one might, death were no divorce.
Alas, as well as other Princes, wee,
(Who Prince enough in one another bee,)
Must leave at last in death, these eyes, and eares,
Oft fed with true oathes, and with sweet salt teares;
  But soules where nothing dwells but love
(All other thoughts being inmates) then shall prove
This, or a love increased there above,
When bodies to their graves, soules from their graves remove.

And then wee shall be thoroughly blest,
  But we no more, than all the rest;
Here upon earth, we'are Kings, and none but wee
Can be such Kings, nor of such subjects bee.
Who is so safe as wee? where none can doe
Treason to us, except one of us two.
  True and false feares let us refraine,
Let us love nobly, and live, and adde againe
Yeares and yeares unto yeares, till we attaine
To write threescore: this is the second of our raigne.

Voice of the Announcer
from *The Fall of the City*

by Archibald MacLeish

We are here on the central plaza.
We are well off to the eastward edge.
There is a kind of terrace over the crowd here.
It is precisely four minutes to twelve.
The crowd is enormous: there might be ten thousand:
There might be more: the whole square is faces.
Opposite over the roofs are the mountains.
It is quite clear: there are birds circling.
We think they are kites by the look: they are very high . . .

The tomb is off to the right somewhere—
We can't see for the great crowd.
Close to us here are the cabinet ministers:
They stand on a raised platform with awnings.
The farmers' wives are squatting on the stones;
Their children have fallen asleep on their shoulders.
The heat is harsh: the light dazzles like metal.
It dazes the air as the clang of a gong does. . . .

News travels in this nation:
There are people here from away off—
Horse-raisers out of the country with brooks in it:
Herders of cattle from up where the snow stays—
The kind that cook for themselves mostly:
They look at the girls with their eyes hard
And a hard grin and their teeth showing. . . .

It is one minute to twelve now:
There is still no sign: they are still waiting:
No one doubts that she will come:
No one doubts that she will speak too:
Three times she has not spoken.

The Tower

William Butler Yeats

I

What shall I do with this absurdity—
O heart, O troubled heart—this caricature,
Decrepit age that has been tied to me
As to a dog's tail?
               Never had I more
Excited, passionate, fantastical
Imagination, nor an ear and eye
That more expected the impossible—
No, not in boyhood when with rod and fly,
Or the humbler worm, I climbed Ben Bulben's back
And had the livelong summer day to spend.
It seems that I must bid the Muse go pack,
Choose Plato and Plotinus for a friend
Until imagination, ear and eye,
Can be content with argument and deal
In abstract things; or be derided by
A sort of battered kettle at the heel.

II

I pace upon the battlements and stare
On the foundations of a house, or where
Tree, like a sooty finger, starts from the earth;
And send imagination forth
Under the day's declining beam, and call
Images and memories
From ruin or from ancient trees,
For I would ask a question of them all.

Beyond that ridge lived Mrs. French, and once
When every silver candlestick or sconce
Lit up the dark mahogany and the wine,
A serving-man, that could divine
That most respected lady's every wish,
Ran and with the garden shears
Clipped an insolent farmer's ears
And brought them in a little covered dish.

Some few remembered still when I was young
A peasant girl commended by a song,
Who'd lived somewhere upon that rocky place,
And praised the colour of her face,

And had the greater joy in praising her,
Remembering that, if walked she there,
Farmers jostled at the fair
So great a glory did the song confer.

And certain men, being maddened by those rhymes,
Or else by toasting her a score of times,
Rose from the table and declared it right
To test their fancy by their sight;
But they mistook the brightness of the moon
For the prosaic light of day—
Music had driven their wits astray—
And one was drowned in the great bog of Cloone.

Strange, but the man who made the song was blind;
Yet, now I have considered it, I find
That nothing strange; the tragedy began
With Homer that was a blind man,
And Helen has all living hearts betrayed.
O may the moon and sunlight seem
One inextricable beam,
For if I triumph I must make men mad.

And I myself created Hanrahan
And drove him drunk or sober through the dawn
From somewhere in the neighbouring cottages.
Caught by an old man's juggleries
He stumbled, tumbled, fumbled to and fro
And had but broken knees for hire
And horrible splendour of desire;
I thought it all out twenty years ago:

Good fellows shuffled cards in an old bawn;
And when that ancient ruffian's turn was on
He so bewitched the cards under his thumb
That all but the one card became
A pack of hounds and not a pack of cards,
And that he changed into a hare.
Hanrahan rose in frenzy there
And followed up those baying creatures towards—

O towards I have forgotten what—enough!
I must recall a man that neither love
Nor music nor an enemy's clipped ear
Could, he was so harried, cheer;
A figure that has grown so fabulous
There's not a neighbour left to say
When he finished his dog's day:
An ancient bankrupt master of this house.

Before that ruin came, for centuries,
Rough men-at-arms, cross-gartered to the knees
Or shod in iron, climbed the narrow stairs,
And certain men-at-arms there were
Whose images, in the Great Memory stored,
Came with loud cry and panting breast
To break upon a sleeper's rest
While their great wooden dice beat on the board.

As I would question all, come all who can;
Come old, necessitous, half-mounted man;
And bring beauty's blind rambling celebrant;
The red man the juggler sent
Through God-forsaken meadows; Mrs. French,
Gifted with so fine an ear;
The man drowned in a bog's mire,
When mocking Muses chose the country wench.

Did all old men and women, rich and poor,
Who trod upon these rocks or passed this door,
Whether in public or in secret rage
As I do now against old age?
But I have found an answer in those eyes
That are impatient to be gone;
Go therefore; but leave Hanrahan,
For I need all his mighty memories.

Old lecher with a love on every wind,
Bring up out of that deep considering mind
All that you have discovered in the grave,
For it is certain that you have
Reckoned up every unforeknown, unseeing
Plunge, lured by a softening eye,
Or by a touch or a sigh,
Into the labyrinth of another's being;

Does the imagination dwell the most
Upon a woman won or woman lost?
If on the lost, admit you turned aside
From a great labyrinth out of pride,
Cowardice, some silly over-subtle thought
Or anything called conscience once;
And that if memory recur, the sun's
Under eclipse and the day blotted out.

III

It is time that I wrote my will;
I choose upstanding men
That climb the streams until

The fountain leap, and at dawn
Drop their cast at the side
Of dripping stone; I declare
They shall inherit my pride,
The pride of people that were
Bound neither to Cause nor to State,
Neither to slaves that were spat on,
Nor to the tyrants that spat,
The people of Burke and of Grattan
That gave, though free to refuse—
Pride, like that of the morn,
When the headlong light is loose,
Or that of the fabulous horn,
Or that of the sudden shower
When all streams are dry,
Or that of the hour
When the swan must fix his eye
Upon a fading gleam,
Float out upon a long
Last reach of glittering stream
And there sing his last song.
And I declare my faith:
I mock Plotinus' thought
And cry in Plato's teeth,
Death and life were not
Till man made up the whole,
Made lock, stock and barrel
Out of his bitter soul,
Aye, sun and moon and star, all,
And further add to that
That, being dead, we rise,
Dream and so create
Translunar Paradise.
I have prepared my peace
With learned Italian things
And the proud stones of Greece,
Poet's imaginings
And memories of love,
Memories of the words of women,
All those things whereof
Man makes a superhuman
Mirror-resembling dream.

As at the loophole there
The daws chatter and scream,
And drop twigs layer upon layer,
When they have mounted up,
The mother bird will rest

On their hollow top,
And so warm her wild nest.

I leave both faith and pride
To young upstanding men
Climbing the mountain-side,
That under bursting dawn
They may drop a fly;
Being of that metal made
Till it was broken by
This sedentary trade.

Now shall I make my soul,
Compelling it to study
In a learned school
Till the wreck of body,
Slow decay of blood,
Testy delirium
Or dull decrepitude,
Or what worse evil come—
The death of friends, or death
Of every brilliant eye
That made a catch in the breath—
Seem but the clouds of the sky
When the horizon fades,
Or a bird's sleepy cry
Among the deepening shades.

Chapter Eight

THE POEM
IN COUNTERMOTION

A poem, by the very fact of its existence in time rather than in space, has *duration* and *pace*. Since a good poem does not move throughout at exactly the same pace (unless the poet is trying for a special effect, and doubtfully then), the poem must also have *change of pace;* one part moves more rapidly or more slowly than another. All such changes of pace, it must be noted, are relative to one another: an anapest introduced into an iambic line accelerates that part of the line; an anapest in an anapestic line sustains the already accelerated pace, but does not accelerate it further. All the rhythms of poetry achieve their effect by the way they play against one another. They exist in countermotion.

Similarly, *all* the elements of a poem are engaged in a series of countermotions. Meter and rhythm are only two of the elements that may be involved. Diction, imagery, rhyme, line length, vowel quantities, consonant sequences, and grammatical structure are some of the other principal elements. From these elements the poem builds complexes of poetic structures, each related to all the others. The motion of these poetic structures, each against the others, is what ultimately determines the poem's performance. One simple rule seems to apply to the play of all such countermotions: *whenever in the course of a poem the poet changes either his tone or his attitude, some change will occur in the handling of the technical elements.* That change in the technical handling of the poem may be slight or it may be marked, but some change must occur. Conversely, any change in the handling of the technical elements in the course of the poem will indicate that a change has taken place in the poet's tone or attitude. Attitude, one will recall, is taken to signify "the way the poet takes his subject"; tone, "the way he takes himself."

The following little poem will serve as a convenient first illustration:

The Span of Life

Robert Frost

The old dog barks backward without getting up.
I can remember when he was a pup.

Note that neither line is a poem by itself. It is not a poem to say "The old dog barks backward without getting up." That much is only a statement. Nor is it a poem to say "I can remember when he was a pup." That much is only a comment. But a poem does happen when the two lines are said one after the other. It must follow that the poem exists in the countermotion of the two lines, in the way the second line (in this case the comment) makes something of what has been established in the first line (in this case the statement). Nor do the two lines simply run together: there is some point of balance between the end of the first and the beginning of the second, a pause, a meditative silence iike a rest in music. The poem enters that pause with one attitude (in this case a relatively detached specific observation of the old dog) and after a moment of meditation it comes out of the pause with a different attitude (in this case a double change involving, first, a fonder, a sadder, and a more general recollection of the dog, and, second, a metaphoric implication, as reinforced by the title, that the comment is not only about the old dog but about all of life).

For convenience such a point of balance (and silence) may be called a *fulcrum* and may be indicated by the symbol $<$. Thus:

> The old dog barks backward without getting up.
> $<$
> I can remember when he was a pup.

Such countermotion is inseperable from "what the poem is" and "what the poem means"; it is in fact "*how* the poem means." In briefest form, *a poem is one part against another across a silence*. To understand this characteristic of the poem is to understand the theory of poetic form. To be able to respond to it in a poem is to understand the practice of poetry.[1]

[1] It was pointed out earlier that every shift in tone or attitude is accompanied by some shift in the handling of the technical elements. That shift is relatively difficult to establish in so brief a poem since it involves the metrical differences between two lines each of which is unusual. The norm is, of course, anapestic, and one will do well to note at least some of the ways in which these lines vary in their play against that norm. The first line may be scanned:

The old dog barks back ward wi thout ge tting up.

Yet certainly there is good reason for wishing to distribute the stress of the first foot over both "old" and "dog," thus:

The old dog barks back ward wi thout ge tting up.

The fact that one must pause after saying "old" in order to form the "d" sound of dog, tends to force a heavy stress on both words. The similarity of the vowels tends to make the words equal. And the repetition of "b" and "k" sounds around a similar (not identical) vowel sound in "barks back" once more heightens the pattern. Thus one is tempted to cluster four heavy accents on "old dog barks back."

The second line, on the other hand, has only one complication and that in the first (monosyllabic) foot. After the first foot the line progresses to the close in flawless anapests (the norm).

I can re mem ber when he was a pup.

Note the unusually heavy accent at the beginning of the second line (in this case a monosyllabic foot). Though it is not an invariable rule, there is a strong tendency in English and American poetry for the line after a fulcrum to begin with an unusually heavy stress, a monosyllabic foot, a spondee, a reversed foot, or some combination of these accents that produces a cluster of heavy stresses.

The Frost poem is as simple an example of poetic countermotion as one may well find. The following poem will illustrate the same sort of countermotion with rather more marked changes occurring across the fulcrum. The poem is one of the most memorable of the anonymous ballad snatches surviving from the early sixteenth century or perhaps earlier. Like most folk balladry, it survives in variant forms. The following is a modernized version.

O Western Wind

Anonymous

O Western wind, when wilt thou blow
   That the small rain down may rain?
                                   <
Christ, that my love were in my arms,
   And I in my bed again.

As indicated by the fulcrum, the poem, like "The Span of Life," consists of two parts. The first two lines are a cry of anguish to the Western wind (in England, the wind of Spring). The lament issues without any statement of cause for the speaker's anguish. The second two lines snap off that generalized lament and utter an angry and specific protest. The poet's tone has undergone an emphatic change.

As in "The Span of Life," one may note at once that neither of the halves is a poem. Whatever is being experienced is not complete in either the first two or the last two lines, but achieves its completion only in their countermotion across the silence of the fulcrum. Now if one will study the differences in technical handling on either side of the fulcrum, and if he will then relate them to the emotional force of the poem, he will be approaching the poem as its own performance, as its own act of itself, without resort to confusion by paraphrase.

For though paraphrase may be useful in helping to explain a specific difficulty in the phrasing of a poem, it is unfailingly a destructive method of discussion if one permits the illusion that the paraphrase is more than a momentary crutch, or that it is in any sense the poem itself. No poem "means" anything that any paraphrase is capable of saying. For, as noted, the poem exists in time and it exists in balance and countermotion across a silence. That timing and that counterthrust are inseparable from the emotional force of the poem, and it is exactly that timing and counterthrust that paraphrase cannot reproduce. The question to put to the poem is not "What does it mean?" but "How does it mean?" "What does it mean?" inevitably invites paraphrase and inevitably leads away from the poem. "How does it mean?" is best asked by absorbing the poetic structure as a poetic structure, *i.e.*, as a countermotion across a silence, and thus leads the analysis to the poem itself.

In "O Western Wind" the two most notable differences between the lines before and after the fulcrum are (1) the pace, as determined by the metrics, by the consonant-vowel sequences, and by the rhetorical structure; and (2) the diction, which changes from formal-hortatory in the first two lines, to colloquial in the second two.

The shift in the quality of the diction is clear enough. The first two lines are a generalized hortatory question phrased in terms that might do for an invocation to some minor deity of the wind; the second two lines are specific and bitter exclamation phrased in the simplest language of common speech.

It is the metric pattern accompanying that shift of diction that is worth special attention:

> O Wes / tern wind, // when wilt / thou blow
> That the small / rain down / may rain?
> Christ // that my love / were in / my arms
> And I / in my bed / again.

The first two lines make use of two spondees in seven feet, and of two series of three heavy stresses in a row. The second two lines make use of no spondees, there is no point in them where even two heavy stresses fall together, there are two anapests in them as opposed to one in the first line, and there is a pyrrhic to add two more unstressed syllables between accents. The only unusual emphasis in the second two lines occurs in the monosyllabic foot at the beginning of line three.[1] After that initial emphasis the meter becomes not only smooth but accelerated. It is as if that initial stress had consumed all the force of despair and passion, after which the voice can only slide forward into its grief.

Thus, one has located a first difference in the technical handling: the first two lines are metrically impeded and the second two lines are not only smooth but slightly accelerated. Having located that difference, one who wishes to experience poetry rather than simply to talk around it, will do well to consider that a fast passage in music is not the equivalent of a slow one, nor of the same passage repeated slowly. In the same way, a good poem does not change its pace without meaning something by that change. The rhythm is one part of the performance of the poem's "meaning."

The first two lines of the present poem, moreover, are impeded not only by the meter but by the six lingering "w" sounds followed by the open vowels of "thou blow" (which pick up the open vowel of the vocative at the beginning of the line), thus:

O WEHstern WInd HWEn WIlt thOU blOW.

---

[1] See Frost's use of the same device after the fulcrum in "The Span of Life" and see the note on page 995.

With this much observed, one may identify the essence of the poem's performance of itself. It begins with a heavily impeded generalized invocation to the Western wind of Spring. The poet draws out his cry as if tortured by the thought, carrying it on a rising inflection throughout the first two lines and leaving it suspended. The cry ends and the poet pauses, silent. Suddenly, within that silence, the terms of his grief change inside him. A second voice of his despair surges in him and lashes forth with a cry to Heaven. The voice resumes with a hammer-beat of anguish on the first syllable. Then, as if that first hammered syllable had drained the last strength of the speaker's anger, the voice slides off into a numb personal statement of the poet's exact grief, that grief now simply stated, no longer volatile and angry but defeated, and the metric line accordingly runs smooth and even accelerates in response to the fact that the poet no longer struggles against the truth, but closes on a dying fall.

The foregoing paragraph is not a paraphrase of the poem, but rather a simplified description of the details of the poetic performance. The function of such description is not to replace the poem but to direct the attention to it by pointing out the emotional sequences of the poem in time and the accompanying shifts in technical management. The question to be addressed is always "How"—not "What"—does a poem mean?

In both "The Span of Life" and "O Western Wind" the poetic structure is built across a single fulcrum and the units on either side of the fulcrum are equal in length. The following poem will illustrate a different case. Before one reads it, he needs to know that the poet served as an Instructor in Aerial Gunnery during World War II and that an essential part of such gunnery training consisted of memorizing the nomenclature of the many parts of a Browning .50 Caliber Machine Gun. Obviously a Gunner must be able to order repair parts from rear area depots, and if he is to receive the right part he must be able to give its exact technical name, no matter how complicated. The "belt feed lever" and the "belt holding pawl" of the last line are two of the many items of nomenclature that student-gunners were required to study. The poet is bemused by the resemblance of such vocabulary exercises from the school-for-death to the exercises all children are assigned in the school-of-innocence.

The Fury of Aerial Bombardment

Richard Eberhart

You would think the fury of aerial bombardment
Would rouse God to relent; the infinite spaces
Are still silent. He looks on shock-pried faces.
History, even, does not know what is meant.
<₃

FROM *Selected Poems,* by Richard Eberhart. 1951. Reprinted by permission of Oxford University Press, Inc.

You would feel that after so many centuries
God would give man to repent; yet he can kill
As Cain could, but with multitudinous will,
No farther advanced than in his ancient furies.

_{<2}

Was man made stupid to see his own stupidity?
Is God by definition indifferent, beyond us all?
Is the eternal truth man's fighting soul
Wherein the beast ravens in his own avidity?

_{<1}

Of Van Wettering I speak, and Averill,
Names on a list whose faces I do not recall.
But they are gone to early death, who late in school
Distinguished the belt-feed-lever from the belt-holding-pawl.

The principal fulcrum of this poem quite clearly occurs, as marked, be.
tween the third and the fourth stanzas. There are lesser fulcrums within
the first three stanzas, but they are better left for later discussion. The
point to note is that there is no reason for two statements to be of the
same length in order to have the same emotional weight. It is a working
convention of the English sonnet, for example, to balance the final couplet
against the twelve preceding lines, the couplet usually reversing the tone
and attitude. Thus the main fulcrum would occur, in such sonnets, be-
tween the first twelve lines and the last two.

The first three stanzas of "The Fury of Aerial Bombardment" are made
up of enormous rhetorical statements and questions addressed to no less
a subject than man's fate upon the planet. In stanza four the address sud-
denly changes from a rhetoric for abstract-man to an understated elegy
for two boys named Van Wettering and Averill, boys who sought no
universal meaning but simply distinguished the belt-feed-lever from the
belt-holding-pawl, and died of their schooling into the anonymities of fate.
They are not even faces: they are names on a list. The only point at which
they touch larger significance is that they are gone to early death. Thus,
they are unknowing heirs to all human waste: their death is their one real
illustration of the universal questions the poem begins with. Yet the implica-
tion is clear that their death is both man's tragedy and failure. The boys are
the least of men in one sense, faceless and forgotten; yet their deaths accuse
all of mankind, the more so in that these who die are so insignificant.

There can be no mistaking that the author has changed both his atti-
tude toward the subject and his personal tone in going from one side of
the fulcrum to the other. The opening attitude is one of the most intense
moral indignation; the opening tone is rhetorical and resonant enough for
the loftiest pulpit. The closing attitude drops the high moral indignation
in favor of the simplest sort of sorrow, and the tone changes from high
rhetoric to a conversational understatement. Inevitably the whole quality
of the language changes from the Latinate diction of moral abstraction to
the colloquial and less Latinate diction of simple statement.

The change in the pace and the rhythm is as marked as the change in diction. Each of the first three stanzas divides between masculine and feminine rhymes, the effect of the feminine rhymes being to leave the voice suspended on a rising inflection. The fourth stanza uses no feminine rhymes, each line closing on a masculine word. The voice is brought down firm to the falling inflection.

The change in the quality of the metrics from one side of the fulcrum to the other is even more emphatically marked. Eberhart's meter is unusual for the number of light syllables allowed into a single foot. One should sense at once that the poem is written in pentameters. And despite great variation, that the norm is iambic. (The next to last line, though lengthened to a hexameter, is made up entirely of iambics, and may be taken as the rest-line of the poem, the line in which the norm is most clearly asserted. When in doubt it is wise to look for such rest lines.) Against that norm, however, the voice must swallow many accelerated syllables. So in the opening line:

$$\text{You would think / the fu ry / of ae / ri al / bom bard ment}$$

Line nine can be scanned only by allowing a double feminine foot at the end:

$$\text{Was man / made stu / pid to see / his own / stu pid it y.}$$

And line ten runs to seven light accents in the second and third feet:

$$\text{Is God / by de fin i tion / in di fe rrent, // beyond / us all?}$$

The characteristic of Eberhart's metric in the first three stanzas is extraordinary acceleration checked by relatively heavy caesura. The voice is thus required to lash out and stop, lash out and stop. The metric effect, when combined with the voice-thrust suggested by the vastness of the concepts being declared, is clearly oratorical. The rhythm thrusts like the voice of a man delivering a powerful, outraged sermon, and being carried away by it. Note also that the sermon concludes with the voice rising on a double feminine, appropriately in a question:

$$\text{Where in / the Beast / ra vens / in his own / a vi di ty?}[1]$$

Across the fulcrum, on the other hand, there is only one case in which three light syllables fall together. The extraordinary accelerations have disappeared, the metric is much smoother, and the pace is further slowed by the fact that the last two lines have become hexameters. The extra foot of the hexameter in English seems almost invariably to slow the pace by drawing out the line.

$$\text{Of Van / We tter ing / I speak, / and A / ver ill,}$$

[1] The first foot may with equal reason be taken as a pyrrhic. The syllables are equal whether taken as stressed or unstressed.

Names / on a list,// whose faces / I do not / recall.[1]
But they / are gone / to ear / ly death,// who late / in school
Dis tin / guished the belt / feed le ver // from the / belt hold / ing pawl.

Were the discussion of the poem to stop here, it would still be apparent that such changes in pace are not only relevant to the "meaning" of the poem, but so inseparably involved in the meaning that there can be no communication of the poem's essential experience until the voice has responded to the changes. Many sensitive readers are able to make such a response without being able to analyze why they have so responded; such attunement is the happy result of extensive and sensitive reading. It is possible, that is to say, to receive a poem without this sort of analysis. It is not possible, however, to *discuss* the poetic structure meaningfully without recognizing the countermoving balance of that structure across the fulcrum and the attendant change in the handling of the poetic elements. It is precisely because paraphrase is incapable of taking these elements and their counterweights into account that one must go the long way round to the discussion if he truly wishes to know what the poem is doing with itself.

There still remains to be considered the matter of the lesser fulcrums in the structure of Eberhart's poem, the fulcrums numbered 2 and 3 as distinct from the major fulcrum numbered 1. Thus far the discussion has all been of central fulcrum points, of the poem divided in two. The suggested image of the poetic structure has been that of a scale-arm balanced across a single fulcrum. That image needs now to be expanded into something more like a piece of mobile sculpture, a structure possessing, to be sure, a single main point of balance, but containing further lesser balances within the parts.

Those lesser balances can become so intricate that to pursue all of them would lead to more confusion than clarity. Certainly, however, one may readily note that the first three stanzas of the Eberhart poem, though they constitute a single side of the central balance, are themselves divided into two units, one of which is divided once again. Represented as a diagramatic mobile sculpture, with the numbers on the weights corresponding to the stanza numbers and F labeling the main fulcrum, the poem might be imagined thus:

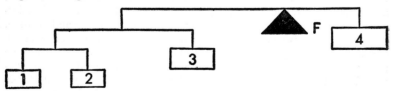

[1]The beginning of line two may be scanned more regularly as a trochee followed by an iamb. There can be no doubt however that the normal speech rhythm of English makes "on a list" an anapest.

One has only to observe the carefully repeated pattern of stanzas one and two to recognize their close relationship. The first line of each stanza is a run-on and the voice continues without pause to a caesura after the third foot of the second line. After that caesura, the second line of each stanza again runs on, the voice in both cases coming to rest after the second foot of the third line. Then once more the voice moves forward for three feet and comes to rest again. And though the fourth line of the first stanza differs from the fourth line of the second by a small caesural effect around "even," the two lines are still more than sufficiently close to keep the pattern firm. Leaving that small caesural ripple around "even" out of consideration, one may diagram the pattern thus:

```
_____    m    f
_____//_____      f    m
_____//_____//      f    m
_____//        m    f
```

The rhyme ("m" for masculine and "f" for feminine) changes position from the first stanza (first column) to the second stanza in a perfect reversed pattern. As if to leave no possible doubt that the stanzas are exactly related, the poet has added an unmissable and unusual internal rhyme, "relent—repent," just before the first caesura in each stanza.

Such patterning of pauses and effects may again be recognized as characteristic of the rhetorician. The very parallel construction of the sentences—"You would think" in the first stanza, "You would feel" in the second, and again "Would rouse God" in the first, and "God would give" in the second—is a device of the same rhetorical impulse.

Then, having established his pattern with such care, the poet breaks from it. The third stanza has a much more definite tendency to run the line straight to a full end-stop without internal pause, and thus the whole pattern of the pauses changes. A principal point of the present discussion, to repeat once again, is that such changes can only happen in response to a change in the poet's tone or attitude or both. He may realize exactly what change he is making, or he may simply follow the dictates of his feelings without analysis or need for analysis, but the changes themselves do not occur without cause. One can, of course, see at a glance that the voice has changed from making statements to asking questions. But given no more than the scansion of the poem and its pattern of pauses, without a word of the text, one would still be able to tell that the voice had undergone some change in response to a change in the poet's tone and attitude.

If every poem is constructed on such countermotions across a fulcrum, and if the handling of the technical elements always changes from one unit of the poetic structure to another, the method of analysis here suggested must inevitably lead to a fuller understanding of that poetic structure. One need only locate the principal fulcrum, the lesser fulcrums within the main units of the structure, and then analyze the differences in the handling of the poetic elements within each unit and sub-unit. To do that much, however, is not to have achieved the poem, but rather to have prepared oneself to achieve it. Any method of analysis is designed only to assure one that he is giving his human attention to the poem itself rather than to some non-poetic paraphrase of its unenacted "meaning." In every good poem there is some final echo of nuance and feeling that lies beyond explanation and analysis.

Not all poems, however, make their countermotions immediately apparent. So it is necessary to distinguish between what may be called *balanced* and *truncated* poems. Balanced poems are of the order already discussed: they exist in countermotion across inner fulcrum points. Truncated poems, on the other hand, travel in a straight line outward from the opening statement and seem to lack the counterthrust of an opposing passage. The following is an example.

My Papa's Waltz

Theodore Roethke

The whiskey on your breath
Could make a small boy dizzy;
But I held on like death:
Such waltzing was not easy.

We romped until the pans
Slid from the kitchen shelf;
My mother's countenance
Could not unfrown itself.

The hand that held my wrist
Was battered on one knuckle;
At every step I missed
My right ear scraped a buckle.

You beat time on my head
With a palm caked hard by dirt,
Then waltzed me off to bed
Still clinging to your shirt.

Despite its seeming lightness, "My Papa's Waltz" is a poem of terror, all the more terrible because the boy is frightened and hurt by the father even in play. "We romped," the poet says, but the romp is a dizzying succession of painful glimpses: the house is shaking, the mother is frowning, the father's hand is scarred by violence, every misstep in the dance scrapes the father's belt-buckle painfully across the boy's ear, and the boy's head is being pounded by that huge, hard palm. It is a romp, but the boy must cling like death until he is finally dumped into bed.

The terror, however, mounts in a straight line, detail upon detail, with no countermotion across a fulcrum *because there is no change either in tone or in attitude.* The poem clearly breaks into four parts, as indicated by the stanza breaks, but the parts follow one another with no sense that one stanza break is more important than another. And as one might suspect in such a case, there is no marked difference in the handling of the poetic elements from stanza to stanza. Metrics, pace, diction, imagery, grammatical structure—all are very nearly constant throughout. Even the pattern of pauses is the same from stanza to stanza with only one variation in the extra pause at the end of the third line of stanza one: with that exception all the stanzas move without pause to the end of the second line, and then move forward again without pause to the end of the fourth line. And though there are two feminine rhymes in the first and third stanzas, even they fall into a neatly repeated pattern. The whole, disregarding the extra pause in stanza one, may be diagrammed thus:

```
_ _ _ _ _ _ _ _ _ _ _ _ _ _ _ _ _ _ _ _ _ _ _ _ _ _ _ _ _ _ _   m   m   m   m
_ _ _ _ _ _ _ _ _ _ _ _ _ _ _ _ _ _ _ _ _ _ _ _ _ _ _ _ _ _ //   f   m   f   m
_ _ _ _ _ _ _ _ _ _ _ _ _ _ _ _ _ _ _ _ _ _ _ _ _ _ _ _ _ _ _   m   m   m   m
_ _ _ _ _ _ _ _ _ _ _ _ _ _ _ _ _ _ _ _ _ _ _ _ _ _ _ _ _ _ //   f   m   f   m
```

The poem seems to lack a fulcrum. The fact is that the poem does indeed work against a fulcrum, but that *the fulcrum occurs after the last line.* Imagine, as a horrible example, that the poet had written an additional summarizing stanza in his first draft, and imagine that it had run to some such sad stuff as the following:

> Ah, that was long ago.
> Now, his first terrors shed,
> This dancer turns to go
> Calm, to the fearless dead.

Miserable and cliché-ridden poeticizing to be sure, but had such a stanza existed one would have had no hesitation in placing the fulcrum between it and the preceding poem, or in identifying the metric shift wherein three of the last four lines begin with monosyllabic feet.

The poet may very well have been tempted at first writing to add some such summarizing stanza. If so, he wisely put by the temptation in the secure sense that nothing could be said in such an addition that was not already better said by silence worked upon by the implications of the preceding lines. For silence, too, is communication when placed in context. Thus *the fulcrum exists outside the poem, between the enacted experience and the silence that follows it.*

The following poem, on the other hand, is a fair example of a poem that over-ran its silence into six lines of "tacked-on moral," all the more painful in view of the extraordinary sharpness and economy of most of the poem up to those last six lines:

Before Disaster
Yvor Winters

Evening traffic homeward burns,
Swift and even on the turns,
Drifting weight in triple rows,
Fixed relation and repose.
This one edges out and by,
Inch by inch with steady eye.
But should error be increased,
Mass and moment are released;
Matter loosens, flooding blind,
Levels driver to its kind.

Ranks of nations thus descend,
Watchful to a stormy end.
By a moment's calm beguiled,
I have got a wife and child.
Fool and scoundrel guide the State.
Peace is whore to Greed and Hate.
Nowhere may I turn to flee:
Action is security.
Treading change with savage heel,
We must live or die by steel.

A metric note is necessary before the discussion of the countermotions of this poem. The pattern of scansion for all lines is the same and may be represented thus:

$$/ - / - / - /$$

Each line, that is, begins and ends with a heavy stress and each consists of four such heavy stresses enclosing three unstressed syllables. In such a case one may be uncertain whether to take the line as iambic or trochaic. The fact is that many English poets who have written in tetrameters have welcomed this effect as pleasing. The voice begins and ends each line on a stressed syllable and proceeds through each line without internal pause, the metronomic quality of such metrics producing an especially incanta-tory effect. It is relevant that this stress-to-stress pattern of the tetrameter line rarely, if ever, occurs when caesuras are used.

Traditionally such lines are referred to as *catalectic* (noun form: *cata-lexis*) from Greek roots signifying "to stop short." Since what is stopped short of must come at the end, catalexis implies a trochaic base with some-thing missing from the last foot:

$$\acute{E}ve\ ning/\ tr\acute{a}\ ffic/\ home\ ward/\ burns$$
$$Swift\ and/\ e\ ven/\ on\ the/\ turns.$$

The terms of Greek prosody cannot, however, be indiscriminately applied to English prosody. In English the base is (more plausibly) iambic, with a truncated first foot. One has only to add an unstressed syllable at the beginning of each line to see that iambic pattern:

$$\bar{\text{As}} \; \acute{\text{eve}}/ \; \bar{\text{ning}} \; \acute{\text{tra}}/ \; \bar{\text{ffic}} \; \acute{\text{home}}/ \; \bar{\text{ward}} \; \acute{\text{burns}}$$
$$\bar{\text{So}} \; \acute{\text{swift}}/ \; \bar{\text{and}} \; \acute{\text{e}}/ \; \bar{\text{ven}} \; \acute{\text{on}}/ \; \bar{\text{the}} \; \acute{\text{turns.}}$$

But these light syllables are excess baggage. Moreover, they interfere with the particular emphasis of the stress-to-stress pattern, loosening the incantatory effect. With something like its tolerance for feminine syllables before a pause, the English ear welcomes the dropping of these initial light syllables. Most precisely scanned, therefore, this tetrameter line may be represented as follows:

$$, / -/ -/ -/$$

In such a special case of metronomic meter, it is unlikely that one will find any significant metric variation across the fulcrums of the poem. The only marked technical differences one may find between the poem and the last six lines are in the quality of the diction. With the last six lines omitted, however, the poem comes to a triumphant major balance (fulcrum) against its own following silence, and may be divided thus:

> Evening traffic homeward burns,
> Swift and even on the turns,
> Drifting weight in triple rows,
> Fixed relation and repose.
> This one edges out and by,
> Inch by inch with steady eye.
> But should error be increased,
> Mass and moment are released;
> Matter loosens, flooding blind,
> Levels driver to its kind.
> $<_2$
> Ranks of nations thus descend,
> Watchful to a sudden end.
> $<_2$
> By a moment's calm beguiled,
> I have got a wife and child.
> $<_1$

A note on the diction of this poem: Is "error" justifiable in Line 7? Is it "error" that is being "increased"? If it is to be increased there must have been some degree of starting error, but is not the whole force of the preceding description the precision with which the dangerous traffic moves, swiftly, evenly, in fixed relation, steadily? The force the poem seems to require is more nearly "should error be introduced" rather than "increased." On the other hand, note the happy ambiguity of "moment," in line 8, as both "momentum" and "the moment of time."

The large fulcrum after the last couplet is labeled 1 to indicate that it is the major point of balance. The lesser fulcrums are both labeled 2 to indicate that they are of equal value. One may, if he wishes, argue for a lesser fulcrum after the sixth line, but it seems more important to stress that the first ten lines are a single unit.

That first unit of the poem is a dispassionate description of evening traffic seen primarily as a problem in physics: the tone of the passage is set by the implicit image of physical particles (detached from all human feeling) in motion. Rank on rank the particles move forward in their dangerous precision.

Across the first of the lesser fulcrums, the poet suddenly strikes a balance against his first image, amplifying the idea from literal description of traffic to an image-related idea of the condition of nations. "Nations" must certainly receive an unusually heavy stress by the logic of the implicit parallel construction. "Ranks of particles move toward collision and ranks of *nations* do exactly the same thing." The first shift then is from description to comment.

Having made a first comment on the largest scale, the poet pauses, and suddenly strikes a further balance with his material by applying it wryly to himself in the most personal terms. "By a moment's calm (fixed relation and repose) and like 'nations,'" the poet says, "*I* have also been beguiled." The three operative emphases are *physical particles, nations,* and *I.*

A triumphant poem thus far, a poetic structure lodging itself in a powerfully suggestive way against its following silence.

But at the end the moralist triumphs over the poet and the poem is blurred by six empty lines of abstract moralizing. "Fool," "scoundrel," "State," "Peace," "Greed," "Hate" (and capitalized for emphasis) are terms that might have tempted such a pompous moralizer as Henley. There can certainly be no doubt that they constitute a change in the quality of the diction, but they are unfortunately a change for the worse.

For a poem must finally be seen as a formal structure in which the countermotions of the units *release into the silences they create a force of contained emotional perception beyond the power of statement.* The key terms are: *release into silence, contained emotional perception,* and *statement.* The poetic structure *releases* its "meaning"; it does not *say* it.

Poems for Study—Countermotion

A number of the following poems have specific suggestions for study attached. In all of them, whether or not accompanied by specific notation:

1. Mark the fulcrums, identify their relative importance, and identify the poem as balanced or truncated.

2. In your own words and as economically as possible, identify the tone and attitude of each division of the poem.

3. Identify every technical device you can locate in each division.

4. Identify and specify every change in the handling of given technical devices across the fulcrum.

5. Reread the poem with these analyses accomplished.

Those who desire further exercises in analyzing the countermotions of poetry may apply these measures to any poem in the present volume, though it may be found that the length of the narrative poems in Part One makes such analysis of them cumbersome.

On the Vanity of Earthly Greatness

Arthur Guiterman

The tusks that clashed in mighty brawls
Of mastodons, are billiard balls.

The sword of Charlemagne the Just
Is ferric oxide, known as rust.

The grizzly bear whose potent hug
Was feared by all, is now a rug.

Great Caesar's bust is on the shelf,
And I don't feel so well myself.

QUESTIONS

1. The humor of this poem is obviously a result of its countermotions. Each couplet builds up to its dividing comma in the largest possible diction, and then counterthrusts with an idea that seems incongruously small by comparison.

2. Is there any progression in this series of thrusts and counterthrusts?

3. See the somewhat similar series of thrusts and counterthrusts in Reed's "Naming of Parts," page 832.

January 1940

Roy Fuller

Swift had pains in his head.
Johnson dying in bed
Tapped the dropsy himself.

From the book *Gaily The Troubadour* by Arthur Guiterman. Copyright, 1936, E. P. Dutton & Co., Inc. Reprinted by permission of the publishers.

From *The Middle of the War,* by Roy Fuller. Reprinted by permission of The Hogarth Press Ltd., London.

Blake saw a flea and an elf.
Tennyson could hear the shriek
Of a bat. Pope was a freak.
Emily Dickinson stayed
Indoors for a decade.
Water inflated the belly
Of Hart Crane and of Shelley.
Coleridge was a dope.
Southwell died on a rope.
Byron had a round white foot.
Smart and Cowper were put
Away. Lawrence was a fidget.
Keats was almost a midget.
Donne, alive in his shroud,
Shakespeare in the coil of a cloud,
Saw death very well as he
Came crab-wise, dark and massy.
I envy not only their talents
And fertile lack of balance
But the appearance of choice
In their sad and fatal voice.

Donne, alive in his shroud: The Sunday before his death, John Donne, then Dean of St. Paul's, arose from his death bed and, dressed in his shroud, preached what amounted to his own death sermon.

QUESTIONS

1. Everything in Fuller's catalogue of the oddness of the English and American poets is true, at least in some sense, but it is stated in the most irreverent terms. How does the poem develop from its irreverence to its final tone?

2. Why the irreverence?

It's No Use Raising a Shout

W. H. Auden

It's no use raising a shout.
No, Honey, you can cut that right out.
I don't want any more hugs;
Make me some fresh tea, fetch me some rugs.
Here am I, here are you:
But what does it mean? What are we going to do?

A long time ago I told my mother
I was leaving home to find another:

I never answered her letter
But I never found a better.
Here am I, here are you:
But what does it mean? What are we going to do?

In my spine there was a base;
And I knew the general's face:
But they've severed all the wires,
And I can't tell what the general desires.
Here am I, here are you:
But what does it mean? What are we going to do?

In my veins there is a wish,
And a memory of fish:
When I lie crying on the floor,
It says, "You've often done this before."
Here am I, here are you:
But what does it mean? What are we going to do?

A bird used to visit this shore:
It isn't going to come any more.
I've come a very long way to prove
No land, no water, and no love.
Here am I, here are you:
But what does it mean? What are we going to do?

QUESTION

1. An anthologist once classified this poem as Light Verse. What is there in the poem that might lead an insensitive reader to take it as light verse, and what is there that would prevent a more careful reader from so taking it?

Lucifer in Starlight

George Meredith

On a starr'd night Prince Lucifer uprose.
    Tired of his dark dominion swung the fiend
Above the rolling ball in cloud part screen'd,
Where sinners hugg'd their spectre of repose.
Poor prey to his hot fit of pride were those,
    And now upon his western wing he lean'd,
    Now his huge bulk o'er Afric's sands careen'd,
Now the black planet shadow'd Arctic snows.
Soaring through wider zones that prick'd his scars
    With memory of the old revolt from Awe,

He reach'd a middle height, and at the stars,
Which are the brain of heaven, he look'd, and sank.
Around the ancient track march'd, rank on rank,
    The army of unalterable law.

the black planet: Lucifer himself.

QUESTION

1. What is the effect of the sequence of related "a" sounds in the last line? Note that the mouth must open wide to make these sounds. And note that each is a heavily stressed syllable in a flow of accelerated syllables.

The Artist

William Carlos Williams

Mr. T
                bareheaded
                        in a soiled undershirt
his hair standing out
                on all sides
                        stood on his toes
heels together
                arms gracefully
                        for the moment
curled above his head.
                Then he whirled about
                        bounded
into the air
                and with an *entrechat*
                        perfectly achieved
completed the figure.
                My mother
                        taken by surprise
where she sat
                in her invalid's chair
                        was left speechless.
Bravo! she cried at last
                and clapped her hands.
                        The man's wife
came from the kitchen:
                What goes on here? she said.
                        But the show was over.

Herself

John Holmes

Herself listening to herself, having no name,
She walked in an airy April sun, clothes close on her
And thin and of some printed green;
A girl came nearer and nearer, came
Carrying white and yellow flowers.

Girls are smooth with sleep in the morning
And before they dress up out of naked bed,
Stand open to all airs,
Next to the world's body as the world's to theirs.
In the evening and at midnight, light
Curves round a girl, reaches to brush her cheek,
Her lips, loose hair, or breast or knee.
Outlining her with shining that cannot speak.

Ann at midnight and three midnights heard a voice
Saying, When you come back you will not find me here.
Or Hulda. Not Ruth. Perhaps Elizabeth
Who read next year's news in a letter, all the accidents
Postmarked, and lost it. No one believed her.

It was a dead man if you know what it is to be dead.
Eleanor, he said, or Janet Janet Janet do you dream me?

QUESTIONS

1. What is the force of "printed green" in line 3? "Printed" green as
distinct from what other kind of green?

2. The third stanza may reasonably be taken as a reconstruction of the
dream life of "Herself" ("At midnight and three midnights heard a
voice"). What is the effect of running so many girls' names in, as if at
random?

Landscape as Metal and Flowers

Winfield Townley Scott

All over America railroads ride through roses.

I should explain this is thoroughly a matter of fact.
Wherever sandy earth is piled to make a road for train tracks

FROM *The Double Root,* by John Holmes. Twayne Publishers, Inc. Reprinted by per-
mission of the author.
FROM *Wind the Clock,* copyright 1941 by Winfield Townley Scott. Reprinted by per-
mission of the author.

The banks on either side are covered with wild, sweet
Pink rambler roses: not because roses are pretty
But because ramblers grow in cheap soil and will hold
The banks firm against rain—therefore the railroad roses.

All over America the steel-supporting flowers,
Sometimes at village depots covering the shingled station,
Sometimes embracing watertanks, but mostly endless tendrils
Out of which locomotives and pullmans flash the morning—
And tunnels the other way into whose firm, sweet evening
The whistle fades, dragging freight cars, day coaches and the caboose.

My Luve

Robert Burns

O my luve is like a red, red rose,
   That's newly sprung in June:
O my luve is like a melodie,
   That's sweetly played in tune.

As fair art thou, my bonie lass,
   So deep in luve am I;
And I will luve thee still, my dear,
   Till a' the seas gang dry.

Till a' the seas gang dry, my dear,
   And the rocks melt wi' the sun:
And I will luve thee still, my dear,
   While the sands o' life shall run.

And fare thee weel, my only luve!
   And fare thee weel a while!
And I will come again, my luve,
   Tho' it were ten thousand mile.

Ozymandias

Percy Bysshe Shelley

I met a traveler from an antique land,
Who said: Two vast and trunkless legs of stone
Stand in the desert. Near them, on the sand,
Half sunk, a shattered visage lies, whose frown,
And wrinkled lip, and sneer of cold command,
Tell that its sculptor well those passions read,

Which yet survive, stamped on these lifeless things,
The hand that mocked them, and the heart that fed:
And on the pedestal these words appear:
"My name is Ozymandias, King of Kings:
Look on my works, ye Mighty, and despair!"
Nothing beside remains. Round the decay
Of that colossal wreck, boundless and bare
The lone and level sands stretch far away.

The Solitary Reaper

William Wordsworth

Behold her, single in the field,
Yon solitary highland lass!
Reaping and singing by herself;
Stop here, or gently pass!
Alone she cuts and binds the grain,
And sings a melancholy strain;
O listen! for the vale profound
Is overflowing with the sound.

No nightingale did ever chaunt
More welcome notes to weary bands
Of travelers in some shady haunt,
Among Arabian sands:
A voice so thrilling ne'er was heard
In spring-time from the cuckoo-bird,
Breaking the silence of the seas
Among the farthest Hebrides.

Will no one tell me what she sings?—
Perhaps the plaintive numbers flow
For old, unhappy, far-off things,
And battles long ago:
Or is it some more humble lay,
Familiar matter of today?
Some natural sorrow, loss, or pain,
That has been, and may be again?

Whate'er the theme, the maiden sang
As if her song could have no ending;
I saw her singing at her work,
And o'er the sickle bending;—
I listened, motionless and still;
And, as I mounted up the hill
The music in my heart I bore,
Long after it was heard no more.

The Passionate Shepherd to His Love
Christopher Marlowe

Come live with me and be my love,
And we will all the pleasures prove,
That valleys, groves, hills and fields,
Woods or steepy mountain yields.

And we will sit upon the rocks,
Seeing the shepherds feed their flocks
By shallow rivers, to whose falls
Melodious birds sing madrigals.

And I will make thee beds of roses,
And a thousand fragrant posies,
A cap of flowers and a kirtle
Embroidered all with leaves of myrtle;

A gown made of the finest wool,
Which from our pretty lambs we pull;
Fair-linèd slippers for the cold,
With buckles of the purest gold;

A belt of straw and ivy buds,
With coral clasps and amber studs;
And if these pleasures may thee move,
Come live with me and be my love.

The shepherd swains shall dance and sing
For thy delight each May morning;
If these delights thy mind may move,
Then live with me and be my love.

The Nymph's Reply to the Shepherd
Sir Walter Raleigh

If all the world and love were young
And truth in every shepherd's tongue,
These pretty pleasures might me move
To live with thee and be thy love.

Time drives the flocks from field to fold
When rivers rage and rocks grow cold,
And Philomel becometh dumb;
The rest complain of cares to come.

The flowers do fade and wanton fields
The wayward winter reckoning yields;
A honey tongue, a heart of gall,
Is fancy's Spring, but sorrow's Fall.

Thy gowns, thy shoes, thy beds of roses,
Thy cap, thy kirtle, and thy posies
Soon break, soon wither, soon forgotten,
In folly ripe, in reason rotten.

Thy belt of straw and ivy buds,
Thy coral clasps and amber studs,
All these in me no means can move
To come to thee and be thy love.

But could youth last and love still breed,
Had joys no date nor age no need,
Then these delights my mind might move
To live with thee and be thy love.

The Baite

John Donne

Come live with mee, and bee my love,
And wee will some new pleasures prove
Of golden sands, and christall brookes,
With silken lines, and silver hookes.

There will the river whispering runne
Warm'd by thy eyes, more than the Sunne.
And there the'inamored fish will stay,
Begging themselves they may betray.

When thou wilt swimme in that live bath,
Each fish, which every channell hath,
Will amorously to thee swimme,
Gladder to catch thee, than thou him.

If thou, to be so seene, beest loath,
By Sunne or Moone, thou darknest both,
And if myself have leave to see,
I need not their light, having thee.

Let others freeze with angling reeds,
And cut their legges, with shells and weeds,
Or treacherously poor fish beset,
With strangling snare, or windowie net:

Let coarse bold hands, from slimy nest
The bedded fish in banks out-wrest,
Or curious traitors, sleavesilk flies
Bewitch poore fishes wandering eyes.

For thee, thou needst no such deceit,
For thou they self are thine owne bait;
That fish that is not catch'd thereby,
Alas, is wiser farre than I.

Many readers have trouble reading John Donne because they fail to solve his grammatical sense (which is not a random eccentricity but a device for forcing voice emphasis primarily through the weight of parallel constructions and balanced antitheses). The last line of the third stanza, for example, is a parallel construction. Rendered with all its implications stated it would read: "[Each fish will be] gladder to catch thee, than thou [wilt be to catch] him." With that understood, the voice must punch the parallel elements with unusual emphasis, thus: "Gladder to catch *thee*, than *thou* him." No poet in English has used grammatical structure so extensively for metric effect.

That grammatical control of voice stresses can be confusing, the first two lines of the fourth stanza attest. Certainly the grammar instructs the voice to read with the stress as follows:

> If THOU, to be so SEENE, beest *loath*,
> By *Sunne* or *Moone,* thou *dark*nest BOTH.

The italicized syllables receive normal stress, those printed in capitals acquire especially heavy stresses because of the grammatical force. Unfortunately some grammatical difficulty is likely to follow, but a willing reader should not find Donne's grammar a stumbling block for long. As an illustration of this sort of difficulty, these two lines may be taken to mean, in more usual grammar: "If thou beest loath to be so seene by either the Sunne or the Moone (a double meaning here equivalent in the second sense to "by day or night") then thou darknest both (and in both senses).

Hawk's Way

Theodore Olson

This was the hawk's way. This way the hawk
Nested a moment on the incredible
Crag of the wind, sitting the air like rock.
This was the perilous, lovely way the hawk fell

REPRINTED by permission of *The Saturday Review* and of the author.

Down the long hill of the wind, the anarch air
Shaped by his going: air become visible, bent
To a blade of beauty, cruel and taut and bare,
A bow of ecstasy, singing and insolent.

And the heart, too, bent to breaking; the heart was rent
Like a cloth, and did not care.

Then air deployed again, and was only air
On the empty way the hawk in his beauty went.

Compare this poem with Yvor Winters', "Before Disaster." The editor
believes that this poem, like Winters', could be much more effective with-
out the added comment. The first two stanzas capture the hawk's way of
going in a magnificent rhythm that closes upward on the rising inflection
of "singing and insolent." Had the poem been brought firmly to rest
against its own charged, following silence, could the reader fail to sense
that the author was indeed moved and that the air seemed empty once
the hawk was gone from it? Could a poet capture the dive of a hawk into
so moving a rhythm unless his "heart" was involved?

To His Coy Mistress

Andrew Marvell

Had we but world enough, and time,
This coyness, lady, were no crime.
We would sit down, and think which way
To walk, and pass our long love's day.
Thou by the Indian Ganges' side
Should'st rubies find: I by the tide
Of Humber would complain. I would
Love you ten years before the Flood,
And you should, if you please, refuse
Till the conversion of the Jews.
My vegetable love should grow
Vaster than empires, and more slow.
An hundred years should go to praise
Thine eyes, and on thy forehead gaze:
Two hundred to adore each breast:
But thirty thousand to the rest;
An age at least to every part,
And the last age should show your heart.
For, lady, you deserve this state,
Nor would I love at lower rate.
But at my back I always hear
Time's wingèd chariot hurrying near:

And yonder all before us lie
Deserts of vast eternity.
Thy beauty shall no more be found;
Nor, in thy marble vault, shall sound
My echoing song: then worms shall try
That long-preserved virginity,
And your quaint honor turn to dust,
And into ashes all my lust.
The grave's a fine and private place,
But none, I think, do there embrace.
   Now, therefore, while the youthful hue
Sits on thy skin like morning dew,
And while thy willing soul transpires
At every pore with instant fires,
Now let us sport us while we may;
And now, like amorous birds of prey,
Rather at once our Time devour,
Than languish in his slow-chapt power.
Let us roll all our strength and all
Our sweetness up into one ball,
And tear our pleasures with rough strife
Thorough the iron gates of life.
Thus, though we cannot make our Sun
Stand still, yet we will make him run.

You, Andrew Marvell

Archibald MacLeish

And here face down beneath the sun
And here upon earth's noonward height
To feel the always coming on
The always rising of the night

To feel creep up the curving east
The earthly chill of dusk and slow
Upon those under lands the vast
And ever-climbing shadow grow

And strange at Ecbatan the trees
Take leaf by leaf the evening strange
The flooding dark about their knees
The mountains over Persia change

And now at Kermanshah the gate
Dark empty and the withered grass

FROM *Collected Poems 1917–1952*, by Archibald MacLeish. Reprinted by permission of Houghton Mifflin Company.

And through the twilight now the late
Few travelers in the westward pass

And Baghdad darken and the bridge
Across the silent river gone
And through Arabia the edge
Of evening widen and steal on

And deepen on Palmyra's street
The wheel rut in the ruined stone
And Lebanon fade out and Crete
High through the clouds and overblown

And over Sicily the air
Still flashing with the landward gulls
And loom and slowly disappear
The sails above the shadowy hulls

And Spain go under and the shore
Of Africa the gilded sand
And evening vanish and no more
The low pale light across that land

Nor now the long light on the sea—

And here face downward in the sun
To feel how swift how secretly
The shadow of the night comes on. . . .

The Tyger

William Blake

Tyger! Tyger! burning bright
In the forests of the night,
What immortal hand or eye
Could frame thy fearful symmetry?

In what distant deeps or skies
Burnt the fire of thine eyes?
On what wings dare he aspire?
What the hand dare seize the fire?

And what shoulder, and what art,
Could twist the sinews of thy heart?
And when thy heart began to beat,
What dread hand? and what dread feet?

What the hammer? what the chain?
In what furnace was thy brain?
What the anvil? what dread grasp
Dare its deadly terrors clasp?

When the stars threw down their spears
And watered heaven with their tears,
Did he smile his work to see?
Did he who made the Lamb make thee?

Tyger! Tyger! burning bright
In the forests of the night,
What immortal hand or eye
Dare frame thy fearful symmetry?

Sailing to Byzantium

William Butler Yeats

I

That is no country for old men. The young
In one another's arms, birds in the trees,
—Those dying generations—at their song,
The salmon-falls, the mackerel-crowded seas,
Fish, flesh, or fowl, commend all summer long
Whatever is begotten, born, and dies.
Caught in that sensual music all neglect
Monuments of unaging intellect.

II

An aged man is but a paltry thing,
A tattered coat upon a stick, unless
Soul clap its hands and sing, and louder sing
For every tatter in its mortal dress,
Nor is there singing school but studying
Monuments of its own magnificence;
And therefore I have sailed the seas and come
To the holy city of Byzantium.

III

O sages standing in God's holy fire
As in the gold mosaic of a wall,
Come from the holy fire, perne in a gyre,
And be the singing-masters of my soul.
Consume my heart away; sick with desire

And fastened to a dying animal
It knows not what it is; and gather me
Into the artifice of eternity.

IV

Once out of nature I shall never take
My bodily form from any natural thing,
But such a form as Grecian goldsmiths make
Of hammered gold and gold enameling
To keep a drowsy Emperor awake;
Or set upon a golden bough to sing
To lords and ladies of Byzantium
Of what is past, or passing, or to come.

The Second Coming

William Butler Yeats

Turning and turning in the widening gyre
The falcon cannot hear the falconer;
Things fall apart; the centre cannot hold;
Mere anarchy is loosed upon the world.
The blood-dimmed tide is loosed, and everywhere
The ceremony of innocence is drowned;
The best lack all conviction, while the worst
Are full of passionate intensity.

Surely some revelation is a hand;
Surely the Second Coming is at hand.
The Second Coming! Hardly are those words out
When a vast image out of *Spiritus Mundi*
Troubles my sight: somewhere in the sands of the desert
A shape with a lion body and the head of a man,
A gaze blank and pitiless as the sun,
Is moving its slow thighs, while all about it
Reel shadows of the indignant desert birds.
The darkness drops again; but now I know
That twenty centuries of stony sleep
Were vexed to nightmare by a rocking cradle,
And what rough beast, its hour come round at last,
Slouches toward Bethlehem to be born?

perne in a gyre: "To perne" is a term from falconry signifying the mounting flight of
the falcon in rising spirals. "Gyre" is a multiple and special term for Yeats but may be
taken here to signify a spiral.

Spiritus Mundi: The Spirit of the World. Yeats was a believer in a mystical system
largely of his own invention. In that system *Spiritus Mundi* is the name of a place
somewhere between the Earth and Sun. It is there the souls of the dead go.

FROM *Collected Poems,* by William Butler Yeats. Used with permission of The Mac-
millan Company.

INDEX OF AUTHORS AND TITLES